The Connected Customer

The Changing Nature of Consumer and Business Markets

The
Connected
Customer

The Changing Nature of Consumer and Business Markets

Edited by
Stefan Wuyts • Marnik G. Dekimpe • Els Gijsbrechts • Rik Pieters

Routledge
Taylor & Francis Group
New York   London

Routledge
Taylor & Francis Group
270 Madison Avenue
New York, NY 10016

Routledge
Taylor & Francis Group
27 Church Road
Hove, East Sussex BN3 2FA

© 2010 by Taylor and Francis Group, LLC
Routledge is an imprint of Taylor & Francis Group, an Informa business

Printed in the United States of America on acid-free paper
10 9 8 7 6 5 4 3 2 1

International Standard Book Number: 978-1-84872-837-0 (Hardback)

Library of Congress Cataloging-in-Publication Data

The connected customer : the changing nature of consumer and business
markets / editors, Stefan Wuyts ... [et al.].
p. cm.
Includes bibliographical references and index.
ISBN 978-1-84872-837-0 (hardcover : alk. paper)
1. Consumer behavior. 2. Branding (Marketing) 3. Marketing. I. Wuyts,
Stefan.

HF5415.32.C6536 2010
658.8'342--dc22   2009043127

Visit the Taylor & Francis Web site at
http://www.taylorandfrancis.com

and the Psychology Press Web site at
http://www.psypress.com

Contents

Foreword, by Dominique M. Hanssens..xi
Preface xiii
Editors' Bios xv
Contributors...xvii

Chapter 1 Introduction 1
Stefan Wuyts, Marnik G. Dekimpe, Els Gijsbrechts, and Rik Pieters
References 4

SECTION I   Connectivity and the New Reality of Markets

Chapter 2 Opportunities and Challenges in Studying
Customer Networks 7
Christophe Van den Bulte
Social Contagion...8
Brand Communities..14
Valuing Networks and Communities....................................16
Horizontal and Vertical Networks...17
Getting Data: Opportunities and Caveats 21
Conclusion...28
References..30

Chapter 3 Understanding the Relational Ecosystem in a
Connected World 37
Conor M. Henderson and Robert W. Palmatier
Customer's Relational Ecosystem.. 43
Relational Entities... 46
Relational Channels 61

Research Directions 69

References 72

Chapter 4 Connectivity, Control, and Constraint in Business
Markets 77

Stefan Wuyts

Connectivity and Control 78

Connectivity and Constraint.. 90

Connectivity, Control, and Constraint: Directions for
Future Research 95

Notes...98

References 99

SECTION II   Leveraging Vertical Connectivity
With Channel Partners and Brands

Chapter 5 The Connected Patient 107

Nuno Camacho, Vardit Landsman, and Stefan Stremersch

From a White-Coat Model to Shared Decision
Making..109

Antecedents of the Evolution to Shared Decision
Making..112

Clinical and Relational Consequences 122

Considering Patient Types in Patient-Centered
Marketing 125

Strategic Implications of Patient Connectedness...............132

Notes.. 134

References 135

Chapter 6 Is Mr. Spock a Good Candidate for Being a
Connected Customer? The Role of Emotion in
Decision Making 141

Baba Shiv

The Connected Customer and the Customer Value
Proposition 142

The CVP: A Historical Perspective 142
The Third-Wave View of the CVP: The Power of Brand
Emotion 144
The Story of Phineas Gage...145
More Evidence From Neurological Patients........................147
Decision Quality, Emotions, and the Brain........................148
Back to the CVP and the Connected Customer 154
A View Into the Future...155
Some Final Words 158
Notes..159
References..160

Chapter 7 God and Mammon: The Influence of Religiosity on
Brand Connections 163

Aric Rindfleisch, Nancy Wong, and James E. Burroughs
Competing Views on the Role of Religiosity on Brand
Connections 165
Fundamentalism: Religiosity as a Desire for
Conservation..167
Spirituality: Religiosity as a Desire for Transcendence......168
Study 1: United States 170
Study 2: Singapore 179
General Discussion 187
Conclusion..194
References..194
Appendix 199

Chapter 8 Brand Platforms as Strategic Investments: Leveraging
Customer Connections to Manage Profitability,
Growth, and Risk 203

Rajendra K. Srivastava and Thorsten Wiesel
The Nature of Strategic Marketing Investments............... 205
The Concept of Product Platforms....................................... 207
Customer and Brand Platforms... 208
Customer and Brand Platforms and Business
Performance 210
References..212

SECTION III   Leveraging Horizontal Connectivity Among Customers

Chapter 9 The Shadow of Other People: Socialization and Social Comparison in Marketing.................................. 217

Ronald Burt
Socialization Mechanism, Connectivity Criterion............218
Equivalence Criterion, Social Comparison Mechanism... 223
Equivalence and Connectivity Often Make the Same
Predictions.. 225
Contradictory Predictions 226
How the Mechanisms Combine.. 240
Closing 247
Acknowledgments.. 248
Notes.. 249
References...252

Chapter 10 Viral Marketing: What Is It, and What Are the Components of Viral Success? 257

Ralf van der Lans and Gerrit van Bruggen
What Is Viral Marketing? 258
How Does Information in Viral Marketing Spread?......... 262
Drivers of Viral Marketing Campaign Success.................. 264
Tracking Viral Campaign Success.....................................270
Conclusions...278
Note 281
References...281

Chapter 11 Social Connectivity, Opinion Leadership, and Diffusion.. 283

Jacob Goldenberg, Sangman Han, and Donald R. Lehmann
Product Diffusion: A Social Process................................. 284
Different Kinds of Influentials.. 285
The Social Hub: The Key to Network Processes................ 287
Social Hubs Activate the Network by Seeking and
Conveying Attractive Information 288

Social Hubs Are Attractive Information Sources 291

Bridging the Chasm 294

Activating the Social Network..295

Social Hubs Are Not Early Adopters, but They Adopt
Early...296

Tracking the Influence of Social Hubs 297

Discussion... 300

Notes.. 302

References 302

Chapter 12 The Effect of Negative Word-of-Mouth in Social
Networks... 307

Andre Bonfrer

What We Have Learned About Word-of-Mouth................ 311

Discussion... 326

Conclusion...332

Notes...333

References 334

Author Index.. 337

Subject Index..347

Foreword

Today's marketers face an environment in which the rapid changes in communications technology and globalization of markets are creating *communities* of customers and prospects rather than a multitude of isolated customers. This state of affairs was revealed by the biennial Research Priorities survey conducted by the Marketing Science Institute (MSI) when I served as its executive director between 2005 and 2007. I am very pleased that the Tilburg University marketing faculty chose this "connected customer" theme for its Lustrum Conference in 2008 and the subsequent publication of a collection of essays presented at the conference.

MSI explored the connected customer theme in three directions, which are also reflected in the content of the chapters in this book. First, business customers and consumers alike are increasingly connected to their suppliers and competitors, not only by traditional one-to-many mass marketing but also by one-to-one and many-to-many marketing techniques. This evolution—and the increasing power of consumers who control the time and place of their media consumption—raises new questions about the management of customer and prospect touch points. Of particular importance is the integration of interactive media in the communications mix of our companies. New search capabilities are changing the decision-making processes of individual and business customers. As one example, marketers must consider the impact of their positioning on search engines such as Google as part of their marketing mix. Indeed a new discipline called *search engine optimization* has emerged from this need. In business-to-business and business-to-consumer markets, buyers and sellers are meeting in unparalleled ways at auctions. Part 1 of this volume describes several important aspects of this changed landscape.

Second, business customers and consumers are digitally connected to each other, resulting in countless special-interest groups that cross national borders. Opinion leadership and word-of-mouth are not new concepts, but the speed and the power of their effects on individual behavior are dramatically increased. In this social network context, "weak ties" become significant as marketers seek to identify individuals with broad influence through many network connections. This highlights a seemingly counterintuitive phenomenon: Loyal customers, whose network is composed of like-minded counterparts, may be less effective than occasional customers in expanding markets via word-of-mouth. In addition, a new distinction is made between marketing-induced and organic word-of-mouth. Marketers may create buzz by investing in social networks that augment their marketing efforts. Organic, or spontaneous, word-of-mouth is less amenable to management control, so marketers need to understand how it is generated and how it impacts their business performance. Parts 2 and 3 of this volume focus on the critical dimensions of this phenomenon.

Finally, the MSI survey revealed that business customers and consumers are increasingly connected to third-party information providers, through a variety of product review and price comparison services. The resulting transparency in our markets challenges prevailing beliefs about the importance of brand image and the role of personal selling. It also expands the definition of *best value*, as consumers now have access to aggregated information, for example, about the customer satisfaction levels with different retailers. The relationship between a retailer's customer satisfaction score and its ability to charge a price premium is but one important research question that may be addressed.

In this connected environment, customers are better informed and harder to please, but they also leave a more visible *evidence trail* in the form of vastly improved databases. This explosion in potential customer information challenges traditional analytical and reporting techniques that turn such information into insights and market intelligence. The scope, pace, and sources of this new information also create opportunities for better and more timely marketing decision support to drive profitable growth. As such, the connected customer era may *change the paradigm for effective marketing strategy*. The essays in this volume represent leading-edge scholarly thinking in this new arena, and I commend the editors on their pioneering effort.

Dominique M. Hanssens
Bud Knapp Professor of Marketing, UCLA Anderson School of Management

Preface

The nature of consumer and business markets is changing: Decision makers no longer act independently of one another but are increasingly connected with other consumers, with other channel members, and with brands. Novel database marketing techniques enable firms to develop closer contacts with customers; customers develop increasingly close connections with brands; customers communicate through electronic and other media with other customers and with firms; firms in turn seek central positions in business networks. The intricate networks that business customers and consumers are part of both shape marketing and are shaped by it. The theme of the connected customer has triggered the interest of marketing scholars and marketing practitioners alike. From beneath the development of new theories and experimentation in practice, a new marketing logic is slowly emerging.

That observation stimulated us to organize a conference on "The Connected Customer" to celebrate the 80th birthday of Tilburg University. At this conference, the breakthrough ideas that were presented and the vivid discussions with the audience highlighted the need for a book that may guide and inspire marketers and marketing scholars in dealing with the new reality of connected consumers and business markets. The presenters at the conference embraced the idea to collect the emerging insights into an edited volume, and several other authors joined in as well. The result is a collection of chapters that deal with the rich facets of connectivity. The book may serve as a source of inspiration for academics in marketing and related fields who wish to contribute to the development of this exciting stream of research. It is a great source of research ideas and fresh theory building. The book is also intended for marketing practitioners who are eager to take up the challenge and adapt their marketing strategies to the changing nature of consumer and business markets.

We are grateful to Tilburg University, and in particular to the executive board and to Professor van der Duyn Schouten (then Rector Magnificus of Tilburg University), for fully supporting the conference. We also thank ABN AMRO and the Dutch province of North Brabant for generously sponsoring the event. The phrase "the connected customer" was also used to designate one of the most important challenges for future marketing research and practice by the Marketing Science Institute—the world's leading research institute in the field—and we are grateful to Professor Dominique Hanssens, executive director of MSI at that time, for writing the foreword to this book. We also want to thank Anne Duffy, Erin Flaherty, and Christopher Myron (at Routledge, Taylor & Francis) for their continuous support in the process.

Finally, this project would not have been realized without the involvement of the many contributing authors. We requested the authors to contribute their breakthrough ideas and cutting-edge research. The authors went a step further. Rather than importing ideas on connectivity into the marketing domain, they pushed the boundaries of thought on connectivity itself. Through the following chapters, they show that the marketing field is at the forefront of this interdisciplinary research domain.

We invite you to take a look, share our enthusiasm, find inspiration, and take the ideas developed in this book a step further tomorrow.

Stefan Wuyts
Marnik G. Dekimpe
Els Gijsbrechts
Rik Pieters

Editors' Bios

Stefan Wuyts is an associate professor of marketing at Tilburg University, the Netherlands. After studying business engineering and marketing, he joined the Tinbergen Institute (Erasmus University Rotterdam) as a doctoral student. His doctoral dissertation was awarded by the Dutch Royal Society for Economics. Stefan's research interests include B2B markets, channel management, innovation, and social networks. His work in these areas has appeared in the *Journal of Marketing*, the *Journal of Marketing Research*, and the *International Journal of Research in Marketing*, among others. In 2007, he was named a Marketing Science Institute (MSI) Young Scholar and published a monograph with Christophe Van den Bulte titled "Social Networks and Marketing" (MSI, 2007). Stefan serves as an area editor for the *International Journal of Research in Marketing* and a reviewer for the *Journal of Marketing*, the *Journal of Marketing Research*, *Management Science*, the *Journal of Operations Management*, and the *Journal of International Business Studies*. He has collaborated with several B2B companies such as ASML and Nexans.

Marnik G. Dekimpe (PhD, UCLA) is Research Professor of marketing at Tilburg University, the Netherlands, and professor of marketing at the Catholic University of Leuven, Belgium. His work has been published in *Marketing Science, Management Science,* the *Journal of Marketing Research,* the *Journal of Marketing,* the *International Journal of Research in Marketing,* and the *Journal of Econometrics,* among others. He has won best-paper awards from *Marketing Science* (1995, 2001), the *Journal of Marketing Research* (1999), the *International Journal of Research in Marketing* (1997, 2001, 2002), and *Technological Forecasting and Social Change* (2000). He became the editor of the *International Journal of Research in Marketing* in October 2009. He also serves on the editorial board of *Marketing Science,* the *Journal of Marketing Research,* the *Journal of Marketing,* the *Journal of Interactive Marketing,* and *Marketing Letters.* He is an academic trustee with both the Marketing Science Institute and AiMark.

Els Gijsbrechts is a professor of quantitative marketing at Tilburg University, the Netherlands. She received a PhD in applied economic sciences from the University of Antwerp, Belgium, and previously held positions at the University of Antwerp, FUCaM, and the Catholic University of Leuven. She is an area editor for the *International Journal of Research in Marketing*, the official journal of the European Marketing Academy. Her research focuses on modeling consumers' shopping behavior and their responses to retailer and manufacturer decisions such as shelf layout, price (promotions), branding, stock-outs, and assortment decisions. She has been involved in research and teaching programs for various companies, such as GfK, Janssen Pharmaceutica, Heineken, and Delhaize, to name just a few. Her research has been published in leading journals such as the *Journal of Marketing Research*, the *International Journal of Research in Marketing*, and the *Journal of Retailing* and received several nominations, including nominations for the IJRM Best Paper Award, the Davidson Award, and the William F. O'Dell Award.

Rik Pieters is a professor of marketing at Tilburg University, the Netherlands, and guest professor at the Robert H. Smith School of Business at the University of Maryland. He holds a PhD in psychology from Leiden University, the Netherlands. His work has appeared in the *Journal of Marketing*, the *Journal of Marketing Research*, *Marketing Science*, *Management Science*, the *Pint Bulletin*, the *Journal of Personality and Social Psychology*, and the *Journal of the American Statistical Association*, among others. He is an area editor of the *Journal of Marketing Research*. Together with Michel Wedel, he organized the first conference on visual marketing at the University of Michigan. His research interests are the effectiveness of marketing communication, the social and cognitive psychology of consumer behavior, and visual marketing. When not doing research, he collects data in various fields.

Contributors

Andre Bonfrer
Singapore Management
    University
Singapore

James E. Burroughs
Associate Professor of Commerce
University of Virginia
Charlottesville, Virginia

Ronald Burt
Hobart W. Williams Professor of
    Sociology and Strategy
University of Chicago
Chicago, Illinois

Nuno Camacho
Doctoral Student
Erasmus School of Economics
Erasmus University Rotterdam
The Netherlands

Marnik G. Dekimpe
Marketing Department
Tilburg University
The Netherlands

Els Gijsbrechts
Marketing Department
Tilburg University
The Netherlands

Jacob Goldenberg
Hebrew University of Jerusalem
Israel

Sangman Han
Sungkyunkwan University
Seoul, Korea

Dominique M. Hanssens
Bud Knapp Professor of Marketing
UCLA
Los Angeles, California

Conor M. Henderson
University of Washington
Seattle, Washington

Vardit Landsman
Assistant Professor of Marketing
Erasmus University Rotterdam
The Netherlands

Donald R. Lehmann
Columbia University
New York, New York

Robert W. Palmatier
Evert McCabe Research Fellow
    and Assistant Professor of
    Marketing
University of Washington
Seattle, Washington

F. M. G. (Rik) Pieters
Marketing Department
Tilburg University
The Netherlands

Aric Rindfleisch
Professor of Marketing
University of Wisconsin-Madison
Madison, Wisconsin

Baba Shiv
Professor of Marketing
Stanford University
Stanford, California

Rajendra Srivastava
Singapore Management University
Singapore

Stefan Stremersch
Chaired Professor of Marketing
and the Desiderius Erasmus
Distinguished Chair of
Economics
Erasmus University Rotterdam
The Netherlands

Gerrit van Bruggen
Erasmus University Rotterdam
The Netherlands

Christophe Van den Bulte
University of Pennsylvania
Philadelphia , Pennsylvania

Ralf van der Lans
Erasmus University Rotterdam
The Netherlands

Thorsten Wiesel
University of Groningen
The Netherlands

Nancy Wong
Associate Professor of Consumer
Science
University of Wisconsin-Madison
Madison, Wisconsin

Stefan Wuyts
Marketing Department
Tilburg University
The Netherlands

1

Introduction

Stefan Wuyts, Marnik G. Dekimpe,
Els Gijsbrechts, and Rik Pieters

These are exciting times for marketing practitioners and marketing academics alike: Much of the discipline's received wisdom is undergoing reconsideration as the nature of marketing is changing fundamentally. A key concept in this discussion is the general notion of "connectivity." Consumers are increasingly interconnected through various sorts of social networks, a trend that is facilitated by recent advances in electronic media and telecommunication. Initiatives on the Internet, for example, have created ample opportunity for consumers to connect with other consumers through social networking sites (MySpace, Facebook, Cyworld), information sharing sites (YouTube), (anti-)brand communities (MyStarbucksIdea. com versus iHateStarbucks.com), and so on. Also among business customers, a trend is apparent toward higher connectivity resulting from externally oriented strategies such as e-business, supply chain integration, and alliance networks. This requires a fresh perspective on analyzing both consumer and business markets, as decision makers no longer function independently of one another. Also, novel perspectives are needed on how customers connect with brands and with products, because customers are becoming more participative in some decision environments (e.g., health care) and more emotionally connected in others (e.g., brand evaluations). One of the clearest examples of how such increased connectivity changes marketing practice is the recent revival of word-of-mouth. The increased connectivity of customers with brands engenders brand communications, and the increased connectivity among customers amplifies the impact of such communications, which has important consequences for the spread of products, ideas, and information. "Buzz marketing" is now a central concept in the marketer's tool kit, and "social contagion" is firmly on top of many marketing scholars' research agenda.

We have now well passed the stage of acknowledging that these are important developments. Having witnessed an explosion of research initiatives in academia and quite some experimentation in marketing practice, we need to both take inventory and look ahead. Exactly how does connectivity change the reality of consumer and business markets? What are the most recent insights regarding vertical connections between customers and channel partners or between customers and brands, and how can (should) marketers leverage such connectivity? What are the boundaries of current marketing thought regarding horizontal connectivity among customers, and how can the marketer exploit such connectivity? These questions are addressed in the chapters of this book, which gathers breakthrough ideas as well as empirical evidence presented by thought leaders in the field.

The marketing community has been alerted to the likely changes brought about by connectivity in the seminal book *Networks in Marketing*, edited in 1996 by Dawn Iacobucci. In the subsequent decade, connectivity increasingly influenced marketing theory and practice. In 2007, Christophe Van den Bulte and Stefan Wuyts published a monograph that served as a primer on social networks for marketers, providing a tool kit for practitioners and an overview of the foundations of network theory. The objective of the present book is to take the next step in understanding the connected customer. The contributors to this book are internationally renowned scholars who share their thoughts and vision on the impact of the phenomenon of connectivity on marketing thought and marketing practice.

The book is organized along the following three main themes. Section I deals with connectivity and the new reality of markets. In Chapter 2, Christophe Van den Bulte kicks off with a critical reflection on how customer networks affect customer behavior and marketing practice. He devotes attention to both horizontal networks (as in social contagion and brand communities) and vertical networks (as in channel settings), as well as to the challenge of gathering network data. In Chapter 3, Conor Henderson and Robert Palmatier discuss the increased complexity of customers' relational environments and introduce the notion of "relational ecosystems," consisting of different objects (brands, boundary spanners, social in-groups, marketplace network) and the channels that bind them. They argue that studying ecosystems allows capturing the complexity, dynamics, and multiple subnetworks that define a customer's environment and, hence, is indispensible to fully understand customer decision making. In Chapter 4, Stefan Wuyts focuses on connectivity, control, and constraint in business markets. He discusses the effectiveness of alternative network control mechanisms but also shows that social networks can constrain economic optimality in business markets.

Section II deals with leveraging vertical connectivity between customers and channel partners or brands. In Chapter 5, Nuno Camacho, Vardit Landsman, and Stefan Stremersch observe a fundamental shift in the role of the patient in medical decision making. They propose a customer-centered marketing approach to leverage the increased participation of the patient. In Chapter 6, Baba Shiv questions conventional wisdom that analytical decision making is superior to emotional decision making. On the basis of a detailed overview and critique of the concept of "customer value propositions," he argues that to truly connect a customer, a firm must acknowledge the power of brand emotion. In Chapter 7, Aric Rindfleisch, Nancy Wong, and James Burroughs examine the influence of religiosity on connections that customers form with brands. Their empirical studies, conducted in the United States and Singapore, demonstrate that fundamentalism and spirituality strongly bear on brand loyalty and self-brand connections across multiple product categories, which opens up new opportunities for target marketing. Chapter 8 concludes Section II. Rajendra Srivastava and Thorsten Wiesel underscore the strategic importance of customer connections in managing profitability, growth, and risk. They advocate that marketers should think in terms of brand platforms, much similar to product platforms, to develop sustainable long-term connections with customers.

Section III collects new insights on how to leverage horizontal connectivity among customers. In Chapter 9, Ronald Burt discusses socialization and social comparison, the main network mechanisms that lie beneath the popular metaphors about contagion. Rather than arguing for one or the other, he examines how both mechanisms combine in a predictable way as they generate contagion in different network settings. In Chapter 10, Ralf van der Lans and Gerrit van Bruggen distinguish the key components that determine the spread of viral marketing campaigns (number of seeded customers, seeding acceptance, forward rate, viral acceptance, and response time). They illustrate the practical relevance of these drivers on the basis of two real-life viral marketing campaigns. In Chapter 11, Jacob Goldenberg, Sangman Han, and Donald Lehmann discuss the critical role of "social hubs" in social systems (i.e., individuals with an exceptionally large number of social ties). They point to the importance of identifying such social hubs for accelerating the diffusion of products. Finally, in Chapter 12, Andre Bonfrer discusses the origins and impact of negative word-of-mouth. He elaborates on how marketers can manage and control this dark side of the word-of-mouth phenomenon.

We are truly excited about the chapters that are collected in this book, and we are grateful to the contributors for enthusiastically sharing their ideas and vision about the connected customer. The chapters not only explore and extend the boundaries of marketing thought but also translate these new insights into recommendations for marketing practice. We are highly indebted to all contributors for the time and energy they have put in their respective contributions. We are convinced that marketing academics and practitioners will find inspiration in the book for more effectively addressing the phenomenon of increased connectivity in consumer and business markets.

REFERENCES

Iacobucci, D. (1996). *Networks in marketing*. Thousand Oaks, CA: Sage.
Van den Bulte, C., & Wuyts, S. (2007). *Social networks and marketing* (Relevant Knowledge series). Boston, MA: Marketing Science Institute.

Section I

Connectivity and the New Reality of Markets

2

Opportunities and Challenges in Studying Customer Networks

Christophe Van den Bulte

In this chapter, I approach the theme of the connected customer from a network perspective. That is, I look at the issue by explicitly considering the structure of connections or ties among customers. In a few instances, I also consider the structure of connections with other market participants, such as suppliers or intermediaries.

Social networks among customers are receiving much attention from managers and researchers nowadays. Yet, current practice does not capitalize on existing network theory and research developed outside marketing. Conversely, some developments in customer networking are ahead of empirical research, and a few seem ahead even of accepted theory. In this chapter, I describe some research opportunities and challenges in developing a richer understanding of how customer networks affect customer behavior and can affect managerial practice. The objective is to raise questions of substantive interest, in the hope that they will generate research that provides answers to them. I also touch on some issues of obtaining network data but steer clear of technical issues involved in analyzing such data (e.g., Carrington, Scott, & Wasserman, 2005).

I first focus on social influence or social contagion dynamics among customers. This seems to be the network phenomenon of greatest interest among marketing researchers and practitioners today. I then turn to brand communities and network valuation, two areas where hardly any research has been conducted so far from a network perspective. Next, I discuss some possible applications of network research involving both horizontal customer-to-customer networks and vertical networks involving both customers and parties upstream in the value chain. Finally, I offer some reflections on strengths and weaknesses of different ways to obtain network data.

SOCIAL CONTAGION

The network phenomenon that enjoys the most attention from marketing researchers and practitioners today is how connections among customers affect word of mouth, i.e., information sharing and influence about products and brands. Because this process is akin to the spread of a virus within a population, some researchers refer to it as social contagion. Here, I offer a few ideas about how we might learn more about this important phenomenon.

Some Skeptical Questions About Social Contagion

Marketers are increasingly experimenting with various forms of network marketing for new products. The rationale of many such strategies rests on three key assumptions: (a) Social contagion among customers is at work, (b) some customers' adoptions and opinions have a disproportionate influence on others' adoptions, and (c) firms are able to identify and target those influentials or opinion leaders. These assumptions are quite reasonable, as the first two are consistent with several sociological and marketing theories, and all three have been supported in at least some studies (e.g., Godes & Mayzlin, 2009; Goldenberg, Lehmann, Shidlovski, & Barak, 2006; Rogers, 2003; Valente, Hoffman, Ritt-Olson, Lichtman, & Johnson, 2003; Weimann, 1994).

Managers would be remiss, however, to simply take those three assumptions for granted. For instance, Van den Bulte and Lilien (1997, 2001) showed that contagion need not be as important as reported in prior studies, Becker (1970) and Watts and Dodds (2007) raised doubts on the importance of opinion leaders in speeding up the acceptance of new products, and Rogers and Cartano (1962) noted already long ago a disagreement on whether to identify opinion leaders based on self-reports or based on their centrality in social networks. More recent research by Coulter, Feick, and Price (2002) and Godes and Mayzlin (2009) provides conflicting answers to the question whether heavy users are more influential than light users, an issue of obvious relevance to the identification and targeting of likely influentials.

Marketers would benefit from studies critically assessing each of the three assumptions fundamental to many "viral" or "word-of-mouth" network marketing efforts. First, when can one expect social contagion to be operating over social ties and affect customer behavior over and above the effect of traditional marketing efforts? Standard diffusion theory suggests some answers, but they are not always nuanced. For instance, one would expect potential customers to turn to others for guidance when they do not feel comfortable with their own judgment. But if the perceived risk is very high, people may prefer not to think about purchasing the product altogether. This line of reasoning implies some nonlinear relationship between perceived risk and the importance of social influence, and it might explain some puzzling research findings. More generally, there is plenty of opportunity to go beyond accepted diffusion theory as codified by Rogers (2003) and to combine more fundamental theories from sociology and other social sciences with rich multicountry or multiproduct data sources that are becoming more readily available to generate richer insights on when can one expect social contagion to be operating in new product diffusion (e.g., Steenkamp & Gielens, 2003; Van den Bulte & Stremersch, 2004).

Second, is it really true that some customers' adoptions and opinions have a disproportionate influence on others' adoptions? And to what extent can one profile those influentials, influencers, or opinion leaders? Although several authors provide answers to these questions (e.g., Rogers, 2003), I am afraid the situation is less rosy than often described. For instance, quite a bit of research on opinion leadership uses self-reported measures. Are people who claim to be opinion leaders really influential? I doubt it, given the prevalence of the better-than-average effect or Lake Wobegon syndrome where people overestimate their own achievements and capabilities (Lake Wobegon is a fictional place invented by writer Garrison Keillor where "all the women are strong, all the men are good looking, and all the children are above average"). To what extent is someone's self-reported leadership correlated with the number of others who report seeking information or guidance from that person? Oddly enough, we do not know, apart from a recent study of physicians in three cities reporting correlations of about 0.30, which is quite low (Iyengar, Valente, and Van den Bulte, 2008). Another issue, distinct from measurement and profiling, is the degree to which opinion leaders exert their influence across the board or not. In spite of claims to the contrary by some peddlers of commercial services, there is no evidence of such a thing as a generalized opinion leader whose influence spans a wide variety of product categories (for a review, see Weimann, 1994). Who exerts influence, even within a category, is likely to depend on what people seek from those they turn to. However, little is known about how the identity of influentials changes depending on, say, whether the perceived risk that consumers try to manage is functional, financial, or social. We also know very little about how the identity of influentials changes depending on whether consumers seek general-technical versus use-situational information. Recent work by Goldenberg and his associates (2006) suggests that considerations of general expertise ("this person knows a lot about the product's features and performance") and representativeness ("this person is like me, and so his advice will be more relevant to me") may lead people to seek advice from different sources. Marketers would benefit from more research into what type of person is influential when and for whom.

The third key question that we would like to know the answer to before designing network marketing campaigns is whether marketers are able to identify and target those influentials or opinion leaders. As noted previously, using self-reports may not be very attractive for that purpose. Using general demographic profiles is not very useful either, research clearly indicates (Weimann, 1994). That would leave one with sociometric methods, something that several pharmaceutical companies are working with and is also taken into account by Tremor and Vocalpoint, the two word-of-mouth marketing services operated by Procter & Gamble. Doubts on marketers' ability to effectively identify influentials using sociometric methods, however, have arisen recently following a simulation study by Watts and Dodds (2007) showing that the customers critical in generating a sudden burst in the speed of diffusion need not necessarily be the best connected. Although this possibility has been already long known to network and diffusion researchers (e.g., Becker, 1970; Locock, Dopson, Chambers, & Gabbay, 2001), the recent simulation results have created a heated debate among marketing practitioners (Thompson, 2008). Much of that debate seems to ignore that the study by Watts and Dodds was only a simulation demonstrating a possibility, not an empirical study providing actual evidence in support of that possibility. Still, the simulation results do bring to the fore potential difficulties marketers may face in identifying key influentials using sociometric methods. This is clearly another area where important research advances can be made.

How to Leverage Social Contagion

The three previous questions challenged the key assumptions underlying network marketing. Several other questions exist about what marketers can do to boost the effectiveness of word-of-mouth, given that it matters.

- How can influentials be persuaded to serve as advocates for one product rather than another? More generally, what makes people spend time and energy to share information and advice? Answers might involve building, maintaining or enhancing social status, maintaining or enhancing self-respect, feelings of benevolence, a sense of moral obligation, generalized reciprocity, or simply calculative give-and-take. There is already some research on this topic (e.g., Walsh, Gwinner, & Swanson, 2004), but it seems to focus on consumer markets and simple products. What about situations where opinion leaders are professionals with heavy demands on their time? Or business markets where influentials may have some reticence about helping out a competitor? Are professionals and businesses more reticent to assist others than consumers, or do the rewards of providing information and guidance to others remain sufficiently appealing (Zuckerman and Sgourev, 2006)? As often in research, looking at contingencies may sharpen our insights.

- How can preexisting social ties be activated to maximum effect? One way to increase the effectiveness of each tie would be to have a "buzz-worthy" message. But what makes messages more likely to be passed along? What makes an overall campaign more likely to be talked about, blogged about, and so on? There are some obvious answers such as relevance, surprise, shock value, and so on, but is that all? Existing research indicates that it is not only the message that affects the transmission rate, but also the nature of tie between potential sender and receiver (e.g., De Bruyn & Lilien, 2008; Frenzen & Nakamoto, 1993). Another refinement on how to activate ties consists of creating specific situations rather than messages. One example is to use medical education seminars featuring influential physicians. This is a well-established practice, but more sophisticated companies are now experimenting with not simply bringing together an influential and other physicians but specifically "matching" speakers and invitees, that is, to invite physicians to a seminar given by their "own" influential who they turn to for advice in their regular practice as well. Some research in health sciences has suggested that bringing together preexisting combinations of opinion leaders and seekers may be more effective than using speakers who are respected for their general expertise but have no genuine tight connection to their audience (Valente et al., 2003).

- How effective are "viral-for-hire" services such as BzzAgent, Matchstick, SheSpeaks, Tremor or Vocalpoint that artificially create buzz for payment (in cash, free product samples, or coupons) compared to genuine word-of-mouth? I know of only one peer-reviewed study (Godes & Mayzlin, 2009), and more such work would be quite welcome, as it might lead not only to more confidence about the average difference in effectiveness, but also to insights about differences across product categories. A question that practitioners and academics seem to have ignored so far is that of persistence: Does paid-for word-of-mouth die out faster than naturally occurring word-of-mouth, because the word-of-mouth mercenaries move on to touting the next product once the commercial contract has expired and the campaign has been terminated? Conversely, can paid-for word-of-mouth campaigns be used to rejuvenate and re-energize the buzz once the naturally occurring word of mouth has vanished? Might it be optimal to use pulsing in word-of-mouth marketing?

The Role of Status and Identity in Social Contagion

Marketers and sociologists have long been interested in how consumers use products and brands to build, signal, and maintain a social identity (e.g., Douglas & Isherwood, 1979; Molnár & Lamont, 2002). The idea seems to be enjoying a renaissance lately, among both marketing practitioners and academics (e.g., Berger & Heath, 2007; Holt, 1998; Van den Bulte & Joshi, 2007; Walker, 2008). Status and identity actually are major issues in social networks. Hence, investigating the role of status and identity in the adoption and consumption of products from a network perspective seems to be an interesting venue for future research.

One phenomenon of particular interest is that of positive and negative contagion across groups. The phenomenon is especially interesting when both operate simultaneously: Adoption or consumption by cool or rich consumers may make the products more appealing to more mainstream or less affluent consumers, but once the latter adopt the product, the former find it less attractive. This is the basis for the standard fashion cycle noted more than a century ago by Georg Simmel and is a problem faced by many marketers of "cool" brands such as Vans and Diesel (cool kids vs. dorks) and major luxury brands such as Louis Vuitton and Burberry (upper-middle class vs. riffraff). One question is whether and how such a system can ever be in equilibrium: Will there ever be a state in which no one has an incentive to adopt or disadopt, and what is that state? That question is probably best investigated analytically through a mathematical model rather than empirically through data (e.g., Bakshi, Hosanagar, & Van den Bulte, 2007; Miller, McIntyre, & Mantrala, 1993). But there are many other questions, such as what marketers can do to weaken the negative feedback loop without weakening the positive one. Another set of issues is how the identity signaling game is affected not only by differences in economic capital (how rich one is) but also by differences in cultural capital and the ability to decode subcultural signals, and what all this means for pricing, product design, and communication tactics (e.g., Han, Nunes, & Drèze, 2008; Walker, 2008).

Another question that I would like to see more research about is whether one's propensity to imitate others is a function of one's status. For instance, the so-called middle-status conformity thesis in sociology (e.g., Philips & Zuckerman, 2001) posits that high-status people do not imitate others very much because they feel quite confident in their own judgment and the legitimacy of their actions. Low-status people do not imitate others either because they feel that it will not help them gain more status. It is only middle-status people who feel they need to imitate in an attempt to keep up with those above them. This hypothesis, when combined with the idea that the number of connections one has in the network is a measure of status, implies not only that people with few connections will not be subject to much contagion (as one would expect based on the limited amount of contact with sources of influence) but also that people with many connections would not be subject to much contagion either. Evidence of such behavior would be important as it might help explain the weak correlation between time of adoption and opinion leadership vs. opinion seeking observed in some studies.

A third phenomenon deserving more attention from marketing researchers is the asymmetric nature of social ties. Many social ties have an aspect of deference attached to them, such as "asking advice from" or "looking up to." Such ties tend to be asymmetric or nonreciprocated, that is, Person A sending a tie to Person B tends to go hand in hand with B not sending a tie to A. In such a network, how does a "leader" react when one or more of the "followers" adopts before he or she does? One possibility is that the leader becomes afraid of losing status and feels compelled to adopt as well. But the reverse is also possible: To maintain his or her self-concept, the leader now deems the new product as somewhat unfit for his or her own status and so becomes less likely rather than more likely to adopt (Jasso, 2001). Understanding such dynamics in asymmetric networks in which status games are being played may be especially important for marketers of status goods (e.g., "cool" brands and luxury) as well as marketers of credence goods in business markets (e.g., consulting services or drugs treating complex chronic medical conditions).

An important contribution by Burt (1987) was to point out that contagion need not operate between directly connected members of the network. To the extent that one is concerned about the respect and status one derives from one's direct contacts, one will be concerned about the adoption and consumption behaviors of other people who have connections to the same set of people one is connected to, that is, one will be concerned about falling behind people or firms with a portfolio of ties that highly overlaps with one's own. Such people or firms with overlapping portfolios of ties are said to be "structurally equivalent" in the network. There are several empirical studies documenting situations where contagion operated more strongly between structurally equivalent members of the network than between directly connected members. I am not aware, however, of work providing strong evidence that contagion through structural equivalence is indeed driven by competitive and status considerations rather than other motivations. Documenting this would be a valuable contribution, as it would directly tie commercial arguments of fear, uncertainty, and doubt (known to marketers as "the FUD factor") about being preempted or losing status to considerations on who in the network to target in order to gain extra leverage (e.g., Van den Bulte & Wuyts, 2007). For a detailed discussion of structural equivalence, see Chapter 9 by Ronald Burt.

BRAND COMMUNITIES

Marketing practitioners and branding experts are becoming increasingly interested in how brand identities come to exist and evolve through social practices and how brand cultures engage or disengage from general culture (e.g., Holt, 2004; Walker, 2008). Of more directly practical interest is the appropriation by particular lifestyle groups and subcultures of particular brands. Examples include the importance of the European rave scene early in Red Bull's history and the hijacking of the Tommy Hilfiger brand by rap music and "urban street" style aficionados (e.g., Wipperfürth, 2005). Brand communities are another phenomenon of great interest to marketers where brands, culture, and social interaction come into play (e.g., Muniz & O'Guinn, 2001; Walker, 2008). To date, the literature on social networks does not provide much insight into these issues. It tends to ignore the meaning of ties and the relation between social network structure and cognitive structures. Personally, I find the theoretical discussions on the relation between network analysis and cultural analysis to be abstract and difficult to grasp (Emirbayer & Goodwin, 1994; Nadel, 1957), but there is some research that pertains to network structure and culture and that might serve as a source of inspiration to enterprising marketing scholars (Martin, 2002; McLean, 1998; Sirsi, Ward, & Reingen, 1996). There also are other streams of research offering some more concrete ideas and findings to build on. First, the current literature on consumer and brand culture counts several contributions that clearly connect to macroscopic social structure (e.g., Holt, 1998), and a study by Muniz and O'Guinn (2001) gets close to social network issues conceptually though not operationally. Second, research on recruitment in social movements has long investigated social networks and has paid attention to the role of powerful symbols and cultural frames in the growth of such movements (e.g., Jasper & Poulsen, 1995; McAdam & Paulsen, 1993; Snow, Zurcher, & Ekland-Olson, 1980). Third, there is some work on relating social and cognitive structures by Carley (1986) that has attracted considerable attention in the sociology of knowledge and that might have relevance to brands as well.

Another advance may come from reversing the question. Rather than just asking what networks can do for brands, marketers should also ask what brands can do for their customers' networks, because people use consumption as a means of building and maintaining a social identity. To the extent that consumers can use brand communities and brand cultures as accounting systems and sorting devices in their everyday social networks (e.g., using brand community membership to infer who they would like to socialize with), some brands may be chosen over others. I wonder to what extent efforts to "get more brand engagement," as branding specialists like to put it, can productively be reframed as efforts "to get more brand embeddedness" into customers' networks. Pursuing this idea to the fullest may involve broadening the notion of membership of a network from only people and firms to also include symbols and inanimate objects, as advocated by Michel Callon, Bruno Latour, and other proponents of the so-called actor-network theory (e.g., Latour, 2005).

VALUING NETWORKS AND COMMUNITIES

Over the past 10 years or so, marketers have become increasingly interested in valuing customers and customer bases. As word-of-mouth dynamics have gained more attention, several people have started to wonder how one might incorporate the extent to which a customer influences others into that customer's lifetime value (CLV) (e.g., Hogan, Lemon, & Libai, 2004; Kumar, Petersen, & Leone, 2007; Lee, Lee, & Feick, 2006). The question of how to value entire consumer networks as more than simply aggregates of consumers has gained perhaps even more attention from practitioners after some media and technology companies tried to put a financial value on potential acquisition targets such as MySpace, Facebook, and YouTube and has captured the attention of some academics as well (e.g., Gupta, Mela, & Vidal-Sanz, 2006; Gupta & Mela, 2008).

Both valuation problems may be very hard to crack. Let me focus on the second. Perhaps one effective way to approach it is to ask oneself how the network facilitated and represented by a social networking company such as MySpace is different from a simple aggregation of consumers. That may help answer the question of why the presence of a network might be worth a multiple over and above a standard customer base valuation. An electronic networking site such as MySpace, Facebook, or Bebo is still, I believe, first and foremost a collection of people (and their eyeballs). But there are some notable differences between what happens on those sites and what happens in a group of television viewers or magazine readers. First, users tend to be more highly involved in electronic networking than when watching television or browsing other media (magazines, Web sites). That is worth something. Second, some electronic networking sites collect quite a bit of information that is of commercial value. For instance, marketers might try to infer from my memberships to multiple interest groups and communities on Facebook what my interests are. The information revelation taking place on electronic networking sites further enhances their value. These two sources of additional value over a mere customer base are quantifiable, at least in principle. It is less clear whether the same holds for the third distinctive element of such networks: Is there any value in the network structure itself, that is, the pattern of person-to-person ties?

A highly central and active member may be worth more than others, but can we really impute a financial value to this social influencer? That would require that we can somehow attribute a fraction of the value of the influencees (e.g., their CLV assessed using standard means) to the social influencer. But an influencee may be connected to more than one influencer, so how will we decide what proportion to allocate to each? That is a difficult problem, especially in large networks where people have many connections (Richardson & Domingos, 2002; Trusov, Bodapati, & Bucklin, 2008). And what should we do once we have boosted the value of influencers based on their influencees' CLV and want to proceed with valuing the entire network? Should we deduct that value component attributed to the influencer from the influencees' CLV to avoid double counting? But if we do so, don't we end up negating all additional value from the network as all the additions and subtractions cancel out in the end? It seems to me that social contagion can lead to the equivalent of category expansion, and one may be able to show this based on the so-called network multiplier effect in network autocorrelated regression modeling. But how large the expansion effect is probably depends on the amount of influence in the network, which needs to be estimated. Accepted benchmark values would be helpful here, but we are far away from having the empirical research base to formulate such benchmarks with any degree of justified confidence.

HORIZONTAL AND VERTICAL NETWORKS

Much of the interest that marketers have in networks pertains to how information, attitudes, and behaviors get transmitted across network ties. Areas of applications include phenomena such as "buzz," "viral marketing," and "brand communities." In all those settings, the network is "horizontal" as it consists only of customers and potential customers. There are several other types of applications of network thinking, however, where the network consists of multiple kinds of actors occupying different locations in the industry column or value chain. I call the latter "vertical networks." There are some interesting marketing issues involving the intersection of horizontal and vertical networks that have been ignored so far by network researchers in marketing.

Buying and Selling Teams in Business-to-Business Marketing

Industrial buying is one of the few areas in marketing where the importance of social networks is not only considered received wisdom but also well supported by evidence (Van den Bulte & Wuyts, 2007). In particular, the relation between one's position in the decision-making unit and one's influence and access to resources is well established. Much of the most compelling evidence is a few decades old, however, and extensive reengineering of both firms and supply chains has occurred over the past 15 years. Ties that cross organizational boundaries and connect buyers to other buyer firms, suppliers, or channel partners may be much more important in organizational buying behavior today than the bulk of existing research and frameworks suggests. Research explicitly starting with attention to interconnections between people and departments both within and across company boundaries may provide valuable novel insights.

One topic that I find particularly interesting is how buying teams or decision-making units on the buyer side interact with account teams or problem-solving units on the selling side. The topic is not only of obvious importance to business-to-business (B2B) marketers in high-tech industries and B2B marketers of complex customer solutions but also of considerable theoretical interest as it involves how two networks interact with each other. Although the marketing literature abounds with conjectures that social network structure affects account team effectiveness (e.g., Hutt & Walker, 2006; Jones, Dixon, Chonko, & Cannon, 2005; Üstüner & Godes, 2006), the empirical evidence to date is quite sparse and mostly anecdotal. A central notion in team selling and account management is the need to have a constellation of various kinds of expertise and knowledge bases that have to be combined to develop and deploy a customer solution (e.g., Cunningham & Homse, 1986; Jones et al., 2005). Another key notion is that some member of the selling team, for example, an account manager, has to ensure the coordination within the team and between the selling team and the customer. Similar structural arrangements exist in the buying team. An important idea in the literature on buyer–seller interaction is that having experts from one side of the buyer–seller dyad interact intensely with their counterparts at the other side of the dyad leads to better knowledge sharing and facilitates keeping track of the current status of the project (Cunningham & Homse, 1986; Håkansson & Östberg, 1975; Håkansson, Wootz, Andersson, & Hangård, 1979; Hutt, Johnston, & Ronchetto, 1985). These knowledge transfer, coordination, and monitoring benefits, in turn, should result in more effective customer solutions. But is the presence of such "matching ties" between counterparts with similar domains of expertise in the two firms sufficient? Are there circumstances in which buyers or sellers may actually want to go beyond them? I expect so. For instance, the purchasing manager may want to keep tabs on all members of the selling team when he is concerned about poor coordination among them. But maintaining such a large number of contacts may be quite burdensome, so the purchasing manager may prefer to have those contacts with nonmatching counterparts to be infrequent, in contrast to having the contacts with the matching counterpart be frequent (Murtha, Bharadwaj, & Van den Bulte, 2008).

Another type of research, more fundamental and focusing on network structure itself rather than on its consequences, would be to collect data on actual buying and selling teams and to study the structure of ties. Are there some types of positions that keep occurring and, if so, with what frequency (e.g., Bonacich & Bienenstock, 1997; Marsden, 1989)? Are there particular motifs or subnetwork structures that keep occurring (Gadde & Mattson, 1987; Milo et al., 2002; Wilkinson, 1976)? Is there a systematic association between the frequency of positions or motifs and the country, industry, or product category? Answers to these descriptive questions might raise new questions, which in turn may help to sharpen our understanding of industrial buying and selling.

Horizontal Networks Disciplining Suppliers

A key problem that buyers and sellers in almost any market face is uncertainty about the trustworthiness of their counterparties (e.g., product availability and quality, prompt payment, delivery, etc.). Consumers buying and selling among themselves have long used third parties to reduce that uncertainty by establishing escrow accounts, providing information on seller reliability, and so on. The real estate market is an example. eBay and other e-commerce operators replicate this intermediary role, thus reducing transaction costs (and getting remunerated for it). Networks, however, may to some extent obviate the need for commercial third parties. Using interview data from over 1,400 respondents to the 1996 U.S. General Social Survey, DiMaggio and Louch (1998) found that when people make significant purchases from other consumers rather than commercial establishments, 20% to 40% do so from people with whom they have prior noncommercial relationships, either directly (relatives, friends, or acquaintances) or through a common link (friend of a friend, relative of a friend, etc.). Theory suggests that transacting with people one is connected to is effective because it embeds commercial exchanges in a web of obligations inducing both parties to behave appropriately in the economic transaction. A dense web of interconnections may also foster identification with the group, further facilitating cooperation (Portes & Sensenbrenner, 1993). These arguments imply that exchanges within one's extended ego-network (people to whom one is linked to directly or through a common contact) will be more common for risky transactions that are unlikely to be repeated and in which uncertainty is high than for other transactions. DiMaggio and Louch's data support this prediction. Exchange frequency reduces the extent to which one uses parties from within one's extended ego-network. Furthermore, their findings support the argument that uncertainty about product and performance quality leads people to prefer sellers with whom they have direct or indirect noncommercial ties. Moreover, people who transact with friends and relatives report greater satisfaction with the results than do people who transact with strangers, especially for risk-laden exchanges.

The general principle at work here is that having a densely knit network where many customers interact with many other customers makes it easier to enforce seller discipline because the presence of common third parties supports the emergence and enforcement of norms of cooperation (e.g., Coleman, 1988; Greif, 1993). In a densely knit network, a customer who feels treated improperly can damage the seller's reputation by bad-mouthing him or her among their common contacts, that is, other customers whom the seller is trying to sell to and whom the focal customer interacts with. Conversely, if the seller behaves beyond the call of duty, the customer can boost his or her reputation. Note, the mechanism applies equally well to horizontal consumer-to-consumer networks studied by DiMaggio and Louch (1998) or trader-to-trader networks studied by Greif (1993) as to vertical networks involving both interconnected customers and upstream suppliers. Hence, densely knit customer networks may increase the reward and coercive power of customers toward their suppliers. Marketers seem especially well placed to contribute insights on how network structure may affect the communication of satisfaction versus dissatisfaction and the enforcement of nonopportunistic behavior by sellers.

Channels of Distribution

Social network analysis seems a natural fit for channels research and can be used to investigate brokerage, competition, and coordination issues that go beyond the dyadic level. The competition of two manufacturers vying for the support of the same reseller who controls and brokers access to consumers is rather obvious. A network perspective also highlights coordination issues. For instance, the quality of work and customer satisfaction of a systems integrator may well be enhanced if two key suppliers cooperate with each other, but that same cooperation may diminish the systems integrator's ability to appropriate a large part of the value created. So, network structure may shed a new and more intense light on issues of brokerage, competition, and coordination pertaining to two key issues in marketing strategy: value creation and value appropriation. On the basis of prior theory and research outside marketing, I expect that even relatively small extensions from channel dyads to very small networks with three to five actors may be enough to learn about such complex issues (e.g., Wuyts, Stremersch, Van den Bulte, & Franses, 2004). Stefan Wuyts discusses the implications of such small networks for control and constraint in business markets in Chapter 4.

GETTING DATA: OPPORTUNITIES AND CAVEATS

Unlike most other types of market research, network analysis requires information not only about customers or other market participants but also about connections between those entities. Some connections leave a trace that is easy to capture. In organizational networks, for example, official and other records capture capital investments in ventures, R&D alliances, and, in some cases, commercial transactions. A nice example of the latter are "tombstone ads" published in the Wall Street Journal through which investment banks announced what deals they were involved in as well as other investment banks involved in the same deal (Podolny, 1993).

In personal networks, capturing connections is more difficult. Some ties may be traceable from secondary sources, such as kin relations and people's affiliation to the same organization, such as the hospital they work at or their university and year of graduation (e.g., Cohen, Frazzini, & Malloy, 2008). Some ties are recorded automatically, especially those taking place through electronic media, such as e-mail or hyperlinks. One of the reasons for the rapidly growing popularity of social network research among marketing academics, it seems to me, is the easy availability of these new types of data. Just as marketing scientists piggybacked on the emergence of scanner data in supermarkets in the 1980s, they now jump on the opportunity to do social network research while conveniently capitalizing on new sources of preexisting network data. Other data opportunities exist as well, however. These merit discussion since different kinds of data have different strengths and weaknesses. Being aware of these will help one use the right data for one's research objectives.

Electronic Data

Several kinds of electronic social network data have become available over the past few years. Some researchers investigating intraorganizational networks have access to data on telephone and e-mail interaction or on visits to company intranet sites acting as "live" document-sharing devices or as repositories of technical documents (e.g., Allatta, 2005; Kumar, Krishnan, & Krackhardt, 2008; Rice, 1994). Some researchers investigating consumer networks are using data on telephone calls (e.g., Drèze, Bonfrer, & Chiang, 2008; Hill, Provost, & Volinsky, 2006), "friendships" in social networking sites (e.g., Hinz & Spann, 2008; Katona, Zubcsek, & Sarvary, 2007; Lewis et al., 2008; Trusov, Bodapati, & Bucklin, 2008), "trusted reviewer" links in peer product review sites like Epinions (e.g., Narayan & Yang, 2008), or email recommendations (e.g., Leskovec, Adamic, & Huberman, 2007). Yet other researchers have investigated how the pattern of hyperlinks between e-commerce vendors' sites affects their revenue (Stephen & Toubia, 2008). Such electronic data have the appeal of being cheap to collect and of capturing the entire network, at least in many cases. Whenever one contemplates using such data, however, one must ask to what extent they reflect meaningful ties relevant for one's research problem. If they do not, as Trusov, Bodapati, and Bucklin (2008) found for about 80% of "friendship" ties in an internet social network, one will not be very different from a drunk looking for his lost keys under lampposts simply because that's where the light is. As documented by Páez, Scott, and Volz (2008), including irrelevant network ties in one's analysis of social influence results in biased estimates and erroneous conclusions. Some research projects by marketing academics jumping on the social network bandwagon seem to be mostly exercises in statistical or econometric modeling applied to data of limited substantive richness or interest. There is hope that matters will improve as marketing academics gain access to better network data and become more interested in substantive network phenomena and theory. At the same time, there is also hope that statistical advances may help researchers better deal with shallow network data, as illustrated by Trusov and colleagues (2008).

Geography as a Proxy for Social Networks

A popular alternative to collecting one's own network data is to use physical distance as a proxy for social distance. This often appears to be an appealing compromise. For instance, marketers studying the diffusion of new products have been interested in social contagion processes for decades but have often been forced to assume network structure away because of a lack of data. The typical study assumed that everyone could influence everyone, which requires that the network over which influence processes operate is either fully interconnected or totally random. Of course, assumptions of full interconnectedness or totally random network structure are often quite unrealistic. Some researchers have therefore used geography as a proxy for network structure (e.g., Bell & Song, 2007; Cliff & Ord, 1975).

The argument here is that one's location in physical or geographical space is related to one's location in the social network. The key assumption in this argument is that of the propinquity effect: People who live or work near each other are more likely to interact with each other than people who live or work far from each other. This propinquity effect has been documented in many studies and at several scales. The effect exists at the microlevel, such as the distance within one and the same building. People living on the same floor in a residential building are more likely to know each other and tend to interact more often than people living on different floors. Engineers having offices near each other are more likely to interact with each other than engineers whose offices are distant from each other. The effect also exists at a somewhat coarser scale, such as interactions among people living in different parts of a village, city, or county. The effect, finally, also operates across very large distances of hundreds of miles.

The propinquity effect results partly from constraints that physical distance places on the ability and opportunity to meet and interact (especially face-to-face), as well as from the fact that people who need or would like to interact tend to colocate. In some cases, it is valuable to distinguish between true distance effects versus self-selection in how and why geographical propinquity is associated with social interaction (e.g., Van den Bulte & Moenaert, 1998). In other cases, however, a marketer or analyst does not care much about why the relationship exists and simply uses the pattern of people's location in physical space as a proxy for their location in a social network (e.g., Bell & Song, 2007; Manchanda, Xie, & Youn, 2008).

The main advantage of using geographical distance as a proxy for distance in a social network is that the former is much easier and cheaper to observe than the latter. In addition, physical location—and hence spatial distance between two people or firms—can often be measured for each and every member of the population. These advantages come with a loss of information, however. The first disadvantage, obviously, is that network ties are not determined solely by physical distance, so the mapping between geography and social network is imperfect. This in turn introduces measurement error, which can result in either upward or downward biases in the statistical results. When spatial proximity is measured not using point-to-point distance but only using coarser areal units such as ZIP codes or states, the measurement error is even greater and may mask much differentiation among actors. Let's take ZIP codes as an example. Approximating the social network by ZIP code membership implies that all actors within the same ZIP code are structurally equivalent. That is, each actor or household has the same pattern of ties with all other actors in their own ZIP code and with all other actors in each other's ZIP code.

A second problem with using geography as a proxy for the network is that people and firms tend to colocate with similar others. For instance, income and wealth determine to large degree the kind of neighborhood one lives in. In the United States, where the quality of the public schools varies dramatically across districts, people with children may have a tendency to prefer a particular location because of school quality, whereas singles and empty nesters would not. The outcome of this self-selection process is that spatial proximity correlates highly with similarity in attributes. Proximity and attribute profile may be highly correlated even in the absence of self-selection. National culture and income per capita, for instance, tend to be more similar across nearby, rather than across distant, countries. Unless these attributes are controlled for in the analysis, similarity in behavior across proximate actors cannot be interpreted as valid evidence of social influence (e.g., Arbia, 1989; Dow et al., 1986).

A third disadvantage is that geographical distances, unlike social ties, are symmetric (setting aside oddities such as one-way streets, which can generate asymmetric travel times between two points). As a result, studies substituting geography for actual network data cannot shed light on issues of in-degree versus out-degree (the number of incoming versus outgoing ties) and the related issues of status, power, dependency, and reciprocation. As a final disadvantage, the loss of asymmetry also means that one's statistical analysis is more likely to suffer from network autocorrelation and reflection problems (e.g., Cliff & Ord, 1981).

In short, although geographical distance data are more easily, and more cheaply, obtained than actual network data, using them may imply a significant loss of information. So, the net benefit of using spatial rather than true network data remains an empirical question. How the advantages and disadvantages balance out is likely to vary from situation to situation. One might expect that using geography as a proxy would be more useful in a large population of undifferentiated consumers than in (a) consumer markets with clear opinion leaders or in (b) business markets and professional markets where a small number of accounts can generate a large proportion of total sales and getting the details right on who their contacts are may matter greatly.

Though I tend to be skeptical of studies using geographical data to make network claims, there are cases where the pattern of physical location can be viewed not as a proxy but as the actual pattern of relevant social relationships. One example is the pattern of competitive intensity among supermarkets, car dealerships, or hotels in the same price range (e.g., Barrot et al., 2008; Baum & Mezias, 1998; Bronnenberg & Mela, 2004). Given the importance of competition in theoretical arguments about social contagion (e.g., Hannan & Carroll, 1992) and structurally equivalent positions in a network (e.g., Burt, 1987), it is surprising that marketers have not used geographically referenced data more to study network-theoretical issues in competitive behavior. The expected return on research investment of such efforts seems attractively high.

Network Surveys

Many types of personal connections such as trust, advice, or conflict are very difficult to measure except through direct questioning. Network surveys have the great benefit of allowing one to tailor one's questions such that they capture the type of tie of substantive or theoretical interest. Unfortunately, surveys also present researchers with several challenges. Apart from sometimes being onerous to administer, they tend to suffer from imperfect accuracy stemming from poor memory (Brewer, 2000), differences across respondents' interpretations of questions (Bearman & Parigi, 2004), and even self-report biases as when respondents think they have many friends or have access to powerful others (Feld & Carter, 2002). Over the years, analysts have developed tools and procedures that limit these problems (Marsden, 1990, 2005). Better research is likely to come from using better measurement instruments, and the value of network research in marketing is likely to depend on it.

An additional problem with surveys is that a less-than-perfect response rate can dramatically affect some features of the observed network. Yet, some network statistics are surprisingly robust to imperfect sampling of the network. This need not be very surprising, provided one controls for size artifacts. Obviously, the characteristic scale of the number of ties each person receives will be biased downwards from the true value as the response rate goes down. In network of 300 people, for instance, the highest possible indegree (number of ties received) is 299 but in a 20% sample of 60 physicians it is only 59. This difference in scale, of course, is important for studies that seek to draw inferences about the true network structure, but it is *not* for studies that seek to relate differences in nodes' indegree to differences in nodes' outcomes or behavior (e.g., prestige, income, or time of adoption). For the latter, the correlation between the indegrees in the true and sampled network is what matters.

Some network statistics are remarkably robust in the sense that the statistic from the sampled network is highly correlated with that from the complete network. For instance, an important early study based on the analysis of 59 different social networks by Costenbader and Valente (2003) indicates that in-degree centrality (the number of times others nominate you as a contact) in human networks is a robust metric as long as response rate is higher than 20%. A more recent study of 447 45-person networks by McCarty, Killworth, and Rennell (2007) corroborates that degree centrality (the number of ties one has) is robust even at a random node sampling rate of 20%, and the authors corroborated this again in a second study of 554 45-person networks. Studying five networks each with tens of thousands of nodes, Leskovec and Faloutsos (2006) conclude that, after taking into account scaling, one is able to get good indegree measures using a 15% random node sampling rate. Another recent study by Kim and Jeong (2007) documents a Pearson correlation of more than 90% between true and measured degree under 20% sampling in a simulated Barabási-Albert network, increasing to more than 95% under 40% sampling. Other studies by Lee, Kim, and Jeong (2006) and De Silva et al. (2006) similarly document robustness of network degree under 20% to 40% sampling. So, depending on what the key constructs in one's study are and depending on what response rate one expects, the threat of less-than-perfect response need not be a reason to forego using network surveys as a means of data collection.

Experiments

Another approach to empirically study behavior within networks is to generate network structures as part of an experimental design rather than to measure pre-existing network structures as part of an observational design. One can create "artificial worlds" with varying network structures and investigate how these differences affect people's behavior. As consumer researchers have long understood, experiments often have the benefit of being cheap and, when well designed, allowing one to draw strong causal inferences about what affects what. Conjoint experiments, for instance, are a methodology that is long accepted in both marketing academia and business and that can easily be applied to networks as well (e.g., Wuyts et al., 2004). Other types of experimental designs can be used as well (e.g., Cook, Emerson, Gillmore, & Yamagishi, 1983; Dodds, Muhamad, & Watts, 2003; Frenzen & Nakamoto, 1993). It seems to me that experimental designs have been unduly maligned among business marketing academics and that they hold considerable promise for studying social network phenomena not only in consumer settings but also in business-to-business and channel settings.

Some may view simulation studies as another way to experimentally generate network structures. This view is quite dangerous when it ignores the distinction between empirical and formal analysis. Simulation studies, whether agent-based or other, do not allow one to study how people or firms behave. Rather, they allow one to study how a mathematical model or system behaves. These are two very different things. Not unrelated when the model is behaviorally sound, but quite different nevertheless.

CONCLUSION

Social networks among customers are receiving much attention from managers and marketing academics nowadays. Unsurprisingly for such a new area, current practice does not always appear to capitalize on existing network theory developed outside marketing, while some current developments in customer networking may be ahead of such theory. I have discussed some opportunities and challenges in developing research on how customer networks affect customer behavior and can affect managerial practice. In doing so, I focused on the structure or pattern of customer connections, rather than on customers (the points or nodes in the network) or connections (the lines in the network).

I first discussed the area that enjoys the most attention from marketing researchers and practitioners today: word of mouth about products and brands leading to an epidemic process sometimes referred to as social contagion. I advanced three ideas. First, many campaigns are based on three assumptions: (1) social contagion among customers is at work, (2) some customers' adoptions and opinions have a disproportionate influence on others' adoptions, and (3) firms are able to identify and target those influentials or opinion leaders. These are all reasonable assumptions, but we need to learn much more about when they are likely to hold. The first assumption is critical for any type of word-of-mouth or viral marketing campaign, whereas the latter two affect whether a campaign focusing on influentials or opinion leaders may be more effective than one aimed at generating buzz indiscriminately. This led me to the second idea: Given that contagion matters, there are several things we need to learn about how we can make campaigns more effective. How can influentials be convinced to serve as advocates for one product rather than another? More generally, what makes people spend time and energy to share information and advice? How can pre-existing social ties be activated to maximum effect? How effective are "viral-for-hire" services such as BzzAgent, Tremor or Vocalpoint that artificially create buzz for payment compared to genuine word of mouth? The third idea I advanced was a call for research on the role of identity and status within contagion processes, including the issue of positive and negative contagion across groups. Research on those issues may prove of both theoretical and practical value, not just in the area of new product marketing but also in that of brand management. This led me to discuss the phenomenon of brand communities from a network perspective. That discussion was limited to making a call for action and providing a few pointers to the sociological literature that might prove useful, because the area of brand communities as networks is one in which we have little to no research or theory.

Another issue of great interest where research is sorely lacking is how to value networks and communities. I suggested focusing on how networks and communities differ from mere aggregates as a possibly productive approach to tackle, or at least frame, this difficult problem. I also very briefly sketched out some issues on the related challenge of valuing particular members within networks or communities.

Social influence and word of mouth take place mostly within horizontal networks among customers. However, there are several other interesting phenomena at work in vertical networks, i.e., networks consisting of actors occupying different locations in the industry column or value chain. These seem to have been largely ignored in recent research, and I called attention to three marketing issues involving the intersection of horizontal and vertical networks. The first was the structure of, and interaction between, buying and selling teams in business-to-business marketing. Industrial buying and selling is a very important phenomenon that has not generated much theoretical excitement the last twenty years or so, and a network perspective may bring new developments and insights. The second issue I called attention to was how people and firms use their network connections to discipline suppliers and other commercial actors. This is a major area of investigation in economic sociology that somehow has not been picked up by marketing researchers, in spite of its obvious relevance to marketing practice and several research traditions within marketing. Disciplining upstream vendors in turn led me to the third issue where thinking in terms of vertical networks may lead to new theoretical developments and empirical insights: framing and investigating distribution channels in terms not of independent dyads but of networks, i.e., interconnecting dyads where the pattern of connections matter.

Having discussed several substantive research opportunities and challenges, I turned to methodological ones. More specifically, I offered some reflections on the strengths and weaknesses of different ways to obtain network data, distinguishing between collecting primary data through surveys, capturing data through electronic traces, using geography as a proxy for social networks, and finally using experimental design to purposely generate network structures in which human behavior takes place and is observed. The main point is that all types of data have their strengths and weaknesses, and that making informed decisions about what data to use for what substantive phenomenon and research question is what matters most. I raised some concerns about the popularity of electronic data and spatial data among marketing academics nowadays, noted that surveys can provide richer and sometimes surprisingly robust measures, and also made an argument in favor of more experimental research.

This chapter has offered some ideas on opportunities and challenges in developing a richer understanding of customer networks. I hope those ideas will provide some guidance, or trigger counterarguments, for future research efforts.

REFERENCES

Allatta, J. T. (2005). Worker collaboration and communities of practice. Unpublished PhD Dissertation, University of Pennsylvania.

Arbia, G. (1989). *Spatial data configuration in statistical analysis of regional economic and related problems*. Dordrecht: Kluwer Academic Publishers.

Bakshi, N., Hosanagar, K., & Van den Bulte, C. (2007). New product diffusion with two interacting segments or products. Working Paper, The Wharton School, University of Pennsylvania.

Barrot, C., Rangaswamy, A., Albers, S., & Shaikh, N. I. (2008). The role of spatial proximity in the adoption of a digital product. Presentation at the 2008 INFORMS Marketing Science Conference, June 12–14, 2008, Vancouver, BC, Canada.

Baum, J. A. C., & Mezias, S. (1992). Localized competition and organizational failure in the Manhattan hotel industry, 1898–1990. *Administrative Science Quarterly*, 37 (December), 580–604.

Bearman, P., & Parigi, P. (2004). Cloning headless frogs and other important matters: Conversation topics and network structure. *Social Forces, 83*(2), 535–557.

Becker, M. H. (1970, April). Sociometric location and innovativeness: Reformulation and extension of the diffusion model. *American Sociological Review, 35*, 267–283.

Bell, D. R., & Song, S. (2007, December). Neighborhood effects and trial on the Internet: Evidence from online grocery retailing. *Quantitative Marketing and Economics, 5,* 361–400.

Berger, J., & Heath, C. (2007, December). Where consumers diverge from others: Identity signaling and product domains. *Journal of Consumer Research, 34,* 121–134.

Bonacich, P., & Bienenstock, E. J. (1997). Latent classes in exchange networks: Sets of positions with common interest. *Journal of Mathematical Sociology, 22*(1), 1–28.

Brewer, D. D. (2000). Forgetting in the recall-based elicitation of personal and social networks. *Social Networks, 22*(1), 29–43.

Bronnenberg, B. J., & Mela, C. (2004, Fall). Market rollout and retail adoption for new brands of non-durable goods. *Marketing Science, 23,* 500–518.

Burt, R. S. (1987, May). Social contagion and innovation: Cohesion versus structural equivalence. *American Journal of Sociology, 92,* 1287–1335.

Carley, K. (1986). An approach for relating social structure to cognitive structure. *Journal of Mathematical Sociology, 12*(2), 137–189.

Carrington, P. J., Scott, J., & Wasserman, S. (Eds.). (2005). *Models and methods in social network analysis.* Cambridge: Cambridge University Press.

Cliff, A. D., & Ord, J. K. (1975). Space-time modelling with an application to regional forecasting. *Transactions of the Institute of British Geographers, 64* (March), 119–28.

Cliff, A. D., & Ord, J. K. (1981). *Spatial processes: Models and applications.* London: Pion.

Cohen, L., Frazzini, A., & Malloy, C. (2008). The small world of investing: Board connections and mutual fund returns. *Journal of Political Economy, 116* (October), 951–79.

Coleman, J. S. (1988). Social capital in the creation of human capital. *American Journal of Sociology, 94*(Suppl.), S95–S120.

Cook, K. S., Emerson, R. M., Gillmore, M. R., & Yamagishi, T. (1983). The distribution of power in exchange networks: Theory and experimental results. *American Journal of Sociology, 89*(2), 275–305.

Costenbader, E., & Valente, T. W. (2003). The stability of centrality measures when networks are sampled. *Social Networks, 25,* 282–307.

Coulter, R. A., Feick, L., & Price, L. L. (2002). Changing faces: Cosmetics opinion leadership among women in the new Hungary. *European Journal of Marketing, 36*(11), 1287–1308.

Cunningham, M. T., & Homse, E. (1986). Controlling the marketing-purchase interface: Resource development and organisational implications. *Industrial Marketing and Purchasing, 1*(2), 3–25.

De Bruyn, A., & Lilien, G. L. (2008). A multi-stage model of word-of-mouth influence through viral marketing. *International Journal of Research in Marketing, 25* (September), 151–63.

De Silva, E., Thorne, T., Ingram, P., Agrafioti, I., Swire, J., Wiuf, C., & Stumpf, M. P. H. (2006, November). The effects of incomplete protein interaction data on structural and evolutionary inferences. *BMC Biology, 4,* 39.

DiMaggio, P., & Louch, H. (1998). Socially embedded consumer transactions: For what kinds of purchases do people most often use networks? *American Sociological Review, 63*(5), 619–637.

Dodds, P. S., Muhamad, R., & Watts, D. J. (2003, August). An experimental study of search in global social networks. *Science, 301,* 827–829.

Douglas, M., & Isherwood, B. (1979). *The world of goods.* New York: Basic Books.

Dow, M. M., Burton, M. L., White, D. R., & Reitz, K. (1984). Galton's problem as network autocorrelation. *American Ethnologist,* 11, 754–70.

Drèze, X., Bonfrer, A., & Chiang, J. (2008). Network effects in defection. Working paper, The Wharton School, University of Pennsylvania.

Emirbayer, M., & Goodwin, J. (1994). Network analysis, culture, and the problem of agency. *American Journal of Sociology,* 99(6), 1411–1454.

Feld, S. L., & Carter, W. C. (2002). Detecting measurement bias in respondent reports of personal networks. *Social Networks,* 24(4), 365–383.

Frenzen, J. K., & Nakamoto, K. (1993). Structure, cooperation, and the flow of market information. *Journal of Consumer Research,* 20(3), 360–375.

Gadde, L.-E., & Mattsson, L.-G. (1987). Stability and change in network relationships. *International Journal of Research in Marketing,* 4 (March), 29–41.

Godes, D., & Mayzlin, D. (2009). Firm-created word-of-mouth communication: Evidence from a field test. *Marketing Science, 28,* 721–739.

Goldenberg, J., Lehmann, D. R., Shidlovski, D., & Barak, M. M. (2006). *The role of expert versus social opinion leaders in new product adoption* (Report No. 06-124). Cambridge, MA: Marketing Science Institute.

Greif, A. (1993). Contract enforceability and economic institutions in early trade: The Maghribi traders' coaliton. *American Economic Review, 83,* 525–548.

Gupta, S., & Mela, C. F. (2008). What is a free customer worth? *Harvard Business Review,* 86 (November), 102–109.

Gupta, S., Mela, C. F., & Vidal-Sanz, J. M. (2006). The Value of a 'Free' Customer. Working Paper No. 07-035, Harvard Business School, Harvard University.

Håkansson, H., & Östberg, C. (1975, June). Industrial marketing: An organizational problem? *Industrial Marketing Management, 4,* 113–123.

Håkansson, H., Wootz, B., Andersson, O., & Hangård, P. (1979). Industrial marketing as an organisational problem: A case study. *European Journal of Marketing, 13*(3), 81–93.

Han, Y. J., Nunes, J. C., & Drèze, X. (2008). First impressions: Status signaling using brand prominence. Working paper, The Wharton School, University of Pennsylvania.

Hannan, M. T., & Carroll, G. R. (1992). *Dynamics of organizational populations: Density, legitimation, and competition.* New York: Oxford University Press.

Hill, S., Provost, F., & Volinsky, C. (2006). Network-based marketing: Identifying likely adopters via consumer networks. *Statistical Science* 21 (2), 256–76.

Hinz, O., & Spann, M. (2008). The impact of information diffusion on bidding behavior in secret reserve price auctions. *Information Systems Research,* 19 (September), 351–68.

Hogan, J. E., Lemon, K. N., & Libai, B. (2004). Quantifying the Ripple: Word-of-Mouth and Advertising Effectiveness. *Journal of Advertising Research,* 44 (September–October), 271–80.

Holt, D. B. (1998, June). Does cultural capital structure American consumption? *Journal of Consumer Research, 25,* 1–25.

Holt, D. B. (2004). *How brands become icons: The principles of cultural branding.* Boston: Harvard Business School Press.

Hutt, M. D., Johnston, W. J., & Ronchetto, J. R., Jr. (1985, May). Selling centers and buying centers: Formulating strategic exchange patterns. *Journal of Personal Selling and Sales Management, 5,* 33–40.

Hutt, M. D., & Walker, B. A. (2006). A network perspective of account manager performance. *Journal of Business and Industrial Marketing, 21*(7), 466–473.

Iyengar, R., Valente, T. W., & Van den Bulte, C. (2008). Opinion leadership and social contagion in new product diffusion. Working Paper, The Wharton School, University of Pennsylvania.

Jasper, J. M., & Poulsen, J. D. (1995). Recruiting strangers and friends: Moral shocks and social networks in animal rights and anti-nuclear protests. *Social Problems, 42*(4), 493–512.

Jasso, G. (2001). Studying status: An integrated framework. *American Sociological Review, 66*(1), 96–124.

Jones, E., Dixon, A. L., Chonko, L. B., & Cannon, J. P. (2005, Spring). Key accounts and team selling: A review, framework, and research agenda. *Journal of Personal Selling and Sales Management, 25,* 182–198.

Katona, Z., Zubcsek, P., & Sarvary, M. (2007). Joining the network: Personal influences as determinants of diffusion. Working Paper, INSEAD.

Kim, P.-J., & Jeong, H. (2007). Reliability of rank order in sampled networks. *European Physical Journal B, 55*(1), 109–114.

Kumar, V., Petersen, J. A., & Leone, R. P. (2007). How valuable is word of mouth? *Harvard Business Review,* 85 (October), 139–46.

Kumar, V., Krishnan, R., & Krackhardt, D. (2008). Dynamics of network structure and content in an organizational forum. Working paper, Carnegie Mellon University.

Latour, B. (2005). *Reassembling the social: An introduction to actor-network-theory.* Oxford: Oxford University Press.

Lee, J., Lee, J., & Feick, L. (2006). Incorporating word-of-mouth effects in estimating customer lifetime value. *Journal of Database Marketing & Customer Strategy Management,* 14 (October), 29–39.

Lee, S. H., Kim, P.-J., & Jeong, H. (2006). Statistical properties of sampled networks. *Physical Review E, 73*(1), 016102.

Leskovec, J., Adamic, L. A., & Huberman, B. A. (2007). The dynamics of viral marketing. *ACM Transactions on the Web,* 1 (May), Article No. 5.

Leskovec, J., & Faloutsos, C. (2006). Sampling from large graphs, in *12th ACM SIGKKD International Conference on Knowledge Discovery and Data Mining,* Philadelphia, PA, 631–636.

Lewis, K., Kaufman, J., Gonzalez, M., Wimmer, A., & Christakis, N. (2008). Tastes, ties, and time: A new social network dataset using Facebook.com. *Social Networks,* 30 (4), 330–42.

Locock, L., Dopson, S., Chambers, D., & Gabbay, J. (2001, September). Understanding the role of opinion leaders in improving clinical effectiveness. *Social Science and Medicine, 53,* 745–757.

Manchanda, P., Xie, Y., & Youn, N. (2008). The role of targeted communication and contagion in new product adoption. *Marketing Science, 27,* 961–976.

Marsden, P. V. (1989). Methods for the characterization of role structures in network analysis. In L. C. Freeman, D. R. White, & A. K. Romney (Eds.), *Research methods in social network analysis* (pp. 489–530). Fairfax, VA: George Mason University Press.

Marsden, P. V. (1990, August). Network data and measurement. *Annual Review of Sociology, 16,* 435–463.

Marsden, P. V. (2005). Recent developments in network measurement. In P. J. Carrington, J. Scott, & S. Wasserman (Eds.), *Models and methods in social network analysis* (pp. 8–30). Cambridge: Cambridge University Press.

Martin, J. L. (2002). Power, authority, and the constraint of belief systems. *American Journal of Sociology, 107*(4), 861–904.

McAdam, D., & Paulsen, R. (1993). Specifying the relationship between social ties and activism. *American Journal of Sociology, 99*(3), 640–667.

McCarty, C., Killworth, P. D., & Rennell, J. (2007). Impact of methods for reducing respondent burden on personal network structural measures. *Social Networks, 29*(2), 300–315.

McLean, P. D. (1998). A frame analysis of favor seeking in the renaissance: Agency networks and political culture. *American Journal of Sociology, 104*(1), 51–91.

Milo, R., Shen-Orr, S., Itzkovitz, S., Kashtan, N., Chklovskii, D., & Alon, U. (2002). Network motifs: Simple building blocks of complex networks. *Science, 298*(5594), 824–827.

Miller, C. M., McIntyre, S. M., & Mantrala, M. K. (1993). Toward formalizing fashion theory. *Journal of Marketing Research, 30* (May), 142–57.

Molnár, V., & Lamont, M. (2002). Social categorisation and group identification: How African-Americans shape their collective identity through consumption. In A. McMeekin, K. Green, M. Tomlinson, & V. Walsh (Eds.), *Innovation by demand: An interdisciplinary approach to the study of demand and its role in innovation* (pp. 88–111). Manchester, UK: Manchester University Press.

Muniz, A. M., Jr., & O'Guinn, T. C. (2001). Brand community. *Journal of Consumer Research, 27*(4), 412–432.

Murtha, B. R., Bharadwaj, S. S., & Van den Bulte, C. (2008). Developing and deploying effective customer solutions: The role of networks within and between buying and selling teams. Working Paper, The Wharton School, University of Pennsylvania.

Nadel, S. F. (1957). *Theory of social structure*. Glencoe, IL: Free Press.

Narayan, V., & Yang, S. (2008). Modeling the formation of dyadic relationships between consumers in online communities. Working Paper, Johnson Graduate School of Management, Cornell University.

Philips, D. J., & Zuckerman, E. W. (2001). Middle-status conformity: Theoretical restatement and empirical demonstration in two markets. *American Journal of Sociology, 107*(2), 379–429.

Páez, A., Scott, D. M., & Volz, E. (2008). Weight matrices for social influence analysis: An investigation of measurement errors and their effect on model identification and estimation quality. *Social Networks, 30* (4), 309–17.

Podolny, J. M. (1993). A status-based model of market competition. *American Journal of Sociology 98* (4), 829–72.

Portes, A., & Sensenbrenner, J. (1993). Embeddedness and immigration: Notes on the social determinants of economic action. *American Journal of Sociology, 98*(6), 1320–1350.

Rice, R. E. (1994). Relating electronic mail use and network structure to R&D work networks and performance. *Journal of Management Information Systems, 11* (1), 9–29.

Richardson, M., & Domingos, P. (2002). Mining knowledge-sharing sites for viral marketing. In *Proceedings of the Eighth International Conference on Knowledge Discovery and Data Mining* (pp. 61–70). Edmonton, Canada: ACM Press.

Rogers, E. M. (2003). *Diffusion of innovations* (5th ed.). New York: Free Press.

Rogers, E. M., & Cartano, D. G. (1962, Autumn). Methods of measuring opinion leadership. *Public Opinion Quarterly, 26*, 435–441.

Sirsi, A. K., Ward, J. C., & Reingen, P. H. (1996). Microcultural analysis of variation in sharing of causal reasoning about behavior. *Journal of Consumer Research 22*, (December), 345–72.

Snow, D. A., Zurcher, L. A., Jr., & Ekland-Olson, S. (1980). Social networks and social movements: A microstructural approach to differential recruitment. *American Sociological Review, 45*(5), 787–801.

Steenkamp, J.-B. E. M., & Gielens, K. (2003, December). Consumer and market drivers of the trial probability of new consumer packaged goods. *Journal of Consumer Research, 29,* 368–384.

Stephen, A. T., & Toubia, O. (2008). Deriving value from social commerce networks. Working Paper, Columbia University.

Thompson, C. (2008, February). Is the tipping point toast? *Fast Company, 122,* 74–105.

Trusov, M., Bodapati, A., & Bucklin, R. E. (2008). Determining influential users in Internet social networks, Working Paper, Robert H. Smith School of Business, University of Maryland.

Üstüner, T., & Godes, D. (2006). Better sales networks. *Harvard Business Review, 84*(7–8), 102–112.

Valente, T. W., Hoffman, B. R., Ritt-Olson, A., Lichtman, K., & Johnson, C. A. (2003, November). Effects of a social-network method for group assignment strategies on peer-led tobacco prevention programs in schools. *American Journal of Public Health, 93,* 1837–1843.

Van den Bulte, C., & Joshi, Y. (2007). New product diffusion with influentials and imitators. *Marketing Science, 26* (May), 400–21.

Van den Bulte, C., & Lilien, G. L. (1997). Bias and systematic change in the parameter estimates of macro-level diffusion models. *Marketing Science, 16*(4), 338–353.

Van den Bulte, C., & Lilien, G. L. (2001, March). *Medical Innovation* revisited: Social contagion versus marketing effort. *American Journal of Sociology, 106,* 1409–1435.

Van den Bulte, C., & Moenaert, R. K. (1998). The effect of R&D team co-location on communication patterns among R&D, marketing, and manufacturing. *Management Science, 44*(11), S1–S18.

Van den Bulte, C., & Stremersch, S. (2004, Fall). Social contagion and income heterogeneity in new product diffusion: A meta-analytic test. *Marketing Science, 23,* 530–544.

Van den Bulte, C., & Wuyts, S. (2007). *Social networks and marketing.* Cambridge, MA: Marketing Science Institute.

Walker, R. (2008). *Buying in: The secret dialogue between what we buy and who we are.* New York: Random House.

Walsh, G., Gwinner, K. P., & Swanson, S. R. (2004). What makes mavens tick? Exploring the motives of market mavens' initiation of information diffusion. *Journal of Consumer Marketing, 21* (2), 109–22.

Watts, D. J., & Dodds, P. S. (2007, December). Influentials, networks, and public opinion formation. *Journal of Consumer Research, 34,* 441–458.

Weimann, G. (1994). *The influentials: People who influence people.* Albany: State University of New York Press.

Wilkinson, I. F. (1976). An exploration of methodologies for detecting subgroups, subsystems and cliques of firms in distribution channels. *Journal of the Academy of Marketing Science, 4*(2), 539–553.

Wipperfürth, A. (2005). *Brand hijack: Marketing without marketing.* New York: Penguin Group.

Wuyts, S., Stremersch, S., Van den Bulte, C., & Franses, P. H. (2004, November). Vertical marketing systems for complex products: A triadic perspective. *Journal of Marketing Research, 41,* 479–487.

Zuckerman, E. W., & Sgourev, S. V. (2006). Peer capitalism: Parallel relationships in the U.S. economy. *American Journal of Sociology, 111* (March), 1327–66.

3

Understanding the Relational Ecosystem in a Connected World

Conor M. Henderson and Robert W. Palmatier

Customer decisions are often influenced by multiple sources including brands, salespeople, friends and co-workers, and internet sites. These sources of influence not only affect the customer but can also influence each other and evolve over time. For example, a firm's brand may indirectly influence a customer through the brand's impact on the customer's social in-group without the customer ever seeing any of the firm's advertising. Viewing the customer, the many sources of influence, and all the interconnections between the different sources together is a challenging task since it creates a complex picture with the customer embedded in an inter-tangled web of connections. In this customer-centric web, marketing actions ripple across direct and indirect connections affecting customer's decisions and behaviors. We term this web of customer centric interconnections as the customer's relational ecosystem. *Merriam-Webster's Collegiate Dictionary* (2001) defined an ecosystem as "the complex of a community of organisms and its environment functioning as an ecological unit." Thus, we chose the term *ecosystem* to emphasize the interconnected nature of the relational entities that constitute the environment, which influences the customer as a decision-making unit.

Specifically, we define a *relational ecosystem* as a web of interconnections among relational entities that operate as a system and influence customer decision-making behaviors, where *relational entities* are unique objects perceived by the customer as containing specific information, meaning, and identity (see Table 3.1). The four relational entities with the largest influence on consumption decisions are brands, boundary spanners, social in-groups, and marketplace networks. Brands are all the relevant brands with direct or indirect influence on a customer. Boundary spanners are a firm's employees that reach out and connect with customers, usually

TABLE 3.1

Relational Ecosystem Definitions

Terms	Definitions	Role in customer's relational ecosystem
Relational ecosystem	Web of interconnections between relational entities that operate as a system and influence customer decision making.	Customers are embedded in an evolving relational ecosystem, which influences their decision-making behaviors.
Relational entity	Unique object perceived by the customer as containing specific information, meaning, and identity. Entities share information, meaning, and identity through relational channels.	The customer is the focal relational entity. The four relational entities with the greatest potential influence on consumption decisions are *brands, boundary spanners, social in-groups*, and *marketplace networks*. Selling firms represent a higher-level entity, linked to the customer's relational ecosystem mainly through its brands and boundary spanners.
Relational channel	A component of the customer's relational ecosystem that is the connecting bond or link for transmitting information, meaning, and identity among the relational entities and customers.	Main relational channels connect the four primary entities to the customer. The customers' *associative relational channel* connects them to brands. Customers' *professional relational channel* connects them to boundary spanners. Customers' *in-group relational channel* connects them to their social in-group. The customers' *network relational channel* connects them to the marketplace network. Side relational channels connect the four primary entities with one another.

sales associates. The social in-group is a social network consisting of all the people with whom the customer has a personal social relationship, excluding boundary spanners. The marketplace network is the publicly available content and information and the infrastructure that connects it to the customer.

We term the sources of influence as "relational entities" and the connections between these sources of influence and the customer as "relational channels." Different relational channels connect customers to each relational entity and provide them with access to the specific information, meaning, and identity* a relational entity offers. Side linkages among relational entities allow relational entities to influence each other, and increase the complexity of understanding the aggregate effects on customers. In summary, relational entities and channels form a unit or system and represent the customers' relational ecosystem. The connections among relational entities represent *relational channels*, defined as a connecting bond or linkage for transmitting information, meaning, and identity among relational entities and customers. In addition to the four primary relational entities, companies (i.e., selling firms) represent a higher level relational entity that captures an aggregate of the customer's links to its brands and boundary spanners. Brands and boundary spanners represent the firm in its relationship with customers, where the trust and loyalty a customer has toward a firm's brands and/or boundary spanners, influence the customer's trust and loyalty toward the firm (Martín Gutiérrez, 2006; Palmatier, Scheer, & Steenkamp, 2007).

The focus of this chapter is to describe a customer's relational ecosystem, its components, and how this ecosystem influences a customer's decision making (Figure 3.1). We propose that viewing a customer as embedded within a relational ecosystem provides a lens that can sharpen our understanding of how customers make decisions in the connected world. This big picture view shows that each relational entity is merely a single component of a complex, interconnected, evolving system; highlighting each relational entity's potential to indirectly influence customers, one of a number of insights hidden when each relational entity is viewed separately.

All four primary relational entities in our framework have important effects on customer decision making. First, research on brands reveals their persuasive power to influence customers' purchase behavior (D. A. Aaker, 1992; Court, Freeling, Leiter, & Parsons, 1996; Hoeffler & Keller, 2003; Keller, 1993). Customers who are familiar with a brand and hold favorable (unfavorable), unique brand associations in their memory respond more positively (negatively) to the marketing of that brand than

---

* Information is obtainable knowledge. Meaning is the significance of a thing. Identity is the distinguishing character or personality of a unit. Relational entities are a source of obtainable knowledge, significance, and distinguishing characteristics or personality traits.

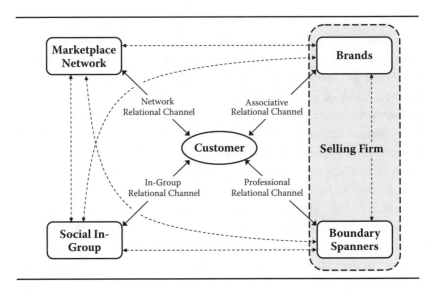

FIGURE 3.1
Customer's relational ecosystem.

if they did not hold this brand knowledge (Keller, 1993). Second, work in relationship marketing reveals that customers believe working with boundary spanners whom they perceive as ethical (Lagace, Dahlstrom, & Gassenheimer, 1991), similar (Crosby, Evans, & Cowles, 1990; Dion, Easterling, & Miller, 1995), trustworthy, committed (Morgan & Hunt, 1994), competent, benevolent, expert, and problem solvers (Sirdeshmukh, Singh, & Sabol, 2002) provides those customers with reduced uncertainty, exchange efficiency, social satisfaction, and other benefits (Dwyer, Schurr, & Oh, 1987). Customers value the benefits provided by these boundary spanners and therefore choose to engage in relationships with them, are influenced by them, and behave in a manner that is beneficial for both the boundary spanner and the boundary spanner's firm (Palmatier et al., 2006). Third, customers' purchase behavior depends on their social network, in the form of prepurchase information sharing, normative pressure, and postpurchase feedback (Bearden & Etzel, 1982; Van den Bulte & Wuyts, 2007). Potential customers look to their social in-group and the network marketplace to find previous customers' product and service evaluations, to find information, and to create expectations (Burnkrant & Cousineau, 1975). Fourth, customers use the marketplace network as a rich source of information for third-party verifications (Klein & Ford,

2003) and comparison shopping (Keeney, 1999). The Internet in particular enables consumers to engage with the marketplace network with maximal convenience, minimal time, and minimal cost (Keeney, 1999).

A review of previous literature reinforces the importance of each of these relational entities. The overwhelming majority of research and practice, however, continues to focus on only one of the relational entities at a time, ignoring how they operate as a complex system with aggregate and synergistic effects on customer decisions. Perhaps this singular focus results from the lack of a comprehensible framework and the difficulty of empirically testing the resultant complex model when accounting for all the relational entities working together to influence customer decisions.

Research in the area of customer/consumer information search has begun to show that not only are customers connected to all of the relational entities but interconnections and relationships also exist between relational entities (Lee & Hogarth, 2000; Mazis, Staelin, Beales, & Salop, 1981; Price, Feick, & Higie, 1987). Information from different sources often acts as a complement or substitute for customers, such that information received from one source likely affects how they interpret information from another (Lee & Hogarth, 2000; Smith, 1993). Customers might use different sources (relational entities) to gather information about the same potential purchase, according to the specific characteristics of the entity (Klein & Ford, 2003). For example, in a study of customers' search for information during automobile purchases, Klein and Ford (2003) showed that customers who research the marketplace network on the Internet spend less time with boundary spanners at the dealership, which indicates relational entities act as substitutes. Customers evaluating a complex offering typically consult different relational entities to obtain information, meaning, and identity about different attributes of that offering (Klein & Ford, 2003). Another study of customers making investment decisions about different financial products shows that they interact with brands (advertisements), boundary spanners (professional financial service providers), social in-groups (family, friends, and colleagues), and the marketplace network (printed literature, information on the Internet, television, and radio broadcasts) (Lin & Lee, 2004). In this study, 42% of customers obtained investment information from at least four sources (Lin & Lee, 2004), demonstrating the pervasive role of the relational ecosystem. The idea that customers connect through multiple relational channels with multiple relational entities to form a higher level system also is gaining momentum as research repeatedly shows that multiple relational entities serve as sources of product and service information for customers (Culnan, 1983; Lee & Hogarth, 2000; Lin & Lee, 2004). Peterson and Merino (2003, p. 100) outlined the need for more research from this perspective, noting that "the manner in which consumers search for, process, and use information is a complex phenomenon that is not completely understood."

Consider an example of how a customer's behavior may be influenced by the aggregate impact of all relational entities working as a unit in a relational ecosystem: A young couple is nervous about purchasing their first house and wants a real estate agent to help them with the process. The couple is influenced by real estate commercials they have seen and their perceptions and associations of different brands. They recognize the name and symbol of the hot air balloon of RE/MAX and are familiar with the gold-colored theme of Century 21. They have strong positive associations toward these brands, but those associations lack a strong enough influence on the couple's decision to focus them solely on these two companies out of the hundreds of brokerages and thousands of agents available. Instead, they search the marketplace network for more information, including searches on Google and Yahoo! to find third-party reviews of agents and brokerages. They used the marketplace network successfully before, when they searched for places to rent, and have some confidence in the objectivity of this relational entity. The marketplace network is virtually limitless and can provide good information, but it is also slightly overwhelming, and the couple is not sure if it provides information that is relevant to their unique situation. The couple would like to validate what they have learned so far by reaching out to their social in-group of friends and family, whom they know can be trusted. It would be easy to look to them for honest answers, but none of the people in this network are experts, in that most have not used real estate agents in this area before. The couple wonders if there are enough informed people within this group who can offer reliable advice. Previously, the couple had a positive personal experience with a Keller Williams agent who was very friendly, returning their dog after it ran over to an open house that the agent was hosting in the neighborhood where they rented. This agent had given them some good advice and seemed knowledgeable. They wonder if they owe this agent any loyalty. At the same time, they question whether this agent is really the best counselor and negotiator, and they feel biased toward agents who represent one of the brands with which they are more familiar and that they have stronger positive associations toward.

Using this web of information and relationships, the young couple makes a decision, for which a side linkage between a member of their social in-group and a boundary spanner turns out to be the key. One of their friends recommends an agent whom he used to work with before the agent got involved in real estate. The couple found positive third-party reviews on the Web and learned that this agent was a top agent for their preferred brokerage, RE/MAX. The linkage with each relational entity aids their decision process, but none of the relationships exist in isolation; instead, they act in concert to influence the couple's decision. As this example reinforces, sellers should take an "ecosystem" perspective when trying to understand customers' decisions.

In the remainder of this chapter, we explore customers' relational ecosystems in an attempt to develop a framework to understand decision processes in a highly connected world. First, we explain the use of the ecosystem. Second, we focus on each entity and its primary role in this connected ecosystem. Third, we examine the relational channels and the interactions and flows that take place among entities, which combine to influence consumer behavior. Fourth, we conclude with a discussion of some potential research directions.

CUSTOMER'S RELATIONAL ECOSYSTEM

In a relational ecosystem, a web of interconnections operates as a system to influence the customer's decisions and behaviors. Our terminology thus borrows from the natural sciences to apply the ecosystem as a metaphor to describe this system. Business professionals and academics often borrow terms from the natural sciences (Lambkin & Day, 1989). Our use of *ecosystem* highlights certain pivotal aspects of this system of relationships (Frels, Shervani, & Srivastava, 2003; Iansiti & Levien, 2004; Moore, 2006; Quinn, 1999). In ecology, an ecosystem, simply put, is a place where living organisms and the physical environment exist together in balance and interact with one another (Xavier, Krishnan, & Borin, 2005). Iansiti and Levien (2004, p. 76) pointed out, "The familiar concept and vivid terminology of the biological ecosystem can help focus managerial attention on features of modern business networks that are often ignored by conventional theories about markets and industry structure but that underlie many drivers of business success and failure."

The simple term *network* also might be used to technically describe the system of connections among relational entities in the customer's relational ecosystem, because a network is a set of nodes (distinct entities) and ties that connect the nodes (Van den Bulte & Wuyts, 2007). The term, however, does not convey the breadth and complexity of the system of relationships among relational entities as effectively as the metaphorical use of the term "ecosystem," for three reasons. First, *ecosystem* better signals that the network is actually a complex, interconnected system in which each entity, and particularly the customer, is influenced by the aggregate effect of all interactions among other entities in the system. Quinn (1999, p. 40) stated, "An ecosystem ... is the most perfect example of pure integration," and just like species in a biological ecosystem, each entity in our relational ecosystem is affected by the aggregate impact of each relationship in the system, whereas outside of the complete system, the entities have little meaning. There are many different types of network structures across a whole spectrum of interconnectedness; ecosystems are at the extreme. Iansiti and Levien (2004, p. 78) warned, "A firm that takes an action without understanding the impact on the ecosystem as a whole is ignoring the reality of the networked environment in which it operates." A complete understanding of the relationship between lions and impalas is impossible without examining the other bonds these animals have within the African savanna ecosystem; it similarly is impossible to understand the buyer–seller relationship without also examining the other relationships that exist in the customer's relational ecosystem. Therefore, our use of the term *ecosystem* emphasizes that the relationships among entities are just as important as any activity that takes place between those entities.

Second, *ecosystem* better highlights the important role of time and evolution. Ecosystems evolve as changes take place in the physical environment or among species in the ecosystem. When one species changes or evolves, other species also evolve to maintain the balance or face extinction, which prompts the whole ecosystem to evolve (Moore, 1993). A customer's relational ecosystem parallels these natural ecosystems, because as one entity's role in the ecosystem changes, other entities must change as well. The Internet, for example, altered many roles. Multiple entities struggle to adapt to the increased importance of the marketplace network, which occurred because the Internet made it much more valuable to customers. Brands and boundary spanners also must adjust and rethink how the increased power of the marketplace network might complement their efforts, as well as the areas in which it fails to satisfy customers as a source of information, meaning, and identity. In analyzing how customer decisions and behaviors occur, we must analyze dynamic effects on the system. When analyzing networks, research is often conducted on static networks; the term ecosystem distinguishes this system as evolving. Researchers acknowledge the need for a more comprehensive model of customer search behavior that incorporates the concept of "ongoing search," or the process by which customers acquire information that may affect their future purchase decisions, even if they have no imminent plans for making such a purchase (Lee & Hogarth, 2000; Schmidt & Spreng, 1996). The ecosystem metaphor naturally incorporates dynamic variables to assess a customer's decisions and behaviors, because ecosystems evolve and experience implications from a single event over many years. As the customer's relationships with each entity evolve, the company's strategy for managing its own resources and handling external resources that influence its relationship with outside entities (i.e., marketplace network and social in-group) also has to evolve.

Third, the term *ecosystem* instead of networks helps provide clarity to the model by emphasizing the diversity of the components that comprise it, some of which are networks themselves (social in-group and marketplace network). When examining a network, we require clear boundaries to distinguish the nodes within it (Van den Bulte & Wuyts, 2007). Van den Bulte and Wuyts point out that relevant boundaries are dependent on the theoretical issue of interest and "there is no standard rule of thumb for the 'boundary specification problem'" (2007, p. 14); although, usually networks and their boundaries tend to be defined so that the nodes and the ties are consistent in nature even if they vary in strength. An ecosystem, however, consists of vastly heterogeneous nodes and diverse ties between mammals, amphibians, plants, fungi, non-living elements. Likewise, in the customer's relational ecosystem each relational entity and their ties are similarly unique. In subsequent sections we analyze in greater depths the distinguishing characteristics of each entity and relational channel; but a quick look here at each one will emphasize their distinct nature. Brands as an entity include the brands that make up a customer's consideration set and the tie is mainly the mental process of building associations with the brands in the consideration set. Boundary spanners include companies' personnel that engage with the customer and the tie is a dyad. Social in-group is the customer's social network, and the ties are all social relationships. The marketplace network is also a network consisting of all publicly available market related messages and the infrastructure that connects it and makes it available serves as the customer's tie to the marketplace network.

The relational ecosystem is a rather diverse system; its own boundaries are restricted by the boundaries and criteria of each of its four main components. In summation, the relational ecosystem could be described as a network, but it is a very specific kind of network and therefore the use of ecosystem as a metaphor is useful as it accentuates certain important characteristics that are less common in the majority of networks.

RELATIONAL ENTITIES

Relational entities in the customer's relational ecosystem are the unique objects perceived by the customer as containing specific information, meaning, and identity. Entities exchange information, meaning, and identity through relational channels, which in aggregate influence the customer's behavior and decisions. We therefore analyze each of the primary relational entities: brands, boundary spanners, social in-group, and marketplace network (Table 3.2 summarizes each relational entity's distinguishing properties). Admittedly there are other ways to categorize unique relational objects that customers perceive as containing information, meaning, and identity; however after reviewing the literature, we believe that categorizing relational objects in these four relational entities supports a parsimonious framework that effectively highlights meaningful distinctions amongst the entities.

Brands

A brand equals the name, symbol, and/or image used to identify the offering of one seller and differentiate it from competing offerings (Kotler, 1991). From a customer's perspective, brands reflect aggregate experience with a product or service, which suggests they are composed of the complete set of associations a customer holds toward that brand (Keller & Lehmann,

TABLE 3.2

Summary of Relational Entities' Distinguishing Properties

Property	Brand	Boundary Spanner	Social In-Group	Marketplace Network
Definition	A brand is the identifying attributes that distinguish an offering of a seller from those of the competitors (Kotler, 1991, p. 442). Brands also are the embodiment of associations toward the offering and thus reflect the complete experience that customers have with the offering (Keller & Lehmann, 2006).	A boundary spanner is the firm's personnel that operate at the periphery of the firm (Singh & Rhoads, 1991). In the customer's relational ecosystem, boundary spanners refer specifically to the selling firm's marketing personnel that engage with customers, most commonly salespeople and customer service representatives.	A social in-group is the network of a customer's friends, family, colleagues, and anyone with whom he or she has a personal relationship who is not associated with the selling firm.	A marketplace network is a network comprised of publicly available content related to the marketplace and the systems and infrastructure that allow for this content to be created and connected for public access.
Unit of analysis	Product or service (Chaudhuri, 1998)	The relationship between parties whether a dyad (Hawke & Heffernan, 2006), a triad (Narayandas et al., 2002), or other structure	Group structure and relationship between actors	Network structure, time spent with various areas of network

Continued

TABLE 3.2 (Continued)

Summary of Relational Entities' Distinguishing Properties

Property	Brand	Boundary Spanner	Social In-Group	Marketplace Network
Relevant theories	Need-press theory (Stanton & Lowenhar, 1974), utility maximization framework in the face of uncertainty (Erdem & Swait, 2004)	Social exchange theory (Bagozzi, 1975), relational contracting theory (Dwyer, Schurr, & Oh, 1987), commitment–trust theory of relationship marketing (Morgan & Hunt, 1994)	Social network theory and group processes (Van den Bulte & Wuyts, 2007)	Network theory
Credibility (trustworthiness and expertise)	Low to medium credibility: medium level of trustworthiness, and low level of expertise.	Medium to high credibility: high level of expertise, and medium of level of trustworthiness. Customers can quickly and confidently decide if an individual boundary spanner is credible.	Medium to high level of credibility: trustworthy source of subjective opinions on experiential attributes. Less able to provide quality objective information and facts. Expertise can vary depending on match between social group's knowledge and specific offering characteristics.	Medium credibility: credible source of objective, functional information. Expert generated content is available through this source, but providers of content can be obscure, anonymous, or unidentified and thus carry more perceived risk (Grant et al., 2007).

Intimacy of relationship	Low to medium level of intimacy: Customers may feel intimate bond with brands, but brands cannot reciprocate at the same level of intimacy because they are impersonal, nonvital entities.	Medium to high level of intimacy: professional and personal relationship. Can reciprocate intimacy and provide social benefits and high level of customization.	Highest level of intimacy through personal social relationship	Lowest level of intimacy because it is an impersonal, public entity
Affiliation	Seller/product affiliated: Information, meaning, and identity in the brand are primarily provided by the selling firm	Seller-affiliated, the selling firms representatives that provide services of seller firm	Independent, associated with social role	Independent third party
Effectiveness	Creating brand loyalty and brand equity; differentiation through associations created by brand elements; specializes as a source of meaning and identity	Reducing uncertainty, managing dependence, customizing bilateral communication, and providing benefits	Influencing customers through word-of-mouth and normative pressures; provides trustworthy information and approval; can be a source of experiential information, identity, and meaning	Providing a wealth of marketplace information to help customers accurately evaluate marketplace offerings and firms in specific and ongoing searches; specializes as a source of information

2006). From the firm's financial perspective, brands are financial assets that hold value and can determine the effectiveness of marketing efforts. As a relational entity, brands included in the customer's consideration set make up the group of brands that are in the relational ecosystem.

Although brands are lifeless and lack objective existence as "simply a collection of perceptions held in the mind of the consumer," they still can serve as partners in a relationship (Fournier, 1998, p. 345). Brands provide customers with information, meaning, and identity, especially when humans anthropomorphize them to animate, humanize, and personalize the brands and facilitate interactions (Fournier, 1998), which in turn allows people to associate human personality characteristics with brands (J. L. Aaker, 1997). The interaction between a brand and customers reflects a relationship because interdependencies exist between both partners; they are both involved in the formation of the relationship, and they both affect, define, and redefine the relationship (Fournier, 1998). Customers often hold similar feelings toward brands and people (e.g., interdependence, commitment, loyalty, love, hate, self-concept) (Aggarwal, 2004; Fournier, 1998; Martín Gutiérrez, 2006). Fournier's (1998) article stimulated vast research that has showed customers engage in relationships with brands, and these relationships often provide a channel for the exchange of information, meaning, and identity.

Brands differ from other relational entities in many ways. One of the key defining aspects of brands as relational entities is their creation and affiliation. The firm's marketing managers play chief roles in constructing the firm's brands and developing brands as relational partners, but customers and other stakeholders also play important roles through different stages of this process (Boyle, 2007). For example, marketing managers make marketing mix decisions that represent the brand's "behaviors," and on the basis of these behaviors, customers make inferences about the traits and personality of the brand (Fournier, 1998). Although the concept of brand cocreation, or the idea that brands result from efforts by multiple stakeholders, including the company and customers, is gaining some momentum among academics (Boyle, 2007), brands as entities remain controlled primarily by the firms that own them and thus are affiliated with the selling firm and its products (Lee & Hogarth, 2000).

Brands appear less credible than other relational entities as a source of expert information because marketing managers create those brands, which implies a potential bias. Customers' belief in the credibility of a brand, which reflects the believability of the brand positioning, remains important, however, when customers form consideration sets and choose from among the options in that set (Erdem & Swait, 2004). Customers worry more about a brand's trustworthiness than its expertise, though both are subdimensions of brand credibility (Erdem & Swait, 2004). Because brands are biased agents, they may not be credible experts, but they still represent current and past marketing strategies, which makes them credible signals of trustworthiness over time (Erdem & Swait, 2004; Herbig & Milewicz, 1995). Even when a firm's employees and strategies change, customers can associate a consistent brand with its current and past behaviors, continue trusting a brand, and expect their associations to stay relatively consistent. For example, Coca-Cola has gone through many different managers and marketing strategies—some of which, such as "New Coke," hurt the brand's trustworthiness—but its marketing behaviors over time have led customers to trust its brand in general, making it one of the strongest in the world. The Coca-Cola brand maintains a lasting history with its customers, so even if a new marketing officer or advertising agency takes over for the brand, customers will continue to trust it on the basis of their history with the brand, which includes both past and current associations.

Yet brands are a relatively impersonal relational entity, which affects their role in the relational ecosystem. Customers can and often do feel close personal attachments to certain brands and even express feelings of lust, love, and commitment—feelings usually reserved for humans (Fournier, 1998). Despite these feelings and the moderate intimacy achieved in brand–customer relationships though, and unfortunately for customers who love certain brands, brands are unable to return these feelings. When Microsoft takes out a full-page advertisement in the *Wall Street Journal* thanking its partners, the brand is not personally engaged but rather just a marionette puppet controlled by the marketing directors. The inability of the brand, despite marvelous advances in technology and customer relationship marketing software, to listen independently and respond empathetically to an individual customer keeps the brand from being as intimate as a relational entity as some more personal entities (e.g., boundary spanners, social in-groups).

In identifying these unique aspects that distinguish brands from other relational entities, we also must try to understand how these aspects may shape the unique role that brands play in a customer's relational ecosystem and how it changes. Typically, brand studies use the product as the unit of analysis (Chaudhuri, 1998). The most relevant theories for explaining brands' influence on customers include the need-press theory, according to which customers try to match needs with the brands they associate with solutions to the need (Stanton & Lowenhar, 1974), and the utility maximization theory, in which customers use brand associations to maximize their utility by limiting uncertainty at the minimum cost (Erdem & Swait, 2004). The main goal of marketing practitioners when they develop and execute brand strategies is to foster brand loyalty among a desired customer base (Chaudhuri, 1998). As a relational entity, brands create differentiation through associations and offer superior sources of meaning and identity, though they are inferior as a source of information (Chaplin & John, 2005; Fournier, 1998; Keller, 1993; Keller & Lehmann, 2006; Kleine, 2006; Sirgy & Danes, 1982).

We believe that brands' roles as relational entities in a customer's relational ecosystem are most pivotal before associations are set, because set brand associations are difficult to change. Brand inertia means firms must address customer–brand relationships in the initial stages, when the associations will influence customer decisions for years to come and may be especially difficult to alter. Therefore, brands continue to play pivotal roles even after associations have been established, though a company's opportunity to establish brand loyalties is greatest at the beginning of the customer relationship. This proposition may help explain why self–brand connections and loyalties begin to develop rapidly between middle childhood and early adolescence, the time when most consumers first begin to encounter brands as individuals (Chaplin & John, 2005).

Boundary Spanners

Boundary spanners are personnel who operate at the periphery of the firm (Singh & Rhoads, 1991); in the customer's relational ecosystem, boundary spanners refer to the selling firm's marketing personnel who engage with the public on behalf of the selling firm, most commonly in the form of salespeople and customer service representatives. For many relationship-oriented firms, the strength of boundary spanners is pivotal to the success of the firm's relationship marketing efforts. When relationship marketing enhances the quality of the relationship between boundary spanners and customers, selling firms experience positive outcomes (Palmatier, Scheer, Houston, et al., 2007).

Customers and selling firms can engage in relationships at three different levels: interpersonal (seller firm's boundary spanners with customer firm's boundary spanners), person to firm, and interfirm (Palmatier, Scheer, Houston, et al., 2007; Palmatier, Scheer, & Steenkamp, 2007). Relationship-oriented customers choose to engage in relationships with boundary spanners because they recognize that boundary spanners offer valuable information, meaning, and identity, such that through the relationship, the customer can receive social, structural, and financial benefits (Palmatier, Scheer, Houston, et al., 2007). The business relationship with a boundary spanner is usually professional in nature, but because it is between people, it is social as well, and friendships may develop between the parties.

Boundary spanners as employees of the seller firm are affiliated with the firm, though they sometimes experience role ambiguity and can feel torn between their loyalty to relational customers and the firm that employs them (Fang, Palmatier, Scheer, & Li, 2008; Stamper & Johlke, 2003). Selling firms may enjoy the benefits of a customer's loyalty directed towards their boundary spanning employees; however, they are also exposed to the risk of losing their customer's loyalty if their boundary spanning employees leave the firm (Palmatier, Scheer, & Steenkamp, 2007).

Customers will judge boundary spanners as credible if they believe their underlying, stable characteristics warrant such a favorable judgment (Campbell, 1958; Hamilton & Sherman, 1996; O'Laughlin & Malle, 2002; Palmatier, Scheer, Houston, et al., 2007). In addition to judging boundary spanners' trustworthiness (Morgan & Hunt, 1994) and expertise (Sirdeshmukh, Singh, & Sabol, 2002), customers consider boundary spanners credible if they seem to be ethical (Lagace et al., 1991), similar (Crosby et al., 1990; Dion et al., 1995), committed (Morgan & Hunt, 1994), competent, and benevolent problem solvers (Sirdeshmukh et al., 2002). Customers who perceive boundary spanners as credible and having those characteristics likely engage in high-quality customer–boundary spanner relationships (Palmatier, Scheer, Houston, et al., 2007). Overall, boundary spanners as entities should appear to be experts; it is their job to have expertise about the offerings to help customers maximize the value of the purchase, consumption, and disposal of the offering. Customers also make quick, strong judgments about each boundary spanner's trustworthiness, unlike judgments about the firm, which is harder to judge because it is an abstract group. Therefore, customers may be more willing to trust and commit to a relationship with an individual boundary spanner than to one with the firm (Hamilton & Sherman, 1996; O'Laughlin & Malle, 2002; Palmatier, Scheer, Houston, et al., 2007).

As entities that consist of people, boundary spanners also can create high levels of intimacy. Customers sometimes express personal feelings— friendship, hate, platonic love—toward certain boundary spanners (e.g., a customer loves her hairdresser, develops a friendship with the sales clerk in Nordstrom's shoe department, and feels safe with her doctor), but unlike brands, boundary spanners can respond in personalized ways. A company with good customer relationship management technologies can send a birthday card with a coupon to valuable customers, but only an actual person can take corporate buyers to a baseball game, buy them their favorite beer, and create memories to share during their next phone call. Boundary spanners thus provide a very personal relational entity.

Studying boundary spanners and their role in relationship marketing programs has grown ever more important in recent decades, as marketers have realized the important role of interpersonal relationships in marketing. The challenge therefore becomes taking all we have learned about boundary spanners and assessing their role as a single entity in the customer's relational ecosystem. Prior research on boundary spanners generally uses the relationship as its unit of analysis, whether a dyad (Hawke & Heffernan, 2006), triad (Narayandas, Caravella, & Deighton, 2002), or some other structure. Several relevant theories have shaped relationship marketing thought, including social exchange theory (Bagozzi, 1975), relational contracting theory (Dwyer et al., 1987), and the commitment–trust theory of relationship marketing (Morgan & Hunt, 1994). When engaging in relationship marketing, both buyers and sellers hope to reduce uncertainty, manage dependence, create efficient exchanges, and enjoy social satisfaction from the association (Dwyer et al., 1987). The parties also may hope to take advantage of the possible "significant gains in joint and consequently individual payoffs" that result from "effective communication and collaboration to attain goals" (Dwyer et al., 1987, p. 79). As a consequence of the collaborative, relational nature of marketing relationships between boundary spanners and customers, boundary spanners are most effective, compared with other relational entities, at manifesting a seller firm's customer orientation in its attempt to personalize its business by providing personal service to customers. As relational entities, boundary spanners specialize in providing information and meaning in the form of the services and relationship benefits they provide. They do not specialize in providing identity though, because of the private, interpersonal nature of their customer linkages.

Finally, the role boundary spanners play in the customer's relational ecosystem depends somewhat on the context (environment, product, and customer characteristics). Because of their ability to customize the interaction for each customer and represent the selling firm throughout a lasting partnership, boundary spanners play more important roles in serving markets in which customers require specialized attention, services, and complex information. If boundary spanners are relationship oriented, the relationship likely requires attention and significant resources from both boundary spanners and the seller firm, which implies each boundary spanner can serve only a limited number of customers. Thus, boundary spanners are powerful information providers and relationship builders but are less able to provide meaning or identity and less capable of efficiently reaching a vast multitude of customers.

Social In-Group

A customer's social in-group consists of the actors (friends, family members, colleagues, associates) and connecting bonds (relationships) in a customer's egocentric social network (Van den Bulte & Wuyts, 2007). Members of a customer's social in-group differ from the boundary spanners with whom a customer may have a relationship, because social in-group members are independent of the selling firm. To clarify, an uncle who works for Dell and advises his niece to buy her first laptop from Dell is a part of the niece's social in-group, not a Dell boundary spanner, because the relationship is independent of the uncle's employment. The uncle's relationship with his niece is not oriented around his employment with Dell and continues even if the uncle quits or is fired. Furthermore, a hairstylist with whom a customer interacts only during a hair appointment is a boundary spanner when they discuss the salon and hair products but could become a member of the consumer's social in-group if the conversation turns to buying a laptop, because the hairstylist–customer relationship is independent of the sale of a laptop. The social in-group therefore comprises individual actors who influence the customer but who also constitute many subgroups (e.g., family, social club, work group, team), each of which is part of the customer's social in-group, which implies that group processes also influence the customer's decisions and behaviors.

Customers engage in relationships with their social in-groups and obtain information from those groups for their decisions (Bearden & Etzel, 1982; Lee & Hogarth, 2000; Stafford, 1966), yet businesses practitioners and some academics still tend to clump customers and their social in-groups within the same category, viewing them as one group because they both represent potential customers. Keller and Lehmann (2006) acknowledged the need for research to understand how marketers can influence a customer's social network and how the social network affects brand equity. Although they considered the firm, boundary spanners, the marketplace network (including competitors), and customers as parts of the complex group of entities that contribute to constructing a brand, they failed, however, to account for noncustomers who still play pivotal roles in shaping the brand through their position in the customer's social in-group. Several authors have encouraged the growing trend of focusing on the effect of the customer's social in-group relationships on customer behaviors (Jones, 2005; Van den Bulte & Wuyts, 2007).

Whether the social in-group is categorized as a social network (Van den Bulte & Wuyts, 2007) or individual members (Culnan, 1983), the defining characteristics of the social in-group and its members are their close relationships with the customer and independence from the seller (Klein & Ford, 2003; Lee & Hogarth, 2000). As a third party to the customer's decision, the social in-group influences the customer and keeps the customer's best interest in mind. The social in-group also commands trust from customers, who recognize that the social in-group is motivated to maintain their relationships and keep the customer healthy, not by self-interest in the outcome of the transaction. Unfortunately though, this trustworthy entity rarely consists of experts, so the social in-group often cannot independently satisfy a customer's need for information. Social in-groups also tend to be rather homogeneous and close, which minimizes the presence of diverse experts who can offer expert advice. Network theory, however, suggests a means to overcome this issue, such that if a customer's social in-group is characterized by a low level of closure, its actors are well connected to other in-groups, so the customer can benefit from the connections with other groups and thus bridge the gap and create more social capital (Van den Bulte & Wuyts, 2007). As an example, if a surfer needs information about wireless Internet routers for his surf shop but associates within a social in-group that is completely made up of other surfers with limited relevant knowledge who are closed off from other social groups, this Internet shopper is out of luck. If one of his friends has a sister who works in the computer science department of MIT though, that relationship can bridge the gap and allow the customer to gain trustworthy information from a third-party expert. Researchers have further speculated that customers look to their social in-group to provide expertise about user experiences but avoid it for objective, specific performance information (Grant, Clarke, & Kyriazis, 2007). A customer may ask a friend how braces feel but will wait to ask the orthodontist how the braces work. Generally, because the social in-group is a very trustworthy entity with some expertise, it represents a highly credible entity.

The social in-group also is capable of the highest level of intimacy, because the connection between the customer, the social in-group, and the actors in that group is purely interpersonal. An actor often develops the most intimate connections with the customer, and the customer serves as a member of the social in-group for the actor when their roles reverse. Family remains one of the primary groups of most customers' social in-groups, with one of the strongest impacts on marketing-related behavior (Gil, Andrés, & Salinas, 2007); intimacy among family members is usually at the highest possible level.

Previous research that relates to the role of a social in-group as an entity in the customer's relational ecosystem focuses on either social networks or social group members' roles in the information search. In either case, the unit of analysis is the structure that connects the actors or the relationship between the actors and the customer, which means the most relevant theories are network theory and social group processes. The social in-group attempts to maintain relational norms and help the customer make utility-maximizing decisions to ensure the health of the relationship and group. As a relational entity, the social in-group specializes in providing information and meaning through word-of-mouth behavior in the form of prepurchase, experiential, subjective information sharing (Grant et al., 2007); postpurchase approval; and normative pressure (Van den Bulte & Wuyts, 2007).

The social in-group thus appears to have a very unique role in the customer's relational ecosystem. It is the one entity that frequently acts as a complement to, rather than a substitute for, other entities, by adding something of value, directing a customer to other entities, or confirming messages delivered from other entities (Klein & Ford, 2003; Ratchford, Talukdar, & Myung-Soo, 2007). The social in-group also appears more important when the customer considers a publicly consumed, as opposed to privately consumed, offering (Ratner & Kahn, 2002). Throughout the different stages of a customer's life cycle, different members within the social in-group probably become more or less important, such as family when customers are dependent on others (young or very old) and friends and coworkers when customers are more independent (adolescent to adult). A final interesting development is that members of society, who often are social in-group members for potential customers, are beginning to participate more and more in the creation of content that previously was the exclusive domain of traditional media powers and companies.

Marketplace Network

The marketplace network is the largest relational entity in the customer's relational ecosystem, comprising all independently created public knowledge, systems, and infrastructure that connect the public to the marketplace and relevant marketplace information. As an example, a multitude of reports on Apple's iPhone 3G appeared published (online and offline in magazines, newspapers, Web sites, blogs, flyers) and broadcasted (television, radio, podcast). The systems and infrastructure that connect marketplace information and make it accessible to the public include cable lines, satellite, wireless, newspaper magazine stands, Internet portals, and search portals (e.g., Google, Yahoo!, MSLive). Recent developments in technology, specifically the increased power of the Internet, also have increased the marketplace network's connective power and, as a result, the importance of the marketplace network.

Yet the marketplace network is the least relationship-oriented entity in the customer's relational ecosystem, though customers still seek out relationships with it. Customers build trust in certain sources of knowledge and become comfortable with engaging with certain systems, infrastructure, and avenues of access, through which they obtain marketplace information.

Public relations firms and departments must pay close attention to customers' trust in different parts of the marketplace network. According to recent studies (Beringer, 2008), customers' relationships with some parts of the network (e.g., dedicated online media channels) are strengthening even as relationships with other parts are weakening (e.g., mainstream media channels, with the exception of radio). Customers characterize online media channels as more accurate, honest, and truthful, but they persist in their relationship with traditional media channels because their history, including the consistent form and availability of these channels, makes them easier to use (Beringer, 2008).

A customer's relationship with the network often is strongest at certain access points, such as a customer's own Web page, which serves as its neighbor and the node through which the customer consistently accesses other parts of the network (Van den Bulte & Wuyts, 2007). The customer grows to trust this access point and engages in a strong relationship with it. For some customers, this access point may be a local newspaper, but by reading the newspaper, they learn of other books, Web sites, and television shows and therefore reach out to those other parts of the network to obtain further value. A company may use a particular website, such as Business.com, as a trusted starting point to access the business-to-business marketplace. Consumers and business-to-business customers value trusted sources that connect them to appropriate solutions. For example, Business.com, Google, Yahoo!, Bing, trade journals, radio stations, newspapers magazines, and many other actors in the marketplace network seek customers and hope to establish relationships in which the customers use them as their initial access point to the rest of the marketplace network. Google and similar companies care little about whether people stay at their Web site; their real value is in connecting the customer with other parts of the marketplace network. These companies earn profits by organizing the network into a user-friendly experience and allowing companies the opportunity to gain a prominent place in the customer's marketplace network search. Google AdWords and other such search advertisement programs, which sell the positions of sponsored ads in search results, also enable companies to connect indirectly with customers through the marketplace network. Companies bid on these positions because they know that customers have relationships with Google and turn to the site as a reliable entity that helps them access the marketplace network.

The marketplace network thus is extremely interconnected and develops ties to all other relational entities, though it is an independent entity. Brands, boundary spanners, and social in-groups may interact with the marketplace network and provide some content, but the network as a whole is not controlled by any one actor; instead, it is created by a multitude of actors and the connections between them. Customers know that even if they come across seller-created information on the marketplace network, other third parties also on the network can offer their opinions and insights regarding the validity of that information.

As an entity, the marketplace network appears largely credible, even if certain actors in the network lack credibility. Every piece of information, opinion, and content is available to the public and thus to public scrutiny; in turn, customers believe that the network undermines poor sources and rewards credible ones. Web sites such as Digg.com use other members of the network to validate their content, so if a member of the marketplace network makes a mistake in one part of the network, other members are quick to find out and identify the mistake. The validity of the marketplace networks comes from the sheer number of sources of content and the power of the interconnections among those sources. Much of what customers find on the network comes from sources that are neither trustworthy nor expert, yet other sources likely will address the flaws and point out the truth. The marketplace network therefore benefits from strength-in-numbers reasoning. As more people grow comfortable with the Internet and its enduring influence on the marketplace network, the marketplace network should become more credible and provide better sources of performance, objective, and factual information used to compare multiple offerings, though not as trustworthy and lacking the expertise provided by the social in-group in experiential, subjective reports on user experience (Grant et al., 2007).

Because the marketplace network is the most public of all relational entities, it is also the least intimate. None of the vast amount of information and content relevant to almost any situation is created for specific users. Even customers participate in the creation of content for the marketplace network, a role previously dominated by traditional media powers and marketers, by posting reviews, ratings, blogs, vlogs, editorials, and more (Kliatchko, 2008). It is important to point out that this user generated content is one part of the marketplace network and not the social in-group. These independent users share their opinions with the marketplace regarding products and services, but do not have a social connection directly with the customer. On the other hand, if a customer is a member of an online community in which the customer has a social online connection with members and shared information is meant for each other, not the public at large then this would be an online social in-group even if members of the "public" could "eavesdrop." The Internet interconnects all aspects of the network, not just media designed for the Web; newspapers, television shows, journals, magazines, radio broadcasts, conference proceedings, and much more all are published on the Web. Marketplace information therefore is available to the public in real time, which has had a profound effect on multiple markets, especially financial markets. Despite its lack of intimacy, such that many customers feel their privacy has been violated when the marketplace network offers individual-specific information, the marketplace network is one of the fastest growing entities in terms of importance because of its power to provide a plethora of valuable content at a minimal resource cost.

Studying the marketplace network has become a top priority in business as the Internet has revolutionized this entity and exponentially increased its value. The traditional unit of analysis was the customer's time spent with a component of the marketplace network, but the Internet has reduced the importance of time spent (Klein & Ford, 2003). The profound impact of the Internet also has prompted reevaluations of several relevant theories, such as information economics and reasoned action. The goal of this entity is to allow actors in the marketplace network to discover, create, and share marketplace-relevant content. As an entity, it specializes in providing objective information that is easily comparable, relevant, and verifiable, as well as a means for people to share information with the public. Therefore, it is most important when customers need factual information to reduce their risk of error or an accurate overview of the whole market. This role may help explain why customers often pay lower prices after they use the Internet to access information about the automobile marketplace network (Ratchford et al., 2007; Zettelmeyer, Scott Morton, & Silva-Risso, 2006).

RELATIONAL CHANNELS

To gain a better understanding of how relational entities operate in a system that collectively influences customer decision making, we also must investigate relational channels, the connecting bonds or linkages that transmit information, meaning, and identity among entities in that relational ecosystem. Four main relational channels connect primary entities to customers: customers' associative relational channel connects them to brands, their professional relational channel connects them to boundary spanners, the in-group relational channel connects them to their social in-group, and customers' network relational channel connects them to the marketplace network. Side relational channels connect the primary entities with one another and tie the relational ecosystem together, such that interactions across them work together to affect customer behavior and decision making. Each relational channel has different characteristics and properties, however, which affects a customer's relationship with a specific relational entity (Table 3.3 summarizes the four primary relational channels' key properties).

Primary Relational Channels

The primary relational channels are the most commonly studied channels in the relational ecosystem because they provide direct connections to and thus directly affect the customer. While the side channels maybe the most interesting channels in that they allow for indirect connections and tie the whole ecosystem together to operate as an intertwined unit, the primary channels are the most important in that they are the channels through which the customer directly participates. Studying each of these channels can help marketers and researchers investigate which relational channel is likely to have the greatest total impact on a customer in specific situations. Knowing which relational channel is most important in a given situation is of greater value to marketers than knowing to which message or content a customer will be most responsive, because if a message or content moves through a channel that a customer generally ignores, it will be useless, no matter how pertinent the message may be (Kliatchko, 2008). Therefore, we evaluate properties, strengths, and weaknesses across different relational channels.

The directionality of interactions tends to be bilateral, as it is in most relationships; the associative and network relational channels, however, are more unilateral than the highly interactive, reciprocal in-group and professional relational channels. The associative relational channel mainly delivers messages and content from the brand to the customer, which customers may use to form associations. The network relational channel mainly features content and messages delivered to the customer from the marketplace network, though the Internet is making this channel more

TABLE 3.3

Summary of Primary Relational Channels' Properties

Property	Associative Relational Channel	Professional Relational Channel	In-Group Relational Channel	Network Relational Channel
Relational entity connected to customer	Brands	Boundary spanners	Social in-group	Marketplace network
Directionality (flow of information, meaning, and identity)	Unilateral from brand to customers	Bilateral and reciprocal two way communication between boundary spanners and customers in real time	Free flowing channel between in-group members and customers	Mainly unilateral from marketplace network to customers, but customers may provide some content to the marketplace network
Target of channel message	Broad target: messages aimed at multiple customers and stakeholders	Specific target: interaction between individuals or small teams of boundary spanners and customers	Specific target: interactions between individuals or small groups	Broad target: messages designed for public consumption
Level of customization for customer	Low: messages meant to appeal to large groups of people	High: can be adapted in real time to customer needs, but boundary spanners may attempt to over-customize and lie	Highest: can be adapted in real time to customer needs, and social in-group members have little motivation to bias information	Low: messages are detailed but often include a lot of extraneous information; costly to find specific customized messages

Continued

TABLE 3.3 (*Continued*)

Summary of Primary Relational Channels' Properties

Property	Associative Relational Channel	Professional Relational Channel	In-Group Relational Channel	Network Relational Channel
Frequency of activity	High: brands are hyper-active in trying to send messages to customers	Varying: activity picks up when service is required or selling firm is attempting to increase business	Normative influences are constant, but specific word-of-mouth behavior is irregular	Varying: marketplace network constantly produces content, and customers easily control when to engage with this channel
Power of activity (impact per message)	Low: plethora of messages often erodes the impact unless customer has a strong identification with the brand	High	Highest	Medium: when messages correctly (incorrectly) provide the information a customer is seeking, it has a high (low) impact

interactive (e.g., Web 2.0). In addition, the customer usually seeks content from the marketplace network through the network relational channel, whereas he or she tends to receive most content and messages passively from brands through the associative relational channel.

The level of customization in each relational channel depends on the level of focus each channel uses to target its interactions. Brands gain the most value when their positive associations are widely and strongly held (Keller, 1993; Keller & Lehmann, 2006), so their messages tend to appeal broadly to a large population, which makes them poorly tailored for individual customers. Messages and content created for the marketplace network may have a specific recipient in mind, but because the public at large may access them, only a small percentage of available messages are relevant to the individual circumstances of members of that public. The network relational channel provides a multitude of specific messages to customers, rarely tailored to a specific situation, such that messages delivered through both channels often end with a suggestion to consult with a boundary spanner who can provide customized, two-way content (e.g., "consult with your doctor before using …"). Finally, boundary spanners and social in-group members connect through their respective channels, which send messages targeted to the individual customer and thus allow a high level of customization in channel interactions.

Two related aspects of the main channels are the frequency and power of activity. A channel's overall impact is a function of the amount of activity and the power of that activity. The associative relational channel is very active, because brands constantly try to grab customers' attention to establish new associations, but it usually is not very powerful. As more and more brands try to use this channel to create favorable brand associations that their target market holds widely and strongly, brands start to sound the same, and customers perceive the messages as just noise. The professional relational channel has less frequent but more powerful interactions, so though customers may be overwhelmed by the amount of boundary spanners trying to establish relationships, once a relationship exists, it has great impact. The in-group relational channel is constantly active as a normative influence; customers observe members of their in-group and are influenced by their behavior. Although it is seldom active as a source of information through word-of-mouth behavior, when it functions, it has significant power. The network relational channel is generally active only when customers decide to engage with the marketplace network, usually in short bursts of activity. The power of the messages delivered through this channel depends greatly on how relevant the message is to the customer.

Side Relational Channels

Side relational channels connect relational entities and enable them to interact with one another; these interactions can shape each relational entity by providing it with additional information, meaning, and identity. By influencing the relational entities, side relational channels indirectly affect the customer's decision making and behavior. Moreover, side relational channels allow the relational entity to influence another entity's connection to the customer by influencing that other entity. For example, a brand's relationship with a customer's family influences family members' relationship with the customer, and through this relationship, the customer often develops similar brand associations and forms relationships with the brands that mimic the family's relationship with the brands (Gil et al., 2007). When business customers look at other companies in their social in-group that have a relationship with a brand, they perceive these relationships as a signal of the brand's level of quality; therefore, the customer company's brand associations depend on the company's relationship with other companies and the other companies' relationship with the brand (Podolny, 2005).

These side channels further allow the entity to play an active role in the customer's relational ecosystem, even if the main relational channel is not open or active. Customers are gatekeepers and may choose to use the main relational channels or block them to avoid the entities' attempts at a relationship. Adblock Plus (one of the most popular add-ons for Mozilla Firefox's Web browser), the National Do Not Call Registry, spam filtering, zapping and zipping commercials with TiVos and DVRs, On Demand television, receptionists, and personal assistants all serve as ways to close some channels. Furthermore, customers realize the entity on the other side of the main relational channel is not willing or able to engage with them. For example, some companies do not worry about branding and have only generic offerings; others ignore the role of boundary spanners and go so far as to eliminate customer service lines or contact information. Sometimes a customer's social in-group cannot provide relevant help regarding offerings, such as information about a local hotel in a small town in Chile. It is even possible that the marketplace network could lack any useful information if the consumer is the foremost expert on the offering or the offering is brand new and no one has used it yet. When a customer blocks a main relational channel or the channel is inactive, other relational channels play a greater role, but all entities still can play a role through their side relational channels.

For example, imagine a woman who finds out from the marketplace network that consuming omega-3 fatty acids, as found in fish oil, is good for people's cardiovascular system, so she discusses this effect with her family doctor, a boundary spanner. When the doctor confirms the potential benefit, she asks him to recommend fish oil capsules to her husband, who has a family history of heart problems, on her husband's visit next week. The doctor agrees, and the husband obediently follows the doctor's orders by purchasing some fish oil from the vitamin and mineral section of the pharmacy. In this example, the husband does not engage with the marketplace network through the network relational channel and has limited activity through the channel connections with his wife, a prominent member of his social in-group; she learned about his family health history but did not give advice directly to him, and he did not seek advice from her. The main relational channel for the husband connects him with his doctor, that is, the professional relational channel, but his behavior was influenced by multiple relational entities that all represent integral parts of the customer's relational ecosystem. Such side relational channels may be especially important to selling firms, because though customers can block main relational channels, they cannot block all side relational channels.

Winning in the Connected World

Some companies have astutely recognized that their customer's exist in a highly connected world and are reaping the benefits by helping customers connect with the relational entities in a manner that is beneficial to the company. Nike has found a way to engage with their customers' relational ecosystems to create an experience that has been beneficial for customers and themselves. This experience creation began when marketing chief Trevor Edwards assembled a cross-specialty, cross-company team with Apple that integrated running, music, and technology to create Nike + in 2006 (Gregory 2007). Nike + began as a tool that communicated data obtained from Nike running shoes' sensor to their iPod nano allowing runners to track their pace, distance, and other running statistics while listening to music (Gregory 2007).

Nike has since developed a growing system that has become bigger than the original idea that started Nike + and is propelling the company's staggering double digit increase in share of the U.S. running shoe market since it introduced Nike + (Greene 2008; Gregory 2007). Nike is connecting with customers' relational ecosystem in new ways that are differentiating it from the competition and providing customers with a reason to try their product in a product category where customers tend to be very loyal to products. By collaborating with Apple, Nike was able to reach a group of runners who enjoyed listening to music while running but previously wore other companies' shoes. The collaboration allowed for Nike to use some customers' strong associative relational channel bond with the Apple brand and the iPod nano to reintroduce itself to the customers. Furthermore, Nike educated its own salespeople and salespeople at retail outlets that carried Nike + so they could inform their customers about the new technology. Nike also realized the Nike + platform presented a great opportunity to facilitate the development of a massive, international community of runners which would provide runners with access to the social benefits that are typically found in team sports such as basketball and soccer but absent in running, a sport that is highly individualistic. They helped develop this community through the creation of a Web site, nikeplus. nike.com, in which runners could automatically upload their running statistics every time they connected their iPods to the computer. This Web site not only served as a place for runners to track their progress but also to connect with other runners by sharing advice and stories on public forms and forming online and potentially real life running groups in which runners would challenge, coach, and push each other to achieve individual and group goals (Greene 2008). The connections runners made with each other fostered excitement about the sport of running and the Nike brand in the marketplace network and in customers' growing social in-groups. By November 2008, Nike + users had already run and logged over 93 million miles on the website (Greene 2008). Although the Web site was a great success, providing runners with a global running club, Nike knew more could be done to enhance its presence in the marketplace network and to connect runners in real world social situations. They planned, promoted and executed the Nike + Human Race, the race of all races. This global event which took place on August 31, 2008 consisted of a 10k race followed by a concert performed by popular artists of 24 cities worldwide. It was a smashing success as 800,000 runners signed up on the nikeplus.nike.com website and participated in the race (Greene 2008). In a sports apparel industry where marketing competition is fierce and traditional strategies are increasingly inefficient, Nike has found a way to win by extending its focus from connecting to customers through its brands or boundary spanners to the entire customer relational ecosystem.

RESEARCH DIRECTIONS

The goal of creating a model of a customer's relational ecosystem is to help facilitate the understanding of how multiple relational entities influence customer decisions and behaviors in a connected world. Each entity influences customers, but we believe it is necessary to step back and view all the entities holistically to develop a clearer picture of the interconnected, complex, and evolving nature of a customer's relational ecosystem.

The relational ecosystem model also allows us to analyze the aggregate role of the relational entities in influencing a customer's total experience. These relational entities provide more than just information; they help give meaning and identity to customers. Not only is the manner in which customers gather and process information a complex phenomenon (Peterson & Merino, 2003) but so is the manner in which they receive meaning and identity from relationships with relational entities. Relational channels connecting customers and the various relational entities differ fundamentally. Furthermore, we argue that the relational ecosystem model conveys the dynamic aspect of customer relationships, such that the relative importance of different entities and channels evolves over time and remains highly dependent on contextual factors.

The relational ecosystem model offers great potential for further research. Studying the role that main relational channels might take as substitutes or complements for providing information, meaning, and identity should offer strong implications for marketing practice. For example, findings that dissect the importance of each channel according to various factors can help companies increase their marketing efficiency. Those factors might relate to the offering (product or service, industry category, complexity, price, stage in product life cycle), the customer (demographics, business or individual), and the company (market share, positioning, dominance in each relational channel). An offering may enjoy the best associations and a dominant position compared with competitors when customers use the associative relational channel but suffer a weak position compared with competitors in the network relational channel. By discovering the relative importance of a channel in certain situations, researchers can arm companies with powerful information that can help them determine how to allocate their marketing resources among various relational entities and channels.

A better understanding of the role of side relational channels also requires further research. Relational channels that connect the relational entities imply that the relational entities have indirect impacts on customers. These indirect channels can provide alternative avenues for companies to deliver information, meaning, and value to consumers. By discovering these indirect avenues and their role, researchers might equip marketers with additional strategies for creating impactful connections with consumers. Combining knowledge about when each main relational channel has greater relative importance with knowledge about the role of potential side relational channels gives marketers the means to use potential side relational channels to connect with customers through their preferred main relational channel, given the specific circumstances. Furthermore, an understanding of how certain entities might indirectly influence customers through side relational channels provides value to companies and researchers who practice integrated marketing communications. Research on every aspect of the ecosystem thus should have important implications for business, because they all affect the consumer's decisions and behavior, but only by taking a holistic view can we understand the aggregate effects.

For business strategy, an understanding of how customers engage in this connected world is critical to creating effective marketing strategies. Businesses should keep an eye on the big picture and see how customers attempt to gain information, meaning, and identity from multiple relational entities. Depending on the circumstances, customers may not be interested in certain main relational channels. If a customer does not want to engage in relationships with boundary spanners for a certain product class, it may be more important to use resources that would have been devoted to the relationship marketing programs to engage with the marketplace network and thereby ensure a positive reputation on the marketplace network and accurate information.

Companies that do not grasp the complexity of the relational ecosystem may become frustrated with the ineffectiveness of their marketing efforts but still fail to realize why their efforts have failed. Customers, overwhelmed by the quantity of brand messages companies try to deliver through the associative relational channel, may close this channel, prompting marketers to change their messaging. Perhaps those marketers, however, should realize that the channel is closed and try to use side channels instead to deliver the brand association messages indirectly in different packages (e.g., brand-sponsored video games, product placement, viral marketing, press releases, pursuing the customer's social in-group). In just this one area, understanding the impact of the customer's relational ecosystem as a whole could be very important to marketers, who can increase the power of their message by sending those messages in unique packages and through indirect channels.

Companies that understand the important role of other entities on customers are starting to investigate how they can engage those other entities to learn about and indirectly influence customers. Just as companies have come to focus on brand equity, they should assign managers to focus on other relational channels and the ecosystem as a whole. In this 21st century, customers' relationships with the marketplace network are becoming just as important as the brand's direct relationship with individual customers. A customer searching for certain solutions, answers, information, or meaning may stumble in millions of directions, depending on the start and each turn taken during the information quest. The information available about a company and its market can range from positive to negative, and though it remains impossible for a company to control all the information available to customers, it can influence the likelihood that customers will find favorable information by directing them toward more positive content.

Overall, an important next step for research is to use more holistic conceptual frameworks to test empirical models that capture the simultaneous influence of the many relational entities and channels and thus realize how a customer's relational ecosystem influences his or her decisions. This effort is especially difficult, because this model is dynamic, requiring a longitudinal perspective to understand how the ecosystem affects a customer's lifetime purchase decisions and the seller's lifetime earnings from that customer.

Moreover, the impact of side channels on a customer's ultimate behavior often occurs outside the customer's and seller's purview, making measurement and control especially complex. Our final appeal asks researchers and managers to view relationship marketing from a holistic perspective, noting that customers have simultaneous relationships with multiple entities and that their attitudes and behaviors depend on the composite influence of their relational ecosystem.

REFERENCES

Aaker, D. A. (1992). The value of brand equity. *Journal of Business Strategy, 13*(4), 27–32.

Aaker, J. L. (1997). Dimensions of brand personality. *Journal of Marketing Research, 34*(3), 347–356.

Aggarwal, P. (2004). The effects of brand relationship norms on consumer attitudes and behavior. *Journal of Consumer Research, 31*(1), 87–101.

Bagozzi, R. P. (1975). Marketing as exchange. *Journal of Marketing, 39*(4), 32–39.

Bearden, W. O., & Etzel, M. J. (1982). Reference group influence on product and brand purchase decisions. *Journal of Consumer Research, 9*(2), 183–194.

Beringer, J. (2008). What do you trust? Understanding information source preference. *Public Relations Tactics, 15*(3), 20–21.

Boyle, E. (2007). A process model of brand cocreation: Brand management and research implications. *Journal of Product and Brand Management, 16*(2), 122–131.

Burnkrant, R. E., & Cousineau, A. (1975). Informational and normative social influence on buyer behavior. *Journal of Consumer Research, 2*(3), 206–215.

Campbell, D. T. (1958). Common fate, similarity, and other indices of the status of aggregates of persons as social entities. *Behavioral Science, 3*(1), 14–25.

Chaplin, L. N., & John, D. R. (2005). The development of self-brand connections in children and adolescents. *Journal of Consumer Research, 32*(1), 119–129.

Chaudhuri, A. (1998). Product class effects on brand loyalty. *Journal of Marketing Management, 8*(2), 66–77.

Court, D., Freeling, A., Leiter, M., & Parsons, A. J. (1996, November). Uncovering the value of brands. *McKinsey Quarterly, 33*(4), 176–178.

Crosby, L. A., Evans, K. R., & Cowles, D. (1990). Relationship quality in services selling: An interpersonal influence perspective. *Journal of Marketing, 54*(3), 68–81.

Culnan, M. J. (1983). Environmental scanning: The effects of task complexity and source accessibility on information gathering behavior. *Decision Sciences, 14*(2), 194–206.

Dion, P., Easterling, D., & Miller, S. J. (1995). What is really necessary in successful buyer/seller relationships? *Industrial Marketing Management, 24*(1), 1–9.

Dwyer, R. F., Schurr, P. H., & Oh, S. (1987). Developing buyer–seller relationships. *Journal of Marketing, 51*(2), 11–27.

Erdem, T., & Swait, J. (2004). Brand credibility, brand consideration, and choice. *Journal of Consumer Research, 31*(1), 191–198.

Fang, E., Palmatier, R. W., Scheer, L. K., & Li, N. (2008, March). Trust at different organizational levels. *Journal of Marketing, 72*, 80–98.

Fournier, S. (1998). Consumers and their brands: Developing relationship theory in consumer research. *Journal of Consumer Research, 24*(4), 343–373.

Frels, J. K., Shervani, T., & Srivastava, R. K. (2003). The integrated networks model: Explaining resource allocations in network markets. *Journal of Marketing, 67*(1), 29–45.

Gil, R. B., Andrés, E. F., & Salinas, E. M. (2007). Family as a source of consumer-based brand equity. *Journal of Product and Brand Management, 16*(3), 188–199.

Grant, R., Clarke, R. J., & Kyriazis, E. (2007). A review of factors affecting online consumer search behaviour from an information value perspective. *Journal of Marketing Management, 23*(5–6), 519–533.

Greene, J. (2008). How Nike's social network sells to runners. *Business Week*. November 17, 2008.

Gregory, S. (2007). Cool runnings. *TIME Magazine*, Vol. 170.

Hamilton, D. L., & Sherman, S. J. (1996). Perceiving persons and groups. *Psychological Review, 103*(2), 336–355.

Hawke, A., & Heffernan, T. (2006). Interpersonal liking in lender–customer relationships in the Australian banking sector. *International Journal of Bank Marketing, 24*(2–3), 140–157.

Herbig, P., & Milewicz, J. (1995). The relationship of reputation and credibility to brand success. *Journal of Consumer Marketing, 12*(4), 5.

Hoeffler, S., & Keller, K. L. (2003). The marketing advantages of strong brands. *Journal of Brand Management, 10*(6), 421.

Iansiti, M., & Levien, R. (2004). Strategy as ecology. *Harvard Business Review, 82*(3), 68–78.

Jones, R. (2005). Finding sources of brand value: Developing a stakeholder model of brand equity. *Journal of Brand Management, 13*(1), 10–32.

Keeney, R. L. (1999). The value of Internet commerce to the customer. *Management Science, 45*(4), 533–542.

Keller, K. L. (1993). Conceptualizing, measuring, and managing customer-based brand equity. *Journal of Marketing, 57*(1), 1–22.

Keller, K. L., & Lehmann, D. R. (2006). Brands and branding: Research findings and future priorities. *Marketing Science, 25*(6), 740–759.

Klein, L. R., & Ford, G. T. (2003). Consumer search for information in the digital age: An empirical study of prepurchase search for automobiles. *Journal of Interactive Marketing, 17*(3), 29–49.

Kleine, R. E., III. (2006). Exploring the co-evolution of possession constellations, self, and identity. *Advances in Consumer Research, 33*(1), 256–257.

Kliatchko, J. G. (2008). Revisiting the IMC construct. *International Journal of Advertising, 27*(1), 133–160.

Kotler, P. H. (1991). *Marketing management: Analysis, planning, and control* (8th ed.). Englewood Cliffs, NJ: Prentice Hall.

Lagace, R. R., Dahlstrom, R., & Gassenheimer, J. B. (1991). The relevance of ethical salesperson behavior on relationship quality: The pharmaceutical industry. *Journal of Personal Selling and Sales Management, 11*(4), 39–47.

Lambkin, M., & Day, G. S. (1989). Evolutionary processes in competitive markets: Beyond the product life cycle. *Journal of Marketing, 53*(3), 4–20.

Lee, J., & Hogarth, J. M. (2000). Relationships among information search activities when shopping for a credit card. *Journal of Consumer Affairs, 34*(2), 330–360.

Lin, Q., & Lee, J. (2004). Consumer information search when making investment decisions. *Financial Services Review, 13*(4), 319–332.

Martín Gutiérrez, S. (2006). A model of consumer relationships with store brands, personnel and stores in Spain. *International Review of Retail, Distribution and Consumer Research, 16*(4), 453–469.

Mazis, M. B., Staelin, R., Beales, H., & Salop, S. (1981). A framework for evaluating consumer information regulation. *Journal of Marketing, 45*(1), 11–21.

Merriam-Webster's Collegiate Dictionary (10th ed.). (2001). Springfield, MA: Author.

Moore, J. F. (1993). Predators and prey: A new ecology of competition. *Harvard Business Review, 71*(3), 75–86.

Moore, J. F. (2006). Business ecosystems and the view from the firm. *Antitrust Bulletin, 51*(1), 31–75.

Morgan, R. M., & Hunt, S. D. (1994). The commitment–trust theory of relationship marketing. *Journal of Marketing, 58*(3), 20–38.

Narayandas, D., Caravella, M., & Deighton, J. (2002). The impact of Internet exchanges on business-to-business distribution. *Journal of the Academy of Marketing Science, 30*(4), 500–506.

O'Laughlin, M. J., & Malle, B. F. (2002). How people explain actions performed by groups and individuals. *Journal of Personality and Social Psychology, 82*(1), 33–48.

Palmatier, R. W., Dant, R. P., Grewal, D., & Evans, K. R. (2006). Factors influencing the effectiveness of relationship marketing: A meta-analysis. *Journal of Marketing, 70*(3), 136–153.

Palmatier, R. W., Scheer, L. K., Houston, M. B., Evans, K. R., & Gopalakrishna, S. (2007, September). Use of relationship marketing programs in building customer–salesperson and customer–firm relationships: Differential influences on financial outcomes. *International Journal of Research in Marketing, 24*, 210–223.

Palmatier, R. W., Scheer, L. K., & Steenkamp, J. B. (2007). Customer loyalty to whom? Managing the benefits and risks of salesperson-owned loyalty. *Journal of Marketing Research, 44*(2), 185–199.

Peterson, R. A., & Merino, M. C. (2003). Consumer information search behavior and the Internet. *Psychology and Marketing, 20*(2), 99–121.

Podolny, J. M. (2005). *Status signals: A sociological study of market competition*. Princeton, NJ: Princeton University Press.

Price, L. L., Feick, L. F., & Higie, R. A. (1987). Information sensitive consumers and market information. *Journal of Consumer Affairs, 21*(2), 328–341.

Quinn, C. (1999). How leading-edge companies are marketing, selling, and fulfilling over the Internet. *Journal of Interactive Marketing, 13*(4), 39–50.

Ratchford, B. T., Talukdar, D., & Myung-Soo, L. E. E. (2007). The impact of the Internet on consumers' use of information sources for automobiles: A re-inquiry. *Journal of Consumer Research, 34*(1), 111–119.

Ratner, R. K., & Kahn, B. E. (2002). The impact of private versus public consumption on variety-seeking behavior. *Journal of Consumer Research, 29*(2), 246–257.

Schmidt, J. B., & Spreng, R. A. (1996). A proposed model of external consumer information search. *Journal of the Academy of Marketing Science, 24*(3), 246–256.

Singh, J., & Rhoads, G. K. (1991). Boundary role ambiguity in marketing-oriented positions: A multidimensional, multifaceted operationalization. *Journal of Marketing Research, 28*(3), 328–338.

Sirdeshmukh, D., Singh, J., & Sabol, B. (2002). Consumer trust, value, and loyalty in relational exchanges. *Journal of Marketing, 66*(1), 15–37.

Sirgy, M. J., & Danes, J. E. (1982). Self-image/product-image congruence models: Testing selected models. *Advances in Consumer Research, 9*(1), 556–561.

Smith, R. E. (1993). Integrating information from advertising and trial: Processes and effects on consumer response to product information. *Journal of Marketing Research, 30*(2), 204–219.

Stafford, J. E. (1966). Effects of group influences on consumer brand preferences. *Journal of Marketing Research, 3*(1), 68–75.

Stamper, C. L., & Johlke, M. C. (2003). The impact of perceived organizational support on the relationship between boundary spanner role stress and work outcomes. *Journal of Management, 29*(4), 569–588.

Stanton, J. L., & Lowenhar, J. A. (1974). A congruence model of brand preference: A theoretical and empirical study. *Journal of Marketing Research, 11*(4), 427–433.

Van den Bulte, C., & Wuyts, S. (2007). *Social networks and marketing.* Cambridge, MA: Marketing Science Institute.

Xavier, M. J., Krishnan, R., & Borin, N. (2005). An integrated model of collaborative value creation for strategic innovation: The case of retail automation in India. *IIMB Management Review, 17*(2), 29–39.

Zettelmeyer, F., Scott Morton, F., & Silva-Risso, J. (2006). How the Internet lowers prices: Evidence from matched survey and automobile transaction data. *Journal of Marketing Research, 43*(2), 168–181.

4

Connectivity, Control, and Constraint in Business Markets

Stefan Wuyts

Much research in the social network literature has argued that firm action is to a large extent socially embedded and that social networks that pervade industry structures have an important bearing on individual firm action (e.g., Braudel, 1985; Granovetter, 1985; Macaulay, 1963). In line with this basic insight, marketing scholars tend to agree that exchange in business markets has a social dimension. Despite the convergence on this general statement, there has been hardly any exploration, let alone systematic evidence, regarding the mechanisms through which social networks impact exchange in business markets. The prior literature is dispersed and lacks focus, particularly regarding the actual mechanisms at work. The first objective of this chapter is to provide an overview of some of the network control mechanisms that have been distinguished in prior literature and discuss the conditions under which different mechanisms are likely to be mobilized and be effective. The second objective of this chapter is to highlight the flipside of control: Social networks can constrain firm behavior and outcomes and lead to inferior exchange conditions. The chapter is organized around these two important themes: (a) connectivity and control and (b) connectivity and constraint.

First, social networks have implications for control in that they can serve in curbing opportunistic tendencies of exchange partners. In view of the scant prior literature on network control mechanisms in marketing, a number of alternative network control mechanisms are described and categorized, and the network-structural and motivational conditions that determine their effectiveness are discussed. Classifying network control mechanisms and reflecting on the conditions under which they are likely to operate successfully may serve as a first step to bridge an important gap in the literature. It is striking that prior marketing channels literature, with its devotion to governance and control, has hardly paid any attention to the mechanisms of network control. Yet, mechanisms such as negative gossip can be quite powerful in terms of curbing an actor's behavior (for an investigation of negative word-of-mouth, see also the discussion by Andre Bonfrer in Chapter 12).

Second, social networks can be constraining. A first form of constraint follows logically from the controlling nature of social networks: Social control can be perceived as constraining by the party that is subject of control. Social networks can, however, also be constraining in a less obvious manner. I will argue next that although social networks can stimulate exchange and provide new exchange opportunities, a downside is that social networks often lead to inferior exchange conditions. As an illustration, I will discuss why biotechnology firms' central social network positions generate more licensing exchange opportunities while also constraining profitability.

I'll conclude the chapter with a reflection on future research directions in the domains of connectivity and control, and connectivity and constraint.

CONNECTIVITY AND CONTROL

After a brief review of the prior literature, I will identify limitations of the literature on network control. One of the limitations is the lack of attention to how network control really works. Subsequently, I will discuss four network control mechanisms: two-step leverage, negative gossip, group norms, and tertius gaudens.

Network Control: Where Do We Stand?

There is a long tradition in the marketing channels literature to study dyadic (one-to-one) exchange.[1] Interestingly, though, a few studies pointed to the importance of considering multiple relations simultaneously. For example, Weiss and Anderson (1992) showed that as customers' loyalty to a dealer increases, so does the manufacturer's satisfaction with the dealer. Such leads, however, were not followed up, and the subsequent rise of transaction cost theory only enforced the focus on dyadic interaction (e.g., Heide & John, 1990). Although Jan Heide pointed out in 1994 that "individual relationships are embedded in a context of other relationships that could have governance implications," these governance implications hardly received attention in the subsequent marketing channels literature. Looking back at almost 40 years of channels literature in marketing, one can conclude only that with its focus on dyadic governance, marketing failed to keep up with sociology. Even though social exchange theory was given a prominent role in the early marketing channels literature, the subsequent marketing channels literature retained a dyadic focus, whereas in sociology, social exchange theory was gradually replaced by network exchange theory (e.g., Cook & Whitmeyer, 1992; Markovsky, Willer, & Patton, 1988). In network exchange theory, exchange networks consist of sets of two or more connected exchange relations, with "connected" referring to one relation being contingent on exchange (or nonexchange) in the other relation (Cook & Emerson, 1978).

This is not to say that network control has been completely overlooked in the marketing literature, however. Recently, a few marketing studies have provided empirical evidence to the claim that networks can have governance implications. In addition, relationship marketing scholars are broadening the conceptualization of exchange beyond the typical buyer–supplier relationship (see Conor Henderson and Robert Palmatier's discussion of ecologies in Chapter 3). As to empirical evidence, Antia and Frazier (2001) found that franchisors are less inclined to enforce contracts if the franchisee has higher network density and centrality, a governance implication they attributed to the franchisor's fear of negative backlash. Wuyts, Stremersch, Van den Bulte, and Franses (2004) found that system buyers prefer to develop a close tie with a systems vendor if the latter has close ties to upstream component suppliers, which they ascribed to hedging tendencies. Wuyts and Geyskens (2005) found that drafting detailed contracts is more effective in terms of curbing opportunism if the buyer–supplier relationship is embedded in a network characterized by high closure, which they argued can be attributed either to the emergence of effective group norms or to a fear of reputational damage as a consequence of negative gossip. Although these empirical findings confirm that networks are important for governing and controlling exchange, there has been no attempt to date to systematically discuss the alternative mechanisms that underlie network governance and the network-structural and motivational conditions under which they are effective.

Although the marketing literature has not systematically discussed network control, network control literature has gained acceptance in related fields, beyond the core discipline of sociology, but is limited in three fundamental ways. First, the prior literature has mainly focused on goal-directed networks as intended organizational forms (e.g., Coleman, 1990; Koza & Lewin, 1999) and has paid far less attention to networks that emerge without ex ante strategic intentions on behalf of their members (see Kilduff & Tsai, 2003).[2] Many complex channel environments, however, emerge from cumulative exchange opportunities rather than an overarching intent to create a specific network structure. Second, many network researchers have focused strongly on network explanations of behavior with little to no attention to the possibility of agency (Emirbayer & Goodwin, 1994; Stevenson & Greenberg, 2000). This is problematic because network positions reveal only the *potential* for action (Wrong, 1961). To fully understand action, we need to consider not only the macrosocial properties of network structure and network position but also the microbehavioral motivational drivers of action (Granovetter & Swedberg, 1992). Third, much attention in the prior network literature has been devoted to abstract-theoretical questions such as whether network control is a hybrid of market and hierarchy (e.g., Park, 1996) or a new form of control (e.g., Newman, 2005; Powell, 1990). Surprisingly little attention has been devoted to down-to-earth questions such as "What are the underlying mechanisms at work?" and "When are these mechanisms effective?"

To address some of these limitations, I will focus on emerging (rather than goal-directed) networks, describe four distinct network control mechanisms, and discuss the network-structural as well as motivational conditions under which they are effective.

Network Control Mechanisms

A Classification of Network Control Mechanisms

To advance the literature on network control mechanisms, we need to take the first step to recognize some of the fundamental differences between alternative network control mechanisms. Among the most important network control mechanisms that have received attention in the prior literature, some are personal in nature in that they are directed to one specific individual actor. Others, however, are impersonal in nature, in that they are directed not to one specific individual actor but to all actors in the social system. An example of the latter is the emergence of group norms such as generalized trust conventions, which are impersonal, as adherence to group norms is not specifically directed toward a prespecified individual actor but generalized across the entire network. Negative gossip on the other hand is directed toward one specific actor. This distinction is important because personal network control mechanisms risk being considered as coercive, which in turn may instigate a vicious circle of retaliation (John, 1984; Lusch, 1976).

Second, network control mechanisms differ in terms of their influencing logic, with some based on a more "positive" logic of alignment and cooperation and some based on a more "negative" logic of retaliation and competition. The group norms and negative gossip mechanisms, for example, differ not only because the first is impersonal in nature and the second is personal in nature but also because they rely on opposing logics. Group norms rely on a positive constructive logic of alignment and cooperation, in that they serve to align behaviors of a collectivity of actors and restrain the individualist pursuit of self-interest. Negative gossip, however, relies on a negative logic of retaliation: It redirects behavior by (the threat of) reputational damage and possible loss of contracts. Arguably, this distinction is more subjective in nature than the distinction between personal and impersonal, and it may even require insight into the exact motivations of the actor that deploys the control mechanism. If the motivation behind sending negative gossip is to protect other members of the network from being harmed, rather than retaliation, negative gossip may be categorized differently. Despite its limitations, the distinction between positive and negative logics is important, as they create different and incompatible atmospheres. The incompatibility of an atmosphere of alignment and cooperation with one of competition and retaliation has consequences for the combined use of different network control mechanisms, as discussed in the following section, "Network Constraint: The Flipside of Control."

A limitation of the two-dimensional framework is that other useful distinguishing dimensions likely exist. One could, for example, make a third distinction between network control mechanisms, on the basis of the level in the network at which they are typically operative. Some network control mechanisms are mostly locally defined, whereas others are mostly globally defined. The distinction between local and global is standard in social network literature (e.g., see Scott, 2000, p. 82). Local refers to the immediate

TABLE 4.1

Classification of Network Control Mechanisms

	Positive (Alignment, Cooperation)	Negative (Retaliation, Competition)
Personal	Two-step leverage	Negative gossip
Impersonal	Group norms	Tertius gaudens

environment, composed of adjacent actors, whereas global refers to the overall structure of the network at large. Even though this distinction may have practical consequences, it is less fundamental, as (a) network control mechanisms that are mostly global in nature such as negative gossip and group norms can perfectly occur at the local level such as in a triad, and (b) the step that represents a fundamental shift in thinking as compared to the dyadic perspective is the step from dyad to triad, as this elementary step opens up the study of control to situations of brokerage, structural balance, and structural unbalance (Wolff, 1950). Therefore, I initially focus on triadic configurations and will only briefly touch on larger network settings in the section titled "Extension to Larger Networks."

Summarizing, the first two dimensions discussed earlier distinguish between alternative network control mechanisms: their personal versus impersonal nature on the one hand and their positive (alignment, cooperation) versus negative (retaliation, competition) logic on the other hand. Along these two dimensions, Table 4.1 classifies the four main network control mechanisms that I will discuss next: two-step leverage, negative gossip, group norms, and tertius gaudens.

In what follows, I discuss each network control mechanism in detail with attention to the triadic and motivational conditions that need to be fulfilled for these network control mechanisms to be effective. As to the triadic conditions, three fundamentally different triadic structures are distinguished, as displayed in Figure 4.1.

When an actor links two unconnected actors, he or she is said to fill a structural hole. Brokerage is observed in markets of complex systems when a systems integrator connects component suppliers with end customers and the end customers do not interact directly with the component suppliers. In that case, the system integrator uniquely links customers and suppliers. Prior research has shown that such a network position conveys brokerage advantage (Burt, 1992). The system integrator can maximize its own interest when selecting component suppliers and play out its suppliers

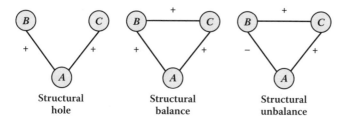

FIGURE 4.1
Fundamental triadic structures.

against its customers or distort information flows as long as customers and suppliers do not interact directly with one another.

When three actors are fully connected and all ties are positive in valence, the triad is said to display structural balance (Heider, 1958). Structural balance is found in close-knit networks and densely connected communities where "a friend of my friend is also my friend."

When three actors are fully connected but two of the three ties are positive in valence and the third one is negative in valence, the triad is said to display structural unbalance (Heider, 1958).[3] Typically, situations of structural unbalance do not last long. For example, it is hard to accept that one's friend is also a friend of one's enemy. Similarly, in business markets, it is not appreciated when a senior consultant provides strategic advice to two competing firms. It is interesting to note that Heider (1958) found evidence of structural balance and unbalance in his study of the psychology of interpersonal relations. The impact that these findings have had in the sociology and social network literatures points to the importance of cross-fertilization between the academic basic disciplines of psychology and sociology (see Chapter 9 by Ronald Burt for an excellent example of this cross-fertilization).

Two-Step Leverage

Two-step leverage is a personal network control mechanism based on alignment logic, aimed to reduce the dependency on an adjacent actor by building ties to other actors that can exert influence on the adjacent actor. Gargiulo (1993) documented this phenomenon in an agro-business cooperative where two-step leverage replaced direct leverage in a dyad. Wuyts et al. (2004) found that a buyer firm's preference for a system integrator that holds intensive ties to component suppliers is increased if the buyer

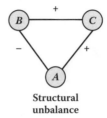

Structural
unbalance

FIGURE 4.2
Triadic condition two-step leverage: structural unbalance.

has direct ties of its own to component suppliers, consistent with the two-step leverage idea. In case the system integrator underperforms, the buyer firm, who may not have sufficient leverage to influence the system integrator directly, may call on the component suppliers to exert influence on the system integrator. Similarly, a consumer can call on the car manufacturer to exert influence on a negligent car dealer.

Triadic conditions for two-step leverage. Two-step leverage is effective if the triad is characterized by structural unbalance (see Figure 4.2). If the tie between A and B is negative in valence (e.g., a customer feels that the car dealer underperforms) and A calls on C (the car manufacturer) to exert influence on B, C should share a positive tie with both A and B in order to be willing and able to exert such influence. Structural unbalance thus provides the opportunity for using two-step leverage as a mechanism to control or redirect a specific actor's behavior.

Motivational conditions for two-step leverage. Although a triadic structure of structural unbalance provides an opportunity for two-step leverage, the effectiveness of two-step leverage is obviously also a function of the willingness of the called-on actor C to exert such influence. This actor must associate either social or economic benefits with exerting influence. For a car manufacturer, the dealer's behaviors toward end customers may determine whether customers are retained or not, providing the car manufacturer with economic benefits to redirect the dealer's misbehavior toward end customers.

Negative Gossip

Negative gossip is a personal network control mechanism based on a negative logic of retaliation. Spreading negative information about an actor

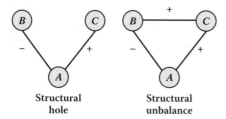

FIGURE 4.3
Triadic condition negative gossip: structural hole and structural unbalance.

can damage its reputation (Dollinger, Golden, & Saxton, 1997), which can cause the loss of future contracts (Greif, 1993; Houston & Johnson, 2000). The phenomenon of negative word-of-mouth is discussed in more detail by Bonfrer in Chapter 12.

Triadic conditions for negative gossip. For negative gossip to be effective, a triadic structure characterized either by brokerage or by structural unbalance is required.

A disgruntled customer, A, may pass on negative information about firm B to either a potential or an existing customer, C, of this firm (respectively, situations of brokerage and structural unbalance; see Figure 4.3). Either way, the threat of losing a (potential) customer may force a firm to avoid misbehavior or correct its behavior toward actor A. To illustrate, Antia and Frazier (2001) found that principals are not eager to strictly enforce contracts if the agent network is denser or when the focal agent is more centrally connected in the agent network. They attributed these findings to the principal accounting for possible retaliation if the word spreads throughout the agent network that the principal's strict enforcement was unfair, consistent with the negative gossip mechanism.

Motivational conditions for negative gossip. Next to triadic conditions, the motivations of the third actor, C, may also influence the effectiveness of the negative gossip mechanism. If C is not motivated to reconsider its (potential) relationship toward firm B after being confronted with the negative news from customer A, negative gossip will have little effect. Negative gossip is likely to be more effective if (potential) customer C has alternative options beyond firm B (i.e., firm B is not a monopolist, switching costs are moderate). Customer C may also perceive social benefits related to passing on information to other actors, for example, if being the source of new information in the social network conveys status benefits. On the contrary, if C has no reasonable alternatives to switch away from firm B and if C also does not perceive any social benefits in passing on the negative gossip, this instrument is unlikely to be effective.

Group Norms

The group norms mechanism is an impersonal network control mechanism based on alignment logic, aimed to control behavior informally through trust and moral obligation (Larson, 1992).

Triadic conditions for group norms. It is well-known that group norms arise in close-knit networks of positive valence. In a triadic sense, a triad characterized by structural balance is a likely condition for the generation and sustainability of group norms (see Figure 4.4). More generally, under conditions of high network density or closure (such as structural balance in a triadic configuration), information regarding the appropriateness of certain behaviors is easily communicated throughout the network (e.g., see Buskens, 1998, on the social structure of trust). In marketing, it also has been argued that closure fosters the emergence of group norms regulating behavior and legitimating group sanctions in case of violations (Wuyts & Geyskens, 2005).

Motivational conditions for group norms. Next to triadic conditions, the effectiveness of group norms in curbing actors' opportunistic tendencies is contingent on these actors' identification with the group. Gould (1993) pointed out that such identification is a boundary condition for behavioral norms, such as fairness norms, to be effective: "Actors [should] perceive themselves as members of an identifiable collectivity" (p. 185). The fact that this is an important boundary condition has been clearly demonstrated in recent research that has shown

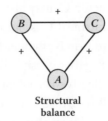

Structural
balance

FIGURE 4.4
Triadic condition group norms: structural balance.

that low levels of identification undermine the effectiveness of group norms and even cause opposite reactions. For individuals who identify less with the social network, group norms can be interpreted as restrictive normative pressure (a more extreme form of constraint), which in turn can cause reactance (i.e., a desire to regain one's lost freedom) (for an application to brand communities, see Algesheimer, Dholakia, & Herrmann, 2005).

Tertius Gaudens

Tertius gaudens is an impersonal network control mechanism based on threat logic, aimed to reduce dependency on adjacent actors by exploitation or by generating competition between these actors (Wolff, 1950). In its strong version, the tertius gaudens principle is also referred to as *divide et impera* (divide and rule), where actors are actively set up against one another. Although the origin of the mechanism is often attributed to the ancient Roman Senate, it has been adopted extensively in warfare, politics, and colonial times. When privileges are granted to some parties but not to others, collusion between the divided parties is unlikely. It is not necessary, however, to actively increase tension and division among actors for the tertius gaudens mechanism to control behavior. The very fact of being connected to competing actors can be sufficient to curb these actors' opportunistic tendencies and even stimulate them to display positive behaviors that will benefit the central firm. One application of the tertius gaudens principle is multisourcing, where a firm cooperates with multiple competing suppliers. Recent research has shown that such a strategy stimulates each supplier to go beyond the call of duty and do more than what is formally required to ensure a favorable share of business (Wuyts, 2007).

Triadic conditions for tertius gaudens. Both structural unbalance and brokerage may provide the opportunity for using the tertius gaudens mechanism. In the case of brokerage, actors B and C are not in contact with one another, providing actor A with brokerage advantage. In the case of structural unbalance (see Figure 4.5), B and C share a negatively valenced tie with one another; they may be direct competitors such that A may play B out against C.

Motivational conditions for tertius gaudens. Next to network conditions that pertain to the triad, the tertius gaudens principle is effective only as long as actors B and C do not consider the option of colluding against

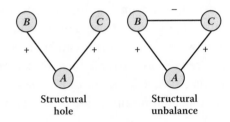

Structural   Structural
hole   unbalance

FIGURE 4.5
Triadic condition tertius gaudens: Structural hole and structural unbalance.

actor A as a beneficial strategy. Collusion would undermine the mechanism, whether in a triadic setting of brokerage or in a structural unbalance. Yet, one could argue that collusion is more of a concern for actor A if the tertius gaudens mechanism is based on brokerage in the triad (as brokerage can be bridged) than when it is based on structural unbalance (as the negative tie between B and C can stand in the way of effective collusion). In a franchise system, for example, a franchisor can retain much power if it succeeds in creating competition for bonuses or other privileges among its franchisees, as long as the franchisees do not collectively stand up against their franchisor, such as by forming franchisee unions. Similarly, strong brand manufacturers can benefit from the heavy competition between large retailers, but recent phenomena such as the formation of buyer groups in European retail can shift the power balance.

Extension to Larger Networks

This discussion of network control mechanisms was limited to triadic network structures. Although further extension to larger networks may not be fundamental in a theoretical sense, it does involve a new complexity: To understand the effectiveness of network control mechanisms at the global network level, we should consider the structure of the global network as well as the network positions of the actors involved.

Two-step leverage and tertius gaudens at the global level. Even though two-step leverage and tertius gaudens are often triadic in nature, quite naturally their application is not restricted to triads. An example of two-step leverage at the global network level is the environmental organization EII's call to consumers to boycott the firm StarKist such that it would refrain from purchasing tuna from foreign firms that use netting methods banned by the United States (Frooman, 1999). The tertius gaudens mechanism can also be effective beyond the confines of a triad. Obviously, multisourcing is not restricted to triadic settings, as many firms build large portfolios of relationships with alternative suppliers and offer the status of preferred supplier only to those that outperform competing suppliers.

Group norms and negative gossip at the global network level. For the mechanisms group norms and negative gossip, the extension to the global network is very intuitive. Perfect connectivity in a network is optimal for rapid diffusion of information. Perfect connectivity is seldom observed, however. Provan and Sebastian (1998) found that group norms develop among firms if there are multiple and overlapping links between organizations ("intensive clique integration"). Such high levels of closure lead to feelings of identification and commonality and hence facilitate the emergence of group norms. Macy and Skvoretz (1998) consistently found that the coordination of effective trust conventions is facilitated in tightly knit networks. Notably, in case of imperfect connectivity, different actors occupy different network positions. If an actor is more centrally positioned in a close-knit network, he or she may be more susceptible to group norms than actors located in the periphery.

Previous research has shown that closure not only enables the emergence of group norms but also facilitates reputation building, which is crucial for the negative gossip mechanism (Buskens, 1998; Jones, Hesterly, & Borgatti, 1997; Raub & Weesie, 1990). Again, in reality social networks are seldom characterized by perfect connectivity. An important observation in the context of the spread of negative gossip (or other simple bits of information) is that many social networks exhibit small-world properties (i.e., high local clustering in combination with short path distances between actors). Watts and Strogatz (1998) found that small deviations from transitivity in combination with local clustering are sufficient conditions for small-world properties. Not only are small-world properties more common, they also enable fast diffusion of information across a network, at least if the network members have a low threshold to acquire and pass on the information (for a similar argument, see Watts, 2002). Notably, as small worlds deviate from perfect connectivity, different actors occupy different network positions. Initiating negative gossip is more effective for those actors that are centrally connected in the global network, as centrality is associated with control (e.g., see Brass, 1984). In particular, a sender's "betweenness centrality" reflects control over the flow of interpersonal information (Dawes, Lee, & Dowling, 1998; Freeman, 1979). Thus, the negative gossip mechanism is likely to be effective in conditions of high closure or in small worlds, where the sender has high betweenness centrality. Importantly, the effectiveness of negative gossip as a control mechanism in social networks that exhibit small-world properties is strongly contingent on the motivations of the actors that serve as linkages between the local clusters (Van den Bulte & Wuyts, 2007). Group norms are less likely to be effective in small worlds because the feeling of identification with the group, a precondition for an actor to be susceptible to group norms, may be lower among members that belong to different local clusters. Although simple bits of information such as negative gossip may easily find their way through a small-world network, norms that regulate behavior likely require more close-knit structures.

CONNECTIVITY AND CONSTRAINT

Thus far, I have focused on how network control mechanisms can enable a firm to control the behavior of its counterparty. A logical next step is to consider the constraining nature of networks. First, the very forces that serve to retain behavior within the range of what is deemed acceptable from the perspective of the controlling actor or collectivity of actors can be perceived as constraining for the actor that is subject of control: Constraint is the flipside of control. Second, networks can also be constraining in a more subtle way: Although social networks are often accredited with providing new exchange *opportunities*, the social layer in which exchange is embedded may cause inferior exchange *conditions*. In this section, I will elaborate on constraint as the flipside of control as well as on the more subtle variants of network constraint.

Network Constraint: The Flipside of Control

Thus far, I have discussed the control consequences of connectivity, particularly the ability of network control mechanisms to curb opportunistic behavior. Control thus goes hand in hand with constraint. The group norms mechanism, for example, relies on a community idea: The behavior of individual actors is influenced by impersonal group norms. Although such norms can effectively curb behavior that goes against group interests, this very control function can be experienced as constraining by those who have reasons to deviate from the collective interest. When network control mechanisms are personal in nature, they can be interpreted as intrusive and cause a circle of retaliation. Prior channels studies have shown that dyadic control mechanisms such as the strict enforcement of contracts can be associated with coercion, which paradoxically increases rather than decreases conflict and opportunism (John, 1984; Lusch, 1976).

Network control mechanisms can also constrain the effectiveness of other network control mechanisms when deployed simultaneously, because different control mechanisms rely on different logics. Whereas two-step leverage and group norms rely on a positive logic of alignment and cooperation (similar to dyadic control mechanisms such as relational norms), negative gossip and the tertius gaudens principle rely on a negative logic of retaliation and competition (similar to dyadic control mechanisms such as taking legal action against very minor deviations from the contract). Past literature has pointed out that the (threat of) strict enforcement of contracts clashes with the use of dyadic alignment mechanisms such as relational norms (Jap & Ganesan, 2000; Macaulay, 1963; Nooteboom, Berger, & Noorderhaven, 1997). Similarly, the tertius gaudens principle (creating an atmosphere of competition) may lead to adverse reactions if the triad is embedded in a close network and behavior is controlled by group norms (requiring an atmosphere of cooperation). Similarly, spreading negative gossip about an actor may go against prevailing group norms.

Finally, network control mechanisms can also constrain the effectiveness of dyadic control mechanisms that are based on a different logic. Let us consider an example. A recent article on the governance of buyer–supplier dyads (Wuyts, 2007) showed that when a buyer firm uses a multisourcing strategy, an example of the tertius gaudens mechanism, suppliers are likely to go beyond the call of duty for the buyer firm and engage in extrarole behaviors that benefit the buyer firm. Arguably, this is caused by the competitive atmosphere that is created by multisourcing. The same study showed that also the creation of a cooperative atmosphere in the dyad stimulates suppliers' extrarole behaviors. Although for that study I did not look into interaction effects, the logic proposed previously suggests that even though both positive (cooperative atmosphere) and negative (multisourcing) control mechanisms may be effective in their own right, their combined use is likely to work counterproductively because of the incompatibility of cooperative and competitive logics. I therefore reanalyzed the same data set including an interaction term between multisourcing and cooperative atmosphere, to examine the consequences for extrarole behaviors if both are deployed simultaneously. The parameter of this interaction term turned out to be negative and significant, consistent with the argument that the tertius gaudens mechanism is incompatible with a cooperative atmosphere: The use of one constrains the effectiveness of the other.

Network Constraint: The Subtle Variant

There is also a more subtle form of constraint that results from increased connectivity. New economic sociology and in particular the discussion on socially embedded exchange (Granovetter, 1985) is built around the premise that social networks stimulate exchange. In view of the controlling nature of social networks discussed previously, however, the same social networks that provide an actor with new exchange opportunities can hinder the actor in maximizing its economic benefits. Combining insights on socially embedded exchange with insights on network control, one can derive a general proposition: Social networks increase exchange opportunities but at *inferior* exchange conditions. In what follows, I will develop the argument for this proposition and provide evidence from business markets.

One of the most important manifestations of the social fabric of exchange in business markets is the phenomenon of interlocked directory boards. At least since the beginning of the 20th century (Dooley, 1969), individuals have simultaneously served on boards of multiple firms. In academia, board interlocks have received much attention across academic fields, especially since the late 1960s. According to Dooley (1969), the creation of exchange opportunities has been among the most important motivations to form board interlocks. Others have attributed board interlocks' positive influence on exchange to coordination and control benefits (Allen, 1974; Ornstein, 1980) and improved information access and transfer (Lang & Lockhart, 1990; Mariolis & Jones, 1982).[4] With a focus on their informational benefits, board interlocks have been attributed an important role in the diffusion of administrative and organizational innovations such as poison pills (Davis, 1991), acquisition activities (Haunschild, 1993), investor relations departments (Hayagreeva & Sivakumar, 1999), and scripts and routines for policy making (Westphal, Seidel, & Stewart, 2001).

Interestingly, the extant board interlock literature not only discusses exchange benefits but also provides evidence of network constraint. At an individual level, if board members support change processes that lead to greater board control over managers, they experience social distancing on other boards (Westphal & Khanna, 2003). At the industry level, board interlocks can disadvantage customer firms. Uzzi and Lancaster (2004) showed that law firms learn through board interlocks about the criteria used to compare bids, enabling them to increase prices. The most important constraint associated with board interlocks is, however, at the firm level: Board interlocks have been associated with reduced autonomy (Dooley, 1969; Lang & Lockhart, 1990). Mizruchi (1996) suggested that a firm's central position in the board interlock network impedes independent decision making and leads to economically suboptimal terms of exchange, a concern that was already voiced in the early 20th century by one of President Woodrow Wilson's chief advisors, Supreme Court Justice Louis Brandeis: "The practice of interlocking directorates is the root of many evils ... it leads to inefficiency; for it removes incentive and destroys soundness of judgement" (Dooley, 1969, p. 314).

Evidence of the Subtle Variant of Network Constraint

Despite the impressive body of literature on board interlocks, previous research has failed to converge when it comes to their consequences for firm performance. An overview article by Mizruchi (1996) underscores the lack of coherence and conflicting evidence regarding this link. Some prior studies reported a positive association between board interlocks and firm profitability (Baysinger & Butler, 1985), whereas other reported a negative association (Fligstein & Brantley, 1992). Considering the different arguments presented previously, a possible explanation for the lack of coherence is that board interlocks, exemplars of interfirm social ties, impact firm performance in two opposite ways. On the one hand, the control and informational benefits of board interlocks create new exchange opportunities (thus indirectly increasing firm performance). On the other hand, as firms become more embedded in a web of social relationships, it becomes harder for them to engage in self-centered behavior because that likely goes against prevailing codes of conduct, reducing firms' autonomy to optimize the terms of trade.

In a recent study, Wuyts and Dutta (2008) investigated the role of board interlock ties in the context of licensing exchange. With a focus on the role of board interlocks as conduits for firm-specific information (Gulati & Westphal, 1999; Haunschild, 1993), they argued that when directors of a biotechnology firm serve on the directory boards of other industry participants, information on the firm's new promising technologies can more easily find its way to other actors. Board interlock ties thus reduce information asymmetry between biotechnology firms and their potential partners. Consistent with this argument, they found that as biotechnology firms are more centrally connected in the social network of board interlocks (higher board interlock [degree] centrality), they obtain more licensing deals. Their results thus provide evidence of the upside of board interlock centrality: Board interlock ties stimulate exchange opportunities, arguably thanks to their role in disseminating firm-specific information throughout the biopharmaceutical industry. They did not, however, investigate the possible constraining nature of board interlock centrality. Controlling for the increased number of licensing deals, do board interlock ties lead to suboptimal terms of trade and hence to reduced profitability?

In an attempt to investigate this downside of board interlock centrality, I specified a profitability equation on the basis of the same data as in Wuyts and Dutta (2008). To assess the impact of board interlock centrality on firm profitability, I accounted for both the indirect effect of board interlock centrality through obtaining more new licensing deals (which should have a positive effect on firm profitability) and the direct effect of board interlock centrality on profitability (expected to be negative because of suboptimal terms of trade). In other words, the two core variables of interest in the profitability equation were the firm's total number of licensing deals and the firm's board interlock centrality.[5] I controlled for a large number of variables that also influence firm profitability.[6] The database used to estimate this profitability equation included observations on 130 public dedicated biotechnology firms in the time period 1994 to 2000, resulting in 433 observations. These firms obtained anywhere between 0 to 15 licensing deals in a given year.

Let us turn to the findings. A first interesting finding was that board interlock centrality and firm profitability were not significantly correlated. At first sight, board interlock centrality is thus not associated with firm profitability. The zero correlation masks two opposing effects, however. First, Wuyts and Dutta (2008) showed a positive effect of board interlock centrality on obtaining new licensing deals, which according to the estimated profitability equation *increases* firm profitability. Thus, board interlock centrality exerts a positive indirect effect on profitability (through its positive effect on the number of licensing deals). Second, I found that board interlock centrality also exerts an additional direct effect on firm profitability that is *negative* (and significant at the .01 level), when controlling for the firm's total number of licensing deals.

The combined findings from Wuyts and Dutta (2008) and the estimation of the profitability equation provide first evidence in favor of the proposition that socially embedded exchange provides new exchange opportunities (here in the form of new licensing deals) but at inferior exchange conditions.

Interestingly, the arguments and findings are in line with insights in other application areas where social networks have been found to stimulate exchange but also to constrain the actors' ability to negotiate optimal terms of trade. DiMaggio and Louch (1998) provided an interesting example in their study of interpersonal exchanges. They found that when exchanges are more uncertain, risky, and unlikely to be repeated (such as when selling a secondhand car), exchange is more often embedded in social networks. Interestingly, although social networks in such markets facilitated exchange and served a control function, a drawback for the seller was that such embedded exchange typically occurred at inferior exchange conditions. Despite the convergence in explanations and even though the findings unequivocally point to an upside as well as a downside of social networks for exchange, more research is required to rule out alternative explanations. In the next section, I will elaborate on this and other promising areas for future research in the domain of connectivity, control, and constraint in business markets.

CONNECTIVITY, CONTROL, AND CONSTRAINT: DIRECTIONS FOR FUTURE RESEARCH

Although the marketing literature has begun to accept sociology as a basic discipline that can help improve the understanding of marketing phenomena, the incorporation, and extension, of social network ideas in the study of business markets and exchange is still in its infancy. A more systematic approach may be warranted to bring this literature one step further. Although social network influences have been taken a step forward in other marketing domains such as the study of word-of-mouth and social contagion, a similar boost in marketing domains related to interfirm exchange is, arguably, still ahead of us. Next, I offer suggestions regarding the directions that future research may take.

The working of network control mechanisms. Experimental methods as well as the study of secondary data sources may aid in investigating the effectiveness of alternative network control mechanisms. Importantly, the network control mechanisms discussed in the section on connectivity and control are not (by far) exhaustive. The set of four control mechanisms needs to be complemented with other mechanisms that facilitate, control, and constrain exchange. For example, whereas the tertius gaudens mechanism is based on the third actor that benefits from competition between other actors, more recently Obstfeld (2005) introduced the notion of tertius iungens, where the third actor plays a role in creating new linkages. The distinction between tertius gaudens and tertius iungens mirrors the distinction between brokerage logic (where a third actor exploits its network position in between unconnected others; see Burt, 1992) and bridging logic (where a third actor uses its network position in between unconnected others constructively; see DiMaggio, 1992). Another interesting way to enrich the study of network control is to look into the role of mobilization in the generation of collective action, as in social movement literature, where much attention has been devoted to the roles and behaviors of cooperators versus shirkers (Gould, 1993; Granovetter, 1978).

The trade-off between opportunity and constraint. Both in marketing and in sociology, little empirical evidence is available to guide firms in making trade-offs between the exchange benefits associated with social networks (such as opportunities for exchange and control) and the constraining nature of such networks (such as reduced economic efficiency). Although previous studies have pointed to the paradox that the same network configurations that enable exchange can also be constraining (e.g., Uzzi, 1997), it is a difficult exercise to strike the balance between opportunity and constraint. The board interlock results reported previously indicate that a central position in the board interlock network has both positive (indirect) and negative (direct) consequences for firm profitability but did not provide insight into how the benefits of such a network position can be materialized while reducing or avoiding its negative consequences. Contingency studies will help in this regard: Under which circumstances do the positive consequences of social networks dominate, and under which conditions do social networks become too constraining? In this regard, it is important to also broaden the study of network constraint by moving beyond the flipside of control. Another form of constraint that follows directly from increased connectivity relates to the lack of attention to information sources beyond the social network (e.g., Uzzi, 1997). This type of myopia can make actors vulnerable to changes in the environment. Moreover, as social networks become increasingly dense, in the situation of intense connectivity, the pool of information that can be accessed and shared is more homogenized and less novel (Uzzi & Spiro, 2005). If you ask your three closest colleagues how to solve a given problem, they are likely to give you similar answers not only because they share experiences from past problems but also because close ties are more likely to develop among similar individuals. Network constraint is thus more than behavioral constraint as the flipside of behavioral control; it also relates to bounded rationality and cognitive biases such as myopia and confirmation bias.

The role of motivations and emotions in network research. The board interlock story assumed that board interlock ties are homogeneous and comparable. This is a serious limitation, as Gulati and Westphal (1999) pointed to the heterogeneous nature of board interlocks. One contingency factor is the valence of the CEO–board relationship. If this relationship is one of control, negative in valence, board interlock ties are less likely to stimulate cooperative forms of behavior. Another contingency factor is the reputation of the external directors on the board, which is particularly important for young firms that are motivated to gain legitimacy and credibility (Y. Deutsch & Ross, 2003). More generally, the study of both intrafirm and interfirm networks requires attention not only to network structures (which represent opportunities for influence or resource access as well as threats of constraint) but also to the motivations of individual actors. Being the sole link between otherwise unconnected others can be considered either as a brokerage opportunity or as an opportunity to constructively bridge unconnected others, depending on the connector's motives. As another example, the extent to which an individual will mobilize her central position in a friendship network when trying to solve a complex task likely depends on her personality: Her score on a personality trait such as self-efficacy determines her felt need to mobilize others as opposed to completing the task by herself.

Understanding new network phenomena. Finally, in business markets several recent phenomena cannot be adequately explained without resorting to a network perspective. For example, European retailers are increasingly collaborating in rather complex buyer groups, leading to an interesting situation of competition where competing retailers join forces to control powerful manufacturers. Furthermore, firms increasingly involve external parties along the consecutive stages of their new product development processes following new trends such as cocreation, supplier involvement, customer participation, open innovation, outsourcing, and crowd-sourcing. As a result, innovative firms face the challenge of coordinating and controlling increasingly complex innovation projects as small-scale networks while retaining optimal access to external resources.

To conclude, as soon as more than two parties are involved in exchange, nowadays arguably the standard rather than the exception, the dyadic approaches to study exchange that have been so popular for decades in marketing need to be replaced by triadic and more complex network approaches. A network perspective would not only advance the marketing literature but also contribute to the network literature where exchange has not received the same attention as in marketing. Blending the insights from marketing regarding the role of economic calculus, motivations, emotions, and attitudes in exchange with insights from the network literature regarding the role of network structures and positions may result in a very valuable cross-fertilization.

NOTES

1. The power and conflict theory that flourished in the 1970s and 1980s (e.g., Gaski, 1984) was grounded in sociological interpretations of dyadic interaction (e.g., M. Deutsch, 1969; Emerson, 1962) and social exchange theory (Thibaut & Kelley, 1959). Also the political economy paradigm mainly focused on dyadic interaction (Stern & Reve, 1980), except for some first references to the importance of the channel environment (Achrol, Reve, & Stern, 1983). The subsequent relationship marketing theory, however, did not elaborate on the channel environment and shifted focus to dyadic relationship development (Anderson & Weitz, 1989; Dwyer, Schurr, & Oh, 1987).

2. For example, prior studies have singled out the world polity as a network governance structure (e.g., Beckfield, 2003; Provan & Milward, 1995). Also the network theory of

organization has focused mainly on enabling coordinated interaction to achieve collective and individual interests (Salancik, 1995). Other studies have discussed alternative approaches to actively govern organizational networks (e.g., through shared governance, brokered governance, separate entities; see Provan & Kenis, 2008).

3. Note that structural balance and structural unbalance in the network literature are in fact more generally defined. Essentially, if the multiplication of signs that characterize the triad is positive, the triad displays structural balance; if it is negative, it displays negative balance. For example, if the tie between A and B is positive, and the ties between A and C and between B and C are negative (my friend's enemies are my enemies), this configuration is categorized as structurally balanced. For reasons of exposition, I limit the discussion to the triadic configuration in Figure 4.2.

4. Interestingly, some more recent evidence shows that board interlocks do not always result from such rational considerations. Westphal and Stern (2006) found that managers who display more ingratiation behaviors toward their CEO are more likely to obtain board appointments at other firms where their CEO serves as a director (i.e., ingratiation behaviors compensate for a lack of an elite background or for belonging to minority groups).

5. I instrumented this variable because it includes the new licensing deals in year t, which was the dependent variable in Wuyts and Dutta (2008) and a function of the firm's board interlock centrality. Instruments include lagged values of centrality in the licensing exchange network as well as all other explanatory variables included in this equation.

6. The variables include the number of different technological domains in which the firm has signed licensing agreements, R&D investments, firm size, firm age, qualifiers of the firm's internal knowledge base based on patents, whether the firm has successfully developed drugs in its lifetime, time trend, and a dummy indicating whether the CEO contract contains a stock option clause.

REFERENCES

Achrol, R. S., Reve, T., & Stern, L. W. (1983, Fall). The environment of marketing channel dyads: A framework for comparative analysis. *Journal of Marketing, 47,* 55–67.

Algesheimer, R., Dholakia, U. M., & Herrmann, A. (2005). The social influence of brand community: Evidence from European car clubs. *Journal of Marketing, 69*(3), 19–34.

Allen, M. P. (1974). The structure of interorganizational elite cooptation: Interlocking corporate directorates. *American Sociological Review, 39*(3), 393–406.

Anderson, E., & Weitz, B. (1989). Determinants of continuity in conventional industrial channel dyads. *Marketing Science, 8*(4), 310–323.

Antia, K., & Frazier, G. L. (2001). The severity of contract enforcement in interfirm channel relationships. *Journal of Marketing, 65*(4), 67–81.

Baysinger, B. D., & Butler, H. N. (1985). The role of corporate law in the theory of the firm. *Journal of Law and Economics, 28*(1), 179–191.

Beckfield, J. (2003, June). Inequality in the world polity: The structure of international organization. *American Sociological Review, 68,* 401–424.

Brass, D. J. (1984). Being in the right place: A structural analysis of individual influence in an organization. *Administrative Science Quarterly, 29*(4), 518–539.

Braudel, F. (1985). *Civilization and capitalism, 15th–18th century: The wheels of commerce* (Vol. 2). London: Fontana Press.

Burt, R. S. (1992). *Structural holes: The social structure of competition.* Cambridge, MA: Harvard University Press.

Buskens, V. (1998). The social structure of trust. *Social Networks, 20*(3), 265–289.

Coleman, J. S. (1990). *Foundations of social theory.* Cambridge, MA: Harvard University Press.

Cook, K. S., & Emerson, R. M. (1978, October). Power, equity, and commitment in exchange networks. *American Sociological Review, 43,* 721–739.

Cook, K. S., & Whitmeyer, J. M. (1992, August). Two approaches to social structure: Exchange theory and network analysis. *Annual Review of Sociology, 18,* 109–127.

Davis, G. F. (1991). Agents without principles? The spread of the poison pill through the intercorporate network. *Administrative Science Quarterly, 36*(4), 583–613.

Dawes, P. L., Lee, D. Y., & Dowling, G. R. (1998, July). Information control and influence in emerging buying centers. *Journal of Marketing, 62,* 55–68.

Deutsch, M. (1969, January). Conflict: Productive and destructive. *Journal of Social Issues, 25,* 7–42.

Deutsch, Y., & Ross, T. (2003). You are known by the directors you keep: Reputable directors as a signaling mechanism for young firms. *Management Science, 49*(8), 1003–1017.

DiMaggio, P. (1992). Nadal's paradox revisited: Relational and cultural aspects of organizational structure. In N. Nohria & R. G. Eccles (Eds.), *Networks and organizations: Structure, form, and action* (pp. 118–142). Boston: Harvard Business School Press.

DiMaggio, P., & Louch, H. (1998). Socially embedded consumer transaction: For what kind of purchases do people most often use networks? *American Sociological Review, 63*(5), 619–637.

Dollinger, M. J., Golden, P. A., & Saxton, T. (1997). The effect of reputation on the decision to joint venture. *Strategic Management Journal, 18*(2), 127–140.

Dooley, P. C. (1969). The interlocking directorate. *American Economic Review, 59*(3), 314–323.

Dwyer, F. R., Schurr, P. H., & Oh, S. (1987, April). Developing buyer–seller relationships. *Journal of Marketing, 51,* 11–27.

Emerson, R. M. (1962, February). Power-dependence relations. *American Sociological Review, 27,* 31–41.

Emirbayer, M., & Goodwin, J. (1994). Network analysis, culture, and the problem of agency. *American Journal of Sociology, 99*(6), 1411–1454.

Fligstein, N., & Brantley, P. (1992). Bank control, owner control, or organizational dynamics: Who controls the large modern corporation? *American Journal of Sociology, 98*(2), 280–317.

Freeman, L. (1979, February). Centrality in social networks: Conceptual clarification. *Social Networks, 1,* 215–239.

Frooman, J. (1999). Stakeholder influence strategies. *Academy of Management Review, 24*(2), 191–205.

Gargiulo, M. (1993). Two-step leverage: Managing constraint in organizational politics. *Administrative Science Quarterly, 38*(1), 1–19.

Gaski, J. F. (1984, Summer). The theory of power and conflict in channels of distribution. *Journal of Marketing, 48,* 9–29.

Gould, R. V. (1993). Collective action and network structure. *American Sociological Review, 58*(2), 182–196.

Granovetter, M. S. (1978). Threshold models of collective behavior. *American Journal of Sociology, 83*(6), 1420–1443.

Granovetter, M. S. (1985). Economic action and social structure: The problem of embeddedness. *American Journal of Sociology, 91*(1), 481–493.

Granovetter, M. S., & Swedberg, R. (1992). *The sociology of economic life.* New York: Westview.

Greif, A. (1993). Contract enforceability and economic institutions in early trade: The Maghribi traders' coalition. *American Economic Review, 83*(3), 525–548.

Gulati, R., & Westphal, J. D. (1999). Cooperative or controlling? The effects of CEO–board relations and the content of interlocks on the formation of joint ventures. *Administrative Science Quarterly, 44*(3), 473–506.

Haunschild, P. R. (1993). Interorganizational imitation: The impact of interlocks on corporate acquisition activity. *Administrative Science Quarterly, 38*(4), 564–592.

Hayagreeva, R., & Sivakumar, K. (1999). Institutional sources of boundary-spanning structures: The establishment of investor relations departments in the Fortune 500 industrials. *Organization Science, 10*(1), 27–42.

Heide, J. B. (1994). Interorganizational governance in marketing channels. *Journal of Marketing, 58*(1), 71–85.

Heide, J. B., & John, G. (1990, February). Alliances in industrial purchasing: The determinants of joint action in buyer–supplier relationships. *Journal of Marketing Research, 27*, 24–36.

Heider, F. (1958). *The psychology of interpersonal relations.* Hillsdale, NY: Lawrence Erlbaum.

Houston, M. B., & Johnson, S. A. (2000). Buyer–supplier contracts versus joint ventures: Determinants and consequences of transaction structure. *Journal of Marketing Research, 37*(1), 1–15.

Jap, S. D., & Ganesan, S. (2000). Control mechanisms and the relationship life cycle: Implications for safeguarding specific investments and developing commitment. *Journal of Marketing Research, 37*(2), 227–245.

John, G. (1984). An empirical investigation of some antecedents of opportunism in a marketing channel. *Journal of Marketing Research, 21*(3), 278–289.

Jones, C., Hesterly, W. S., & Borgatti, S. P. (1997). A general theory of network governance: Exchange conditions and social mechanisms. *Academy of Management Review, 22*(4), 911–945.

Kilduff, M., & Tsai, W. (2003). *Social networks and organizations.* London: Sage.

Koza, M. P., & Lewin, A. Y. (1999). The coevolution of network alliances: A longitudinal analysis of an international professional service network. *Organization Science, 10*(5), 638–653.

Lang, J. R., & Lockhart, D. E. (1990). Increased environmental uncertainty and changes in board linkage patterns. *Academy of Management Journal, 33*(1), 106–128.

Larson, A. (1992). Network dyads in entrepreneurial settings: A study of the governance of exchange relationships. *Administrative Science Quarterly, 37*(1), 76–104.

Lusch, R. F. (1976). Sources of power: Their impact on intrachannel conflict. *Journal of Marketing Research, 13*(4), 382–390.

Macaulay, S. (1963). Non-contractual relations in business: A preliminary study. *American Sociological Review, 28*(1), 55–67.

Macy, M. W., & Skvoretz, J. (1998, October). The evolution of trust and cooperation between strangers: A computational model. *American Sociological Review, 63*, 638–660.

Mariolis, P., & Jones, M. H. (1982). Centrality in corporate interlock networks: Reliability and stability. *Administrative Science Quarterly, 27*(4), 571–585.

Markovsky, B., Willer, D., & Patton, T. (1988). Power relations in exchange networks. *American Sociological Review, 53*(2), 220–236.

Mizruchi, M. S. (1996, August). What do interlocks do? An analysis, critique, and assessment of research on interlocking directorates. *Annual Review of Sociology, 22,* 271–298.

Newman, J. (2005). Enter the transformational leader: Network governance and the micropolitics of modernization. *Sociology, 39*(4), 717–734.

Nooteboom, B., Berger, H., & Noorderhaven, N. G. (1997). Effects of trust and governance on relational risk. *Academy of Management Journal, 40*(2), 308–338.

Obstfeld, D. (2005). Social networks, the *tertius iungens* orientation, and involvement in innovation. *Administrative Science Quarterly, 50*(1), 100–130.

Ornstein, M. D. (1980). Assessing the meaning of corporate interlocks: Canadian evidence. *Social Science Research, 9,* 287–306.

Park, S. H. (1996). Managing an interorganizational network: A framework of the institutional mechanism for network control. *Organization Studies, 17*(5), 795–824.

Powell, W. W. (1990). Neither market nor hierarchy: Network forms of organization. In B. M. Staw & L. L. Cummings (Eds.), *Research in organizational behavior* (Vol. 12, pp. 295–336). Greenwich, CT: JAI Press.

Provan, K. G., & Kenis, P. (2008). Modes of network governance: Structure, management, and effectiveness. *Journal of Public Administration Research and Theory, 18*(2), 229–252.

Provan, K. G., & Milward, H. B. (1995). A preliminary theory of interorganizational network effectiveness: A comparative study of four community mental health systems. *Administrative Science Quarterly, 40*(1), 1–33.

Provan, K. G., & Sebastian, J. G. (1998). Networks within networks: Service link overlap, organizational cliques, and network effectiveness. *Academy of Management Journal, 41*(4), 453–463.

Raub, W., & Weesie, J. (1990). Reputation and efficiency in social interactions: An example of network effects. *American Journal of Sociology, 96*(3), 626–654.

Salancik, G. R. (1995). Wanted: A good network theory of organization. *Administrative Science Quarterly, 40*(2), 345–349.

Scott, J. P. (2000). *Social network analysis* (2nd ed.). Thousand Oaks, CA: Sage.

Stern, L. W., & Reve, T. (1980). Distribution channels as political economies: A framework for comparative analysis. *Journal of Marketing, 44*(3), 52–64.

Stevenson, W. B., & Greenberg, D. (2000). Agency and social networks: Strategies of action in a social structure of position, opposition, and opportunity. *Administrative Science Quarterly, 45*(4), 651–678.

Thibaut, J. W., & Kelley, H. (1959). *The social psychology of groups.* New York: Wiley.

Uzzi, B. (1997). Social structure and competition in interfirm networks: The paradox of embeddedness. *Administrative Science Quarterly, 42*(1), 35–67.

Uzzi, B., & Lancaster, R. (2004). Relational embeddedness and learning: The case of bank loan managers and their clients. *Management Science, 49*(4), 383–399.

Uzzi, B., & Spiro, J. (2005). Collaboration and creativity: The small world problem. *American Journal of Sociology, 111*(2), 447–504.

Van den Bulte, C., & Wuyts, S. (2007). *Social networks and marketing.* Cambridge, MA: Marketing Science Institute.

Watts, D. J. (2002). A simple model of global cascades on random networks. *Proceedings of the National Academy of Sciences of the United States of America, 99*(9), 5766–5771.

Watts, D. J. & Strogatz, S. H. (1998). Collective dynamics of 'small world' networks. *Nature*, *393*(6684), 440–442.

Weiss, A. M., & Anderson, E. (1992). Converting from independent to employee sales forces: The role of perceived switching costs. *Journal of Marketing Research*, *29*(1), 101–115.

Westphal, J. D., & Khanna, P. (2003). Keeping directors in line: Social distancing as a control mechanism in the corporate elite. *Administrative Science Quarterly*, *48*(3), 361–398.

Westphal, J. D., Seidel, M.-D. L., & Stewart, K. J. (2001). Second-order imitation: Uncovering latent effects of board network ties. *Administrative Science Quarterly*, *46*(4), 717–747.

Westphal, J. D., & Stern, I. (2006). The other pathway to the boardroom: Interpersonal influence as a substitute for elite credentials and majority status in obtaining board appointments. *Administrative Science Quarterly*, *51*(2), 169–204.

Wolff, K. H. (Ed.). (1950). Quantitative aspects of the group. In *The sociology of Georg Simmel* (pp. 87–177). New York: Free Press.

Wrong, D. (1961). The oversocialized conception of man in modern sociology. *American Sociological Review*, *26*(2), 183–193.

Wuyts, S. (2007). Extra-role behavior in buyer–supplier relationships. *International Journal of Research in Marketing*, *24*(4), 301–311.

Wuyts, S., & Dutta, S. (2008). Licensing exchange: Insights from the biopharmaceutical industry. *International Journal of Research in Marketing*, *25*(4), 273–281.

Wuyts, S., & Geyskens, I. (2005). The formation of buyer–supplier relationships: Detailed contract drafting and close partner selection. *Journal of Marketing*, *69*(4), 103–117.

Wuyts, S., Stremersch, S., Van den Bulte, C., & Franses, P. H. (2004). Vertical marketing systems for complex products: A triadic perspective. *Journal of Marketing Research*, *41*(4), 479–487.

Section II

Leveraging Vertical Connectivity With Channel Partners and Brands

5

The Connected Patient

Nuno Camacho, Vardit Landsman, and Stefan Stremersch

When in 1992 Laura Landro, a journalist at the *Wall Street Journal*, was diagnosed with chronic myelogenous leukemia, she decided to gather as much information as possible about her disease and to become an *informed patient*. At this time, the use of the Internet was still not sufficiently widespread, and physicians were not accustomed to patients bringing documents and medical data to the medical encounter. As a result, challenging doctors "was no picnic," and to find the "accessible, wonderful, caring doctors" she deserved, Laura had to sever ties with a few more "impersonal physicians and medical workers who were simply annoyed at a patient who was trying to be her own best advocate" (Landro, 1999, p. 56).

At the same time, pharmaceutical companies, perceiving changes in the role of patients in medical decision making, initiated a trend that would soon become controversial. The amount of money invested in direct-to-consumer advertising (DTCA) by the American pharmaceutical industry rose steadily from the mid-1990s onward. Indicative of recent changes in the health care systems, DTCA expenditures reached, in 2006, $4.8 billion (Pharmaceutical Research and Manufacturers of America, 2008).

In this chapter, we review evidence supporting the claim that a fundamental shift in the role of the patient (and, consequently, of the physician) in medical decision making is taking place. There is a trend toward more participatory decision making in which doctors and patients *together* bear responsibility for medical decisions. This change has implications for patient welfare and for firms operating in the life sciences industry.[1]

In this new paradigm, physicians are expected to establish a dialogue with their patients and apply their medical knowledge to connect scientific evidence to patient needs and preferences (Emanuel & Emanuel, 1992; Epstein, Alper, & Quill, 2004; Morgan, 2003). Despite its renewed appeal, this idea of reaping benefits from a strong collaboration between patient and physician has a very long tradition in medicine. For example, in an influential article about patient–physician relationships, Emanuel and Emanuel (1992, p. 225) quoted Plato, who, more than 2,000 years ago, wrote,

> The free physician, who usually cares for free men, treats their diseases first by thoroughly discussing with the patient and his friends his ailment. This way he learns something from the sufferer and simultaneously instructs him. Then the physician does not give his medications until he has persuaded the patient; the physician aims at complete restoration of health by persuading the patient to comply with his therapy.

Until recently, however, the relationship between patients and doctors could still, by and large, be characterized by a *white-coat model*, according to which the physician uses her or his knowledge to prescribe treatments in a paternalistic way (Charles, Gafni, & Whelan, 1999). Limited patient participation in medical decisions was generally accepted because (a) the utility of different health outcomes was considered objective and independent of the subjective thoughts of doctors and/or patients, and (b) society at large empowered physicians to use their knowledge to decide, on behalf of the patient, what treatment and tests were the most appropriate given her or his condition (Emanuel & Emanuel, 1992).

Today, the expectations and views of both physicians and patients regarding medical encounters are changing, and a trend toward *shared decision making* is emerging. These changes are a natural consequence of the significant links found between patient participation in medical decisions and desirable health consequences. For instance, patient participation in medical decisions has been linked to improvements in adherence to treatment plans (Golin, DiMatteo, & Gelberg, 1996; Horne, 2006), patient satisfaction, perceived improvement in symptoms, and general improvement in health condition (Brody, Miller, Lerman, Smith, & Caputo, 1989; Lerman et al., 1990; Little et al., 2001). Yet, the transition toward a more active participation of patients in medical decision making requires a transformation of the tie between patient and doctor, which may entail changes in the amount, content, and directionality of information flow and in the level of reciprocity in the relationship. Neither all doctors nor all patients are equally prepared or motivated for this change.

In this chapter, we review antecedents and consequences of the trend toward increased patient participation in medical decisions. A better

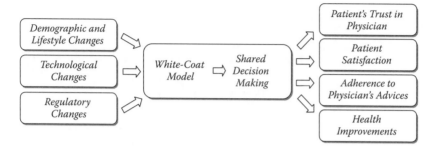

FIGURE 5.1
Antecedent and consequences of increased patient connectedness.

understanding of patient needs and preferences will help us uncover how patient satisfaction, health outcomes, effective health care delivery, and life sciences firms' marketing strategies can be improved. This understanding will also provide insights on several open research topics. Figure 5.1 illustrates a conceptual overview of this chapter.

As can be seen in Figure 5.1, the primary focus in this chapter is the dyadic connectivity between patients and their physicians. To develop a more comprehensive understanding of the underlying processes in these relations, however, we consider—in an admittedly cursory manner—the broader context of these relations and investigate other types of ties in medical decision making. Such "surrounding connections" may be among patients, among physicians, or between heath-related entities (e.g., pharmaceutical companies, health insurance companies) and patients or physicians.

FROM A WHITE-COAT MODEL TO SHARED DECISION MAKING

Figure 5.2 presents a typology for possible models for the patient–physician relationship according to the dual power structure within this relationship. The white-coat model on the lower right part of Figure 5.2 was the mainstream approach until the 1980s and is characterized by a relationship in which the physician takes a paternalistic role and acts as a guardian of the patient and his or her health. Under the white-coat model, the final goal of improving the patient's health status is treated as an objective

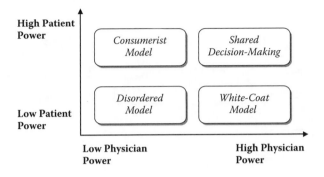

FIGURE 5.2
Models of patient–physician relationships. Adapted from "The Enduring and Evolving Nature of the Patient–Physician Relationship," by D. Roter, 2000, *Patient Education and Counseling, 39*(1), pp. 5–15. Copyright 2000. Adapted with permission from Elsevier.

goal that has priority over both patients' autonomy and personal choices (Emanuel & Emanuel, 1992). In such a model, the patient is expected to cooperate and *comply* with the physicians' orders and recommendations. The relationship usually assumes a biomedical tone, with the emotional and psychosocial components of medical care garnering relatively less importance (Morgan, 2003).

Moving away from the white-coat model, however, is neither easy nor consensual. Different physicians react differently to patient participation in medical decisions. Some argue that there is a lack of practical guidelines to guide physicians in the process of adapting their behavior to the new reality of patient empowerment (Taylor, 2007). Others fear that physicians might start interpreting their role solely as providers of important information to the patient rather than as influencers of patient decisions. In such cases, a *consumerist model* would be established, and patients would turn to physicians for medical information but assume the control of their medical decisions (upper left part of Figure 5.2). Many physicians feel uncomfortable with these challenges, which might explain why today, despite the increasing agreement on the need for more patient participation, many physicians still adopt a white-coat approach to medical care (Young, Bell, Epstein, Feldman, & Kravitz, 2008).

In fact, a risk entailed in the process of empowering patients is that physicians might practice reactive, rather than proactive, medicine. Reactive medical care—a tendency to offer only the advice and information requested by patients—can be particularly undesirable when patients are not able or willing to take the lead in making medical decisions. In effect, if the physician assumes erroneously that the patient wants to make his or her own decisions and prematurely hands over relational power and control to the patient, the patient–physician relationship can suffer from lack of direction. We labeled such situations as a *disordered model*.[2]

This discussion suggests that it is important (a) to distinguish shared decision making from other alternative models of the patient–physician relationship, (b) to better understand how shared decision making can be promoted, and (c) to understand the role of patient expectations in shaping patient–physician relationships. In essence, the *shared decision-making model* entails a *mutual* involvement of patients and physicians in clinical decisions and is increasingly seen as the ideal standard for patient–physician relationships. According to Charles, Gafni, and Whelan (1997, 1999), four necessary conditions must be met for a relationship to be classified as shared decision making:

1. *Mutual participation:* Both the physician and the patient participate in the decision-making process.[3]
2. *Mutual sharing of information:* The physician shares information about existing treatment alternatives and listens to information the patient might have gathered from other sources.
3. *Value sharing:* The patient expresses his or her preferences, and the physician shares his or her knowledge-based values about the best course of action.
4. *Mutual agreement:* This last condition, which focuses on the outcome rather than the decision process, claims that more than mutual participation, the physician and the patient need to reach mutual agreement about the best course of action.

In sum, there is an increased agreement that shared decision making is the ideal model for patient–physician relationships in the 21st century.[4] This paradigm change entails opportunities and challenges for all stakeholders involved in health care. In particular, for life sciences firms, this new model suggests the need to invest in marketing strategies that address the increasingly active role of patients in treatment decisions.

ANTECEDENTS OF THE EVOLUTION TO SHARED DECISION MAKING

Now we turn to the antecedents of the trend from a white-coat model toward a shared decision-making model and address the magnitude of this trend. An insightful way to analyze these antecedents is by broadening the focus of analysis from a dyadic perspective of the patient–physician relationship to a *network perspective* of the social system consisting of physicians and patients.

Taking a network perspective here is consistent with recent calls by marketing scholars to implement a network perspective in the analysis of social systems in knowledge-rich environments (Manchanda et al., 2005; Wathne & Heide, 2004). The network perspective allows us to expand our analysis beyond the patient–physician relationship and also consider social ties among physicians and among patients. Moreover, by using this framework, we can explore the effect of external drivers on the network structure as well as on the nature of ties in the social system.

Figure 5.3 presents a network representation of a basic social system consisting of doctors and patients. Interpersonal networks of physicians and patients have already attracted the attention of scholars in sociology, medicine, and marketing. Existing studies have focused on the influence of interpersonal networks of physicians on their prescription choices

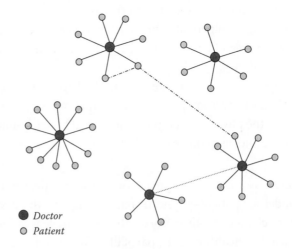

● *Doctor*
○ *Patient*

FIGURE 5.3
The health system: a network of patient–physician relationships.

(Coleman, Katz, & Menzel, 1966; Nair, Manchanda, & Bhatia, 2006) as well as on interpersonal relations among patients and their role, for example, in the spread of infectious diseases (Rothenberg et al., 1998). Many questions remain unanswered, however, particularly in terms of the ties between *physicians* and *patients*, which is the main focus of this chapter.

Patient–physician ties are based on the flow of information between these two actors and are, therefore, directional. That is, one can ask whether the information flows from actor A to actor B, or vice versa. This directionality allows us to look at levels of *reciprocity* or *symmetry* in the patient–physician relationship.[5] Reciprocity can serve as a "starting mechanism" in early relational phases to induce higher levels of cooperation (Gouldner, 1960). Symmetry can also be used to capture the trend toward shared decision making, that is, the extent to which one observes a shift away from a sole focus on the "voice of medicine" to an increasing emphasis on the "voice of the patient" (Morgan, 2003, p. 55).

We can identify three major drivers triggering the move toward more patient autonomy and participation in medical care: (a) demographic changes, (b) technological advances, and (c) changes in the regulatory environment.

Demographic and Lifestyle Changes

Demographic and lifestyle changes are important contributors to the trend toward more patient participation in medical decisions. Ongoing shifts in demography (e.g., an aging population) and lifestyle (such as increased urbanization, exposure to pollutants, or stress) contribute to an increased focus on chronic conditions worldwide (Murray & Lopez, 1996). Leading public health concerns include ischemic heart disease, the continued spread of HIV/AIDS, and several forms of cancer (see Figure 5.4, adapted from Mathers & Loncar, 2006).

The increase in the prevalence and importance of chronic diseases creates two forces that encourage more informed and more connected patients, that is, shared decision making. First, chronic patients have a strong incentive to collect information and discuss their health with friends or through patient support groups; hence, they will typically be more knowledgeable about their diseases than patients suffering from acute diseases. The increased knowledge possessed by chronically ill patients equips such patients with a greater ability to participate in their own medical care. Second, public health initiatives increasingly promote

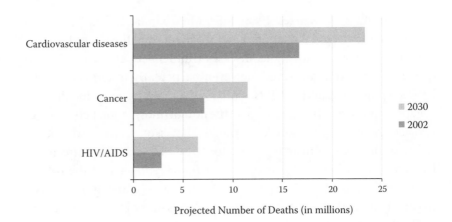

FIGURE 5.4
Projections for major causes of death globally (2002–2030). From "Projections of Global Mortality and Burden of Disease From 2002 to 2030," by C. D. Mathers and D. Loncar, 2006, *PLoS Medicine, 3*(11), e442.

the need for lifestyle changes such as smoking prevention and cessation (Pauwels, Buist, Calverley, Jenkins, & Hurd, 2001) and eating a well-balanced diet (Grundy et al., 2004). This need to persuade healthy consumers to make lifestyle changes (with the objective of avoiding future health hazards) is facilitated by more patient involvement and thus by a shared decision-making approach (Roter & Hall, 2006; Sheridan, Harris, & Woolf, 2004).

Technological Changes

Technological advances also contribute to the obsolescence of the white-coat model. Specifically, two major technological shifts have facilitated the transition toward shared decision making: (a) the advent of the Internet and the consequent democratization of access to medical information, and (b) the sequencing of the human genome, which triggered the emergence of personalized medicine.

The Rise of the Internet and E-health

The first important technological development that impacts patient–physician relationships involves the advent of the Internet and the consequent consumer access to health information. A recent survey conducted by iCrossing (2008), which is a research firm specialized in digital marketing, found that 59% of all American adults look for health information on the Internet. This makes the Internet the most popular source of health information, as 55% stated that they look for health information by visiting their physicians, and only 29% acknowledged looking for such information by talking with friends, relatives, or coworkers. Scholars in medicine have indeed recognized that the massive accessibility of online health information has contributed to the "most important techno-cultural medical revolution of the past century" (Ferguson & Frydman, 2004, p. 1149).

In fact, the Internet affects the structure of the patient–physician network in two ways: It lowers the access barriers to medical information, and it facilitates the connection and sharing of information among actors (i.e., among patients, among physicians, between physicians and patients, and between firms and the other stakeholders). The first effect—easier access to medical information—directly facilitates patient empowerment, because patients can now easily collect information that they can later discuss with their physicians. The second effect—increased connection among actors—also operates by increasing patients' knowledge, but it typically interferes with the patient–physician relationship in an indirect manner. Virtual networking among patients, for example, facilitates the sharing of experiences, information, and support that can help in medical diagnosis and treatment (Mukherjee & McGinnis, 2007). Thus, virtual networking can facilitate patients' input during medical encounters. On the physician side, the advent of e-health care is also strengthening social networks by facilitating the establishment of new ties among physicians and health professionals, allowing for more information to flow directly in the system. The increased importance of such virtual communities of physicians has the potential to improve the lives of many patients (Mukherjee & McGinnis, 2007).

It is important for all stakeholders in the health care industry to understand the implications of these changes and to learn how to leverage the potential of the Internet in general and social media in particular. Marketers, for example, can serve an important role in persuading both patients and physicians to use these new tools to improve the quality of their mutual relationship and promote shared decision making.

Genomics and Personalized Medicine

A second critical technological development in the life sciences has been the sequencing of the human genome and the ensuing rise of *genomics* as a revolution in medicine and drug discovery (Zerhouni, 2003). Genomics is the study of the genetic material of an organism. Launched in 1990 by the U.S. government, the Human Genome Project (HGP) was a large research project involving more than 350 laboratories from several countries to study human genetic material (Enriquez & Goldberg, 2000). In 2003, the HGP completed the mapping of the human genome, which opened a vast array of new possibilities in tailoring medicine to the needs of individual patients.

A good example of the impact of genomics on the prescription drug market is the growth of the biotechnology sector as compared to the pharmaceutical industry overall. Table 5.1 shows the largest 25 companies in the world in terms of sales of human prescription drugs and vaccines. The table shows that biotech companies such as Amgen and Genentech have grown faster than the market and thus have climbed up in ranking. Between 2005 and 2006, for example, the biologics sector grew 17.1% and reached sales figures above $52 billion, whereas the pharmaceutical market as a whole only grew 7% (Pharmaceutical Executive, 2006).

Although the rise of personalized medicine cannot be considered an antecedent of the recent trend toward patient empowerment, we can certainly expect it to reinforce such a trend. Developments in genetics and biotechnology will boost personalized medicine, which requires detailed information flows between patients and their physicians for both diagnosis and treatment decisions. Therefore, we expect the rise of personalized medicine to accelerate the trend toward shared decision making by enhancing the volume and frequency of information flow between patients and physicians.

Regulatory Changes

Increases in patient–physician connectedness have also been triggered by changes in existing regulations. Examples of such changes include greater flexibility in DTCA regulation, especially in the United States and New Zealand, and the increased use of malpractice suits by patients against physicians.

TABLE 5.1

Top 25 Companies in Terms of Prescription Drug Sales

Rank	2001	2002	2003	2004	2005	2006	2007
1	Pfizer	Pfizer	Pfizer	Pfizer	Pfizer	Pfizer	Pfizer
2	Glaxo Smith Kline	Glaxo Smith Kline	Glaxo Smith Kline	Glaxo Smith Kline	Glaxo Smith Kline	Glaxo Smith Kline	Glaxo Smith Kline
3	Merck	Merck	Merck	Sanofi-Aventis	Sanofi-Aventis	Sanofi-Aventis	Sanofi-Aventis
4	AstraZeneca	AstraZeneca	Johnson & Johnson	Johnson & Johnson	Novartis	Novartis	Novartis
5	Bristol-Myers Squibb	Aventis	Aventis	Merck	AstraZeneca	AstraZeneca	AstraZeneca
6	Aventis	Johnson & Johnson	AstraZeneca	AstraZeneca	Johnson & Johnson	Johnson & Johnson	Johnson & Johnson
7	Johnson & Johnson	Novartis	Novartis	Novartis	Merck	Merck	Merck
8	Novartis	Bristol-Myers Squibb	Bristol-Myers Squibb	Bristol-Myers Squibb	Wyeth	Roche	Roche
9	Pharmacia	Pharmacia	Wyeth	Wyeth	Bristol-Myers Squibb	Eli Lilly	Wyeth
10	Lilly	Wyeth	Eli Lilly	Abbott Labs	Eli Lilly	Wyeth	Eli Lilly
11	Wyeth	Eli Lilly	Abbott Labs	Eli Lilly	Abbott Labs	Bristol-Myers Squibb	Bristol-Myers Squibb
12	Roche	Roche	Roche	Roche	Roche	Amgen	Bayer
13	Schering-Plough	Abbott Labs	Sanofi-Synthlabo	Amgen	Amgen	Abbott	Abbott

Continued

TABLE 5.1 (*Continued*)

Top 25 Companies in Terms of Prescription Drug Sales

Rank	2001	2002	2003	2004	2005	2006	2007
14	Abbott Laboratories	Schering-Plough	Boehringer Ingelheim	Boehringer Ingelheim	Boehringer Ingelheim	Boehringer Ingelheim	Amgen
15	Takeda	Sanofi-Synthelabo	Amgen	Takeda	Takeda	Bayer	Boehringer Ingelheim
16	Sanofi-Synthelabo	Boehringer Ingelheim	Takeda	Schering Plough	Astellas	Takeda	Schering-Plough
17	Boehringer Ingelheim	Takeda	Schering-Plough	Schering AG	Schering-Plough	Schering-Plough	Takeda
18	Bayer	Schering AG	Schering AG	Bayer	Bayer	Teva	Genentech
19	Schering AG	Bayer	Bayer	Eisai	Schering AG	Genentech	Teva
20	Akzo Nobel	Amgen	Sankyo	Teva	Genentech	Schering AG	Novo Nordisk
21	Amgen	Sankyo	Eisai	Merck KGaA	Novo Nordisk	Astellas Pharma	Astellas
22	Sankyo	Akzo Nobel	Yamanouchi	Genentech	Eisai	Novo Nordisk	Daiichi Sankyo
23	Merck KGaA	Eisai	Novo Nordisk	Yamanouchi	Teva	Merck KGaA	Merck KGaA
24	Novo Nordisk	Yamanouchi	Merck KGaA	Otsuka	Merck KGaA	Eisai	Eisai
25	Shionogi	Merck KGaA	Teva	Novo Nordisk	Sankyo	Otsuka	Otsuka

Source: *The World's Top 50 Pharmaceutical Companies,* by Pharmaceutical Executive, 2006.

Regulation of Direct-to-Consumer Advertising

DTCA contributes, at least in the United States and New Zealand, to an increased participation of patients in medical decision making. In the United States, from the mid-1990s, the increase in DTCA expenditures became quite evident (see Figure 5.5).

There exists strong controversy about DTCA and the need for stricter regulation. On the one hand, some authors have defended DTCA as a means to educate and empower patients to take a more active role in their treatment (Holmer, 1999). On the other hand, other authors have suggested that such efforts mainly boost consumer demand and distort the role of patients in the (traditional) relationship with their physicians (Hollon, 1999; Moynihan, Heath, & Henry, 2002), which may result in a consumerist or, even worse, a disordered model (see Figure 5.2).

Still, everyone agrees that the main effects of DTCA are to prompt patients to visit their physicians, possibly to request a specific drug (Bell, Wilkes, & Kravitz, 1999). Recently, research in medicine has shown that patient requests stimulate more shared decision-making behaviors from physicians (Young et al., 2008). Along similar lines, Venkataraman and Stremersch (2007) found that patient requests for a certain drug increase

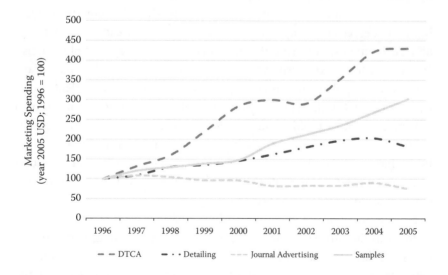

FIGURE 5.5
Growth in annual spending per type of marketing (1996–2005). From "A Decade of Direct-to-Consumer Advertising of Prescription Drugs," by J. M. Donohue, M. Cevasco, and M. B. Rosenthal, 2007, *New England Journal of Medicine, 357*(7), pp. 673–681.

physicians' prescriptions of that drug. Moreover, physicians' refusals to accommodate such requests have been associated with patient dissatisfaction and even with intentions of switching physicians (Bell et al., 1999). Thus, DTCA might contribute to an increase in patient power in medical decisions, leading some scholars to recognize that "DTC advertising has the potential to fundamentally alter the roles of doctor and patient" (Wilkes, Bell, & Kravitz, 2000, p. 122).

A network perspective can help uncover important consequences of DTCA. For instance, social network theory suggests that different network properties, and different positions in a network, can make some actors more or less influential in marketing events (Van den Bulte & Wuyts, 2007). Physician and patient beliefs can be influenced by the decisions of (a) those who are close to them (i.e., contagion by direct contact, which is promoted by cohesion), (b) those who are similar to them (i.e., contagion by structural equivalence), or (c) those who are particularly respected by them (Burt, 1987; Nair et al., 2006). Both the Internet and DTCA can contribute to changes in these properties. In particular, from a social network perspective, we can see the entities behind both DTCA and Internet Web sites targeting patients as additional "actors" who provide patients with information regarding their health conditions.

Thus, DTCA can influence patient power in medical decisions by increasing their *degree centrality* and *closeness centrality* in the social network and, consequently, lowering the informational advantages of physicians.[6] In fact, on top of their specialized training and knowledge, physicians used to monopolize the brokering of information across patients. That is, their contact with many patients gave them yet another informational advantage, that of building knowledge from learning about the experiences of different patients. These bridge positions—that is, network locations that span structural holes in the network—are a typical source of informational advantages (Burt, 1992). DTCA (and the Internet), however, contributes to a new network structure that has fewer structural holes and, as a result, fewer actors occupying bridge positions in the network.

Previous literature has connected informational advantages with power (Brass, Galaskiewicz, Greve, & Tsai, 2004; Podolny, Stuart, & Hannan, 1996). In the patient–physician context, this implies that physicians in the new network structure have less power in their relationship with patients than before. This leads us back to Figure 5.2 and to the general trend toward relationships that are characterized by shared decision making (see also

Figure 5.1). Nonetheless, physicians are still expected to keep their role as major players in patient–physician relationships. Their specialized training is not replaceable by either DTCA or by health information available on the Internet. An ideal patient–physician relationship should be characterized by good interaction between two experts: the physician, who is an expert on diagnoses and treatments, and the patient, who is the expert on his or her values and preferences and how the disease interferes with his or her life (Roter & Hall, 2006). Thus, we anticipate a trend toward shared decision making involving the mutual participation of more informed patients with more facilitative, less authoritative physicians, rather than a shift toward a consumerist model.

Frequency and Severity of Malpractice Suits Against Physicians

Another regulatory factor that may promote patient involvement in medical decisions involves the climate created by increases in the frequency and severity of malpractice claims. In the United States, there are on average 15 claims per 100 physicians per year (Danzon, 2000). Physicians practicing in high-risk specialties, such as surgery or obstetrics, can expect to be sued once every 6 years, and although the vast majority of suits are either dropped or won by physicians, legal defense is still very expensive (Danzon, 2000; Gawande, 2005). This liability climate impacts patient–physician relationships.

First, appropriate involvement of a patient in medical decisions might help the physician share the responsibility of the decisions made with patients and, thus, reduce the likelihood of being sued. Failure to obtain *informed consent* from patients, for example, is treated as medical negligence and can be used in court as equivalent to careless medical practice (Faden & Beauchamp, 1986).[7] Second, a way to reduce the threat of litigation is to promote open communication between the patient and the physician. In fact, when senators Hillary Clinton and Barack Obama proposed the National Medical Error Disclosure and Compensation Bill, they believed in open communication within the patient–physician relationship as a way to reduce litigation (Clinton & Obama, 2006).

In sum, technological, demographic, and regulatory changes affect the structure of the social system of patients and physicians and contribute to increased connectedness in this network. We now turn to the consequences of shared decision making.

CLINICAL AND RELATIONAL CONSEQUENCES

Increased patient connectedness entails structural changes in patient–physician relationships and in the health system that are capable of affecting the performance, productivity, or innovativeness of existing ties. Cohesion in social networks, for instance, can be translated into performance improvements because of the increased capacity of such a network to encourage knowledge transfer, enhanced collaboration, and learning. In a study of the performance of corporate R&D teams, Reagans and Zuckerman (2001) showed that both cohesion and diversity among actors contribute to team productivity. We expect stronger ties between physicians and patients to contribute to improvements in clinical and relational outcomes, including patient trust in physicians, patient satisfaction, adherence to physician recommendations, and general health outcomes.

Trust

In medicine, trust is typically considered to be the cornerstone of the patient–physician relationship (Kao, Green, Zaslavsky, Koplan, & Cleary, 1998). It is also a core construct in relationship marketing, and it can be defined as "a willingness to rely on an exchange partner in whom one has confidence" (Moorman, Zaltman, & Deshpande, 1992, p. 315). The current trend toward more patient involvement has consequences for patient trust in physicians. Partnership-building efforts from physicians, for instance, facilitate the transfer of important information between the patient and the physician, reinforcing the patient's trust in his or her physician (Epstein et al., 2004). Patients also are more likely to trust physicians who explore their disease and illness experience and provide longer consultations (Fiscella et al., 2004). Thus, we expect the trend toward shared decision making to foster patients' trust in their physicians.

Trust has important health, social, and economic consequences. In Kao et al.'s (1998) study, patients with lower trust levels were more than twice as likely to have considered changing physicians. This may have direct implications for managers in the health care industry looking to foster patient loyalty. Patients with a low level of trust are also more likely to report a lower satisfaction with care, weaker intentions to adhere to their physician's recommendations, and lower improvements in health (Thom, Kravitz, Bell, Krupat, & Azari, 2002). Finally, patient trust in physicians promotes the spread of positive word-of-mouth, reduces conflicts between the patient and the physician, and encourages perceived effectiveness of care (Hall, Dugan, Zheng, & Mishra, 2001).

Patient Satisfaction

Increased patient connectedness can also affect a second important health-related outcome, patient satisfaction. Research in medicine has suggested a clear link between a physician's practice style and patient satisfaction. Flocke, Miller, and Crabtree (2002) conducted a study based on 2,881 patients and 138 family physicians to quantify the extent to which the style of interaction between patients and physicians influences patient satisfaction. They classified physicians into four mutually exclusive categories: (a) *person-focused* physicians (49%) were personable, friendly, and more focused on the patient than on the disease; (b) *biomedical* physicians (20%) focused on the disease and were unlikely to invest time exploring biopsychosocial information; (c) *biopsychosocial* physicians (16%) elicited some psychosocial clinical information, such as information on social and psychological issues, but overall were more focused on the disease; and (d) *high-physician-control* physicians (15%) dominated the clinical encounter and disregarded the patient's agenda. They found that patients visiting person-focused physicians were significantly more satisfied with the care they received (Flocke et al., 2002). Therefore, in general, we expect the trend toward shared decision making to lead to higher levels of patient satisfaction.

Adherence to Treatment Plan and Preventive Behaviors

Adherence to treatment plans is a very important health issue for all stakeholders in the medical care system. We adopt the definition of adherence provided by the World Health Organization: "the extent to which a person's behavior—taking medication, following a diet, and/or executing lifestyle changes—corresponds with agreed recommendations from a health care provider" (2003, p. 3). Scholars in medicine have suggested that adherence might be the key mediator between medical practice and health outcomes (Kravitz & Melnikow, 2004). Increased adherence has also been linked to higher patient satisfaction (Dellande, Gilly, & Graham, 2004). Hence, improving patient adherence has the potential to improve societal welfare.

A better understanding of patients, physicians, and the relationships they establish should help in designing better, perhaps branded, adherence programs for patients. Facilitating shared decision making is an important step in this direction. For example, several authors have defended the need to replace terms such as *compliance*, which suggests a passive role for the patient, with the term *adherence*, which implies patient involvement and mutual decision making (Osterberg & Blaschke, 2005). The suggested positive link between shared decision making and adherence to treatment recommendations is supported by medical evidence (Golin et al., 1996; Horne, 2006).

Furthermore, the economic costs of *nonadherence* are very high. In the United States alone, nonadherence causes 33% to 69% of all medication-related hospital admissions and an overall economic burden in excess of $100 billion a year (Dunbar-Jacob & Mortimer-Stephens, 2001). Moreover, lost sales due to nonadherence cost the pharmaceutical industry between $15 billion and $20 billion annually (Wosinska, 2005). Thus, adherence is an important topic for many stakeholders in the health system, such as pharmaceutical firms and insurance companies. Therefore, programs aimed at improving patient adherence, even when promoted by pharmaceutical companies, should be well received by other players in the health system (namely, physicians and regulators). Ongoing regulatory changes in Europe, for example, should facilitate direct targeting of adherence-related information to patients (European Commission, 2008). As such, future research should strive to better understand nonadherence from a social network perspective and to clarify strategies that marketers can use to promote adherence.

Health Improvements

Finally, shared decision making may translate into better health outcomes, such as less patient discomfort, greater alleviation of symptoms, and better general health condition (Brody et al., 1989). Di Blasi, Harkness, Ernst, Georgiou, and Kleijnen (2001) reviewed the results of 25 randomized controlled studies and concluded that there is consistent evidence that physicians who adopt a warm, friendly, and reassuring approach are associated with better patient outcomes—for example, less pain and improved speed of recovery—than physicians who adopt a more formal and less reassuring approach. Still, the authors acknowledged that more evidence is needed to confirm the robustness of these findings.

Indeed, in another review, Guadagnoli and Ward (1998) concluded that although many studies find that shared decision making yields positive consequences, other studies offer conflicting results. These conflicting results might be a reflection of patient heterogeneity. Not all patients seem to be willing to participate in their medical decisions. So, it is important to understand what type of patient–physician relationship is most suitable for different types of patients. We now use existing evidence to suggest new ways of understanding different segments of the patient population.

CONSIDERING PATIENT TYPES IN PATIENT-CENTERED MARKETING

We define *patient-centered marketing* as a strategic orientation whereby life sciences firms aim their marketing efforts at holistically targeting both patients and physicians to (a) provide treatment solutions that match the specific needs of distinctive patient niches; (b) offer objective, unbiased, transparent, and up-to-date information about available treatments; and (c) stimulate patient empowerment. These patient-centered marketing principles should lead to marketing strategies that contribute to improved interactions between patients and their physicians and, ultimately, to improvements in treatment effectiveness and desirable patient behaviors, such as adherence to medical treatment. We argue that the current trend toward shared decision making will accelerate the importance of patient-centered marketing for life sciences firms and influence the ongoing transformation of their business models. To more fully understand these trends, we now analyze market segmentation.

Market segmentation entails the development of specific marketing activities for homogenous subgroups in the consumer population that exhibit significant differences in their consumption patterns (Kamakura & Russell, 1989). Note that in the specific case of prescription drugs, the "consumer" is both the patient and the physician. Traditionally, the pharmaceutical industry has focused on segmentation strategies for the physician side of the market. This focus is coherent with the typical pattern of allocation of marketing resources in the pharmaceutical industry. Despite the significant rise in DTCA expenditures in recent decades, in 2005, DTCA still represented only 14.2% of total industry expenditures in the promotion of prescription drugs in the United States; direct-to-physician efforts such as detailing, journal advertising, and drug samples represented the bulk of pharmaceutical marketing expenditures (Donohue, Cevasco, & Rosenthal, 2007). In most other countries in which DTCA is typically not allowed, direct-to-physician efforts are even stronger.

Pharmaceutical marketers tend to focus on direct communication to physicians, with resource allocation being determined by physician characteristics, such as market potential, prescription volume, responsiveness to marketing, or capacity to influence other physicians. The models used for segmentation in the pharmaceutical industry also tend to be disease focused, with the nature and severity of illnesses together with the nature of third-party payment agreements assuming key roles (Smith, Kolassa, Perkins, & Siecker, 2002). In fact, for a certain *disease category*, the focus of most firms has been to *convince physicians* that they are capable of offering the best-in-class treatment, that is, a treatment alternative that offers superior value for the *average patient* when compared with competing alternatives. We call this type of approach a *mass-therapy marketing approach*; it is depicted in Figure 5.6.

This traditional mass-therapy approach is closely related to the prevailing "blockbuster" model in the pharmaceutical industry; this business model

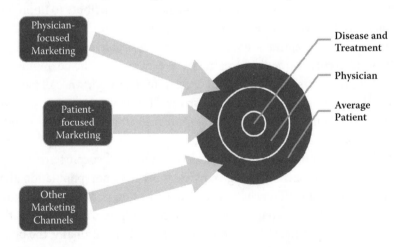

FIGURE 5.6
Mass-therapy marketing approach.

focuses on finding innovative drugs, which are then converted into brands capable of generating annual revenues in excess of US$1,000,000,000. Despite its popularity during the past decades, the blockbuster model seems to be losing its appeal. Recent evidence has suggested that life sciences firms need to shift away from blockbuster drugs to niche remedies and personalized medicine ("Beyond the Blockbuster," 2007).

The current trend toward higher patient connectedness suggests that firms need to segment patients and address each patient niche with customized marketing strategies. There are two particular dimensions of patient heterogeneity worth discussing here: (a) heterogeneity in patient preferences for involvement and (b) heterogeneity in patient goals and expectations from medical treatment. We explore these to suggest how firms can understand underlying patient segments and improve the effectiveness of their marketing activities targeted at patients.

Patient-Level Segmentation Based on the Desired Level of Involvement in Heath Care Decisions

Not all patients are moving toward shared decision making at the same rate. Some patients seek higher involvement in their health decisions, whereas others prefer to maintain a traditional paternalistic relationship with their physicians. Different preferences for involvement translate into differences in patient trust in their physician's capability of making the right choice, patient health information needs, and patient adherence to recommended treatment plans. Thus, segmenting patients according to their desired level of involvement in health care decisions is of great value to marketers. Such an approach can help determine which patients are more responsive to information provided through DTCA or other direct-to-patient channels such as Web sites with health information.

Prior research has already shown that for some segments of patients, DTCA has positive effects, whereas for others it has negative effects (Bowman, Heilman, & Seetharaman, 2004). One important implication for the life sciences industry is that patients who wish to have an active role in medical decisions are the most valuable targets of DTCA. These patients want to play an active role in their own care and, therefore, are more likely to decide to visit their physician after seeing an advertisement. Ironically, however, patients who are more in control of and involved in health decisions are also more likely to actively decide to not fill a prescription or adhere to a treatment regimen (Roselund, Lovich, Lubkerman, & Flanagan, 2004). Therefore, firms need to understand the needs of different patient segments in order to leverage their unique opportunities while addressing their specific threats.

To segment patients based on involvement, pharmaceutical firms must pinpoint what drives involvement preferences. Once such drivers are recognized, pharmaceutical firms can fine-tune their marketing activities to effectively and profitably influence these patient segments. Some demographic characteristics, for instance, have been found to affect the level of patient participation and interest in medical decisions. For example, someone who is white, female, and relatively educated and enjoys a relatively high level of health is likely to have a higher preference for involvement in medical decisions (Flynn, Smith, & Vanness, 2006; Street, Gordon, Ward, Krupat, & Kravitz, 2005). Age also plays a role, with younger patients desiring more active participation in their medical decisions (Cassileth, Zupkis, Sutton-Smith, & March, 1980; Rotter & Hall, 2006). This correlation between age and participation might be explained by physician stereotypes about older patients, their weaker health status, the presence of a visit companion during medical encounters (which is common among older patients), and an unwillingness to challenge the authority of physicians (Roter & Hall, 2006).

Stremersch, Landsman, and Venkataraman (2008) found that physician responsiveness to patient requests is correlated with the demographic composition of the area in which the physician's practice is located, which is consistent with the importance of various patient characteristics.[8] This finding suggests that physicians do not treat all patient requests equally. A recent study using unannounced actors posing as patients showed that primary care physicians engaged in more shared decision-making behaviors in response to patient requests (Young et al., 2008). The authors suggested that this observation is a consequence of a tendency of physicians to interpret overt participatory behaviors of patients, such as medication requests, as an expression of their preference for involvement and to adapt their interaction style accordingly. Combining these results with Stremersch et al. (2008), we suggest that patient demographic characteristics (e.g., education, ethnicity, income) can moderate how physicians interpret and respond to patient requests.

Other, less explored patient characteristics that could lead to different preferences for involvement include differences in attitudes toward health and health providers as well as cultural or individual values. All of these characteristics may vary among people, regions, and countries. Contextual effects, such as the specific condition suffered by a patient, can also trigger higher or lower levels of desired involvement (Cassileth et al., 1980). Under some circumstances, patients might prefer to discuss treatment alternatives and illness-related information but still delegate final medical decisions to the physician.

Patient-Level Segmentation Based on Needs and Expectations

Apart from a patient's desire for involvement, patient health needs and expectations about treatment can distinguish different niches of patients that subsequently can be addressed by distinct marketing strategies. We define patient *needs* as a feeling of dissatisfaction that motivates the patient to set specific goals to be achieved through medical treatment; patient *expectations* comprise the information the patient expects to receive about the treatment, the risks he or she is willing to incur, and the effort he or she is willing to invest in reaching these predefined health goals.

The different psychological reactions of patients to disease, including stress, emotional arousal, and distress, have been related to different health behaviors and distinct ways of coping with disease (Baum & Posluszny, 1999). Similarly, we argue that patients with different lifestyles, family and personal needs, pain tolerance, and risk attitudes will require different types of information and treatment approaches. In terms of marketing strategy, a deeper acknowledgment and integration of this distinction should engender better ways of conveying information and even treatment solutions to different niches of patients.

Toward a Patient-Centered Marketing Approach

The critical and defining characteristic of the patient-centered philosophy is its focus on the patient rather than on the patient's disease or the physician. Yet, by considering the pivotal role of the patient–physician relationship and of mutual participation in treatment decisions, our call for more patient-centered marketing should not be confused with a call for more DTCA or for a more consumerist view of health care. Rather, to adopt a patient-centered marketing philosophy, firms should focus their

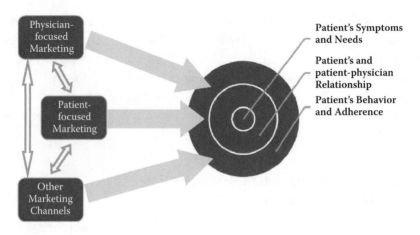

FIGURE 5.7
Patient-centered marketing approach.

strategies, including those directed at physicians, on (a) offering the best treatment for each *patient niche*, (b) promoting more productive *patient–physician relationships*, and (c) achieving more *desirable patient behaviors*, for example, greater adherence to medical recommendations. We depict this approach in Figure 5.7, which summarizes the ideas developed in prior sections.

The challenge for firms is to find creative ways to address both the opportunities and the threats (including regulation, potential for physician backlash and public backlash) that a patient-centered approach yields. The Internet, for example, might still provide many new opportunities for firms to interact with patients and their physicians (Lerer, 2002). AstraZeneca's Web site mysymbicort.com is a good example of how a life sciences company can develop a channel to directly communicate with patients, share information about a specific brand, and promote tips and ideas aimed at increasing patient quality of life and adherence to medical treatment. Life sciences firms are becoming more alert to these challenges. Consulting companies such as DKI Direct and The Patient Practice, for example, are offering services aimed at improving the effectiveness of direct-to-patient marketing efforts.[9] As this trend develops, there are many opportunities for scholarly research to positively impact the transition from a mass-therapy to a patient-centered marketing approach. Firms would certainly benefit from new tools and answers to the many open questions.

Limitations of the Patient-Centered Approach

There are three major barriers that may slow down the transition from a mass-therapy to a patient-centered marketing approach. First, there exists a "clash of mentalities." Sales and marketing managers have developed very high levels of expertise in steering marketing efforts toward physicians; they thus may be reluctant to adopt a patient-centered view. Second, regulators, physicians, and the general population are not used to seeing life sciences firms communicate directly with patients. This is especially true outside the United States and New Zealand. Third, a reinforced focus on the patient suggests that pharmaceutical firms may need to develop new skills and use new, potentially costly, consumer channels to promote their products.

The arguments we have presented suggest that the change toward patient-centered medicine is already in progress. Failure to adapt marketing strategies to this new paradigm for medical practice will be even costlier than investing in these new skills. Therefore, firms should look for opportunities, rather than ruminate on the threats, in these trends. Some opportunities may even help ameliorate the three major barriers just discussed.

First, it is important to integrate patient-directed efforts with existing marketing actions directed at physicians and other stakeholders. Investing in a patient-centered marketing approach should not be seen as a replacement for other marketing channels. On the contrary, the objectives defined earlier for patient-centered marketing can be achieved only by promoting a greater integration between marketing and sales as well as among the different existing channels, which include patients, physicians, hospitals, pharmacies and wholesalers, regulators, and insurers.

Second, marketing researchers in life sciences firms will need to gather information about patient treatment goals and expectations as well as in-depth knowledge about the meanings that patients attach to the biomedical aspects of their diseases. The knowledge they obtain from these research efforts should be used to craft valuable information that is not only targeted at the patient but also coordinated with physicians and the views of other stakeholders. This will help guarantee that the life sciences industry is perceived as a "lifesaving" rather than "sickness-selling" industry.

Third, to gather such information, firms may need to develop further patient-focused market research competencies and invest resources in new marketing and communication channels. Some reallocation of resources from physician channels to patient channels seems appropriate, however, and might appease potential cost concerns that arise with increased patient-level segmentation. The rationale for this substitution lies in the recognition that the law of diminishing returns might already be affecting direct-to-physician marketing. Evidence shows that nowadays, direct-to-physician marketing is not as effective as firms would expect and desire (Kremer, Bijmolt, Leeflang, & Wieringa, 2008; Venkataraman & Stremersch, 2007). Therefore, reallocating marketing resources from direct-to-physician channels to less saturated marketing channels, such as direct-to-patient channels, should bring new profit-improving opportunities for firms. We now conclude with a summary of the key strategic implications of patient connectedness.

STRATEGIC IMPLICATIONS OF PATIENT CONNECTEDNESS

The previous discussion highlights several important research topics that may be of interest to life sciences firms, patients, physicians, and policy makers, as is synthesized in Figure 5.8.

First, more effort needs to be devoted to motivate physicians to encourage patient participation in medical decisions. Most physicians do not initiate shared decision making; rather, patients still play a pivotal role in triggering shared decision-making behaviors (Street et al., 2005; Young et al., 2008). Many physicians may still feel uncomfortable with patient empowerment, and so firms, patients, and policy makers should convince physicians of the importance of shared decision making. Other stakeholders such as payers (insurance companies or governments), financial intermediaries, and life sciences firms will indirectly benefit from increased patient participation in medical decisions.[10]

Second, firms should strive to understand patient needs and preferences regarding participation in medical decisions. Whenever deemed possible and desirable, firms can provide more information to patients to motivate patient participation in medical decisions. This can be accomplished through DTCA by supporting patient organizations or promoting Web sites directed to patients. If firms are too forthright in motivating patients

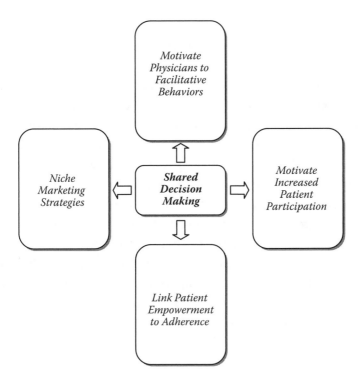

FIGURE 5.8
Policy recommendations to leverage the trend toward the shared decision-making, patient-centered marketing approach.

to participate in treatment decisions without also convincing physicians of the usefulness of such an approach, however, they may be accused of interfering in undesirable ways with the patient–physician relationship (Hollon, 1999; Moynihan et al., 2002; Wilkes et al., 2000). Therefore, it is important to consider all the direct and indirect effects of marketing actions on the health system. Especially during the first trials of new patient-centered marketing strategies, pretesting the proposed marketing actions in limited geographic areas or therapeutic markets may be wise.

Third, firms can use these reinforced patient–physician relationships to promote adherence to treatment and medical advice. This objective is desirable from the perspective of all involved stakeholders (World Health Organization, 2003; Wosinska, 2005). Thus, it is a particularly useful objective to pursue, because more collaboration among all agents involved in the health value chain can be expected as a result. In fact, according to Stremersch and Van Dyck (2009), stimulating patient adherence is one of the research topics with the most potential impact on most impactful research topics in life sciences marketing.

Fourth, given this analysis, firms may choose to focus more on smaller patient niches. Life sciences firms should complement their business model, which still is very dependent on the blockbuster model discussed previously, with niche marketing strategies. This can be achieved through careful patient segmentation in which segments are defined using traditional demographic and health status variables as well as through more psychological constructs such as patients' beliefs, expectations, and needs and their level of involvement in their health in general.

Future research in marketing should address the challenges and opportunities that an increase in patient connectedness will create for life sciences firms. We hope this chapter has at least achieved the following two goals: (a) to stimulate interest among social network scholars to examine patient–physician relationships and (b) to emphasize the role of the patient as increasingly central in medical decision-making research.

NOTES

1. Throughout the chapter, we adopt Stremersch and Van Dyck's (2008) definition of the life sciences industry as an industry that develops science-based knowledge and improves consumers' quality of life. When we refer to "life sciences firms," we refer to pharmaceutical, biotechnology, and therapeutic medical devices companies.
2. Roter (2000) suggested that in such cases, the relationship can be transformed into a *dysfunctional standstill* in which misunderstandings and frustrations can be frequent and often lead to a breach in the relationship.
3. In some cases, other participants, such as relatives, might also play an important role in a medical encounter. These triadic relationships are frequent in the case of older and adolescent patients (Charles, Gafni, & Whelan, 1997).
4. See also the conclusions of an American Healthways and John Hopkins (2003) Outcomes Summit where more than 200 patients and physicians discussed the ideal patient–physician relationship for the 21st century.
5. In our context, reciprocity or symmetry refer to a directed and bidirectional tie between a physician and a patient, that is, a tie that is directed and flows from the physician to the patient as well as from the patient to the physician (Van den Bulte & Wuyts, 2007).
6. Degree centrality reflects the number of ties an actor has in the system. Closeness centrality measures how close the actor is to each of the other actors in the social system (Van Den Bulte & Wuyts, 2007).

7. Informed consent implies that the physician has a duty to provide information to his or her patients. If harm results from a certain medical treatment and the patient is able to show in court that he or she would have opposed that medical decision, then the doctor runs a high risk of being found negligent (Faden & Beauchamp, 1986).
8. We cannot directly infer participatory style from a physician's response to patient requests. Responsiveness to patient requests may occur even if participation is low (such as automatic accommodation of requests in the case of a consumerist relationship), and low responsiveness can also occur under participatory encounters (e.g., a physician may influence a patient against a certain medicine).
9. DKI Direct (www.dkidirect.com) works with pharmaceutical companies to elaborate on profitable patient relationship marketing strategies. The Patient Practice (www.thepatientpractice.com) is a consulting firm specialized in providing advice on how firms and organizations can interact with patients. It was founded by Di Stafford, former head of patient-focused marketing at Pfizer UK.
10. See the value chain in the life sciences industry in Stremersch and Van Dyck (2008).

REFERENCES

American Healthways and Johns Hopkins. (2003, October–November). *Defining the patient–physician relationship for the 21st century*. Paper presented at Third Annual Disease Management Outcomes Summit, Phoenix, AZ.

Baum, A., & Posluszny, D. M. (1999, February). Health psychology: Mapping biobehavioral contributions to health and illness. *Annual Review of Psychology, 50*, 137–163.

Bell, R. A., Wilkes, M. S., & Kravitz, R. L. (1999). Advertisement-induced prescription drug requests. *Journal of Family Practice, 45*(6), 446–452.

Beyond the blockbuster: Drugs firms are rethinking their business model. (2007, June 30). *The Economist.*

Bowman, D., Heilman, C. H., & Seetharaman, P. B. (2004). Determinants of product-use compliance behavior. *Journal of Marketing Research, 41*(3), 324–338.

Brass, D. J., Galaskiewicz, J., Greve, H. R., & Tsai, W. (2004). Taking stock of networks and organizations: A multilevel perspective. *Academy of Management Journal, 47*(6), 795–817.

Brody, D. S., Miller, S. M., Lerman, C. E., Smith, D. G., & Caputo, G. C. (1989). Patient perception of involvement in medical care. *Journal of General Internal Medicine, 4*(6), 506–511.

Burt, R. S. (1987). Social contagion and innovation: Cohesion versus structural equivalence. *American Journal of Sociology, 92*(6), 1287–1335.

Burt, R. S. (1992). *Structural holes: The social structure of competition*. Cambridge, MA: Harvard University Press.

Cassileth, B. R., Zupkis, R. V., Sutton-Smith, K., & March, V. (1980). Information and participation preferences among cancer patients. *Annals of Internal Medicine, 92*(6), 832–836.

Charles, C., Gafni, A., & Whelan, T. (1997). Shared decision-making in the medical encounter: What does it mean? (or it takes at least two to tango). *Social Science and Medicine, 44*(5), 681–692.

Charles, C., Gafni, A., & Whelan, T. (1999). Decision-making in the physician–patient encounter: Revisiting the shared treatment decision-making model. *Social Science and Medicine, 49*(5), 651–661.

Clinton, H. R., & Obama, B. (2006). Making patient safety the centerpiece of medical liability reform. *New England Journal of Medicine, 354*(21), 2205–2208.

Coleman, J. S., Katz, E., & Menzel, H. (1966). *Medical innovations: A diffusion study.* Indianapolis, IN: Bobbs-Merrill.

Danzon, P. M. (2000). Liability for medical malpractice. In A. J. Culyer & J. P. Newhouse (Eds.), *Handbook of health economics.* Amsterdam, North Holland: Elsevier.

Dellande, S., Gilly, M. C., & Graham, J. L. (2004, July). Gaining compliance and losing weight: The role of the service provider in health care services. *Journal of Marketing, 68*, 78–91.

Di Blasi, Z., Harkness, E., Ernst, E., Georgiou, A., & Kleijnen, J. (2001). Influence of context effects on health outcomes: A systematic review. *Lancet, 357*(9258), 757–762.

Donohue, J. M., Cevasco, M., & Rosenthal, M. B. (2007). A decade of direct-to-consumer advertising of prescription drugs. *New England Journal of Medicine, 357*(7), 673–681.

Dunbar-Jacob, J., & Mortimer-Stephens, M. K. (2001). Treatment adherence in chronic disease. *Journal of Clinical Epidemiology, 54*(Suppl.), S57–S60.

Emanuel, E. J., & Emanuel, L. L. (1992). Four models of the physician–patient relationship. *Journal of the American Medical Association, 267*(16), 2221–2226.

Enriquez, J., & Goldberg, R. A. (2000). Transforming life, transforming business: The life-science revolution. *Harvard Business Review, 78*(2), 94–103.

Epstein, R. M., Alper, B. S., & Quill, T. E. (2004). Communicating evidence for participatory decision-making. *Journal of the American Medical Association, 291*(19), 2359–2366.

European Commission. (2008). *Legal proposal on information to patients.* Retrieved from http://ec.europa.eu/enterprise/pharmaceuticals/pharmacos/docs/doc2008/2008_02/info_to_patients_consult_200802.pdf

Faden, R. R., & Beauchamp, T. L. (1986). *A history and theory of informed consent.* New York: Oxford University Press.

Ferguson, T., & Frydman, G. (2004). The first generation of e-patients: These new medical colleagues could provide sustainable healthcare solutions. *British Medical Journal, 328*(7449), 1148–1149.

Fiscella, K., Meldrum, S., Franks, P., Shields, C. G., Duberstein, P., McDaniel, S. H., & Epstein, R. (2004). Patient trust: Is it related to patient-centered behavior of primary care physicians? *Medical Care, 42*(11), 1049–1055.

Flocke, S. A., Miller, W. L., & Crabtree, B. F. (2002). Relationships between physician practice style, patient satisfaction, and attributes of primary care. *Journal of Family Practice, 51*(10), 835–840.

Flynn, K. E., Smith, M. A., & Vanness, D. (2006). A typology of preferences for participation in healthcare decision-making. *Social Science and Medicine, 63*(5), 1158–1169.

Gawande, A. (2005, November 14). The malpractice mess. *The New Yorker,* 62–71.

Golin, C. E., DiMatteo, M. R., & Gelberg, L. (1996). The role of patient participation in the doctor visit: Implications for adherence to diabetes care. *Diabetes Care, 19*(10), 1153–1164.

Gouldner, A. (1960). The norm of reciprocity: A preliminary statement. *American Sociological Review, 25*(2), 161–178.

Grundy, S. M., Cleeman, J. I., Merz, C. N. B., Brewer, H. B., Jr., Clark, L. T., Hunninghake, D. B., Pasternak, R. C., Smith, S. C., Jr., & Stone, N. J. (2004). Implications of recent clinical trials for the National Cholesterol Education Program Adult Treatment Panel III Guidelines. *Circulation, 44*(3), 720–732.

Guadagnoli, E., & Ward, P. (1998). Patient participation in decision-making. *Social Science and Medicine, 47*(3), 329–339.

Hall, M. A., Dugan, E., Zheng, B., & Mishra, A. K. (2001). Trust in physicians and medical institutions: What is it, can it be measured, and does it matter? *Milbank Quarterly, 79*(4), 613–639.

Hollon, M. F. (1999). Direct-to-consumer marketing of prescription drugs creating consumer demand. *Journal of the American Medical Association, 281*(4), 382–384.

Holmer, A. F. (1999). Direct-to-consumer prescription drug advertising builds bridges between patients and physicians. *Journal of the American Medical Association, 281*(4), 380–382.

Horne, R. (2006). Compliance, adherence and concordance: Implications for asthma treatment. *Chest, 130*(1), S65–S72.

iCrossing. (2008). *How America searches: Health and wellness.* Retrieved August 10, 2008, from www.icrossing.com

Kamakura, W. A., & Russell, G. A. (1989, November). A probabilistic choice model for market segmentation and elasticity structure. *Journal of Marketing Research, 26*, 379–390.

Kao, A. C., Green, D. C., Zaslavsky, A. M., Koplan, J. P., & Cleary, P. D. (1998). The relationship between method of physician payment and patient trust. *Journal of the American Medical Association, 280*(19), 1708–1714.

Kravitz, R. L., & Melnikow, J. (2004). Medical adherence research: Time for a change in direction? *Medical Care, 42*(3), 197–199.

Kremer, S. T. M., Bijmolt, T. H. A., Leeflang, P. S. H., & Wieringa, J. E. (2008). Generalizations on the effectiveness of pharmaceutical promotional expenditures. *International Journal of Research in Marketing, 25*(4), 234–246.

Landro, L. (1999). Patient–physician communication: An emerging partnership. *The Oncologist, 4*(1), 55–58.

Lerer, L. (2002). Pharmaceutical marketing segmentation in the age of the Internet. *International Journal of Medical Marketing, 2*(2), 159–166.

Lerman, C. E., Brody, D. S., Caputo, G. C., Smith, D. G., Lazaro, C. G., & Wolfson, H. G. (1990). Patients' perceived involvement in care scale. *Journal of General Internal Medicine, 5*(1), 29–33.

Little, P., Hazel, E., Williamson, I., Warner, G., Moore, M., Gould, C., Ferrier, K., & Payne, S. (2001, October). Observational study of effect of patient centeredness and positive approach on outcomes of general practice consultations. *British Medical Journal, 323*, 908–911.

Manchanda, P., Wittink, D. R., Ching, A., Cleanthous, P., Ding, M., Dong, X. J., Leeflang, P. S. H., Misra, S., Mizik, N., Narayanan, S., Steenburgh, T., Wieringa, J. E., Wosinska, M., & Xie, Y. (2005). Understanding firm, physician and consumer choice behavior in the pharmaceutical industry. *Marketing Letters, 16*(3–4), 293–308.

Mathers, C. D., & Loncar, D. (2006). Projections of global mortality and burden of disease from 2002 to 2030. *PLoS Medicine, 3*(11), e442.

Moorman, C., Zaltman, G., & Deshpande, R. (1992, August). Relationship between providers and users of market research: The dynamics of trust within and between organizations. *Journal of Marketing Research, XXIX*, 314–328.

Morgan, M. (2003). The doctor–patient relationship. In G. Scambler (Ed.), *Sociology as applied to medicine*. London: Saunders.

Moynihan, R., Heath, I., & Henry, D. (2002). Selling sickness: The pharmaceutical industry and disease mongering. *British Medical Journal, 324*(7342), 886–891.

Mukherjee, A., & McGinnis, J. (2007). E-healthcare: An analysis of key terms in research. *International Journal of Pharmaceutical and Healthcare Marketing, 1*(4), 349–363.

Murray, C. J. L., & Lopez, A. D. (1996). Evidence-based health policy: Lessons from the Global Burden of Disease Study. *Science, 274*(5288), 740–743.

Nair, H., Manchanda, P., & Bhatia, T. (2006). *Asymmetric social interactions in physician prescription behavior: The role of opinion leaders*. Unpublished manuscript, Stanford University.

Osterberg, L., & Blaschke, T. (2005). Adherence to medication. *New England Journal of Medicine, 353*(5), 487–497.

Pauwels, R. A., Buist, A. S., Calverley, P. M. A., Jenkins, C. R., & Hurd, S. S. (2001). Global strategy for the diagnosis, management, and prevention of chronic obstructive pulmonary disease: NHLBI/WHO Global Initiative for Chronic Obstructive Lung Disease (GOLD) workshop summary. *American Journal of Respiratory and Critical Care Medicine, 163*(5), 1256–1276.

Pharmaceutical Executive. (2006). *The world's top 50 pharmaceutical companies*. Retrieved September 29, 2008, from http://pharmexec.findpharma.com/pharmexec/data/articlestandard//pharmexec/182006/323799/article.pdf

Pharmaceutical Research and Manufacturers of America. (2008). *The facts about pharmaceutical marketing and promotion*. Washington, DC: Author.

Podolny, J. M., Stuart, T. E., & Hannan, M. T. (1996). Networks, knowledge, and niches: Competition in the worldwide semiconductor industry, 1984–1991. *American Journal of Sociology, 102*(3), 659.

Reagans, R., & Zuckerman, E. W. (2001). Networks, diversity, and productivity: The social capital of corporate R&D teams. *Organization Science, 12*(4), 502–517.

Roselund, T., Lovich, D., Lubkeman, M., & Flanagan, A. (2004). Marketing strategy: Biopharmaceutical marketing excellence; Driving business results. *International Journal of Medical Marketing, 4*(3), 209–218.

Roter, D. (2000). The enduring and evolving nature of the patient–physician relationship. *Patient Education and Counseling, 39*(1), 5–15.

Roter, D., & Hall, J. A. (2006). *Doctors talking with patients/patients talking with doctors: Improving communication in medical visits* (2nd ed.). Westport, CT: Praeger.

Rothenberg, R., Sterk, C., Toomey, K. E., Potterat, J. J., Johnson, D., Schrader, M., & Hatch, S. (1998). Using social network and ethnographic tools to evaluate syphilis transmission. *Sexually Transmitted Diseases, 25*(3), 154–160.

Sheridan, S. L., Harris, R. P., & Woolf, S. H. (2004). Shared decision-making about screening and chemoprevention: A suggested approach from the U.S. Preventive Services Task Force. *American Journal of Preventive Medicine, 26*(1), 56–66.

Smith, M. C., Kolassa, E. M., Perkins, G., & Siecker, B. (2002). *Pharmaceutical marketing: Principles, environment, and practice*. Binghamton, NY: Haworth Press and Pharmaceutical Products Press.

Street, R. L., Gordon, H. S., Ward, M. M., Krupat, E., & Kravitz, R. L. (2005). Patient participation in medical consultations: Why some patients are more involved than others. *Medical Care, 43*(10), 960–969.

Stremersch, S., Landsman, V., & Venkataraman, S. (2008, May). *The connection between patients and their physicians: The consumerization of health care.* Paper presented at the Tilburg Lustrum Conference.

Stremersch, S., & Van Dyck, W. (2009). Marketing of the life sciences: A new framework and research agenda for a nascent field. *Journal of Marketing, 73*(July), 4–30.

Taylor, S. (2007). Approaches to health and illness. In S. Taylor & D. Field (Eds.), *Sociology of health and health care* (4th ed.). Oxford, UK: Blackwell.

Thom, D. H., Kravitz, R. L., Bell, R. A., Krupat, E., & Azari, R. (2002). Patient trust in the physician: Relationship to patient requests. *Family Practice, 19*(5), 476–483.

Van den Bulte, C., & Wuyts, S. (2007). *Social networks and marketing.* Cambridge, MA: Marketing Science Institute.

Venkataraman, S., & Stremersch, S. (2007). The debate on influencing doctors' decisions: Are drug characteristics the missing link? *Management Science, 53*(11), 1688–1701.

Wathne, K. H., & Heide, J. B. (2004). Relationship governance in a supply chain network. *Journal of Marketing, 68*(1), 73–89.

Wilkes, M. S., Bell, R. A., & Kravitz, R. L. (2000). Direct-to-consumer prescription drug advertising: Trends, impact, and implications. *Health Affairs, 19*(2), 110–128.

World Health Organization. (2003). *Adherence to long-term therapies: Evidence for action.* Geneva, Switzerland: Author.

Wosinska, M. (2005). Direct-to-consumer advertising and drug therapy compliance. *Journal of Marketing Research, 42*(3), 323–332.

Young, H. N., Bell, R. A., Epstein, R. E., Feldman, M. D., & Kravitz, R. L. (2008). Physicians' shared decision-making behaviors in depression care. *Archives of Internal Medicine, 168*(13), 1404–1408.

Zerhouni, E. (2003). The NIH roadmap. *Science, 302*(5642), 63–72.

6

Is Mr. Spock a Good Candidate for Being a Connected Customer? The Role of Emotion in Decision Making

Baba Shiv

> *Kirk:* "Have I ever mentioned you play a very irritating game of chess, Mr. Spock?"
>
> *Spock:* "Irritating? Ah, yes—one of your Earth emotions."
>
> **—*Star Trek*, "Where No Man Has Gone Before"**

A popular character in *Star Trek*, Mr. Spock is portrayed as being emotionless and analytical as a result of being half-Vulcan, sharing the Vulcan trait of being devoid of emotion. He is also seen as an embodiment of a "good" decision maker—cold, calculated, and rational—however difficult the decision may be. But is this an accurate portrayal of reality? Is the right approach to making good decisions one where we become analytical, an approach that is rooted in conventional wisdom? Is this the right approach from the point of view of the firm whose goal is to create a connected customer in the form of greater connectedness and loyalty toward the brand? For example, when faced with a decision conflict such as choosing among job or admission offers, should the customer be encouraged to adopt the technique proposed by Benjamin Franklin—list all the positives and negatives of the options and choose the option with the greatest number of positives and the fewest number of negatives? Or is it time to question conventional wisdom and make a case from the point of view of being a connected (i.e., loyal) customer that Mr. Spock, the emotionless half-Vulcan, would end up making "bad" decisions? The thrust of this chapter is to address these questions and, thereby, enrich our understanding of the role of emotion in decision making.

THE CONNECTED CUSTOMER AND THE CUSTOMER VALUE PROPOSITION

It is pretty obvious that to have a connected and loyal customer, a firm needs to create and sustain a competitive advantage by offering a superior customer value proposition (CVP). The greater and more sustained the CVP, the greater is the likelihood that the customer will remain connected to the firm. How has our thinking about the CVP been shaped over the years? What are some of the emerging trends related to the CVP, particularly on the role of emotion in the "branding route" to the CVP? Specifically, will creating Mr. Spocks out of customers be advantageous or disadvantageous in terms of creating the connected customer? We will delve into these questions in the sections that follow. Specifically, the next section will highlight the evolution of the CVP across the years. The subsequent sections will highlight the emergent "third-wave" viewpoint of the CVP, at the core of which is brand emotion and its power in shaping a sustainable CVP.

THE CVP: A HISTORICAL PERSPECTIVE

The traditional view that prevailed until the 1980s and even into the 1990s was that marketers could shape the CVP and, thereby, create a connected (i.e., loyal) customer by focusing on one or both of two routes. One route is the "branding route," where the marketer shapes the CVP through a product differentiation strategy by offering a superior value in terms of the benefits (Vb), both tangible and intangible (e.g., Keller, 1993; Park, Jaworski, & MacInnis, 1986). A second route to shaping the value proposition is the "pricing route," where the marketer shapes the CVP by offering superior value in terms of lower prices (Vp), either momentarily through discounts, rebates, and so on or by adopting a price-leadership strategy (e.g., by eliminating inefficiencies in the supply chain and passing on the reduced costs to customers). Stated differently, as per the traditional viewpoint, the CVP could be captured by the following simple equation: CVP = Vb + Vp. The marketer could, thus, increase the attractiveness of the CVP and, thereby, enhance its competitive advantage by focusing its efforts on Vb through product improvements, more convenient packaging, and so on and/or by focusing its efforts on Vp.

By the end of the 1990s, one additional component began to emerge as part of the branding route, giving rise to the "second-wave" view of the CVP—the explicit appearance of brand emotion (E) in the CVP.[1] Two developments during this period shaped this revision in our thinking of the CVP, wherein CVP = E + Vb + Vp.[2] First was a recognition that emotions are a key component of a brand's inventory (see Keller, 2001, 2002). The second critical development was that brand emotion could be shaped by the marketer through aspects that are completely unrelated to Vb, particularly through the use of emotional advertising (e.g., Batra & Ray, 1986; Mitchell & Olson, 1981). More important was the recognition that such brand emotion, shaped independently of Vb, is often nonconscious (Gorn, 1982; Zajonc, 1980; Zajonc & Markus, 1982) and can have a direct impact on customer choices (Gorn, 1982; Miniard, Sirdeshmukh, & Innis, 1992).

At this point, the reader might wonder why including E as a separate component in the CVP was an important development over the traditional perspective involving only the Vb and Vp components. Consider the following situation in the marketplace: a marketer and a competitor in dead-heat in terms of the CVP, resulting in an equal likelihood of the customer choosing the marketer's and the competitor's brand:

	Branding Route (Vb)	+	Pricing Route (Vp)	= CVP
Marketer	4		4	= 8
Competitor	4		4	= 8

According to the traditional perspective, the marketer had only two options to break the tie: go in for a product differentiation strategy by offering more benefits to the customer through product improvements, adding new attributes, and so on or go in for a pricing strategy by reducing prices either momentarily or for the long haul. The modified CVP with E in the picture afforded the marketer to break the tie and create a competitive advantage by efforts aimed at building brand emotion through emotional advertising, product placements, event sponsorship, and so forth, without the need to engage in expensive product improvements (Vb) or reduced prices (Vp).

Although the emergence of E in the CVP was an important development, note that in the revised formulation, E is treated as an add-on to the value proposition. An important implication of this feature in the revised second-wave view of the CVP is that the marketer has the freedom to focus either on E or on Vb under the branding route. Stated differently, as per the second-wave view, the marketer can completely ignore E and yet expect to enjoy a sustainable competitive advantage as long as Vb + Vp is more favorable for the marketer's brand than the competitors' brands. In the next section, we will delve into the demerits of this rather simplistic viewpoint and argue that brand emotion might actually be essential for and fundamental to creating a sustainable competitive advantage through a superior E-based CVP.

THE THIRD-WAVE VIEW OF THE CVP: THE POWER OF BRAND EMOTION

To frame the discussion in this section, let us revisit a fundamental question that has been debated for centuries from the time of the Greek philosopher Plato through the time of medieval Christian philosophers such as Leibniz and Descartes to modern philosophers such as Hare and Rawls. The question is, are emotions *by and large* beneficial for human decision making, or are they detrimental? The consensus view to this fundamental question that prevailed over the centuries was that emotions are by and large detrimental to human decision making. In other words, if the philosophers of yesteryears had been familiar with the half-Vulcan Mr. Spock in *Star Trek*, they would have argued that the emotionless Mr. Spock would end up making better decisions.

Although this consensus view of the role of emotion in decision making was questioned from time to time across the centuries (e.g., Hume in the 1700s), it was not until the 1970s that a diametrically opposite viewpoint (that emotions by and large are beneficial to decision making) began to gain traction. Notable among the proponents of this diametrically opposite viewpoint were social psychologists such as Robert Zajonc (Zajonc, 1980), moral psychologists such as Lawrence Kohlberg (Kohlberg, 1971), and evolutionary psychologists such as Leda Cosmides and John Tooby (see Cosmides & Tooby, 2000), who made compelling arguments in favor of the evolutionarily adaptive function of emotion in decision making. Although psychologists were building a strong case for the diametrically opposite view, by the 1990s neuroscientists were also beginning to address this issue, notable among the proponents being Antonio R. Damasio and his colleagues (Hanna Damasio and Antoine Bechara, to name a few). Particularly important was that the neuroscientists began to present compelling clinical as well as empirical evidence in support of this diametrically opposite viewpoint (Bechara & Damasio, 2005; A. R. Damasio, Everitt, & Bishop, 1996). Probably the earliest recorded clinical evidence derives from the unfortunate story of Phineas Gage.

THE STORY OF PHINEAS GAGE

The story of Phineas Gage is set in the mid-1800s. Gage was a construction foreman for the Rutland and Burlington Railroad Company in New England and was noted for being very responsible as a manager of people and respectful of authority and for doing reasonably well financially and very well socially. On a fateful day in September 1848, Gage fell victim to an accident, wherein an explosion hurled a tamping iron about an inch in diameter through his left cheek, skull, and finally out of the front of his head. To everyone's surprise, Gage recovered from the accident and was soon able to walk, talk, and even engage in his normal activities. Or was this the case?

Following the accident, Gage's acquaintances began to notice a marked change in his personality. Capturing these marked changes are the following excerpts from the report by Gage's doctor:

> Previous to his injury, although untrained in the schools, he possessed a well-balanced mind, and was looked upon by those who knew him as a shrewd, smart businessman, very energetic and persistent in executing all his plans of operation.

[After the injury] Gage was fitful, irreverent, indulging at times in the grossest profanity (which was not previously his custom), manifesting but little deference for his fellows, impatient of restraint or advice when it conflicts with his desires, at times pertinaciously obstinate, yet capricious and vacillating, devising many plans of future operations, which are no sooner arranged than they are abandoned in turn for others appearing more feasible. (Harlow, 1868, 274–281)

For the purposes of the exposition regarding the power of emotion (E) in the CVP, the focus will be on one part of the doctor's report—the observation that following the accident, Gage became capricious and indecisive, akin to the proverbial Buridan's ass. (For the reader who is not familiar with the story of Buridan's ass, it goes as follows. A completely rational ass was placed between two stacks of hay of equal size and quality. The rational ass starved to death not being able to decide which stack to start eating from.) But, before focusing on that aspect of the report, let's continue with the unfortunate story of Phineas Gage.

Following his tragic accident, Gage went on to live for another 12 years! During this time, he wandered from one job to another, made bad financial and social decisions, and died a pauper financially as well as socially. What might have caused this drastic change in Gage's behaviors? Why did Gage end up making bad decisions following his accident? Preliminary answers to these questions emerged from a study conducted by Hanna Damasio and her colleagues (H. Damasio, Grabowski, Frank, Galaburda, & Damasio, 1994). In this study, Gage's skull, which is still preserved in the Warren Anatomical Museum at Harvard University, was subject to a forensic-neuroscience examination. A series of analyses revealed that the accident had damaged a very critical component of the brain's emotional circuitry, namely, the ventromedial prefrontal cortex.

Recall the original question: Are emotions beneficial or detrimental to human decision making? The story of Gage and the forensic examination of his skull provide a possible answer to this question: Emotions might actually be beneficial to human decision making. Phineas Gage loses a critical component of his brain's emotional circuitry and ends up making bad decisions for the rest of his life. But can one come to this conclusion with just a single data point?

MORE EVIDENCE FROM NEUROLOGICAL PATIENTS

Phineas Gage is not alone in terms of displaying marked changes in behavior following damage to components of the brain's emotional circuitry. Similar "before–after" alternations in behavior have since been observed in several neurological patients with damage to various areas of the brain's emotional circuitry (see Figure 6.1): amygdala, insula, somatosensory cortex, and ventromedial prefrontal cortex.

As with Gage and his doctor's observations, typical changes that are observed in such patients are unrestrained (impulsive) behaviors, the inability to learn from previous "slaps on the wrist," and, most pertinent for this chapter, the inability to make good decisions (Bechara & Damasio, 2005; Naqvi, Shiv, & Bechara, 2006).

By now, the perceptive reader would have noted the use of terms such as "bad decisions" and "good decisions" and begun to wonder, "How does one characterize a decision as being good or bad?" And "Why would damage to the emotional circuitry result in an inability to make good decisions?" These questions will be addressed in the next section, which will be followed by a discussion of the theoretical as well as the

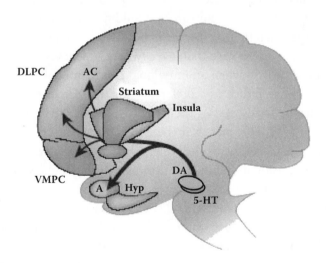

FIGURE 6.1
Areas of the brain's emotional circuitry. A – amygdala; VMPC – ventromedial prefrontal cortex; the somatosensory cortex is located above the insula and the striatum (in the Figure).

managerial implications of this discourse for the CVP and the connected customer.

DECISION QUALITY, EMOTIONS, AND THE BRAIN

In this section, I will first present my perspective on what makes a decision good or bad. I will then revisit observations of individuals with damage to the emotional circuitry and subsequently posit reasons why such individuals end up unable to make good decisions.

When is a decision good or bad? One way of answering this question is to rely on normative benchmarks, violations of which can be characterized as bad decisions. These normative benchmarks include two basic rational axioms of rational preference relations in economics: *dominance* and *transitivity* (Mas-Colell, Whinston, & Green, 1995). Dominance implies that for a set of options a and b, if $a > b$ then a decision is bad when the individual chooses the dominated option b. Stated in simple words, if an individual prefers a Toyota Prius over a BMW but chooses the BMW, then his or her decision should be characterized as being bad. Transitivity implies that a consumer should have a well-defined preference structure, such that for any set of bundles a, b, and c, if $a \geq b$ and $b \geq c$, it must also be the case that $a \geq c$ (where $\geq$ denotes relative preference). In other words, when an individual is presented with a Prius and a BMW, he or she indicates a preference for the former over the latter. When presented with a BMW and a Cadillac, he or she indicates a preference again for the former over the latter. But when presented with a Prius and a Cadillac, if he or she prefers the latter, then one would characterize the decision as being bad (normatively, he or she should prefer the Prius over the Cadillac).

Normative benchmarks exist in other forms as well. Most of the research on heuristics and biases such as the sunk-cost effect rely on the use of normative benchmarks (in the case of the sunk-cost effect, from a normative standpoint, one ought to ignore sunk costs while evaluating options, yet individuals frequently violate this benchmark). For another instance of the existence of a normative benchmark to evaluate the quality of a decision, consider the following task.

You will engage in several rounds of investment decisions. Before you begin to make your decisions, I will endow you will $20 in $1 bills. On each round, you can decide not to invest, in which case I will proceed to the next round. Alternatively, you can invest a dollar, in which case I will toss a fair coin. If the outcome is "heads," you will lose your investment. If the outcome is "tails," I will add $1.50 to your investment of a dollar. In other words, I will give you $2.50.

If you, the reader, were faced with this task, what would you do? We are quite sure that the answer would be, "Keep investing in every single round. The expected value from investing ($1.25) is greater than the expected value from not investing ($1)." Yet, as demonstrated by Uri Gneezy (Gneezy & Potters, 1997) and Baba Shiv (Shiv, Loewenstein, Bechara, Damasio, & Damasio, 2005), individuals often invest in fewer rounds (especially as the task progresses) than that suggested by normative principles.[3]

Decision making in the absence of normative benchmarks.[4] Although we as decision makers do frequently face decisions that offer normative benchmarks, arguably such situations are far less frequent than those that offer no such benchmarks and yet present us with trade-off conflicts (i.e., the choice options *a* and *b* are equally preferred such that *a* = *b*). The question is, how does one go about making good decisions under these circumstances? One perspective on resolving such decision conflicts is to adopt the completeness principle, a notion that is grounded in economics (e.g., Sugden, 1991) and shared by decision-making researchers (e.g., Payne, Bettman, Jamers, & Johnson, 1993). According to this perspective, the way to resolve the conflict is to collect as much information on the options as feasible (with some cutoff rule, if needed). If a dominance structure emerges from this exercise, then choose the dominating option; if the trade-off conflict remains, then decide by simply tossing a coin. Note that this perspective focuses on the "input side" to the decision.

An alternate perspective, which we adopt for the rest of our exposition, focuses on the "output side" to the decision. According to this perspective, a good decision is one where the decision maker is satisfied with, confident about, and, thus, committed to the chosen option.[5] In a sense, this perspective is consistent with how firms would characterize (their) customers' decisions as being good—after all, a satisfied and committed customer is likely to exhibit greater loyalty, fewer cases of product returns (i.e., switching behaviors), and greater word-of-mouth.[6] Interestingly, this perspective is in line with the Latin root of the word decision, *decidere*, which in turn is derived from *caedere*, which means *to cut* (words such as *excise* and *circumcise* share the same Latin root). This Latin root implies that when one is faced with a trade-off conflict, one has made a decision if one cuts oneself from the past, cuts oneself from reexamining the decision, and, thus, is no longer in a state of indecision. *State of indecision:* Does this remind the reader of the proverbial Buridan's ass that was featured earlier in this chapter? Well, let us get back to the proverbial Buridan's ass and to the story of Phineas Gage.

Compromised emotional circuitry and the inability to make good decisions. Recall the following observation made by Gage's doctor: "[After the injury] Gage was … capricious and vacillating, devising many plans of future operations, which are no sooner arranged than they are abandoned in turn for others appearing more feasible." Similar observations have been made by Damasio and his colleagues on patients with damage to the emotional circuitry (A. R. Damasio, 2000). When faced with trade-off conflicts, such patients have been observed to exhibit a lack of commitment to the chosen option following a decision, resulting in considerable vacillation, frequent changes of mind, and, thus, the inability to make good decisions (as viewed from the output side and particularly as viewed from the Latin root of the word *decision*).[7]

Evidence from "normal" individuals. It is not just patients who exhibit the inability to make good decisions. In a study that we conducted with normal individuals, we examined if those with a more "muted" emotional circuitry (we termed such individuals as "vulcans" in our research) would exhibit greater inability to make good (i.e., committed) decisions compared to those (i.e., the "emotionals") with a more sensitive emotional circuitry. To categorize individuals as either vulcans or emotionals, we first administered the Affect Intensity Measure scale (Larsen, Diener, & Emmons, 1986) as part of a purportedly unrelated series of studies. After a short filler task, participants moved on to the next task, which was an adaptation of Wilson et al.'s (1993) change-of-mind experimental paradigm. In this task, participants first chose among eight Stanford memorabilia (as a token of our appreciation for their participation in this study). After a brief filler task and prior to being thanked and debriefed, participants were told that we were about to place the order for the item they had previously selected. Participants were asked if they would like to revisit the options before making up their minds. The proportion of participants who decided to revisit the options and the proportion of participants who changed their minds (i.e., ended up selecting an option that was different from the one previously selected) served as the key dependent variables. The results from this study are presented as follows:

	Vulcans	Emotionals
Percentage revisiting	40.4	17.5
Percentage changing minds	21.4	5.0

Consistent with observations on Phineas Gage and patients with damage to the emotional circuitry, the results from this study suggest that vulcans, compared to emotionals, have a greater propensity to vacillate and change their minds and, thus, a greater propensity to make bad (i.e., less committed) decisions. The question is, why? What do emotions have to do with the ability to make good (i.e., committed) decisions?

Emotions and the ability to make good decisions. The *somatic marker hypothesis* posited by Damasio and his colleagues (Bechara & Damasio, 2005; A. R. Damasio et al., 1996) provides potential answers to why emotions are crucial for and fundamental to making good (i.e., committed) decisions. According to the somatic marker hypothesis, the way the brain goes about resolving trade-off conflicts is *not* as shown in Figure 6.2a. That is, the brain does not follow the economist's perspective of what makes good decisions, which is following the completeness principle by engaging in an unbiased acquisition and evaluation of information until, one hopes, a dominance structure emerges. Instead, the brain seems to resolve trade-off conflicts in an arguably more efficient manner.

As shown in Figure 6.2b, the brain might begin the decision-making process through an unbiased information acquisition and evaluation process ("might," because this step can be skipped if one of the options is already enriched with positive emotions); as the process begins to unfold, however, a positive emotional signal (somatic marker) gets generated in favor of one of the options. The source of this emotional signal is a prior positive or negative experience that becomes associated with a particular thought or scenario conjured up during the pondering of a decision. Thereafter, often unbeknownst to the decision maker, the process that ensues becomes biased toward the emotionally enriched option. In other

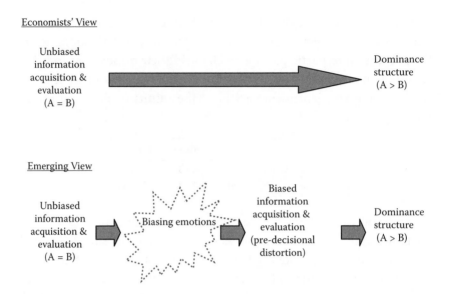

FIGURE 6.2

Figure 6.2a (top panel) and 6.2b (bottom panel). Emerging view of the decision-making process contrasted with the traditional (economists') view.

words, the brain engages in what Jay Russo and his colleagues termed "pre-decisional distortion" (Russo, Meloy, & Medvec, 1998; Russo, Meloy, & Wilks, 2000), wherein the brain shifts the evaluation of attribute information in favor of the emotionally enriched option and against the emotionally impoverished option. Stated differently, the biased emotional signal triggers a selective exposure to and evaluation of information that is acquired subsequently (see Pala, 2008, for a similar conceptual model for biased decisions). The biased processing that is rooted in an emotion now enables the brain to create a clear dominance structure (i.e., $a > b$) and, thus, make good (i.e., committed) decisions.

The propositions stated previously can account for why individuals with a muted emotional circuitry exhibit indecisiveness in the form of vacillation, which can manifest in the form of trade-off aversion (see Luce, 1998), changes of mind, and a lack of commitment to the option that is chosen following the decision. With no biasing emotional signals to trigger the biased processing and, in turn, to create the dominance structure, such individuals are left to the mercy of the "rational" brain; unless the information being acquired clearly favors one of the options, such individuals are stuck where they started, namely, $a = b$, hence, the ensuing vacillation, trade-off aversion, changes of mind, and inability to make good (i.e., committed) decisions.

Preliminary evidence from a study that we conducted using the predecisional distortion paradigm seems to support these propositions. Participants in this study were first categorized as being either vulcans or emotionals (as described earlier). The participants were then taken through a task adapted from the work by Russo and his colleagues (e.g., Russo et al., 1998). Specifically, one group (treatment condition) was asked to imagine the task as being a horse race and told that after each piece of information on two smart phones A and B, they would rate by how much one option was ahead of the other in the race (on a 11-point scale). Another group (control condition) rated a set of binary smart phone options (again on a 11-point scale), which were labeled differently across the pieces of attribute information (e.g., A and B, followed by T and U).

The level of distortion in the treatment condition (across the various attributes) was computed by comparing the ratings given by each participant on each attribute in the treatment condition with the mean ratings for the same attribute across all participants in the control condition. A comparison of the results on the cumulative distortion across the sequence of attributes that were presented in the treatment conditions revealed a clear predecisional distortion among emotionals; vulcans on the other hand barely distorted the information—their ratings were no different from those in the control condition. More important, participants in the treatment condition were asked to choose between the smart phones and then asked to rate how satisfied they were with their selection. It is not surprising that vulcans were less satisfied, compared to emotionals, with their chosen option.

The evidence from this preliminary study suggests the following. Emotionals in the treatment condition seem to have generated stronger biased emotional signals resulting in heightened predecisional distortion in favor of the front-runner. In other words, they seem to have selectively distorted information about the two options in favor of the front-runner, ending up with a clear dominance structure in favor of A (A > B in Figure 6.2b). Thus, they were more satisfied with and potentially more committed to the front-runner. Vulcans on the other hand seem to have generated more muted biased emotional signals, resulting in less predecisional distortion in favor of the front-runner, ending up with a less clear dominance structure in favor of A (A potentially equal to B in Figure 6.2b).

Thus, being stuck at where they started, namely, an indifference between the two smart phones, vulcans expressed greater dissatisfaction with their choices as compared to emotionals.

BACK TO THE CVP AND THE CONNECTED CUSTOMER

It is time to get back to where we started: the CVP and the connected customer. More specifically, the role of emotion (E) in creating the connected customer, one who is not only brand loyal but also an advocate of the brand. Recall an important development in the 1980s related to the CVP, namely, the emergence of E as an explicit component in the second-wave view of the value proposition. Also recall E being treated as an add-on to the value proposition, implying that the marketer can completely ignore E as part of the branding route and yet expect to enjoy a sustainable competitive advantage as long as Vb + Vp is more favorable for the marketer's brand than the competitors' brands. Now juxtapose this second-wave view with the exposition in the previous section: It would become readily apparent to the reader why the second-wave view, the notion that E is merely an add-on to the CVP—although a significant development over the traditional first-wave view—is quite simplistic. The growing evidence seems to point to the notion that E, rather than being an add-on, is interactive, shaping Vb and Vp through predecisional distortion processes. In sum, E might actually be essential for and fundamental to creating a connected customer who is satisfied and committed to the chosen options, resulting in a *sustainable* competitive advantage through greater brand loyalty, favorable word-of-mouth, and fewer product returns. Stated differently, encouraging customers to become analytical like Mr. Spock could actually backfire on the firm that is trying to create a connected customer!

This exposition thus far has attempted to convince the reader of the power of emotional branding in the third-wave view of the CVP—its power to shape the CVP by setting into motion mental processes that yield a satisfied and committed customer. Let's now shift gears and examine the potential future of this third-wave view in terms of both academic research and managerial applications.

A VIEW INTO THE FUTURE

This section will highlight some promising opportunities related to the third-wave view, wherein E plays a more central and powerful role than previously envisaged in shaping the CVP. These opportunities include (a) developing appropriate measures for the E component, (b) examining the array of tactical means of shaping E, and (c) gaining richer insights into the CVP by adding β-weights to the various components (i.e., E, Vb, and Vp) and examining the nature of these weights for different product categories, including those in the B-to-B space.

Developing Appropriate Measures for the E Component

Given how central E is to the third-wave view of the CVP and the creation of the connected customer, developing appropriate measures related to this component is likely to become more important that ever in the near future. The primary challenge is that with most of the brain's emotional processes arguably being inaccessible to our conscious awareness (e.g., Kihlstrom, Mulvaney, Tobias, & Tobis, 2000), traditionally used self-reported measures might be tapping into merely the tip of the emotional iceberg. The question is, how can we gain access to nonconscious emotional processes? Advances in neuroimaging (e.g., functional magnetic resonance imaging) might provide an answer to the question, but the costs involved in using this relatively modern technology and the complexity involved in executing the studies as well as interpreting the data are formidable enough that we are unlikely to see a widespread use of this approach in the near future.

A promising direction might come from making traditional measures of the physiological correlates of E more accessible and user friendly to marketing researchers. These measures include face tracking, cardio activity, and skin conductance, apart from scalp-recorded brain electrical activity, which have been shown to be sensitive to measuring both the valence and the arousal dimensions of emotions (e.g., Cacioppo et al., 2000). The rationale behind these physiological measures is that emotional processes that occur in the brain and the viscera manifest themselves in the form of changes to the facial musculature, heart rate, skin conductance, and so on.

One promising approach to making such traditional physiological measures more accessible and user friendly has been developed by a team of

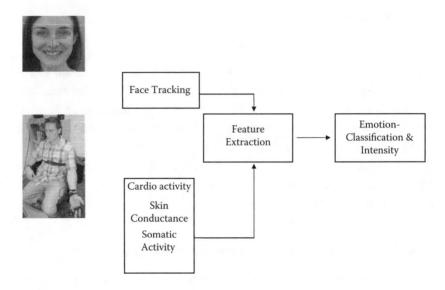

FIGURE 6.3

Measuring (non-conscious) emotions through facial feature tracking and physiological changes (Bailenson et al. 2008).

researchers at Stanford University (Bailenson et al., 2008). A schematic of this approach presented in Figure 6.3 combines face tracking with other physiological measures, all of which are automatically fed into an algorithm that yields two dimensions of the emotions being experienced in real time by the individual: valence and intensity of the experienced emotions.

Exploring Tactical Approaches to Shaping E in the Age of the Internet

Since E emerged as a separate component of the CVP in the 1980s, considerable research has been conducted on the effectiveness of various means of shaping this component. The notion behind the use of these tactics is as follows. Emotions that are triggered by a stimulus (e.g., an attractive celebrity, music, humor, etc.) in the presence of the featured brand have the potential to get associated with the brand (for a recent exposition on this notion, see Niedenthal, 2007). In this regard, the consensus has been that the most effective media vehicle to shape E is audiovisual advertising, given the range of executions it offers. Although this consensus view has been prevalent now for more than two decades, more research is needed on media and execution-related factors that are likely to engender the most favorable and the most intense brand emotion in the quickest and most cost-effective fashion. Identifying such factors is likely to gain in urgency given the shift in media consumption behavior—the emergence of the notion of "wee-wee-wee," with technological advances giving customers the option of consuming what they want, where they want, and when they want.

Apart from audiovisual advertising, other tactics that can shape E and, thus, the CVP merits consideration in future research. First is the use of outdoor and in-store signage, event sponsorship, and so on that are known to enhance brand salience (i.e., the top-of-mind awareness of the brand name, logos, etc.). Although brand salience is believed to be critical in the formation of the consideration set (see Keller, 2003), it may also shape E through the mere-exposure effect (Zajonc, 1980), which was built on Titchener's (1910) thesis on familiarity. Titchener argued that we, as decision makers, have an inherent preference for familiar options because such options give us a "glow of warmth, a sense of ownership, a feeling of intimacy" (p. 411). Titchener's thesis needs further testing, especially given the advances in the measurement of emotions.

A second approach that offers rich opportunities for future research is the use of tactics that enhance a feeling of ownership, often termed the "endowment effect" in the literature (Kahneman, Knetsch, & Thaler, 1991). These tactics could include putting in effort by consumers for an option through contests, opportunities to customize options, and so on. A recent piece of work on the "IKEA effect" (Norton, Mochon, & Ariely, in press) provides evidence in support of the notion that effort increases the value of the option the effort was directed toward. In one study, participants were asked to create an origami frog or crane and then asked to buy their creations with their own money. These participants, in general, bid higher amounts than a different set of participants who did not put in effort to create the objects. Future research needs to delve deeper into the underlying mechanism giving rise to the IKEA effect. Our thesis is that effort put into an option enhances predecisional distortion toward the option, resulting in greater willingness to pay and greater commitment to the chosen option.

Promising opportunities are also likely to emerge by focusing not merely on the encoding (of advertising, creation of options, etc.) stage but also on the retrieval stage—identifying factors that will be most effective at retrieving E during the decision-making process so as to increase chances that biased predecisional distortion processes will ensue (see Keller, 1987).

Adding β-Weights to the Components of the CVP

In the formulation at the beginning of the chapter, the CVP was expressed as E + Vb + Vp. This was later modified to the interactive effect of E on Vb and Vp, yielding a formula such as E + Vb + Vp + E*(Vb) + E *(Vp). The more interesting questions that are likely to arise are when β-weights are added to the various components. One can begin to explore the following. Which product categories are likely to have bigger betas, both in terms of the main effects and in terms of the interactions, and why? How will these betas manifest for products in the B-to-B space? Are these betas likely to be small, or, counterintuitively, are these betas likely to be large? Are there diminishing returns to scale in terms of investing in E, and is there a possibility of a saturation or a supersaturation effect? Is there a threshold effect for E before it really becomes important? Are there asymmetric effects for increases versus decreases in E? Finally, what are the situational and individual-difference factors that are likely to moderate these β-weights? For example, can tactics focusing on Vp (e.g., rebates, coupons, discounts, etc.) not only enhance price sensitivity in the form of greater β-weights on this component but also enhance "vulcanism" leading to reduced β-weights on the interaction of E with Vb, increased indecisiveness, and reduced commitment to the chosen options? Addressing these questions can yield significant insights not merely into the strategic and tactical aspects of the CVP but also into the underlying processes giving rise to good decisions.

SOME FINAL WORDS

The broad objective of this chapter was to take the reader on a journey involving the CVP and the connected customer, a journey that was aimed at unraveling the importance of emotion in creating a connected customer, who is not only brand loyal but also an advocate of the brand. The thrust was on highlighting the notion that emotion should be treated not merely as an add-on to the CVP as previously envisaged in the second-wave view but as a component that can actively shape Vb and Vp through predecisional distortion and, thereby, enhance the chances of creating a connected customer. We also presented empirical evidence in support of the third-wave view of the CVP and highlighted some promising opportunities for the future. Most important, we hope that this journey has left the reader with a desire to learn more about the disadvantages of being like Mr. Spock—becoming a Buridan's ass, indecisive, uncommitted, and, most important for the firm, an unconnected customer.

NOTES

1. In all fairness to the traditional perspective, emotion was implicitly considered part of the CVP, albeit as arising from Vb elements (e.g., design, packaging, etc.).

2. The components of this equation can also be construed in terms of constructs in the attitude literature. For instance, E shares kinship with affective attitudes, Vb shares kinship with multiattribute cognitive attitudes (attributes with the exception of price-related attributes), and Vp can be construed as cognitive attitudes related to price, momentary incentives such as rebates, and so on.

3. My view of normative principles is that they are not only rooted in rational economic theory but also rooted in internalized sociocultural norms. For instance, the decision by a substance abuser to abuse rather than abstain would be considered by most of us as violating a normative benchmark, this time as defined by internalized social norms.

4. An emphasis on "absence" is important for the viewpoint that I present in this section. If there are normative benchmarks, then, in my opinion, these benchmarks dominate the discourse in this section regarding what makes decisions good or bad.

5. This output perspective is bound to raise criticisms from readers. For example, if one falls prey to an escalation of commitment, where one becomes very committed to a course of action despite negative feedback, the output perspective would view one's decision as being good. In the same vein, if an addict chooses to abuse himself rather than abstain and is happy about the decision, the output perspective would view his decision as being good. Yet, most of us would agree that such decisions are bad. Rather than entering into debate on this issue, we qualify this "output-side" perspective as being applicable to decisions where a normative benchmark, as broadly defined by axioms of rational choice, by the society (e.g., substance abuse is not normatively advantageous), and so on, does not exist yet the decision maker is confronted with a trade-off conflict. In other words, as stated in note 4, normative benchmarks, if they exist, ought to dominate the output-side perspective in determining the quality of a decision.

6. From the point of view of the marketer, however, having customers making bad decisions from a normative viewpoint but making good decisions from an output-side perspective would not be controversial, in general.

7. It should be noted that when such patients face choice options with a clear dominance structure, they have little problem in making good (i.e., committed) decisions.
It is when they face trade-off conflicts, wherein the choice options are equally preferred (i.e., there is no dominance structure), that their ability to make good decisions
breaks down.

REFERENCES

Bailenson, J. N., Pontikakis, E. D., Mauss, I. B., Gross, J. J., Jabon, M. E., Hutcherson, C. A.
C., Nass, C., & John, O. (2008). Real-time classification of evoked emotions using
facial feature tracking and physiological responses. *International Journal of Human-
Computer Studies, 66*(5), 303–317.
Batra, R., & Ray, M. L. (1986). Affective responses mediating acceptance of advertising.
Journal of Consumer Research, 13(2), 234–249.
Bechara, A., & Damasio, A. R. (2005). The somatic marker hypothesis: A neural theory of
economic decision. *Games and Economic Behavior, 52*(2), 336–372.
Cacioppo, J. T., Tassinary, L. G., & Berntson, G. G. (2000). *Handbook of psychophysiology.*
New York, NY: Cambridge University Press.
Cosmides, L., & Tooby, J. (2000). Evolutionary psychology and the emotions. In M. Lewis &
J. M. Haviland-Jones (Eds.), *Handbook of emotions* (2nd ed.). New York: Guilford.
Damasio, A. R. (2000). *Descartes' error: Emotion, reason, and the human brain.* New York:
Harper Perennial.
Damasio, A. R., Everitt, B. J., & Bishop, D. (1996). The somatic marker hypothesis and the
possible functions of the prefrontal cortex. *Philosophical Transactions: Biological
Sciences, 351*(1346), 1413–1420.
Damasio, H., Grabowski, T., Frank, R., Galaburda, A. M., & Damasio, A. R. (1994). The
return of Phineas Gage: Clues about the brain from the skull of a famous patient.
Science, 264(5162), 1102–1105.
Gneezy, U., & Potters, J. (1997). An experiment on risk taking and evaluation periods.
Quarterly Journal of Economics, 112(2), 631–645.
Gorn, G. J. (1982). The effects of music in advertising on choice behavior: A classical condi-
tioning approach. *Journal of Marketing, 46*(1), 94–101.
Harlow, J. M. (1868). Recovery from the passage of an iron bar through the head. *Bulletin
of the Massachussetts Medical Society,* reprinted in *History of Psychiatry, 4*(14),
274–281.
Kahneman, D., Knetsch, J. L., & Thaler, R. H. (1991). The endowment effect, loss aversion,
and status quo bias. *Journal of Economic Perspectives, 5*(1), 193–206.
Keller, K. L. (1987). Memory factors in advertising: The effect of advertising retrieval cues
on brand evaluations. *Journal of Consumer Research, 14*(3), 316–333.
Keller, K. L. (1993). Conceptualizing, measuring, managing customer-based brand equity.
Journal of Marketing, 57(1), 1–22.
Keller, K. L. (2001). Building customer-based brand equity. *Marketing Management, 10*(2),
14–19.
Keller, K. L. (2002). Branding and brand equity. In B. A. Weitz & R. Wensley (Eds.),
Handbook of marketing (pp. 151–178). London: Sage.

Keller, K. L. (2003). *Strategic brand management: Building, measuring, and managing brand equity.* New York: Prentice Hall.

Kihlstrom, J. F., Mulvaney, S., Tobias, B. A., & Tobis, I. P. (2000). The emotional unconscious. In E. Eich, J. F. Kihlstrom, G. H. Bower, J. P. Forgas, & P. M. Niendenthal (Eds.), *Cognition and emotion* (pp. 30–86). New York: Oxford University Press.

Kohlberg, L. (1971). From is to ought: How to commit the naturalistic fallacy and get away with it in the study of moral development. In T. Mischel (Ed.), *Cognitive development and epistemology* (pp. 151–235). New York: Academic Press.

Larsen, R. J., Diener, E., & Emmons, R. A. (1986). Affect intensity and reactions to daily life events. *Journal of Personality and Social Psychology, 51*(4), 803–814.

Luce, M. F. (1998). Choosing to avoid: Coping with negatively emotion-laden consumer decisions. *Journal of Consumer Research, 24*(4), 409–433.

Mas-Colell, A., Whinston, M. D., & Green, J. R. (1995). *Microeconomic theory.* New York: Oxford University Press.

Miniard, P. W., Sirdeshmukh, D., & Innis, D. E. (1992). Peripheral persuasion and brand choice. *Journal of Consumer Research, 19*(2), 226–239.

Mitchell, A. A., & Olson, J. C. (1981). Are product attribute beliefs the only mediator of advertising effects on brand attitude? *Journal of Marketing Research, 18*(3), 318–332.

Naqvi, N., Shiv, B., & Bechara, A. (2006). The role of emotion in decision making: A cognitive neuroscience perspective. *Current Directions in Psychological Science, 15*(5), 260–264.

Niedenthal, P. M. (2007). Embodying emotion. *Science, 316*(5827), 1002–1005.

Norton, M. I., Mochon, D., & Ariely, D. (in press). The IKEA effect: When labor leads to love. *Journal of Consumer Research.*

Pala, Ö. (2008). *Selective exposure to information in the context of escalation of commitment.* Unpublished doctoral dissertation, Radboud University Nijmegen, the Netherlands.

Park, C. W., Jaworski, B. J., & MacInnis, D. J. (1986). Strategic brand concept-image management. *Journal of Marketing, 50*(4), 135–145.

Payne, J. W., Bettman, J. R., & Johnson, E. J. (1993). *The adaptive decision maker.* Cambridge: Cambridge University Press.

Russo, J. E., Meloy, M. G., & Medvec, V. H. (1998). Predecisional distortion of product information. *Journal of Marketing Research, 35*(4), 438–452.

Russo, J. E., Meloy, M. G., & Wilks, T. J. (2000). Predecisional distortion of information by auditors and salespersons. *Management Science, 46*(1), 13–27.

Shiv, B., Loewenstein, G., Bechara, A., Damasio, H., & Damasio, A. R. (2005, June). Investment behavior and the negative side of emotion. *Psychological Science, 16,* 435–439.

Sugden, R. (1991). Rational choice: A survey of contributions from economics and philosophy. *Economic Journal, 101*(407), 751–785.

Titchener, E. B. (1910). *A textbook of psychology.* New York: Macmillan.

Wilson, T. D., Lisle, D. J., Schooler, J. W., Hodges, S. D., Klaaren, K. J., & LaFleur, S. J. (1993). Introspecting about reasons can reduce post-choice satisfaction. *Personality and Social Psychology Bulletin, 19*(3), 331–339.

Zajonc, R. B. (1980). Feeling and thinking: Preferences need no inferences. *American Psychologist, 35*(2), 151–175.

Zajonc, R. B., & Markus, H. (1982). Affective and cognitive factors in preferences. *Journal of Consumer Research, 9*(2), 123–131.

7

God and Mammon: The Influence of Religiosity on Brand Connections

Aric Rindfleisch, Nancy Wong, and James E. Burroughs

Religiosity may seem like an odd topic for a book about the connected customer. As evidenced by the other chapters in this volume, current perspectives on customer connections are strongly secular in nature. This secular quality reflects the broader marketing literature, which has paid scant attention to religiosity. Like many social scientists, marketing scholars may doubt the appropriateness of religiosity as a topic for scientific inquiry (Ebaugh, 2002). We have no such doubt, and we suggest that religiosity is a highly relevant topic for marketing scholarship in general and for understanding the connected customer in particular. Thus, we ask, "What is the influence of religiosity on the strength of the connections that customers form with their brands?" Although our predictor (i.e., religiosity) is rather distinctive, our outcome (i.e., customer-brand connections) is quite consistent with many of the other chapters in this collection.

Our research question is motivated by everyday observations of the important role of religiosity in many aspects of contemporary social life, including the design of educational curriculum (Alphonso & Bonoguore, 2007), the electability of political candidates (Turley, 2007), and the causes of global terrorism (Hadiwinata, 2002). These heated social debates signify that religiosity is a key element in the lives of many of our world's inhabitants (including members of modern consumer societies in North America, Western Europe, and East Asia). For example, recent national surveys reveal that over 90% of Americans believe in God, and approximately 70% believe in the Devil (Harris Interactive, 2003; Pew Forum, 2008). And although America is clearly more religious than Western Europe, survey research has indicated that the majority of inhabitants of highly secular societies such as France and Germany express a belief in God or some other form of spiritual presence (Eurobarometer, 2005). In sum, religiosity is an important, but understudied, aspect of contemporary social life.

The influence of religiosity on social behavior was a central area of inquiry among many early social scientists, including Durkheim (1912), Marx (1912), and Weber (1930). In ensuing decades, however, the combination of rapid advances in scientific knowledge mixed with the explosive growth of technology and rapid industrialization led many social scientists to believe that secularization was an inevitable outgrowth of modernization (Ebaugh, 2002). Thus, for most of the 20th century, religion was considered a taboo subject for scientific inquiry. After "years of relative neglect" (Zinnbauer, Pargament, & Scott, 1999, p. 911), however, the study of religion appears to be in revival across a broad swath of social science. For example, in recent years, scholars have proposed that religiosity shapes the ethical decision making of corporate executives (Weaver & Agle, 2002), facilitates economic growth (Barro & McCleary, 2003), influences the voting behavior of members of Congress (Fastnow, Grant, & Rudolph, 1999), and enhances psychological well-being (Francis & Kaldor, 2002). As noted by Ebaugh (2002, p. 388), this growing body of research suggests that "religious variables are central in explanations of human behavior."

Despite its enormous social import, as well as its resurgence in social science discourse, religiosity has received scant attention from marketing scholars. This is likely a result of marketing's growth as a social science at a time when religious considerations were eschewed by the academic community in general (Bartels, 1976). Hence, an extensive search reveals only a handful of studies on this topic in the marketing literature (e.g., Delener, 1994; Hirschman, 1981; LaBarbera & Gurhan-Canli, 1997; McDaniel & Burnett, 1990; Sood & Nasu, 1995; Tellis, Stremersch, & Yin, 2003; Wilkes, Burnett, & Howell, 1986). Moreover, much of this research focuses on understanding the role of religious affiliation in product preference (for notable exceptions, see Belk, Wallendorf, & Sherry, 1989; Muñiz & Schau, 2005; O'Guinn & Belk, 1989; Sherry & Kozinets, 2007). Consequently, the influence of religiosity on the connections that customers form with their brands remains an open empirical question. This question is intriguing because brands are increasingly imbued with religious themes (e.g., "Jesus Is My Homeboy" T-shirts, Mecca Cola, True Religion jeans), and religion is increasingly marketed as a brand (e.g., Joel Osteen's Lakeland Church, T. D. Jake's Potter's House, Rick Warren's Saddleback Church).

Thus, religiosity and brands are currently comingling to form an intriguing nexus.

To understand the role of religiosity on the strength of the connections that customers form with their brands, we reviewed of a broad swath of religiosity research (e.g., Spilka, Hood, & Gorsuch, 1985; Stark & Glock, 1968; Wuthnow, 1998). This research suggests that religiosity is a multidimensional construct and that these dimensions vary in their impact on social behavior. Thus, we examine the influence of two related but distinct dimensions of religiosity in the forms of fundamentalism and spirituality. Recent research suggests that these two forms of religiosity differ in the degree to which they resonate with an individual's broader array of life values (Roccas, 2005; Saroglou & Muñoz-García, 2008). Thus, our conceptualization of the influence of religiosity on brand connections largely draws from values theory research (i.e., Schwartz, 1992). On the basis of this research, we contrast the role of fundamentalism (i.e., religiosity as a desire for conservation) with that of spirituality (i.e., religiosity as a desire for transcendence) on the strength of the connections that consumers form with their brands. To test these two competing views, we conducted an initial survey among 363 Americans and a second survey among 300 Singaporeans. Our combined results suggest that the influence of fundamentalism trumps spirituality and that the desire for conservation and need for predictability encourages consumers to form strong connections to their brands.

COMPETING VIEWS ON THE ROLE OF RELIGIOSITY ON BRAND CONNECTIONS

As noted previously, religiosity is a complex construct and composed of multiple dimensions (Cornwall, Albrecht, Cunningham, & Pitcher, 1986; Spilka et al., 1985; Stark & Glock, 1968). Although the number of dimensions and their labels vary from one study to another, almost all of these dimensions can be grouped into either (a) religious cognitions (e.g., fundamentalist beliefs, moral standards), (b) religious affect (e.g., feelings of spirituality, communal affiliation), or (c) religious behavior (e.g., religious worship, prayer). Although these three dimensions are empirically distinct, they are positively correlated. Because of this correlation, studies of the influence of religiosity should assess all three dimensions to avoid the risk of spurious interpretations. Therefore, although our conceptualization focuses on the influence of fundamentalism versus that of spirituality, for the sake of completion, we also empirically assess (and control for) the influence of religious behavior.

Our conceptualization focuses on fundamentalism and spirituality because these two particular aspects of religion have received substantial attention in recent years (Hill & Pargament, 2003; Saroglou & Muñoz-García, 2008). In addition, a focus on fundamentalism and spirituality is congruent with Wulff's (1997) influential work on the psychology of religion, which argues that religiosity can be boiled down to two essential tensions: the inclusion versus exclusion of transcendence (i.e., spirituality) and the literal versus symbolic interpretations of religious experiences (i.e., fundamentalism). In addition to this conceptual grounding in the religiosity literature, our focus on fundamentalism versus spirituality also aligns with a considerable body of research on the role of cognition and affect on consumer behavior (Bettman, Luce, & Payne, 1998; Garbarino & Edell, 1997; Zajonc & Markus, 1982). This literature suggests that consumer behavior is influenced by two related but distinct psychological mechanisms: cognitive (i.e., thoughts) and affective (i.e., feelings), which may have differing effects on persuasion, product choice, and brand preference (Petty, Cacioppo, & Schumann, 1983; Shiv & Fedorikhin, 1999).

Thus, we conceptualize that fundamentalism and spirituality exert divergent influences on the connections that consumers form with their brands. This assertion is congruent with prior research that suggests that although spirituality and fundamentalism are positively associated, they are nomologically distinct (Hill & Pargament, 2003; Saroglou & Muñoz-García, 2008). Specifically, on the basis of an assessment of prior research in religiosity and values theory, we suggest that fundamentalism is associated with conservation values and, thus, should have a positive influence on brand connections. In contrast, we suggest that spirituality is associated with transcendence values and, thus, should have a negative influence on brand connections. A large body of prior research also indicates that conservation and transcendence values are orthogonally aligned (Schwartz, 1992; Schwartz & Huismans, 1995). In the remainder of this conceptualization, we present the theoretical rationale for each perspective.

FUNDAMENTALISM: RELIGIOSITY AS A DESIRE FOR CONSERVATION

We define *fundamentalism* as the strength of belief in the correctness of one's religious worldview (Balmer, 2006). Fundamentalists typically regard their religious texts as the literal word of God and, thus, believe in strict adherence to the doctrines of their faith. For example, Carpenter (1997, p. 69) characterized Christian fundamentalists as individuals who deeply believe "that the Bible communicated God's sure, clear, and unchanging will." Because of this strong belief in the correctness of their religious worldview, fundamentalists are often characterized as having closed-minded and dogmatic personalities (Delener, 1994; Stark & Glock, 1968). This view, however, has received mixed empirical support, as the association between fundamentalism and personality appears modest at best (Saroglou & Muñoz-García, 2008; Schwartz & Huismans, 1995).

Given this mixed empirical support for personality correlates, researchers interested in uncovering religiosity's broader nomological network have recently turned to values theory (e.g., Roccas, 2005; Saroglou, Delpierre, & Dernelle, 2004; Saroglou & Muñoz-García, 2008; Schwartz & Huismans, 1995). According to this theory, values are desirable guiding life principles that shape perceptions and motivate action (Rokeach, 1973; Schwartz, 1992). As suggested by Roccas (2005, p. 748), "Values express what people believe to be good or bad and what they think should or should not be done." For many individuals, religion plays a similar role as a life-guiding mechanism (Smith, 1991). Hence, values and religiosity appear to serve congruent functions.

The emerging literature on values and religiosity provides consistent and compelling evidence that individuals strongly committed to their religious beliefs (regardless of their specific tradition) exhibit values that emphasize conservative tendencies (e.g., Roccas, 2005; Roccas, Sagiv, Schwartz, & Kanfo, 2002; Saroglou & Muñoz-García, 2008; Saroglou et al., 2004). For example, Schwartz and Huismans's (1995) study of the value profiles of Jews, Greek Orthodox, Protestants, and Roman Catholics reveals that the degree of orthodoxy is positively correlated with the value placed on tradition and conformity and negatively correlated with the value placed on hedonism and stimulation. On the basis of these findings, they suggested that this dimension of religiosity encourages individuals to "favor conserving the status quo" (p. 103). This interpretation has received recent support by Saroglou and Muñoz-García (2008), who similarly found that the importance placed on religiosity is positively associated with conformity and tradition and negatively associated with hedonism and stimulation (see Saroglou et al., 2004, for a meta-analysis of this literature).

Because values guide behavior across a broad variety of contexts (Schwartz, 1992), this underlying emphasis on conserving the status quo should also influence the secular behavior of fundamentalists. Although empirical research in this domain is scant, it appears to support this proposition. For example, Djupe (2002) found that individuals who strongly subscribe to their religious beliefs are also more committed to their political ideologies and less likely to switch party membership. Likewise, Delener (1990) showed that strongly held religious beliefs are negatively related to an individual's level of risk tolerance. This preference for established offerings was also evidenced by Wilkes et al. (1986), who documented a positive relationship between degree of religious commitment and preference for well-known brands. Collectively, this diverse body of research suggests that the fundamentalism dimension of religiosity encourages individuals to value things that are familiar and discourage variety seeking. Thus, this perspective implies that religiosity (in the form of fundamentalism) should *strengthen* the connections that consumers form with the brands they own.

SPIRITUALITY: RELIGIOSITY AS A DESIRE FOR TRANSCENDENCE

We define *spirituality* as "the degree to which one feels God's presence in one's life" (Zinnbauer et al., 1999, p. 895). The feeling of being in the presence of God is often described as a sacred and transcendent experience in which one attains a sense of communal connection with a supreme being (Spilka et al., 1985; Zinnbauer et al., 1999). For example, Saroglou and Muñoz-García (2008, p. 88) suggested that spirituality entails a "connection with transcendence, others, and the world in general."

Although spirituality is generally viewed as an integral and essential component of religiosity, extant research on the psychology of religion has typically focused on religiosity's cognitive dimension (cf. Saroglou et al.,

2004). Consequently, the values associated with spirituality have received scant attention. The one exception is a recent study by Saroglou and Muñoz-García (2008), which found that spirituality is positively associated with the value placed on benevolence and negatively associated with the value placed on power. According to Schwartz's (1992) value framework, individuals who value benevolence place importance on transcending worldly and material concerns, whereas individuals who value power display the opposite orientation.

This pattern of value correlates is conceptually congruent with the notion of spirituality as a transcendent experience and is typically viewed as an escape from the everyday world and its profane and secular nature (Gorsuch & Miller, 1999). This viewpoint is shared by scholars in both religion and marketing. For example, Schwartz and Huismans (1995, p. 91) argued that transcendence is opposed to both "self-indulgent materialism" and "happiness in the pursuit and consumption of material goods." Similarly, Belk et al.'s (1989) vanguard Consumer Odyssey revealed that material objects such as branded products are generally considered to be embodiments of the profane. Thus, the transcendent aspect of religiosity appears conceptually at odds with the notion of being tightly connected to branded products, as the search for the sacred typically requires divestment of the profane (Smith, 1991).

The notion that material objects are obstacles to spiritual transcendence is a hallmark of many of the world's religions (Smith, 1991). In Christianity, for instance, several passages in the New Testament note the dangers of trying to balance both spirituality and worldliness. For example, John the Apostle admonished, "Do not love the world or the things in the world" (I John 2:15). The distinction between the sacred world of God and the profane world of material objects is also clearly evident in the writings of evangelical Christian author John Kavanaugh (1991), who viewed religiosity and marketing as "two competing gospels" (p. 22) and suggested that "the very nature of our economic system provides a faith challenge for those who wish to lead the Christian life" (p. 59). He went on to argue that Christians must resist the temptation to become attached to mass-marketed products. Such admonitions are not unique to Christianity. For example, Buddhists also view the elimination of object desire as a prerequisite to enlightenment (Zimmer, 1993).

The proposition that religious transcendence conflicts with attachment to material objects has received indirect support in research by Burroughs and Rindfleisch (2002), who found a negative relationship between religiosity and materialism. Their research suggests that the theoretical driver of this negative association is internal value conflict, as individuals who attempt to adhere to both types of values experience considerable psychological stress. Likewise, Guth, Green, Kellstedt, and Smidt (1995) noted that the search for spiritual transcendence is sometimes taken to such an extreme that adherents generate an attitude of almost complete disinterest (if not contempt) for worldly objects, issues, and events. The oppositional nature of spiritual transcendence and worldly indulgence led Elkins, Hedstrom, Hughes, Leaf, and Saunders (1988, p. 11) to suggest, "The spiritual person can appreciate material goods ... but does not seek ultimate satisfaction from them." Thus, this perspective implies that religiosity (in the form of spirituality) should *weaken* the connections that consumers form with the brands they own.

STUDY 1: UNITED STATES

Participants and Procedures

We assessed these two competing perspectives in a nationwide (U.S.) mail survey to obtain results that were as generalizable as possible. We purchased a mailing list that included 2,000 American adults age 20 and older. We mailed each individual a survey, a cover letter explaining the importance and confidentiality of our research, and a postage-paid reply envelope. As an incentive to participate, we also included a sweepstakes entry form that respondents could return for a chance to win a $300 gift card for Best Buy.

Fifty-six surveys were returned as undeliverable, reducing our effective sampling frame to 1,944 potential respondents. We received responses from 382 individuals, for a 20% response rate. This response rate is comparable to other recent mail surveys targeted to the general U.S. population (e.g., Burroughs & Rindfleisch, 2002; Wong, Rindfleisch, & Burroughs, 2003). After eliminating 19 surveys because of severe missing data, we were left with a final sample of 363 respondents across 46 states. Of these 363 respondents, 51% were female, 82% were White, 6% were African American, 3% were Hispanic, and 2% were Asian. The mean age of our respondents was 48 (range 20 to 87), their average household income was $52,000, and 43% had earned at least a bachelor's degree. In terms of religious affiliation, 55% of our respondents were Protestants, 24% were Catholics, and 21% were non-Christians. Moreover, 35% of our respondents attend religious services at least once a week. Other than education (which is slightly higher than national norms), the demographic composition and religious affiliation and practice of our sample closely mirrors that of the U.S. adult population (U.S. Bureau of the Census, 2000).

Measures and Validation

Construction of our survey instrument began with a careful review of the extant literature to find relevant measures for our key constructs. We were able to find existing measures that we could either directly apply or slightly adapt to fit our research goals. We pretested our instrument among 45 American adults, which revealed that our measures were generally sound.

Two product categories were the focus of this study: (a) automobiles and (b) jeans. We selected automobiles and jeans because of their high penetration rate among the U.S. population and because they represent two different types of product categories (i.e., a commonly purchased item vs. a big-ticket investment). In addition, our pretests indicated that both product categories exhibited considerable variance in their degree of brand connections. Of our 363 respondents, 339 owned a car, and 294 owned a pair of jeans. The measures used to assess our constructs are described next. Unless stated otherwise, these measures were assessed using a 7-point Likert scale (7 = *strongly agree*). Summary statistics are provided in Table 7.1.

Brand connection. According to Keller (2003), consumers may form a variety of different types of connections with their brands. Specifically, he suggested that the two most common forms of brand connections are cognitive preference (i.e., brand loyalty) and emotional bonding (i.e., self-brand connection). Thus, these are the two forms of brand connections that we assess.

We define *brand loyalty* as the intent to repurchase a preferred brand in the future (Oliver, 1999) and measured this construct using a four-item scale developed by Chadhuri and Holbrook (2001). This scale contains items that tap both behavioral intent and attitudinal loyalty and displayed

TABLE 7.1

Key Measure Summary Statistics

	Mean	SD	(1)	(2)	(3)	(4)	(5)	(6)
Automobiles (Study 1)								
Fundamentalism (1)	3.48	1.90						
Spirituality (2)	5.02	1.69	.59**					
Brand loyalty (3)	4.17	1.79	.04	−.02				
Brand connection (4)	3.43	1.81	−.02	−.02	.60**			
Product satisfaction (5)	5.67	1.27	−.03	.07	.70**	.45**		
Jeans (Study 1)								
Fundamentalism (1)	3.48	1.90						
Spirituality (2)	5.02	1.69	.57**					
Brand loyalty (3)	4.29	1.70	.13*	.02				
Brand connection (4)	2.91	1.72	.26**	.06	.56**			
Product satisfaction (5)	5.39	1.20	.12*	.10	.71**	.49**		
Watches (Study 2)								
Fundamentalism (1)	4.79	1.49						
Spirituality (2)	5.10	1.37	.87**					
Brand loyalty (3)	4.06	1.57	.25**	.24**				
Brand connection (4)	3.84	1.53	.16**	.15*	.82**			
Product satisfaction (5)	4.88	1.28	.19**	.26**	.64**	.61**		
Need for order (6)	4.88	1.28	.48**	.42**	.22**	.28**	.23**	
Need for predictability (7)	4.68	1.22	.40**	.35**	.30**	.35**	.25**	.77**
Cell phones (Study 2)								
Fundamentalism (1)	4.79	1.49						
Spirituality (2)	5.10	1.37	.87**					
Brand loyalty (3)	4.66	1.49	.17**	.08				
Brand connection (4)	4.06	1.59	.25**	.20**	.75**			
Product satisfaction (5)	4.93	1.30	.23**	.22**	.72**	.60**		
Need for order (6)	4.88	1.28	.48**	.42**	.30**	.33**	.34**	
Need for predictability (7)	4.68	1.22	.40**	.35**	.28**	.42**	.29**	.77**

Note: $*p < .05$, $**p < .01$.

strong reliability ($CR_{automobiles} = .95$, $CR_{jeans} = .87$). We define *self-brand connection* as a personal and special attachment to a brand (Keller, 2003) and measured this construct using Escalas and Bettman's (2003) five-item measure of self-brand connection. This measure assesses the degree to which a consumer has integrated a brand into part of his or her self-concept and displayed strong reliability ($CR_{automobiles} = .98$, $CR_{jeans} = .98$).

Fundamentalism. This aspect of religiosity refers to the degree of conviction in one's beliefs about the absolute correctness and inherent truth qualities of a religion's teachings and scriptures (Stark & Glock, 1968). We measured fundamentalism using six items from the Religious Fundamentalism Scale (Altemeyer & Hunsberger, 1992). This measure was developed to capture fundamentalist beliefs across a wide variety of religions. Thus, its items are general in nature and do not focus on the tenets of any specific faith. The reliability of this measure was quite strong (CR = .98). This measure represents the religion-as-conservation perspective.

Spirituality. This aspect of religiosity refers to the value placed on the transcendent aspect of religion (Seidlitz et al., 2002). We assessed spirituality using eight items from the Spiritual Transcendence Index (STI) developed by Seidlitz et al. (2002). Unlike most other measures of spirituality, the STI was designed to be applicable across a broad range of religions. Thus, it does not contain items that refer to beliefs or experiences associated with any specific religion; instead, it focuses on spiritually related beliefs and experiences common to most religions. This measure displayed high internal consistency (CR = .96) and represents the religion-as-transcendence perspective.

Values. To validate the conceptual distinction between our two forms of religiosity, we assessed four fundamental life values (i.e., benevolence, hedonism, power, and tradition). These four values were drawn from Schwartz's (1992) typology of 10 universal values, which has been validated across thousands of participants and dozens of cultures. This typology suggests that these values are structured by two underlying dimensions: (a) self-transcendence versus self-enhancement and (b) conservation versus openness to change. According to Schwartz, benevolence and hedonism largely align with self-transcendence versus self-enhancement, whereas tradition and power largely align with conservation versus openness to change. We used Schwartz's (1992) measures to assess each value: benevolence (three items, CR = .82), hedonism (two items, CR = .70), power (three items, CR = .78), and tradition (three items, CR = .94).

Control variables. We also collected data on a number of control variables. Specifically, we used self-report single-item measures to assess respondents' age, gender, education, and income because prior research has shown that these variables are often related to religiosity (Francis & Kaldor, 2002; Graduate Center of the City University of New York, 2001). In addition, to avoid the dangers of social desirability response (SDR) bias (Mick, 1996), we assessed SDR using 15 items from Paulhus's (1992) Balanced Inventory of Desirable Responding (CR = .68). To account for alternative influences on brand connections, we also assessed respondents' level of satisfaction with their brand using five items from the Consumption Satisfaction Scale developed by Oliver (1997, p. 343). This scale displayed strong reliability ($CR_{automobiles}$ = .96, CR_{jeans} = .96).

Finally, we assessed our respondents' degree of religious practices in order to control for any effect that these activities may have on brand connections. On the basis of prior research, we identified three common practices associated with individuals high in religiosity: (a) attendance at religious services, (b) prayer, and (c) reading of religious texts (Francis & Kaldor, 2002; Greely, 1963; Poloma & Pendelton, 1990). Following these prior studies, we summed a set of single-item self-reported measures of each type of behavior (on a 5-point scale where 1 = *never* and 5 = *daily*). Because these measures represent formative indicants, assessment of internal consistency is inappropriate (Jarvis, MacKenzie, & Podsakoff, 2003).

Measure validation. We validated our multi-item reflective measures by using confirmatory factor analysis (CFA) using LISREL 8 (Jöreskog & Sörbom, 1993). Specifically, we conducted three sets of CFA on theoretically similar sets of measures as a means of examining maximally similar constructs. As noted by Campbell and Fiske (1959), this grouping of similar constructs provides a stringent test of construct validity. These three sets consisted of (a) brand-related, (b) religiosity-based, and (c) life values measures. Details for these sets of analyses are provided in the appendix.

Our brand-related CFA included brand loyalty, self-brand connection, and product satisfaction. For the validation of our brand-related measures, we specified two separate measurement models for the two product categories (automobiles and jeans) used in this study. The fit for both models was acceptable (automobiles: χ^2 (69) = 182, CFI = .98, NNFI = .97, RMSEA = .071; jeans: χ^2 (69) = 257, CFI = .96, NNFI = .94, RMSEA = .098), and all items displayed strong factor loadings and composite reliabilities.

Our religiosity CFA included our two religiosity measures (i.e., fundamentalism and spirituality). This model revealed that one item from our spirituality scale ("My spirituality gives me a sense of fulfillment") displayed poor fit compared to the rest of the items. After removing this item, the religiosity measurement model exhibited good fit (χ^2 (76) = 253, CFI =

.96, NNFI = .95, RMSEA = .083), and all items had strong factor loadings and composite reliabilities.

Our life values CFA included benevolence, hedonism, power, and tradition. The fit for this model was acceptable (χ^2 (33) = 128, CFI = .94, NNFI = .90, RMSEA = .087), and all items displayed strong factor loadings and composite reliabilities. As a means of assessing the predictive validity of both religiosity measures, we assessed the level of religious practices among respondents high versus low (based on a median split) on fundamentalism and spirituality. As expected, respondents high in spirituality or fundamentalism engaged in more frequent religious practices than respondents with low levels of either religious value ($M_{\text{(high spirituality)}}$ = 3.76, $M_{\text{(low spirituality)}}$ = 2.28, $p < .001$; $M_{\text{(high fundamentalism)}}$ = 3.61, $M_{\text{(low fundamentalism)}}$ = 2.28, $p < .001$). These results suggest that our religiosity measures have predictive validity.

We tested the discriminant validity of our measures by employing Fornell and Larcker's (1981) test of shared variance between each pair of latent constructs. The results of this test reveal that the squared correlations between these pairs of constructs do not exceed the average variance extracted for any single latent construct ($p < .001$). Thus, we concluded that our measures display adequate discriminant validity.

Finally, because cross-sectional, self-report surveys are susceptible to common method variance (CMV) bias, we assessed the potential for this bias by conducting Harmon's one-factor test as recommended by Podsakoff and Organ (1986). This test involves entering all of the items for our latent variables into a single factor using CFA procedures. The fit statistics for this model were quite poor (automobiles: χ^2 (324) = 6,541, CFI = .31, NNFI = .26, RMSEA = .33; jeans: χ^2 (324) = 5,344, CFI = .33, NNFI = .28, RMSEA = .34), indicating that there is no general factor that accounts for the majority of covariance in these variables and providing evidence against the presence of CMV bias in this sample.

Results and Discussion

Before undertaking our main analysis of the influence of religiosity on brand connections, we conducted a couple of precursory analyses: (a) an empirical test of the conceptual distinction between fundamentalism and spirituality, and (b) an assessment of the specific brands owned by our participants.

Analysis of the distinction between fundamentalism and spirituality. Recall that we posited that fundamentalism represents a desire for conservation, whereas spirituality represents a desire for transcendence. Hence, these two forms of religiosity should empirically align with values that respectively represent these desires. We tested this premise through multidimensional scaling (MDS) analysis. MDS provides a graphical representation of how respondents perceive constructs relative to one another in conceptual space and helps uncover their underlying dimensions. Each construct is represented as a point in multidimensional space, and the distances between these points reflect their intercorrelations. The specific constructs included in our MDS were fundamentalism, spirituality, benevolence, hedonism, tradition, and power. We conducted this analysis using the standardized values for each construct and employed the ALSCAL algorithm to compute proximities (Kruskal & Wish, 1978).

The results of this analysis reveal that a two-dimensional solution explains a high proportion of variance (RSQ = .98) and has a low degree of stress (Kruskal's stress = .06). Both of these fit indices surpass recommended standards (Kruskal & Wish, 1978). As shown in Figure 7.1, spirituality is located along the X-axis in close proximity to benevolence (i.e., self-transcendence) and directly opposed to power (i.e., self-enhancement). In contrast, fundamentalism aligns near the Y-axis in much closer proximity to tradition (i.e., conservation) than to hedonism (i.e., change). In sum, this MDS analysis supports our contention that fundamentalism

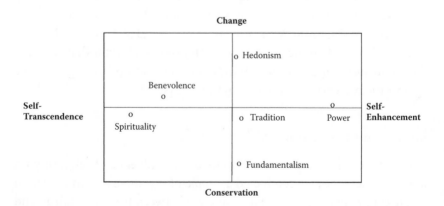

FIGURE 7.1
Multidimensional scaling plot of the structure of religiosity and values (Study 1).

and spirituality represent two different dimensions of religiosity and serve distinct sets of life values.

Analysis of brand ownership. Because our research objective is to investigate the impact of religiosity on brand connections in general (rather than specific brand preferences), we tried to avoid product categories laden with religious connotations. If highly religious individuals systematically prefer certain brands, our results could be confounded. To assess this potential risk, we examined whether specific brand preferences vary by degree of religiosity. Specifically, we selected the top five reported brands for both product categories and used discriminant analysis to test whether religiosity (both fundamentalism and spirituality) was a significant predictor of our respondents' specific brand ownership. Neither fundamentalism nor spirituality appears to influence either the specific brand of vehicle driven or the jeans worn among our respondents (Wilks's $\lambda > .90$ across all four groups, $p = ns$). Thus, we concluded that our results are not confounded by religious connections to specific brands.

Analysis of the effect of religiosity on brand loyalty and self-brand connections. Finding that religiosity is unrelated to specific brand preferences, we next examined the influence of religiosity on brand connections through structural equation modeling using LISREL 8 (Jöreskog & Sörbom, 1993). We specified separate models for each product category. In these models, our two measures of religiosity were the key exogenous variables, and age, gender, education, income, product satisfaction, SDR, and religious practices were entered as control variables (also specified as exogenous variables). Our endogenous variables were brand loyalty and self-brand connection. The fit indices for both models met recommended standards (automobiles: χ^2 (445) = 899, CFI = .95, NNFI = .94, RMSEA = .057; jeans: χ^2 (445) = 942, CFI = .93, NNFI = .92, RMSEA = .063].

As shown in Table 7.2, fundamentalism is positively related to brand loyalty for both automobiles ($\gamma = .13, p < .05$) and jeans ($\gamma = .18, p < .01$) and also positively related to self-brand connection for jeans ($\gamma = .37, p < .01$). By contrast, spirituality is negatively related to brand loyalty for automobiles ($\gamma = -.23, p < .05$) but unrelated to brand loyalty for jeans ($\gamma = -.05, p = ns$) and self-brand connection for both automobiles ($\gamma = -.06, p = ns$) and jeans ($\gamma = .06, p = ns$). In sum, fundamentalism appears positively related to both brand loyalty and self-brand connection, whereas spirituality appears to be either negatively related or unrelated to these constructs.

TABLE 7.2

Coefficient Estimates for Study 1 (United States)

	Brand Loyalty	Self-Brand Connection
Automobiles		
Fundamentalism	.13 (.06)*	−.05 (.08)
Spirituality	−.23 (.11)*	−.06 (.08)
Product satisfaction	.72 (.05)**	.46 (.06)**
Social desirability response	.05 (.07)	−.03 (.07)
Sex	−.13 (.06)*	−.03 (.06)
Age	.19 (.06)**	.12 (.06)*
Education	.00 (.06)	−.03 (.06)
Income	.04 (.06)	.03 (.06)
R^2	.51	.21
Jeans		
Fundamentalism	.18 (.07)**	.37 (.08)**
Spirituality	−.05 (.11)	.06 (.12)
Product satisfaction	.66 (.07)**	.46 (.06)**
Social desirability response	.08 (.07)	−.07 (.07)
Sex	−.04 (.06)	.01 (.06)
Age	−.06 (.06)	−.12 (.06)*
Education	−.14 (.06)*	−.17 (.06)**
Income	.11 (.06)	−.11 (.06)
R^2	.47	.33

Note: $*p < .05, **p < .01$.

Among our control variables, satisfaction has the strongest relationship with both brand loyalty (automobiles: $\gamma = .72, p < .01$; jeans: $\gamma = .66, p < .01$) and self-brand connections (automobiles: $\gamma = .46, p < .01$; jeans: $\gamma = .46, p < .01$). Beyond satisfaction, the only other control variables with significant effects on either construct were age and education (automobiles: $\gamma_{\text{age-loyalty}} = .19, p < .01, \gamma_{\text{age-connection}} = .12, p < .05$; jeans: $\gamma_{\text{age-connection}} = -.12, p < .05, \gamma_{\text{education-loyalty}} = -.14, p < .05, \gamma_{\text{education-connection}} = -.17, p < .01$).

Overall, our results suggest that the religiosity-as-conservation perspective trumps the religiosity-as-transcendence perspective in terms of explaining religiosity's influence on brand connections. The results of this initial study are limited, however, by both its scope and its sample. Our study investigated only two product categories, and our sample consisted primarily of Christians. Consequently, the robustness of these findings across other product categories and religious traditions remains to be seen. Furthermore, although the results of this initial study clearly point to a relationship between fundamentalism brand connections, they provide limited insight into the cognitive mechanism that may underlie this association.

STUDY 2: SINGAPORE

Objective

The findings from Study 1 suggest that religiosity in the form of fundamentalism is positively associated with both brand loyalty and self-brand connections and that religiosity in the form of spirituality *may* exhibit a negative association with these constructs. In this second study, we seek to clarify and enrich these findings in three ways. First, we examine the degree to which this pattern is replicable across other cultural settings and religions (i.e., Buddhism, Christianity, and Islam). Second, we test the robustness of these effects using two new product categories (i.e., watches and cell phones). Third, we seek to shed additional light on the underlying cognitive mechanism behind these effects.

As noted earlier, our conceptualization of the influence of religiosity on brand connections is grounded largely in values theory. According to this theory, values represent desirable goals and, thus, serve as motives for action (Roccas, 2005; Schwartz, 1992). Our results from Study 1 suggest that the main motive behind the influence of religiosity on brand connections is a desire for conservation. To enrich our understanding of the nature of this motive, Study 2 examines its underlying *cognitive traits*. As noted by Roccas et al. (2002), cognitive traits influence values because of the need for individuals to maintain cognitive consistency. Although values represent what individuals desire (i.e., who they want to be), traits indicate how they actually think and behave (i.e., who they are) (Saroglou & Muñoz-García, 2008). Thus, an inquiry into fundamentalism's traits should provide additional insights into the cognitive mechanism behind its association with brand connections.

The psychological literature is replete with a plethora of various cognitive traits (e.g., need for cognition, style of processing, coping style, etc.). Many of these traits would likely provide interesting insights into the nature of the association between fundamentalism and brand connections. One particularly intriguing trait is the need for cognitive closure (NFCC) (Kruglanski, 1989; Kruglanski et al., 1997; Kruglanski & Webster, 1996; Neuberg, Nicole, & West, 1997; Webster & Kruglanski, 1994). NFCC is conceptualized as a stable individual difference in an individual's cognitive motives and is defined as "the desire for a definite answer on some topic ... as opposed to confusion and ambiguity" (Kruglanski, 1989, p. 14). In other words, NFCC represents an aversion to ambiguity and a strong desire for certainty and influences how individuals process information. Specifically, individuals high in NFCC try to attain certainty by urgently *seizing* incoming information when faced with a new decision and then permanently *freezing* this information once a decision is reached (Kruglanski & Webster, 1996). NFCC has received considerable attention among cognitive psychologists, who have found that this trait is a strong predictor of information processing and decision-making styles (e.g., Kruglanski et al., 1997; Neuberg et al., 1997). In addition, recent research has also found that some dimensions of NFCC (i.e., needs for order and need for predictability) are positively associated with religiosity (Saroglou, 2002).

The usefulness of NFCC for understanding customer behavior has recently captured the attention of marketing scholars (e.g., Houghton & Grewal, 2000; Kardes, 1996; Vermeir, Van Kenhove, & Hendrickx, 2002). For example, Vermeir et al. (2002) showed that individuals high in NFCC have greater confidence in their brand choice decisions compared to individuals low in NFCC. Moreover, NFCC has been shown to be conceptually and empirically valid across multiple cultures (Kossowska, Van Hill, Chun, & Kruglanski, 2002). Thus, NFCC appears to be a generalizable concept that may be useful for understanding the cognitive traits underlying fundamentalism's association with brand connections. Although the religiosity and branding literatures differ widely in their objectives and substantive focus, scholars in both traditions have suggested that individuals highly committed to either religion or brands exhibit a high need for cognitive certainty, predictability, and stability (e.g., Chadhuri & Holbrook, 2001; Fournier, 1998; Francis, 2001; Stark & Glock, 1968). Thus, we suggest that NFCC is a cognitive trait that underlies the association between fundamentalism and brand connections.

Participants and Procedures

We selected Singapore as the setting for our second study because it is one of the few places where the populace contains sizable percentages of adherents to three of the world's leading religions (i.e., Buddhism, Christianity, and Islam). In addition, English is the official language of Singapore, which minimizes concerns about language translation issues.

Because mail surveys are rare in Singapore, we decided to conduct a mall intercept study (e.g., Wong et al., 2003). We hired a leading Singaporean research firm to conduct a stratified survey of 300 respondents with equal representation of Christians, Muslims, and Buddhists. Interviewers were situated at centrally located shopping malls, where they approached a total of 1,170 individuals, of whom 300 agreed to participate (26% response rate). Fifty-one percent of the respondents were female, their median age was 37 (range 18 to 67), their median household income was $23,000, and 26% had earned at least a bachelor's degree. In terms of ethnicity, 66% were Chinese, 30% were Malay, and 3% were Indian. In terms of religious service attendance, 21% of the Buddhists, 68% of the Christians, and 91% Muslim respondents attend services once a week or more. In general, the demographic composition and religious practices of this sample closely matches Singapore's population statistics (Statistics Singapore, 2000).

Measures and Validation

Our survey instrument contained many of the same measures used in Study 1, along with measures of NFCC (see appendix). As before, we assessed two specific product categories: (a) cell phone and (b) wristwatch. All 300 respondents owned both products.

Brand loyalty and self-brand connection. For comparability purposes, we employed the same two measures used in Study 1. Both measures displayed strong reliability (loyalty: $CR_{watch} = .94$, $CR_{phone} = .96$; connection: $CR_{watch} = .97$, $CR_{phone} = .98$).

Fundamentalism and spirituality. As before, we assessed fundamentalism using the Religious Fundamentalism Scale. This measure displayed good reliability ($CR = .97$). Spirituality was again assessed using the Spiritual Transcendence Index. This measure displayed good reliability

($CR = .96$) and has been successfully employed in prior studies among Asian respondents (Kim & Seidlitz, 2002).

Need for cognitive closure. The NFCC was originally intended to assess five separate cognitive traits (i.e., need for order, need for predictability, closed-mindedness, intolerance of ambiguity, and decisiveness) that were combined into an overall indicant of need for closure. Subsequent research has shown, however, that these five dimensions do not load on a single construct, and there has been considerable debate as to how to most appropriately employ this measure (e.g., Neuberg et al., 1997). It is now widely recommended that each dimension be analyzed as a separate component of NFCC, with the choice of dimensions being guided by one's research objectives. Because brand loyalty and self-brand connection are fundamentally about stability and security (Escalas & Bettman, 2003; Chadhuri & Holbrook, 2001), we focused on *need for order* (NFO) and *need for predictability* (NFP) as our key dimensions. Moreover, these two needs have been shown to be the NFCC dimensions most strongly related to religiosity (Saroglou, 2002). Because of a number of psychometric challenges with NFCC's original format, we used a refined measure of NFO and NFP developed by Houghton and Grewal (2000). These two dimensions displayed good reliability ($CR_{order} = .96$, $CR_{predictability} = .97$).

Control variables. We assessed respondent's age, gender, education, income, and SDR as control measures ($CR = .62$). To account for alternative influencers of brand connections, we assessed product satisfaction (for both watches and cell phones) using the same measure as in Study 1 ($CR_{phone} = .97$, $CR_{watch} = .98$). In addition, because watches and cell phones are often purchased as gift items, we included a question that asked participants if they purchased the focal brand themselves or received it as a gift. As before, we also controlled for degree of religious practices by summing three formative items (on a 5-point scale where $1 = never$ and $5 = daily$) similar to those used in Study 1. These three items were the frequency of (a) attending church, mosque, or temple; (b) praying or meditating; and (c) reading Holy Scriptures. We added meditation along with prayer to accommodate our Buddhist respondents, who typically meditate rather than pray.

Measure validation. We assessed the validity of our multi-item measures using the same procedure as in Study 1. We specified three sets of models among maximally similar constructs: (a) brand-related measures, (b) religiosity measures, and (c) cognitive trait measures. Specific details for these analyses are provided in the appendix.

Following Study 1, our brand-related CFA included brand loyalty, self-brand connection, and product satisfaction. As before, we specified two separate models for our two product categories. Both models displayed good fit statistics (cell phones: χ^2 (69) = 181, CFI = .97, NNFI = .96, RMSEA = .074; watches: χ^2 (69) = 178, CFI = .96, NNFI = .95, RMSEA = .075), and all items had strong loadings and good composite reliabilities. Our second CFA, for religiosity (i.e., spirituality and fundamentalism), also displayed good fit statistics (χ^2 (71) = 165, CFI = .98, NNFI = .97, RMSEA = .067), and strong factor loadings and composite reliabilities, after the removal of the one bad spirituality item discussed in Study 1. Our third CFA included our two dimensions of NFCC. This model had good fit statistics (χ^2 (19) = 53, CFI = .97, NNFI = .96, RMSEA = .081) and strong factor loadings and composite reliabilities.

We assessed the predictive validity of our religiosity measures by examining the relationship between these measures and our measures of religious practice. As before, respondents high in fundamentalism or spirituality engaged in more frequent religious practices than respondents with low levels of either dimension ($M_{(high\ fundamentalism)}$ = 3.73, $M_{(low\ fundamentalism)}$ = 2.55, $p < .001$; $M_{(high\ spirituality)}$ = 3.84, $M_{(low\ spirituality)}$ = 2.43, $p < .001$). These results suggest that our religiosity measures exhibit predictive validity among Singaporeans. Once again, we tested the discriminant validity of our measures by applying Fornell and Larcker's (1981) test of shared variance between each pair of latent constructs. The results of this test reveal that the squared correlations between each pair of constructs do not exceed the average variance extracted for each single latent construct ($p < .001$). Thus, we concluded that our measures display adequate discriminant validity.

Finally, we assessed the potential for CMV bias in our sample by conducting a Harmon's one-factor test in which we entered all of the items for our latent variables into a single factor using CFA. The fit statistics for this model were quite poor (cell phones: χ^2 (560) = 6,282, CFI = .35, NNFI = .31, RMSEA = .30; watches: χ^2 (560) = 4,967, CFI = .43, NNFI = .39, RMSEA = .25), indicating that there is no general factor that accounts for the majority of covariance in these variables and providing evidence against the presence of CMV bias in this sample.

Results and Discussion

As before, we first conducted a discriminant analysis to see if brand preferences are influenced by religiosity. This analysis revealed no significant differences in brand ownership of either cell phones or watches based on levels of either fundamentalism or spirituality (Wilks's λ > .90 across all four groups, p = ns).

Replication of Study 1. We examined the relationship between religiosity and brand connections using structural equation modeling via LISREL 8. We specified separate models for each product category. As before, our two measures of religiosity were the key exogenous variables and age, gender, education, income, product satisfaction, SDR, religious practices, and mode of acquisition (self purchase or gift) were entered as control variables (also specified as exogenous variables). Our endogenous variables were brand loyalty and self-brand connection. The fit indices for both models met recommended standards (cell phones: χ^2 (732) = 1,542, CFI = .91, NNFI = .90, RMSEA = .064; watches: χ^2 (732) = 1,458, CFI = .91, NNFI = .89, RMSEA = .057).

The results of this analysis are reported in Table 7.3. As shown in this table, fundamentalism is positively and significantly related to both brand connection measures for both cell phones (loyalty: γ = .37, p < .01; connection: γ = .37, p < .01) and watches (loyalty: γ = .39, p < .01; connection: γ = .36, p < .01). In contrast, spirituality is significantly and negatively related to only brand loyalty for cell phones (γ = –.39, p < .05). Among our control variables, satisfaction has the strongest relationship with both brand loyalty (cell phones: γ = .75, p < .01; watches: γ = .67, p < .01) and self-brand connection (cell phones: γ = .60, p < .01; watches: γ = .68, p < .01). Beyond satisfaction, the only other control variables with significant effects on either brand measure were age and education (cell phones: $\gamma_{education\text{-}connection}$ = –.13, p < .05; watches: $\gamma_{age\text{-}loyalty}$ = .14, p < .05). Collectively, these results largely replicate our findings from Study 1 and lend further support to the religion-as-conservation perspective.

Testing robustness across religions. In addition to replicating our results in another culture, a second objective of this study was to examine the robustness of the effect of fundamentalism across different religions. Recall that our sample consisted of 100 respondents per religion (i.e., Buddhists, Christians, and Muslims). Given the large number of variables in our model, our sample size per religion does not meet the five-to-one

TABLE 7.3

Coefficient Estimates for Study 2 (Singapore)

	Brand Loyalty	Self-Brand Connection
Watches		
Fundamentalism	.39 (.12)**	.36 (.12)**
Spirituality	−.11 (.13)	−.15 (.13)
Product satisfaction	.67 (.07)**	.68 (.06)**
Social desirability response	.10 (.11)	−.02 (.11)
Sex	.09 (.07)	.06 (.07)
Age	.14 (.06)*	.11 (.06)
Education	−.10 (.06)	−.10 (.06)
Income	.05 (.06)	.07 (.06)
R^2	.51	.50
Cell Phones		
Fundamentalism	.37 (.11)**	.37 (.12)**
Spirituality	−.39 (.11)**	−.20 (.13)
Product satisfaction	.75 (.06)**	.60 (.06)**
Social desirability response	.01 (.10)	.07 (.10)
Sex	−.08 (.06)	−.11 (.06)
Age	−.11 (.06)	.03 (.06)
Education	−.07 (.06)	−.13 (.06)*
Income	−.06 (.06)	−.11 (.06)
R^2	.59	.43

Note: $^*p < .05$, $^{**}p < .01$.

ratio required for estimation using an *SEM* approach (Bentler & Chou, 1987). Thus, we conducted a series of regression analyses for each specific religion, in which brand loyalty and self-brand connection were the dependent variables and fundamentalism was the key independent variable. In addition, all regressions included the control variables discussed earlier. This analysis revealed that among Christians, fundamentalism is positively related to both brand loyalty to cell phones ($b = .33$, $p < .001$) and self-brand connection to watches ($b = .23$, $p < .10$). Among Buddhists, fundamentalism is positively related to both brand loyalty to watches ($b = .20$, $p < .10$) and self-brand connection to watches ($b = .20$, $p < .10$). Fundamentalism, however, exhibits no significant relationship to either brand loyalty or self-brand connection among Muslims.

Collectively, these religion-specific results appear weaker than our overall findings. We believe this discrepancy is largely due to the greater degree of variation in fundamentalism when all three religions are combined (M = 4.79, SD = 1.49), compared to when they are examined separately (Buddhists: M = 3.80, SD = 1.28; Christians: M = 4.56, SD = 1.35; Muslims: M = 6.01, SD = 0.81). This limited variance may attenuate the relationship between fundamentalism and religiosity among these subgroups. This attenuation is particularly noticeable among Muslims, where the lowest level of fundamentalism among our 100 individual respondents is 4.00 (out of a possible 7.00).

This pattern in fundamentalism across religions (i.e., low among Buddhists, moderate among Christians, high among Muslims) is congruent with prior research (e.g., K. Armstrong, 2001) and suggests that Muslims should display considerably higher levels of brand connections than either Buddhists or Christians. To test this assumption, we conducted a MANOVA in which brand loyalty and self-brand connections (for both cell phones and watches) were our dependent variables and religious affiliation (i.e., Buddhist, Christian, or Muslim) was our grouping variable. Results reveal that Muslims, compared to Buddhists and Christians, exhibit significantly ($p < .01$) higher levels of brand connections to both watches and cell phones. For example, the average level of brand loyalty to their watch was 4.53 among Muslims but only 3.87 among Christians and 3.77 among Buddhists. These religion-based differences provide convergent support for the positive relationship between fundamentalism and brand connections among our combined sample and lend additional credence for the religiosity-as-conservation perspective.

Examining the role of NFCC. To probe more deeply into the nature of fundamentalism's influence on brand connections, we examined fundamentalism's underlying cognitive traits, namely, the need for order (NFO) and the need for predictability (NFP). To assess the potential influence of NFO and NFP, we compared the fit indices and coefficient estimates of the causal paths between a direct effect model (i.e., the effect of fundamentalism on brand connections) and an expanded model (i.e., with NFO and NFP included as antecedents to these constructs). When these two cognitive traits are included, the fit indices improved significantly (watches: χ_d^2 (6) = 130, $p < .01$; cell phones: χ_d^2 (6) = 106, $p < .01$), indicating that these cognitive traits play an important role in explaining the influence of fundamentalism on brand connections.

As noted earlier, fundamentalism has a positive effect on brand loyalty (cell phones: γ = .37, $p < .01$; watches: γ = .39, $p < .01$) and self-brand connection (cell phones: γ = .37, p < .01; watches: γ = .36, p < .01). After we account for the influence of NFO and NFP, however, fundamentalism still exerts a positive effect on brand loyalty (cell phones: γ = .25, p < .01; watches: γ = .30, p < .01) but not on self-brand connection (cell phones: γ = .04, p = *ns*; watches: γ = –.05, p = *ns*). Thus, NFCC appears to underlie the *connections* that fundamentalists form with their brands. Conversely, the brand *loyalty* of fundamentalists appears to have little to do with their underlying NFO or predictability.

A closer examination revealed that the effects of NFCC are most strongly attributable to NFP (see coefficients in Table 7.3). The pattern of results suggests, therefore, that the driving cognitive trait behind fundamentalism's impact on brand connections is a desire for predictability. Figure 7.2 shows the relationships between fundamentalism and brand connections after controlling for the potential effects of NFP for both product categories. As shown in this figure, NFP has a direct effect on self-brand connection for cell phones but not for watches and has no direct influence on brand loyalty for either product category.

GENERAL DISCUSSION

Collective Findings and Theoretical Implications

Like many social scientists, marketing scholars appear to have assumed that secularism was an inevitable outgrowth of modernization and that religiosity had little relevance for theories of social behavior. This assumption has proved premature, as modern education, politics, and warfare are all intimately tied to religious issues (K. Armstrong, 2001). As shown in our two studies involving hundreds of respondents across three religious traditions, two cultures, and four product categories, religiosity also plays an important role in the connections that consumers form with their brands. In aggregate, we found that fundamentalism is consistently and positively related to brand loyalty and self-brand connections (see Table 7.4 for a summary of our main effects across both studies). Thus, it appears that individuals who hold a fundamentalist religious orientation are more likely to exhibit stronger connections to their brands compared to individuals lacking this orientation.

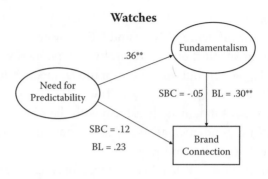

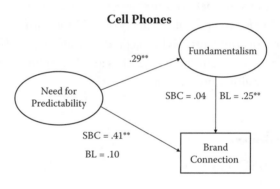

Note:*p < .05, **p < .01

FIGURE 7.2
The influence of need for predictability on religious fundamentalism and brand connection (Study 2). SBC = self brand connection. BL = brand loyalty.

At the surface, the positive relationship between fundamentalism and brand connections may seem incongruent. Despite their differences, the world's major religions all appear united in their admonitions about the hazards of becoming overly attached to fleeting material objects (Smith, 1991). Thus, fundamentalists, who are usually quite adamant about the importance of following the tenets of divine scripture in a highly literal fashion, might be expected to exhibit relatively weak connections to worldly possessions such as cars, clothing, and fashion accessories. So why does our evidence so consistently suggest exactly the opposite?

TABLE 7.4

Summary of the Direct Effects of Religiosity Across Studies 1 and 2

	Automobiles	Jeans	Watches	Cell Phones
Fundamentalism (+)				
Brand loyalty	+	+	+	+
Self-brand connection	Ø	+	+	+
Spirituality (–)				
Brand loyalty	–	Ø	Ø	–
Self-brand connection	Ø	Ø	Ø	Ø

Note: + denotes hypothesized positive relationship is supported, – denotes hypothesized negative relationship is supported, Ø denotes hypothesized relationship is not supported.

These findings appear much more orderly upon closer inspection of the cognitive motives underlying the recent rise in worldwide religious fundamentalism. As documented by K. Armstrong (2001), fundamentalism is in large part a reaction against the fears and anxieties associated with rapid technological, social, and cultural changes, as fundamentalists "feel that they are battling against forces that threaten their most sacred values" (p. xviii).

As evidenced by our MDS results (Study 1), for fundamentalist consumers, this battle appears to be viewed as a war between conservation and change. Thus, fundamentalists seek the protection and security of familiar entities, including branded objects. The notion that brands provide a sense of meaning and security is a growing theme among consumer researchers (Escalas & Bettman, 2003; Fournier, 1998; Holt, 2002). For example, Fournier (1998) demonstrated that stable consumer–brand relations promote a sense of meaning. Our results support this perspective, as it appears that brands provide fundamentalists with a means to express their beliefs and make sense of their experience in a seemingly hostile and uncertain world. Although fundamentalists may seek to avoid particular brands (e.g., the Playboy Channel), widespread brand proliferation makes it possible for them to seek security and predictability in brands closely aligned with their belief system (e.g., the Christian Broadcasting Network).

As a means of further diagnosing fundamentalism's underlying cognitive traits, we examined the influence of two aspects of an individual's NFCC (i.e., NFO, NFP). This analysis reveals that among these two cognitive traits, NFP is most closely associated with fundamentalism. Thus, individuals high in fundamentalism appear to be strongly motivated by a "desire for certainty in their lives" (Webster & Kruglanski, 1994, p. 1050). This finding challenges traditional stereotypes that regard fundamentalists as simply closed-minded dogmatists. Instead, our results suggest that fundamentalists are seekers of a predictable set of responses to life's uncertainties. Thus, traditional notions about the motives underlying fundamentalism may be incomplete.

This recent upswing in fundamentalism can no longer be relegated to the sidelines of our attention, as persuasively argued by Armstrong (2001). She noted this rise of fundamentalism has been seen across every major world religion, and in some cases (such as among Muslims in Singapore) this tide of fundamentalism is quite high. This is an important development for social scientists interested in the influence of religion on human behavior. As shown by our results, fundamentalism is empirically distinct from spirituality and appears to dominate spirituality in terms of how individuals relate to branded products. Thus, we encourage marketing scholars interested in understanding the role of religiosity to use caution in employing global measures of religiosity, as such an approach may mask important nuances in religiosity's specific dimensions.

The importance of examining multiple dimensions of religiosity is evident when attempting to decipher the relationship between spirituality and brand connections. As shown in both Tables 7.2 and 7.3, our *SEM* models, which account for the influence of both spirituality and fundamentalism, suggests that spirituality is unrelated (and at times negatively related) to both brand loyalty and self-brand connections. In contrast, the bivariate correlations shown in Table 7.1 provide the impression that spirituality is *positively* related to these two forms of brand connections. This "reversal paradox" (Messick & van de Geer, 1981) is a classic example of how bivariate relationships can be misleading because of a failure to account for the influence of a suppressor variable (in this case fundamentalism). To examine this issue, we reanalyzed the bivariate relationships between spirituality and both measures of brand connection across all four product categories using a partial correlation analysis controlling for the influence of fundamentalism. These analyses revealed that after accounting for fundamentalism, spirituality is statistically unrelated to brand loyalty or self-brand connections ($r < .05$, $p = ns$). Burroughs and Rindfleisch (2002) recently suggested that values such as religiosity exhibit a dynamic and interactive quality. Our research supports and extends their work by showing that religiosity is a multifaceted construct and that both the spirituality and the fundamentalism facets need to be simultaneously incorporated in order to obtain a richer understanding of how religiosity influences consumer behavior.

Beyond those interested in religiosity per se, we believe that our findings should also be of interest to brand management scholars, who have long searched for a means to identify individuals whose connection to brands transcends multiple product categories (e.g., Frank, 1967; Tucker, 1964). Oliver (1999) referred to these individuals as the "inherently loyal" and noted that the search for individual difference markers of such individuals has been empirically bankrupt. Similarly, Fournier (1998) acknowledged that consumer researchers know little about why some consumers become emotionally connected to their brands whereas others do not. Prior searches for general predictors of brand connections (i.e., loyalty) have often focused on demographic or lifestyle differences but have had very little success identifying systematic effects for these types of variables (e.g., Cunningham, 1956; Frank, 1967). Likewise, prior studies of the influence of religious affiliation or church attendance have exhibited inconsistent relations to brand behavior (McDaniel & Burnett, 1990; Wilkes et al., 1986). Our results provide a fresh direction to this search by suggesting that the desire for conservation, as expressed through fundamentalism, serves as one possible marker of propensity to form brand connections.

Managerial Implications

Our findings suggest that product managers need to carefully consider the influence of religiosity on customer behavior. As noted by Wuthnow (1998), "The dry spell of secularism is over" (p. 1). Although this may be true, it appears that for residents in modern industrial societies, religiosity is a supplement, rather than a substitute, to secularism. Thus, religion's spiritual dimension, which has traditionally encouraged transcendence from worldly objects, may be giving ground to the fundamental dimension, which appears to foster both cognitive loyalty and strong emotional connections to branded products. Thus, a strong base of fundamentalist customers should be viewed as a potentially important brand franchise. Moreover, the fertility rate of fundamentalist Christians is far above national averages (Hout, Greeley, & Wilde, 2001), which suggests that this segment will only grow larger in the years ahead.

In general, firms appear to pay attention to fundamentalists only when an organized group of these individuals boycotts its products or raises religious-based objections. The recent case of the meetings between the "Big Three" U.S. automobile manufacturers and the Evangelical Environmental Network (www.whatwouldjesusdrive.org) is a good example of this catch-as-catch-can perspective. On the basis of our findings, firms may wish to take a much more proactive stance in developing relationships with fundamentalists. A healthy body of research on NFCC suggests that once individuals with a high need for predictability make a preference decision, they exhibit considerable confidence in their choice and are resistant to persuasion attempts to the contrary (e.g., Kossowska et al., 2002; Kruglanski et al., 1997; Kruglanski & Webster, 1996). As noted by Kruglanski and Webster (1996, p. 278), these individuals prefer to "fight rather than switch." Thus, once fundamentalists are attracted to a brand, they are likely to avoid and discount discrepant information such as appeals to switch to a new cellular phone service. As noted by Oliver (1999), this ability to remain vigilant to a particular brand and shun competitive appeals is an increasingly valuable commodity in a fragmented and hypercompetitive marketplace.

Given our findings about fundamentalism's underlying cognitive motives and traits, appeals to tradition and predictability may be a particularly effective means of marketing to these individuals. For example, campaigns that stress how a product or service delivers consistent and predictable performance should help attract these individuals to a brand and maintain them as part of its franchise. Although fundamentalism is clearly not as outwardly identifiable as traditional demographically based segmentation variables, individuals high in fundamentalist religious values should be easily reachable through one of the many mass media channels or programs that cater to them (e.g., the 700 Club, Focus on the Family, etc.). Marketers could also target social activities and organizations that appeal to individuals with strong fundamentalist religious values (e.g., Promise Keepers, Young Republicans, etc.).

Limitations and Future Research Directions

Although our findings appear quite consistent across two countries, three religions, and four product categories, all of the products we examined could be considered durable goods. It remains to be seen if religious fundamentalism also engenders commitment to nondurables. On the one hand, nondurables generally lack the deep symbolic and psychological meanings found in automobiles and clothing. On the other hand, consumers appear to exhibit considerable loyalty and connection to several nondurable brands (e.g., Coke vs. Pepsi). Moreover, recall that fundamentalists' underlying motive appears to be a need for predictability in their lives. Thus, fundamentalists may actually exhibit even stronger brand commitment for nondurable products because these items are purchased relatively frequently and, thus, provide a means for ensuring predictability in one's daily routine. Nevertheless, an investigation of the role of religiosity on commitment to nondurable brands would complement and extend our research.

Our initial investigations of the possible cognitive traits underlying the relationship between religiosity and brand connections reveals that the need for predictability, rather than the need for order, underlies the influence of fundamentalism's relationship to self-brand connections but not its relationship to brand loyalty. Although prior research on cognitive motives has shown that needs for predictability and order are strongly related (Neuberg et al., 1997), our results reveal that these two cognitive traits have differential impacts on brand connections. Likewise, brand researchers have suggested that brand loyalty and self-brand connections are highly related (Escalas & Bettman, 2003). Our results suggest that despite this relationship, these brand-related constructs may have different antecedents. Future research would be helpful in elucidating the differences between predictability and order as well as the distinctions between the cognitive traits and motives underlying cognitive preferences versus emotional connections.

Our results suggest that the need for cognitive closure plays an important role by motivating an individual to adopt religious fundamentalism. It is possible that this need for closure may also motivate other forms of fundamentalism such as conservative political or family ideologies. Thus, it may be possible to expand our findings into of other types of fundamentalism such as the influence of political conservatism on brand connections. Furthermore, it is also possible that other cognitive traits such as risk aversion or a need for control might also play an important role in influencing the connection between religiosity and brand connections. Future research can make a useful contribution by examining these possibilities.

CONCLUSION

By exploring religiosity's influence on brand connections, this chapter expands the conceptual boundaries of the connected customer and complements several of the other chapters in this collection, especially Baba Shiv's (Chapter 6) essay on the emotional basis of brand connections and Nuno Camacho, Vardit Landsman, and Stefan Stremersch's examination of the connections between patients and physicians (Chapter 5). In contrast to marketing's decidedly secular focus, our research suggests that religiosity plays an important role in shaping the strength of the connections that customers form with their brands. We hope that our research will inspire both marketing scholars and practitioners to more closely examine the interesting and intricate nexus between God and Mammon.

REFERENCES

Alphonso, C., & Bonoguore, T. (2007, September 15). Creationism raised as Ont. election issue. *Globe and Mail.*

Altemeyer, B., & Hunsberger, B. (1992). Authoritarianism, religious fundamentalism, quest, and prejudice. *International Journal for the Psychology of Religion, 2*(2), 113–133.

Armstrong, K. (2001). *The battle for God: A history of fundamentalism.* New York: Ballantine.

Balmer, R. (2006). *Mine eyes have seen the glory.* New York: Oxford University Press.

Barro, R. J., & McCleary, R. M. (2003, October). Religion and economic growth across countries. *American Sociological Review, 68*, 760–781.

Bartels, R. (1976). *The history of marketing thought* (2nd ed.). Columbus, OH: Grid.

Belk, R. W., Wallendorf, M., & Sherry, J. F., Jr. (1989, March). The sacred and the profane in consumer behavior: Theodicy on the odyssey. *Journal of Consumer Research, 15*, 1–38.

Bentler, P. M., & Chou, C. P. (1987, August). Practical issues in structural modeling. *Sociological Methods and Research, 16*, 78–117.

Bettman, J. R., Luce, M. F., & Payne, J. W. (1998, December). Constructive consumer choice processes. *Journal of Consumer Research, 25*, 187–217.

Burroughs, J. E., & Rindfleisch, A. (2002, December). Materialism and well-being: A conflicting values perspective. *Journal of Consumer Research, 29*, 348–370.

Campbell, D. T., & Fiske, D. W. (1959, March). Convergent and discriminant validity by the multitrait-multimethod matrix. *Psychological Bulletin, 56*, 81–105.

Carpenter, J. A. (1997). *Revive us again: The reawakening of American fundamentalism.* New York: Oxford University Press.

Chadhuri, A., & Holbrook, M. B. (2001, April). The chain of effects from brand affect to brand performance: The role of brand loyalty. *Journal of Marketing, 65*, 81–93.

Cornwall, M., Albrecht, S. L., Cunningham, P. H., & Pitcher, B. L. (1986). The dimensions of religiosity: A conceptual model with an empirical test. *Review of Religious Research, 27*(3), 226–244.

Cunningham, R. M. (1956, January–February). Brand loyalty: What, where, and how much? *Harvard Business Review, 34*, 116–128.

Delener, N. (1990). The effects of religious factors on perceived risk in durable goods purchase decisions. *Journal of Consumer Marketing, 7*, 27–38.

Delener, N. (1994). Religious contrasts in consumer behaviour patterns: Their dimensions and marketing implications. *European Journal of Marketing, 28*(5), 36–53.

Djupe, P. A. (2002). Religious brand loyalty and political loyalties. *Journal for the Scientific Study of Religion, 41*(1), 78–89.

Durkheim, E. (1912). *The elementary forms of religious life*. London: Allen and Unwin.

Ebaugh, H. R. (2002). Presidential address 2001 return of the sacred: Reintegrating religion in the social sciences. *Journal for the Scientific Study of Religion, 41*(3), 385–395.

Elkins, D. N., Hedstrom, L. J., Hughes, L. L., Leaf, J. A., & Saunders, C. (1988, Fall). Toward a humanistic-phenomenological spirituality: Definition, description, and measurement. *Journal of Humanistic Psychology, 28*, 5–18.

Escalas, J. E., & Bettman, J. R. (2003). You are what they eat: The influence of reference groups on consumer connections to brands. *Journal of Consumer Psychology, 13*(3), 339–348.

Eurobarometer. (2005). *Social values, science, and technology*. European Commission. Retrieved from http://ec.europa.eu/public_opinion/archives/ebs/ebs_225_report_en.pdf

Fastnow, C. J., Grant, T., & Rudolph, T. J. (1999, December). Holy roll calls: Religious traditions and voting behavior in the U.S. House. *Social Science Quarterly, 80*, 687–701.

Fornell, C., & Larcker, D. F. (1981, February). Evaluating structural equation models with unobserved variables and measurement error. *Journal of Marketing Research, 28*, 39–50.

Fournier, S. (1998, March). Consumers and their brands: Developing branding theory in consumer research. *Journal of Consumer Research, 24*, 343–373.

Francis, L. J. (2001). Christianity and dogmatism revisited: A study among 15- and 16-year-olds in the United Kingdom. *Religious Education, 96*, 211–226.

Francis, L. J., & Kaldor, P. (2002). The relationship between psychological well-being and Christian faith and practice in an Australian population sample. *Journal of the Scientific Study of Religion, 41*(1), 179–184.

Frank, R. E. (1967). Correlates of buying behavior for grocery products. *Journal of Marketing, 31*(2), 48–53.

Garbarino, E. C., & Edell, J. A. (1997, June). Cognitive effort, affect, and choice. *Journal of Consumer Research, 24*, 147–158.

Gorsuch, R. L., & Miller, W. R. (1999). Assessing spirituality. In W. R. Miller (Ed.), *Integrating spirituality into treatment* (pp. 47–64). Washington, DC: American Psychological Association.

Graduate Center of the City University of New York. (2001). *American religious identification survey*. Retrieved from www.gc.cuny.edu/faculty/research_briefs/aris.pdf

Greely, A. (1963, October). A note on the origins of religious differences. *Journal of the Scientific Study of Religion, 3*, 21–31.

Guth, J. L., Green, J. C., Kellstedt, L. A., & Smidt, C. E. (1995, May). Faith and the environment: Religious beliefs and attitudes on environmental policy. *American Journal of Political Science, 39*, 364–382.

Hadiwinata, B. S. (2002, December 5). Terrorism, religion, and global politics. *Jakarta Post*.

Harris Interactive. (2003). *American belief poll*. Rochester, NY: Harris Research.

Hill, P. C., & Pargament, K. I. (2003, January). Advances in the conceptualization and measurement of religion and spirituality. *American Psychologist, 58*, 64–74.

Hirschman, E. C. (1981, Summer). American Jewish ethnicity: Its relationship to some selected aspects of consumer behavior. *Journal of Marketing, 45*, 102–110.

Holt, D. B. (2002, June). Why do brands cause trouble? A dialectical theory of consumer culture and branding. *Journal of Consumer Research, 29*, 70–90.

Houghton, D. C., & Grewal, R. (2000, November). Please, let's get an answer—any answer: Need for consumer cognitive closure. *Psychology and Marketing, 17*, 911–934.

Hout, M., Greeley, A., & Wilde, M. J. (2001, September). The demographic imperative in religious change in the United States. *American Journal of Sociology, 107*, 468–500.

Jarvis, C. B., MacKenzie, S. B., & Podsakoff, P. M. (2003, September). A critical review of construct indicators and measurement model misspecification in marketing and consumer research. *Journal of Consumer Research, 30*, 199–218.

Jöreskog, K., & Sörbom, D. (1993). *LISREL 8 user's reference guide*. Chicago: Scientific Software International.

Kardes, F. R. (1996). In defense of experimental consumer psychology. *Journal of Consumer Psychology, 5*(3), 279–296.

Kavanaugh, J. F. (1991). *Following Christ in a consumer society: The spirituality of cultural resistance* (Rev. ed.). Maryknoll, NY: Orbis Books.

Keller, K. L. (2003). *Building, measuring, and managing brand equity* (2nd ed.). Upper Saddle River, NJ: Prentice Hall.

Kim, Y., & Seidlitz, L. (2002, June). Spirituality moderates the effect of stress on emotional and physical adjustment. *Personality and Individual Differences, 32*, 1377–1390.

Kossowska, M., Van Hill, A., Chun, W. Y., & Kruglanski, A. W. (2002). The need for cognitive closure scale: Structure, cross-cultural invariance, and comparison of mean ratings between European-American, and East Asian samples. *Psychologica Belgica, 42*(4), 267–286.

Kruglanski, A. W. (1989). *Lay epistemics and human knowledge: Cognitive and motivational bases*. New York: Plenum.

Kruglanski, A. W., Atash, M. N., DeGrada, E., Mannetti, L., Pierro, A., & Webster, D. M. (1997). Psychological theory testing versus psychometric nay-saying: Comment on Neuberg et al.'s (1997) critique of the need for closure scale. *Journal of Personality and Social Psychology, 73*(5), 1005–1016.

Kruglanski, A. W., & Webster, D. M. (1996, April). Motivated closing of the mind: "Seizing" and "freezing." *Psychological Review, 103*, 263–283.

Kruskal, J. B., & Wish, M. (1978). *Multidimensional scaling*. Beverly Hills, CA: Sage.

LaBarbera, P. A., & Gurhan-Canli, Z. (1997). The role of materialism, religiosity, and demographics in subjective well-being. *Psychology and Marketing, 14*(1), 71–97.

Marx, K. (1912). *Capital: A critique of political economy*. Chicago: Charles H. Kerr.

McDaniel, S. W., & Burnett, J. J. (1990). Consumer religiosity and retail store evaluative criteria. *Journal of the Academy of Marketing Science, 18*(2), 101–112.

Messick, D. M., & van de Geer, J. (1981). A reversal paradox. *Psychological Bulletin, 90*(3), 582–593.

Mick, D. G. (1996, September). Are studies of dark side variables confounded by socially desirable responding? *Journal of Consumer Research, 23*, 106–119.

Muñiz, A. M., Jr., & Schau, H. J. (2005, March). Religiosity in the abandoned Apple Newton brand community. *Journal of Consumer Research, 31*, 737–747.

Neuberg, S. L., Nicole, J. T., & West, S. G. (1997, June). What the need for closure scale measures and what it does not: Toward differentiating among related epistemic motives. *Journal of Personality and Social Psychology, 72*, 1396–1412.

O'Guinn, T. C., & Belk, R. W. (1989, September). Heaven on earth: Consumption at Heritage Village, USA. *Journal of Consumer Research, 16*, 227–238.

Oliver, R. L. (1997). *Satisfaction: A behavioral perspective on the consumer.* New York: McGraw-Hill.

Oliver, R. L. (1999). Whence consumer loyalty [Special issue]? *Journal of Marketing, 63*, 33–44.

Paulhus, D. L. (1992). *The balanced inventory of desirable responding reference manual, BIDR version 6.* Vancouver: University of British Columbia.

Petty, R. E., Cacioppo, J. T., & Schumann, D. (1983, September). Central and peripheral routes to advertising effectiveness: The moderating role of involvement. *Journal of Consumer Research, 10*, 135–146.

Pew Forum. (2008). *U.S. religious landscape survey.* Washington, DC: Author.

Podsakoff, P. M., & Organ, D. W. (1986). Self-reports in organizational research: Problems and prospects. *Journal of Management, 12*(4), 531–544.

Poloma, M. M., & Pendleton, B. F. (1990). Religious domains and general well-being. *Social Indicators Research, 22*(3), 255–276.

Roccas, S. (2005). Religiosity and value systems. *Journal of Social Issues, 61*(4), 747–759.

Roccas, S., Sagiv, L., Schwartz, S. H., & Kanfo, A. (2002, June). The big five personality factors and personal values. *Personality and Social Psychology Bulletin, 28*, 789–801.

Rokeach, M. (1973). *The nature of human values.* New York: Free Press.

Saroglou, V. (2002). Beyond dogmatism: The need for closure as related to religion. *Mental Health, Religion and Culture, 5*(2), 184–194.

Saroglou, V., Delpierre, V., & Dernelle, R. (2004). Values and religiosity: A meta-analysis of studies using Schwartz's model. *Personality and Individual Differences, 37*(4), 721–734.

Saroglou, V., & Muñoz-García, A. (2008). Individual differences in religion and spirituality: An issue of personality traits and/or values. *Journal of the Scientific Study of Religion, 47*(1), 83–101.

Schwartz, S. H. (1992). Universals in the content and structure of values: Theoretical advances and empirical tests in 20 countries. In M. Zanna (Ed.), *Advances in experimental social psychology* (pp. 1–65). Orlando, FL: Academic Press.

Schwartz, S. H., & Huismans, S. (1995). Value priorities and religiosity in four Western nations. *Social Psychology Quarterly, 58*, 88–107.

Seidlitz, L., Abernathy, A. D., Duberstein, P. R., Evinger, J. S., Chang, T. H., & Lewis, B. L. (2002). Development of the spiritual transcendence index. *Journal for the Scientific Study of Religion, 19*(1), 60–67.

Sherry, J. F., Jr., & Kozinets, R. V. (2007). Comedy of the commons: Nomadic spirituality and the burning man festival. *Consumer Culture Theory: Research in Consumer Behavior, 11*, 119–147.

Shiv, B., & Fedorikhin, A. (1999, December). Heart and mind in conflict: The interplay of affect and cognition in consumer decision making. *Journal of Consumer Research, 26*, 278–292.

Smith, H. (1991). *The world's religions.* San Francisco: HarperSanFrancisco.

Sood, J., & Nasu, Y. (1995, September). Religiosity and nationality: An exploratory study of their effect on consumer behavior in Japan and the United States. *Journal of Business Research, 34*, 1–9.

Spilka, B., Hood, R. W., Jr., & Gorsuch, R. (1985). *The psychology of religion: An empirical approach.* Englewood Cliffs, NJ: Prentice Hall.

Stark, R., & Glock, C. Y. (1968). *American piety: The nature of religious commitment.* Berkeley: University of California Press.

Statistics Singapore. (2000). Retrieved from www.singstat.gov/sg/stats/themes/people/demo.html

Tellis, G. J., Stremersch, S., & Yin, E. (2003). The international takeoff of new products: Economics, culture, and country innovativeness. *Marketing Science, 22*(2), 188–208.

Tucker, W. T. (1964, August). The development of brand loyalty. *Journal of Marketing Research, 1*, 32–35.

Turley, J. (2007, November 19). When religion becomes fair game. *USA Today*, p. 15A.

U.S. Bureau of the Census. (2000). *Resident population estimates of the United States.* Retrieved from www.census.gov/population/estimates/nation/intfile2-1.txt

Vermeir, I., Van Kenhove, P., & Hendrickx, H. (2002). The influence of need for closure on consumer's choice behavior. *Journal of Economic Psychology, 23*(6), 703–727.

Weaver, G. R., & Agle, B. R. (2002). Religiosity and ethical behavior in organizations: A symbolic interactionist perspective. *Academy of Management Review, 27*(1), 77–97.

Weber, M. (1930). *The Protestant ethic and the spirit of capitalism* (T. Parsons, Ed.). Boston: Unwin Hyman.

Webster, D. M., & Kruglanski, A. W. (1994). Individual differences in need for cognitive closure. *Journal of Personality and Social Psychology, 67*(6), 1049–1062.

Wilkes, R. E., Burnett, J. J., & Howell, R. D. (1986, Spring). On the meaning and measurement of religiosity in consumer research. *Journal of the Academy of Marketing Science, 14*, 47–56.

Wong, N., Rindfleisch, A., & Burroughs, J. E. (2003, June). Do reverse-worded items confound measures in cross-cultural consumer research? The case of the material values scale. *Journal of Consumer Research, 30*, 72–91.

Wulff, D. M. (1997). *Psychology of religion: Classic and contemporary* (2nd ed.). New York: Wiley.

Wuthnow, R. (1998). *After heaven: Spirituality in America since the 1950s.* Berkeley: University of California Press.

Zajonc, R. B., & Markus, H. (1982). Affective and cognitive factors in preferences. *Journal of Consumer Research, 9*, 123–131.

Zimmer, H. (1993). Buddhahood. In R. Eastman (Ed.), *The ways of religion* (2nd ed., pp. 65–73). New York: Oxford University Press.

Zinnbauer, B. J., Pargament, K. I., & Scott, A. B. (1999, December). The emerging meanings of religiousness and spirituality: Problems and prospects. *Journal of Personality, 67*, 889–919.

APPENDIX

Measurement Items

	United States				Singapore			
	Automobile		Jeans		Watches		Cell Phones	
	Loading	CR	Loading	CR	Loading	CR	Loading	CR
Brand Loyalty (Chadhuri and Holbrook 2001)		.95		.87		.94		.96
1. The next time I am in the market for a vehicle, I plan to buy the same brand I currently own.	.92		.65		.86		.87	
2. I intend to keep buying the same brand of vehicle for the foreseeable future.	—		.77		—		.96	
3. I am committed to my current brand of vehicle.	.97		—		.97		—	
4. Next time I shop for a vehicle, I would be willing to pay more for my current brand than other brands.	.76		.74		.69		.86	
Brand Connection (Escalas and Bettman 2002)		.98		.98		.97		.98
1. This brand reflects who I am.	.92		.91		.98		.91	
2. I can identify with this brand.	.97		.92		.96		.95	
3. I feel a personal connection to this brand.	—		.96		—		—	
4. I (can) use this brand to communicate who I am to other people	.92		.96		.87		.92	
5. I consider this brand to be "me".	.92		—		.83		.94	

Continued

APPENDIX (*Continued*)

Measurement Items

| | United States | | | | Singapore | | | |
| | Automobile | | Jeans | | Watches | | Cell Phones | |
	Loading	CR	Loading	CR	Loading	CR	Loading	CR
Product Satisfaction (Oliver 1997)		.96		.96		.98		.97
1. This is one of the best vehicles I could have bought.	.88		.86		.86		.86	
2. This vehicle is exactly what I need.	.68		.87		.98		.98	
3. I am satisfied with my decision to buy this vehicle.	.94		.83		.93		.90	
4. I have truly enjoyed owning this vehicle.	.97		—		—		—	
5. Owning this vehicle has been a good experience.	—		.95		.99		.91	

| | United States | | Singapore | |
	Loading	CR	Loading	CR
Religiosity—Fundamentalism (Altemeyer and Hunsberger 1992)		.98		.97
1. To lead the most meaningful life, one must belong to the one true religion.	.98		—	
2. Whenever science and sacred scripture conflict, science must be wrong.	.83		.72	
3. My religion teaches, without error, God's truths.	.99		.96	
4. God will severely punish those who abandon his true religion.	.91		.88	
5. My religion shows the best way to serve God and should not be compromised.	—		.88	
6. It is not enough to be a good person, one must also believe in the right religion.	.95		.96	

	λ	CR	λ	CR
Religiosity—Spirituality (Siedlitz et al., 2002)		.96		.96
1. I maintain an inner awareness of God's presence in my life.	.89		.76	
2. Even when I experience problems, I can find a spiritual peace within.	.93		.72	
3. I try to strengthen my relationship with God.	.93		—	
4. Maintaining my spirituality is a priority for me.	1		.89	
5. God helps me to rise above my immediate circumstances.	.98		.95	
6. My spirituality helps me to understand my life's purpose.	—		.87	
7. I experience a deep communion with God.	.96		.94	
Need for Order (Kruglanski, Webster, and Klem 1993)				.96
1. I find that establishing a consistent routine enables me to enjoy life.			—	
2. I enjoy having a clear and structured mode of life.			.91	
3. I like a well ordered life with regular hours.			.94	
4. I like having a place for everything and everything in its place.			.83	
Need for Predictability (Kruglanski, Webster, and Klem 1993)				.97
1. I like predictable situations.			—	
2. I don't like o be with people who are capable of unexpected actions.			.89	
3. I prefer to socialize with familiar friends because I know what to expect of them.			.90	
4. I like the certainty of going into a situation and knowing what will happen.			.95	

Note: CR = Composite reliability.

8

Brand Platforms as Strategic Investments: Leveraging Customer Connections to Manage Profitability, Growth, and Risk

Rajendra K. Srivastava and Thorsten Wiesel

Making marketing accountable has become a critical focus of most firms as they struggle to show how major investments lead to increased performance and shareholder value. The study of marketing metrics has been the top research priority of the Marketing Science Institute for the past 6 years. Yet, what is not measured is not tracked. What is not tracked is not managed and nurtured. Consequently, market-based off-balance sheet assets such as brands and customers that drive cash flow continue to be a "blind spot" in senior management decisions ranging from resource allocation to M&A valuations. And, all too often, companies focus on identifying marketing actions that can deliver acceptable short-term metrics rather on developing strategies to outdistance competitors. Others try to come up with a silver bullet—and fail.

This myopic perspective is especially surprising given the strong linkage between customer equity and brand equity (Hogan et al., 2002; Keller, 1993) as well as the link between customer connectivity and financial performance (Gupta, Lehmann, & Stuart, 2004; Reinartz, Thomas, & Kumar, 2005) in the marketing literature. Thus, customer-centric brands provide a platform to develop sustainable long-term connections with customers that, in turn, improve long-term performance and value. With such a perspective, which underscores the strategic importance of customer connections in managing profitability, growth and risk are especially important if marketing is to earn a seat in the boardroom.

Marketing professionals have historically found it difficult to measure and communicate to other disciplines and to top management the value created by marketing activities. All too often, justification of marketing and communication initiatives is restricted to their impact on revenue generation. But marketers do create value in other ways. Marketing actions do lead to an acceleration of the market's acceptance of new products, to enhanced customer retention and loyalty, to an improvement in the size and quality of customer bases, and to price premiums and other desirable payoffs. Such financial outcomes suggest that marketing activities are often strategic investments, not tactical, intangible expenses. Yet, this reality is in conflict with another. The "depreciation schedule for brands and customers" is but a single year (as marketing is a "cost" center; expenses are written off and depreciated right away). Ironically, brands and customers are among a very small set of business assets that appreciate.

Much has been achieved in theory development and empirical research since Srivastava, Shervani, and Fahey (1997, 1998, 1999) suggested that the effectiveness of marketing initiatives should be evaluated on the basis of their impact on the basic drivers of shareholder value—increase in levels of cash flow, acceleration and growth of cash flows, and reduction in volatility and vulnerability of cash flows. In addition, as per proponents of the resource-based view (RBV) of competition, investments in "rare" business assets that provide companies with sustainable competitive advantages (Hunt & Morgan, 1995; Srivastava, Fahey, & Christensen, 2001; Wernerfelt, 1984) can be expected to enhance shareholder value. Much of this recent work has focused on the impact of marketing versus R&D spend on risk and return or abnormal returns associated with marketing activities and communications such as new product announcements and strategic alliances. Results show, for example, that market-based activities and investments enhance returns and reduce both systematic and idiosyncratic risk. There are, however, two recurring limitations linked to a majority of this work. First, academic research on marketing's impact on business performance has focused on aggregate analyses using data at the *firm* level. Although these findings are helpful, most marketing strategy decisions are made at the *product-market* or *customer-segment* level. Second, when the focus has been at the more disaggregate product market or segment level, the majority of the work has leveraged short-term performance data (e.g., marketing mix models examining the relative impact of price promotions and advertising; analyses related to brand and customer equity). Third, although many marketing investments are made with an eye on future payoffs, we invariably use metrics that are backward looking. We must distinguish between backward-looking measures of the past to monitor performance and forward-looking measures to plan the future (Ambler & Roberts, 2006). Of course there are many exceptions such as Sood and Tellis's (in press) recent research examining the impact of innovation on stock returns. A good review of the current state of research on marketing's impact on firm value can be found in Srinivasan and Hanssens (in press).

The objective of this chapter is not to criticize what we are doing. Rather the goal is to identify a useful area of inquiry that deserves attention and that will enhance the strategic, as opposed to tactical, role of marketing within business organizations. Much as the research, development, and engineering community has focused on product platforms to help justify investments in projects that have long-term, uncertain, and intangible pay-offs, marketers can position brands, customers, and channels as platforms that enhance profitability and growth while mitigating risk. For example, strong brands enhance productivity of marketing spend (Boulding, Lee, & Staelin, 1994; Keller, 1993), provide avenues for future growth through brand extensions, reduce volatility in returns through persistent sales based on higher levels of brand loyalty, and are less vulnerable to competitive moves (Srivastava et al., 1998).

In this chapter, we first briefly examine the strategic role of marketing investments and how they vary over the life cycle. Next we take a quick look at the concept of product platforms and how the engineering professionals have leveraged them to better justify investments in product platforms. We then focus on how customer-centric brand platforms provide much the same benefits albeit by different mechanisms. Finally we outline propositions linking customer-centric brand platforms to business and financial performance that provide fodder for future research.

THE NATURE OF STRATEGIC MARKETING INVESTMENTS

Figure 8.1 presents a framework centered around a typical product or industry life cycle. As illustrated in Figure 8.1, the impact of marketing on shareholder value can be captured through influence on enhancing, accelerating, and sustaining cash flows during introduction, growth, maturity,

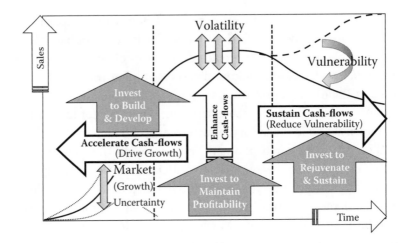

FIGURE 8.1
Investing to manage profitability growth and risk over the product life cycle.

and decline phases of a product life cycle. Each phase of this life cycle poses different challenges. The early (introduction and growth) stages are fraught with uncertainty while brimming with opportunity. Risks in early stages of the life cycle can be reduced or managed through a variety of ways. Market intelligence and agility can help shift resources from poor performing innovations that should be rationalized to ones that are performing better than expected and should be nurtured. This is indeed the logic behind exit and growth options, respectively, in the realm of real options. Investments in marketing activities such as advertising and promotions can help accelerate adoption and cash-flow cycles. Furthermore, existing market-based assets such as brands and channels can be leveraged to speed up adoption while simultaneously enhancing the likelihood of success—a strategy managed to distinction by the likes of Apple.

During the maturity phase, market-based assets serve to reduce volatility as investments in strategies, as increasing customer-switching costs serves to stabilize sales and profitability. Furthermore, as the product-market focus shifts from innovation to efficiency, it is the less established and midrange brands that are more susceptible to competitive inroads. Finally, during the decline phase, market-based assets help enhance the longevity of cash flows.

Although many marketing-based assets such as brands, customers, channels, and innovations have long-term implications, their impact on business processes and performance is often assessed based on short-term quarterly metrics. Much can be learned from the engineering community regarding communicating the value of intangibles. A technology that does not exist, with unproven applications and hidden competition, is no more tangible than future customers with suspect loyalties and ever-increasing price sensitivity.

THE CONCEPT OF PRODUCT PLATFORMS

Product platforms, which are component subsystem assets shared across a line of products, have been glorified in the popular business press for their cost- and time-saving benefits (Kogut & Kulatilaka, 1994; Krishnan, 2003). The concept of a product platform is embedded in the answer to the following question: How do you park six Hondas in one garage? Well, it is not a six-car garage but multiple Honda products—car, motorbike, personal watercraft, snowmobile, lawn mower, scooter, and snowblower all squeezed into a garage. All these products ride on Honda's small-engine expertise. They share some common modular components; some are modified depending on the application (carburetors for watercrafts have to be protected from water) whereas others are unique (bikes need wheels, watercrafts need hulls, snowmobiles need skis). This allows product platforms to exploit internal firm synergies such as shared manufacturing capacity, inventories, economies of scale, and purchasing power in sourcing components to increase efficiency and contain costs. By spreading the cost of product innovation of modularized components across multiple end products, companies leveraging product platforms can outspend competition and end up with better differentiated products. Finally, by creating products as combinations of modular component parts, companies such as Dell are able to deliver greater variety at lower costs based on the concept of mass customizations (Sanchez, 1999).

Importantly, product platforms can also help companies bring product innovations to market more quickly, especially of technology from the older generation that can be reused for the next generation. This in turn provides a cycle-time advantage that, even if small, is critical because it can be compounded over multiple generations. A fast-cycle competitor can therefore overtake a pioneer. A strategy based on frequent cycles such as that implemented by Intel with the x86 and Pentium platform will reinforce the advantage.

Product platforms can thus be leveraged to reduce both time to market and time to volume, the latter helping in accelerating the experience curve, thereby reducing costs. Products brought to market faster and at a lower cost are bound to have a distinct competitive advantage.

Sustainability is enhanced and competitive risks are mitigated by staying ahead of competition through better differentiation and lower total cost of ownership associated with greater experience in the supply chain. Finally, because future generations have to build on existing products, investments in current R&D can be justified by the promise of fruits in the future. For example, many electronic components that might go into a digital camera (sensors, microcontroller, microprocessors) can be justified based on camera applications designed for use with personal computers, still cameras, mobile cameras in cell phones, and movie cameras. Thus the engineering community is able to use "technology road maps" or future visions to justify investments in product platforms.

CUSTOMER AND BRAND PLATFORMS

If Intel's x86 and Pentium product platform provide a compelling illustration for the viability of product platforms, Microsoft's investments in building and nurturing a customer base provide an even more compelling argument for customer-centric brand platforms. Microsoft "invests" in a customer platform by frequently distributing beta samples and using viral marketing. Although Intel is known for its time-to-market culture and competence, Microsoft is known for often being late to market. But Microsoft is able to leverage its customer-installed base to X-sell related products and accelerate time-to-market penetration. For example, Microsoft is able to leverage customer relationships and experience in the Windows and Office product markets to force an entry into an "adjacent" Windows Mobile market for 3G phones. Microsoft's strategy of developing customer bases, up-selling and cross-selling, retaining through bundling and experience-based switching costs, and expanding into adjacent markets enables controlled growth while mitigating risk.

The customer-installed base then becomes a cash machine. Furthermore, customer-centric brand platforms result in a more diversified business portfolio and therefore reduce volatility and vulnerability. For example, although Intel's main strengths are mostly restricted to the PC area, Microsoft has leveraged its customers and brand to cover product markets ranging from operating systems in PC (Windows) and server (Windows NT) markets, PC applications, entertainment (Xbox), telecommunications (Windows Mobile), MSN, Explorer, and the newly emerging search-engine- and social-network-centered markets. The growing importance of social networks in influencing choice through peer-to-peer communications further underscores the value of customer-centric marketing practices that represent future battlegrounds for Google, Microsoft, MySpace, and Facebook.

Table 8.1 summarizes and compares benefits associated with product platforms as well as customer-centric brand platforms (of course, nothing prevents a firm from implementing strategies encompassing both). This same logic can be, and is, implemented in the services and business-to-business sectors under the label of customer solutions. General Electric (GE) famously shifted from a product and manufacturing orientation to a service-oriented company during the mid- to late '90s. This enabled GE to focus on its customers' problems rather than on selling specific products. In the process, GE serviced its competitors' products as well as its own. Resulting improvements on earning were due to a better utilization of service capacity, synergies in cross-selling equipment, consumables,

TABLE 8.1

Product and Brand/Customer Platforms

Concept	Product Platform	Brand/Customer Platform
Cost containment	Reuse, experience, modular design, shared inventory	Shared sales, service, and support; solution bundling
Growth prospects	Scalability, supply-side synergies	X-sell, up-sell, demand-synergy
Velocity	Time to market and time to volume	Time-to-market penetration
Sustainability	Differentiation, TCO	Switching cost, loyalty
Investment	Tangible (patents) and intangible know-how	Intangible (brand equity) and tangible (distribution NWs)

Note: TCO = total cost of ownership; NW = network.

components for repair and maintenance, and an enhancement of customer-switching costs (often customers such as hospitals outsourced the entire imaging [X-ray, CT scan, MRI] processes to GE and hence became dependent on GE for future expansions and improvements) and therefore loyalty. Perhaps the icing on the cake was that instead of meeting quarterly sales goals, GE now had multiple-year contracts resulting in an ever-increasing share of cash flows from recurring business—a metric that the investment community loves and that is associated with higher price-earnings multiples in the service sector. Thus GE's customer-centric solutions approach resulted not only in higher earnings but also in higher PE ratios that ran up GE's market valuation more than threefold from 1995 to 1999. Other companies have been able to reduce risk and enhance profitability by shifting from price-picking "transactional" customers to service-oriented "relationship" customers.

CUSTOMER AND BRAND PLATFORMS AND BUSINESS PERFORMANCE

Although much has been accomplished in exploring the marketing-finance interface at the aggregate/firm level, we now need to shift attention to more disaggregate analyses linking customers and brands to business performance. There is an ongoing debate regarding customer and brand equity. Rather than getting embroiled in that exchange, however, we recognize that there is considerable overlap between the two concepts. Strong brands do help in customer acquisition and retention. And customer-focused service strategies build strong brands. Therefore we posit in Table 8.2 the propositions for "customer-centric brands." These propositions provide a perspective that allows marketing managers to focus on what brand, customers, and other market-based assets bring to future performance and shift attention away from short-term metrics such as margins, sales, and return on marketing investments to longer term metrics linking the impact of these assets on long-term performance and value.

Table 8.2 summarizes the value of customer connections in enhancing business performance. Although customer connectivity and brand reputation are expected to translate into a revenue premium (incremental share and/or price), their value reflected in speed and/or risk containment is

TABLE 8.2

Research Propositions Linking Customer-Centric Brand Assets Strategies and Business Performance

1. The stronger the market-based assets (brands, customers, channels), the faster the ability to penetrate markets and the lower the risk associated with market entry.

2. The stronger a customer-centric brand, the faster the rate of market penetration and growth in cash flows in (a) emerging/geographical markets, (b) related categories, and (c) electronic channels.

3. The stronger a brand, the lower the volatility (the higher the persistence) of market share and profitability.

4. The lower the share of transactional customers, the lower the volatility in sales and profitability and the higher the market valuation ratios (P/E and M/B or Tobin's Q).

5. The greater the focus on development and implementation of customer solutions, the higher the level and the lower the volatility in cash flows.

6. The greater the level of customer–vendor interaction and the more positive the experience, the higher the customer-switching costs and the lower the vulnerability of cash flows to competitive actions.

7. The greater the focus on better serving high-value customers, the lower the turnover and the higher the customer lifetime value of customers and the higher the value of business.

8. The higher the customer turnover, the higher the cost of capital and the lower the value of business.

9. Customer-centric brand platforms reduce product-market entry risks in dynamic emerging markets by offering increased agility and trust.

10. Companies adopting customer-centric approaches are better able to expand their share of customer requirements while reducing their vulnerability to competitive actions, resulting higher levels of more persistent cash flows and in higher market valuations.

11. The stronger a customer-centric brand, the lower the vulnerability to competition and the greater the longevity of positive cash flows. In mature and declining markets, the stronger the market-based assets, the greater the longevity of positive cash flows and the lower the cost of capital and the lower idiosyncratic risk relative to peer companies in the same industry.

often ignored. For example, when a strong, existing brand can be leveraged to launch new products, the result is often faster market penetration (Proposition 1 [P1]). This ability to penetrate markets quickly is the difference between successful and less successful products in short-cycle markets. Indeed Apple could present a master class on how to leverage iPod and iPhone brands to successfully introduce new products. In addition, strong brands can be used to leverage existing customer connections to enter adjacent markets (category extensions) and markets (P2) with lower risk (P9).

Strong brand and customer relationships can be used to reduce volatility and vulnerability while enhancing profitability and market value (see P3 and P5, respectively) and shifting from transactional customers to relationship customers (P4)—a strategy used by companies as diverse as GE and Coca-Cola.

Strong customer–vendor interactions accompanied by positive experience help build stronger relationships and therefore switching costs, which results in ties that bind vendors and customers, reducing vulnerability to competitive moves (P6). These interactions also result in better customer insights and identification of more (or less) value customer. Subsequently, companies that use this information better to take care of their most valuable customers are able to reduce customer churn and cost of capital to enhance business value (see P7 and P8).

Finally, customer-centric brand platforms not only provide opportunities for growth but also reduce vulnerability to competition (P10) thereby enhancing longevity of cash flows, reducing risks and cost of capital, and driving business value (P11). This is reflected in strategies adopted by GE and IBM Global Services.

REFERENCES

Ambler, T., & Roberts, J. (2006). *Beware the silver metric: Marketing performance measurement has to be multidimensional* (Report 06-113). Cambridge, MA: Marketing Science Institute.

Bharadwaj, S., & Bhattacharya, C. (2009). *Persistent superior performance: The role of brand and category level correlates.* Unpublished manuscript, Emory University.

Boulding, W., Lee, E., & Staelin, R. (1994, May). Mastering the mix: Do advertising, promotion, and sales force activities lead to differentiation? *Journal of Marketing Research*, *31*, 159–172.

Gupta, S., Lehmann, D., & Stuart, J. A. (2004). Valuing customers. *Journal of Marketing Research*, *41*, 7–18.

Hogan, J., Lehmann, D., Merino, M., Srivastava, R., Thomas, J., & Verhoef, P. (2002). Linking customer assets to financial performance. *Journal of Services Research*, *5*(1), 26–38.

Hunt, S. D., & Morgan, R. M. (1995, April). The comparative advantage theory of competition. *Journal of Marketing*, *59*, 1–15.

Keller, K. L. (1993). Conceptualizing, measuring, and managing customer-based brand equity. *Journal of Marketing*, *57*(1), 1–22.

Kogut, B., & Kulatilaka, N. (1994, Winter). Options thinking and platform investments: Investing in opportunity. *California Management Review*, *36*, 52–71.

Krishnan, V. (2003). *Profiting from platforms: Realizing the potential and avoiding the pitfalls.* Unpublished manuscript, University of Texas at Austin.

Reinartz, W., Thomas, J., & Kumar, V. (2005). Balancing acquisition and retention resources to maximize customer profitability. *Journal of Marketing, 69*, 63–79.

Sanchez, R. (1999). Modular architectures in the marketing process [Special issue]. *Journal of Marketing, 63*, 92–111.

Sood, A., & Tellis, G. J. (in press). Do innovations really pay off? Total stock market returns to innovation. *Marketing Science.*

Srivastava, R., Shervani, T., & Fahey, L. (1997). Driving shareholder value: The role of marketing in reducing vulnerability and volatility of cash flows. *Journal of Market Focused Management, 2*, 49–64.

Srivastava, R., Shervani, T., & Fahey, L. (1999). Marketing, business processes, and shareholder value: An organizationally embedded view of marketing activities and the discipline of marketing [Special issue]. *Journal of Marketing, 63*, 168–179.

Srivastava, R. K., Shervani, T. A., & Fahey, L. (1998). Market-based assets and shareholder value: A framework for analysis. *Journal of Marketing, 62*(1), 2–18.

Srivastava, R. K., Fahey, L., & Christensen, H. K. (2001). The resource-based view and marketing: The role of market-based assets in gaining competitive advantage. *Journal of Management, 27*(6), 777–802.

Srinivasan, S., & Hanssens, D. M. (in press). Marketing and firm value: Metrics, methods, findings, and future directions. *Journal of Marketing Research.*

Wernerfelt, B. (1984). A resource-based view of the firm. *Strategic Management Journal, 5*, 171–180.

Section III

Leveraging Horizontal Connectivity Among Customers

9

The Shadow of Other People: Socialization and Social Comparison in Marketing

Ronald Burt

Voluminous marketing data record the opinion and behavior of individual customers as they state intentions and make purchases. Much of what determined the intentions and purchases, however, remains unrecorded. In shadow lies the opinion and behavior of other people—friends, neighbors, colleagues, and others. Those other people are variably connected in the surrounding social network so as to affect what any one individual can do, what he or she feels obligated to do, and what he or she feels inclined to do. Something about the network around two people makes the opinion and behavior of one contagious for the other, an effect familiar in popular metaphors about word-of-mouth advertising, building the buzz, and viral marketing.

This chapter is an overview of the two network mechanisms—socialization and social comparison—that lie beneath the popular metaphors about contagion. I have two goals for the chapter: distinguish the two mechanisms by the network conditions in which they occur, and describe how the mechanisms combine in a predictable way as they generate contagion. Neither mechanism is the whole story; at the same time, neither is completely wrong. Socialization turns out to describe the occasional, critical instance of opinion and behavior brokered between groups. Social comparison describes the more frequent instance of interpersonal influence within groups and indifference beyond the group. The only course of action that is clearly wrong is to ignore either one of the two mechanisms— and that is a course too often taken. I begin with introductions to the network mechanisms and the early research in which they were conceptualized and follow that with summary evidence on the way they combine in the actual diffusion of opinion and behavior, which connects back to the two-step flow of information discovered long ago in the influential stream of marketing research from Columbia University's Bureau for Applied Social Research and connects forward to social capital applications of network theory in contemporary research on competitive advantage. Given the role of this chapter in this book, I put aside network analyses of buyer–seller relations (e.g., DiMaggio & Louch, 1998; Frenzen & Davis, 1990) to focus on the way networks create contagion among potential buyers. Furthermore, to focus on the network mechanisms, I put aside significant differences between contagions such as the risk they pose (e.g., Van den Bulte & Lilien, 2001) or their complexity (e.g., Centola & Macy, 2007). Finally, I focus on contagion at the person-to-person level because that is where the social psychology of the network mechanisms is most intuitive. I hasten to note that such a focus comes at the cost of putting aside most studies of contagion between organizations, which are some of the most sophisticated empirical studies available (see Strang & Soule, 1998, for a review; see also Davis, Morrill, Rao, & Soule, 2008).

SOCIALIZATION MECHANISM, CONNECTIVITY CRITERION

When available data are insufficient to decide on an appropriate judgment or course of action, we can turn to friends and colleagues to discuss the matter and come to a better sense of our own position. As we talk and exchange views, we socialize one another such that we eventually express similar opinions and act in similar ways. The network prediction is that people connected by a strong relationship are likely to share similar opinion and behavior.

How It Works

The connectivity criterion—also discussed as a "cohesion" or "structural cohesion" criterion—comes to contemporary network analysis from an influential series of marketing studies conducted in the 1940s and 1950s at Columbia University. Precedent for the studies came from Muzafer Sherif's (1935, 1936) experiment on social norms among college students at Columbia University.[1] The study was based on a psychophysics experiment using a stimulus selected for its ambiguity. Students were asked to judge the distance moved by a point of light projected from 15 feet away in a dark room. The point of light was stationary but appeared to move because of random noise in human sight combined with the lack of visible reference points in the dark room (autokinetic effect; Sherif, 1936, pp. 91–92).

When students were alone and asked to evaluate the extent to which the point of light moved, evaluations converged toward a standard for each person; less than 1 inch for some students and over 7 inches for others, with 3.3 inches the average across individuals (Sherif, 1936, pp. 102–103). As Sherif (1936, p. 97) quoted from participants, the lack of a reference point made the evaluation difficult (e.g., "It was difficult to estimate the distance the light moved because of the lack of visible neighboring objects"), so people relied on their prior evaluations as the best available frame of reference (I "compared with previous distance"), which resulted in different individuals converging on different standards.

When Sherif's students made evaluations in groups of three, group standards emerged. Individual evaluations quickly converged to a group standard consistent across the individuals in the group, and the group standard persisted when the participants returned later to repeat the experiment alone. Zucker (1977) took up the persistence result to show that the arbitrary group standard could be expected to persist for a dramatically longer period of time if evaluations were embedded in a simple organizational routine (from persistence across 7 sessions in Sherif's design to persistence beyond 38 sessions if the group standard is embedded in a simple organizational routine; Zucker, 1977, p. 735).

Outside the lab, sources of contagious opinion and behavior were measured with sociometric choice data. Survey respondents were asked to name their friends or the people with whom they discuss things, then asked about the opinions or behavior of the cited people. A body of research emerged in which people connected by a sociometric link were reported to have similar opinions and behaviors. In the more influential studies (see Rogers, 1962/2003, for broad review), connected people have similar presidential preferences (Berelson, Lazarsfeld, & McPhee, 1954; Lazarsfeld, Berelson, & Gaudet, 1944), similar student opinion and activity (Festinger, Schachter, & Back, 1950), similar consumer preferences (Katz & Lazarsfeld, 1955), and similar professional practices (Coleman, Katz, & Menzel, 1957).

Following the precedent of Sherif's study, the survey research focused on ambiguous stimuli, stimuli that had no obvious empirical referent, because ambiguous stimuli were likely to reveal social forces at work. Festinger, Schachter, and Back (1950, pp. 168–169) gave a working definition often cited in subsequent work:

> If a person driving a car down a street is told by his companion that the street ends in a dead end, this piece of information may be easily checked against physical "reality." He has only to drive on and soon he will find out whether or not the street really does end in this manner. ... The situation with regard to social opinions and attitudes is quite different, however. There is no such "physical reality" against which to check. If one person offers the opinion to another that if the democratic candidate for president is elected economic ruin may be expected, the second person may agree or not but he cannot definitely check this opinion against "reality." ... The "reality" which settles the question in the case of social attitudes and opinions is the degree to which others with whom one is in communication are believed to share these same attitudes and opinions.

In subsequent work, Schachter (1959, p. 126) noted that our wide variation in emotions is generated by a narrow range of physiological states occurring in a wide variety of social situations. Emotion is physiology matched to a situation. There can be ambiguity in identifying the emotion appropriate to a situation. I feel anxious. Is it excitement about the task at hand? Am I afraid? Angry? How should I interpret this feeling? The answer lies in connecting with people who are going through the same experience, which leads to Schachter's results showing that people afraid of an event are drawn to affiliate with people facing the same event (also see Schachter & Singer, 1962). Schachter (1959, p. 129) concluded, "The emotions or feelings, like the opinions and abilities, require social evaluation when the emotion-producing situation is ambiguous or uninterpretable in terms of past experience." Toward the end of the era, Coleman, Katz, and Menzel (1966, pp. 118–119) offered a similar description of doctors influencing one another's decision to begin prescribing a new antibiotic:

> Confronted with the need to make a decision in an ambiguous situation—a situation that does not speak for itself—people turn to each other for cues as to the structure of the situation. When a new drug appears, doctors who are in close interaction with their colleagues will similarly interpret for one another the new stimulus that has presented itself, and will arrive at some shared way of looking at it.

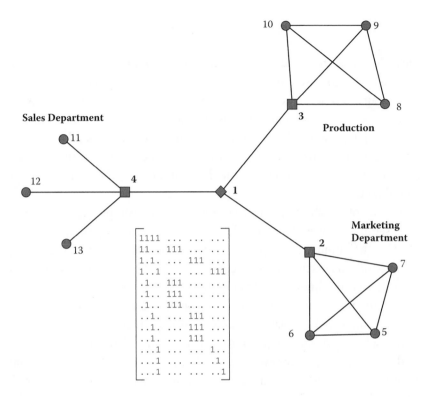

FIGURE 9.1

Discussion network in a hypothetical organization. Connectivity criterion predicts similarity between people connected by a line.

Empirical Evidence

It will be useful to have a simple, concrete example. Figure 9.1 is a sociogram of a hypothetical organization. Lines indicate close relations. Contagion in this context refers to the spread of opinion and practice between employees. Examples would be getting employees to adopt a new practice in human resources, getting employees to be more frugal with business travel costs, or getting employees to implement an efficiency program such as Six Sigma.

To predict ego's opinion or behavior under a connectivity criterion, look at the people with whom ego has close relations—the lines in Figure 9.1. Given variable Y measuring individual responses to an idea or practice spreading through a population, the connectivity criterion says that ego's response can be predicted from the weighted average of responses by ego's discussion partners:

$$yi^* = \Sigma j \ wij \ yj, \ i \neq j$$

where yj measures discussion partner j's response, yi^* is the average response by ego's discussion partners, ego i's response yi is excluded from the average, and network weight wij is a fraction increasing with the extent to which ego's connection with j is stronger than ego's connection with other people ($\Sigma j \ wij = 1$). Alternative definitions of the network weight wij can be compared for the extent to which ego and her peers make similar evaluations. The more accurate the definition of wij, the more similar yi should be to yi^*.

In much of the above-cited survey research, for example, network weight wij is set to $1/N$ for each contact that ego cites as a close discussion partner, and N is the number of people that ego cited, whereupon yi^* is the average response of ego's discussion partners. With respect to the network displayed in Figure 9.1, the lines indicate close relationships, and socializing discussion occurs in close relations, so similar opinion and behavior is predicted between connected people. The salesmen discuss their work only with the head of sales, so wij would equal 1.0 for each salesman i's relationship with the head of sales j and zero for everyone else in the network. The marketing staff discuss their work with one another and the head of marketing, so wij would equal 0.25 from individual contributor i to each of their four colleagues j in marketing. Across the network, there would be a typical response to a new company policy from the production employees, which could be different from the typical response by employees in the marketing department.

Figure 9.2 contains illustrative evidence. Heinz, Laumann, Nelson, and Salisbury (1993) described the social system of elite lobbyists active in U.S. government policy in agriculture, energy, health, and labor during the early 1980s. Ronald Reagan had been elected U.S. president. Conservative ideals had popular support. Among the elite lobbyists were a few that Heinz et al. (1993, Chap. 10) described as notables because of their special prominence as representatives. The 63 notables are the study population here (see Burt, 2009, Figure G3, for more detail on the lobbyist network and evidence of interpersonal influence). The vertical axis in Figure 9.2 measures lobbyist opinion on national policy. Each lobbyist was asked to express on a scale from 1 to 5 his or her agreement with eight opinion items concerning government policy. The vertical axis in Figure 9.2 is the factor-score average of the eight items that Heinz et al. (1993) discussed as lobbyist economic ideology, which ranges from extremely conservative (high score) to

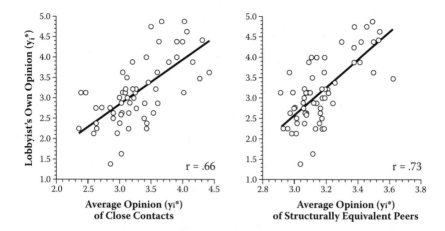

FIGURE 9.2
Economic opinions of notable American lobbyists relative to the social opinion around them (Higher scores indicate more conservative opinion. Data are from Heinz, Laumann, Nelson, and Salisbury, 1993.)

welfare-state liberalism (low score). Network data were obtained by asking each lobbyist to look over a roster of other lobbyists and indicate which were close contacts: "Please place a check by the names of people you know well enough to be confident that they would take the trouble to assist you briefly (and without a fee) if you requested it." The horizontal axis of the graph to the left in Figure 9.2 is the average opinion of a lobbyist's contacts (y_i^* in the previous equation with w_{ij} equal to 1 over the number of contacts j cited by lobbyist i). There is strong correlation between a lobbyist's expressed opinion and the average opinion of his or her close contacts ($r = .66$). With cross-sectional data as in Figure 9.2, it is impossible to know whether close relations developed between lobbyists with similar opinion or whether similar opinion emerged from discussion between closely connected lobbyists, but there is clearly a correlation between similar opinion and close relations—which is the connectivity criterion for contagion.[2]

EQUIVALENCE CRITERION, SOCIAL COMPARISON MECHANISM

Connectivity is one of the two network criteria by which individuals are combined into socially similar kinds of people. The other is equivalence.

Two people are equivalent when they have identical patterns of relationships. Equivalent people do not have to have a relationship with one another, though they often do. The equivalence criterion emerged in the 1970s as contemporary network analysis evolved from sociometry, so it was not a consideration in the research just discussed. The connectivity and equivalence criteria are network instances of an ancient distinction: classifications based on similarity within a category versus similarity beyond the category. Is a bug to be classified into a category because the bug looks like other bugs in the category or because it has similar relations with related categories of predators, hosts, and competitors? Should this variable be considered an indicator of concept A because it is correlated with other indicators of the concept (factor analysis, internal consistency) or because it resembles other indicators of A in its correlations with key concepts related to concept A (canonical correlation, construct validity)? With respect to network analysis, the long-standing distinction became explicit with the emergence of structural equivalence in the 1970s, first in Lorrain and White's (1971) theoretical treatment, then in White, Boorman, and Breiger's (1976) operational treatment. In fact, research on interpersonal influence between equivalent people was already well established in social psychology, but socialization fit more easily into the sociometric concepts popular after World War II, so the early researchers assumed that socialization was responsible for the network effects observed in the spread of opinion and behavior. Before turning to that fact, let me quickly illustrate overlap and contradiction between the two network criteria for interpersonal influence.

Distinguishing the Equivalence Criterion

The equivalence criterion is illustrated in Figure 9.3. Structural and role equivalence are illustrated. Two people are structurally equivalent when they have identical relations with the same people. Two people are role equivalent when they have identical relations with the same kinds of people. The two spatial maps in Figure 9.3 are multidimensional scalings of distances measuring the extent to which the people in Figure 9.1 are structurally equivalent (map to the left in Figure 9.3) or role equivalent (map to the right).[3] People are close together to the extent that they are equivalent.

Structural Equivalence

Role Equivalence

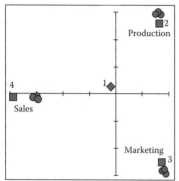

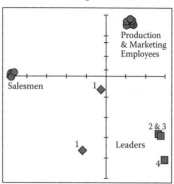

FIGURE 9.3

Equivalence criteria applied to Figure 9.1 network (equivalence criterion predicts similarity between people close together; multidimensional scaling, see note 4).

EQUIVALENCE AND CONNECTIVITY OFTEN MAKE THE SAME PREDICTIONS

When equivalent people have strong relations with each other, equivalence predicts contagion exactly where it is predicted by connectivity. In Figure 9.1, the three individual contributors in production are connected with one another. In Figure 9.3, they are right on top of one another as equivalent people. You can see their structural equivalence in the Figure 9.1 matrix of connections. Look down the rows of columns 8, 9, and 10, which are the columns of relations to the three production staff. Entries are identical across the columns. Persons 8, 9, and 10 are all connected to their supervisor and all connected to one another. The three are all disconnected from everyone else in the organization. Similarly, rows 8, 9, and 10 of the matrix are identical. In sum, persons 8, 9, and 10 are structurally equivalent because they have identical relations to (rows) and from (columns) everyone in the network. Relations are symmetric in Figure 9.1, so identical rows mean identical columns, but relations are often asymmetric in actual networks (the people who Bob names as close friends need not all name Bob as one of their close friends). Returning to Figures 9.1 and 9.3, both connectivity and equivalence predict that persons 8, 9, and 10 are contagious for one another so they are expected to express similar opinion and display similar behavior. The story just told about the three individual contributors in production also describes the three individual contributors in marketing.

The lobbyist network of close contacts discussed with respect to Figure 9.2 is composed of distinct, cohesive groups that correspond to policy domains (see Burt, 2009, Figure G3, for a sociogram). Lobbyists in each group are similarly close to one another and similarly less close to lobbyists in most other groups. In such a network, equivalence and connectivity make similar predictions. The point is illustrated by the second graph in Figure 9.2. The vertical axis is a lobbyist's opinion on national economic policy, and the horizontal axis is the average opinion of the lobbyist's structurally equivalent peers.[4] The correlation is strong ($r = .73$), about the same as the correlation with the average opinion of a lobbyist's close contacts ($r = .66$). Not surprisingly, the average opinion of close contacts is strongly correlated with the average opinion of structurally equivalent peers ($r = .89$).

CONTRADICTORY PREDICTIONS

Network structure among the notable lobbyists was relatively simple. Table 9.1 shows contagion correlations for more complex networks in which the equivalence criterion contradicts connectivity—and better predicts contagion. The first row of the table refers to the lobbyists in Figure 9.2.

The second row refers to managers in Galaskiewicz's (1985) study of corporate philanthropy in Minneapolis and St. Paul (with a follow-up survey described in Galaskiewicz, 1997). Galaskiewicz interviewed the manager in charge of his or her company's contribution to local nonprofit organizations. The manager was asked to indicate where he or she was personally acquainted with the other managers and was asked for his or her evaluation of local nonprofit organizations as potential recipients for corporate philanthropy. Relative to the lobbyists, the managers were less likely to reciprocate their citations to contacts (55% versus 69%) and were more often connected indirectly through more than a single intermediary (51% versus 33%). The contagion question was whether managers expressed evaluations similar to their close contacts versus their structurally equivalent peers (for details, see Burt, 2009, Figure G2; Galaskiewicz & Burt, 1991).

TABLE 9.1

Network Structure and Contagion in Three Study Populations

	Reciprocal Connections	Percentage of Population Beyond Friends of Friends	Contagion Measure	Correlation for Contagion by Connectivity Criterion	Correlation for Contagion by Equivalence Criterion	Correlation Between Connectivity Versus Equivalence Predictors
Lobbyists (Figure 9.2)	69%	33%	Similar economic ideology	.66	.73	.89
Managers	55%	51%	Similar opinions of other organizations	.22	.54	.34
Doctors	24%	85%	Similar dates for prescribing new drug	–.01	.35	.31

Table 9.1 shows that evaluations were more similar between structurally equivalent peers and that the equivalence and connectivity predictors are much less similar among the managers than they were among the lobbyists (correlation of .34 versus .89 for the lobbyists).

The third row of Table 9.1 refers to doctors in the classic diffusion study, *Medical Innovation*, by Coleman et al. (1957, 1966). Doctors in four Illinois communities were asked to name the doctors with whom they discussed cases and to whom they turned for advice. Prescription records were searched to determine the date at which each doctor had begun prescribing a new antibiotic. The contagion question was whether doctors began prescribing the new drug about the same time as the people with whom they discussed cases or about the same time as their structurally equivalent peers in the community. The study was the first to combine mathematical models with extensive network data and a behavioral measure of adoption. The study is often cited for its evidence of discussion partners beginning to prescribe the new drug at about the same time. Table 9.1 shows that equivalence better predicts where contagion occurred between the doctors and that connectivity has no predictive value at all. The data are ancient history in terms of contemporary medicine, but the analysis is an exemplar for academic research and practitioners (e.g., Sawai, 1994) and has continuing policy relevance (e.g., Carrin, 1987).[5]

Although the communities of lobbyists, managers, and doctors were about the same size (respectively, 63, 61, and an average of 66 for the doctors), they were very different social environments. In particular, the manager and doctor networks are in two ways different from the lobbyist network.

The manager and doctor networks are first of all more complex, which is associated with weaker evidence of contagion. The more complex the network, the less clear the social pressure on opinion and behavior (Burt, 2009, Figure G7; Burt & Janicik, 1996). Complexity increases, and contagion decreases, down the rows in Table 9.1. The lobbyists were connected by close, symmetric relations and show the strongest evidence of contagion. The doctors were connected by long chains of asymmetric relations and show the weakest evidence of contagion. The doctors often cited discussion partners and advisors who did not reciprocate the citation (24% reciprocated, versus 55% and 69% among the managers and lobbyists, respectively), and connections with other doctors in the same community tended to be long and indirect (85% longer than friend of friend, versus 51%

and 33%, respectively, among the managers and lobbyists). The manager network is between the extremes of the doctor and lobbyist networks.

Second, the manager and doctor networks differ from the lobbyist network in that equivalence more often contradicts the contagion predicted by connectivity. A particularly important contradiction occurs when equivalence predicts contagion between people who do not talk to each other. The three salesmen in Figure 9.1 illustrate the contradiction. The salesmen are structurally equivalent in Figure 9.3 but disconnected from each other in Figure 9.1. By structural equivalence, contagion is expected between the salesmen. By connectivity, contagion is expected between each salesman (persons 11, 12, and 13) and the head of sales (person 4). There are several instances of groups like the salesmen among the managers and doctors (Burt, 2009, Figures G3 and G5). These instances involve equivalence contradicting connectivity, but the contagion correlations in Table 9.1 show that equivalence is the better predictor. Contagion exists between equivalent managers and doctors even in the absence of direct communication.

One could argue that equivalence and connectivity make the same predictions, but connectivity is indirect. Here is the argument: Because all three salesmen are predicted by connectivity to be influenced by their discussions with the head of sales, they should end up expressing similar opinion and behavior—which is the prediction by equivalence. Here is the fly in the ointment: If the similarity between the salesmen results from their similar discussions with the head of sales, then their opinion and behavior similarity to the head of sales should be stronger than their similarity to one another. Their similarity to the head of sales is the direct result of socializing discussion, whereas their similarity with one another is an indirect result of that discussion. In fact, as shown next, similarity between equivalent people exists regardless of direct, indirect, or no connection between the people. Equivalence itself triggers contagion.

Role equivalence makes more obvious the contradiction to connectivity. Structural equivalence is the usual criterion used in contagion studies, but I mention role equivalence because it is an intuitive concept, it is easily measured, and it makes more obvious the contradiction between equivalence and connectivity as contagion predictors. Role equivalence is an abstract form of structural equivalence. Two people are role equivalent when they have identical relations with the same kinds of people—not the same individuals, but the same kinds, where kinds are distinguished by network structure. For example, two fathers are role equivalent in having children, but they are not structurally equivalent because they are not father to the same children. The presidents of two universities cannot be structurally equivalent because they manage different groups, but they can be role equivalent if they manage the same kinds of groups. Returning to the concrete example in Figure 9.1, the individual contributors in marketing and production are role equivalent across the two functions, whereas structural equivalence occurs only within each function. The spatial map to the left in Figure 9.3 shows marketing separate from production. The map to the right shows marketing right on top of production. The marketing and production people are role equivalent because they are similar in having relations with people who are strongly connected. Pick any one of the three individual contributors in marketing—persons 5, 6, or 7. Each of their contacts is connected with every other of their contacts. Each of the three marketing people works in a closed network. The same is true in production. Thus, the marketing and production staffs are role equivalent across functions in that their surrounding network is completely closed. In contrast, the salesmen—persons 11, 12, and 13—are not role equivalent to the marketing and production staff. The network of indirect relations through the head of sales that defines a salesman's role in the organization is different from the closed-network, direct-contact pattern that defines the role played by staff in marketing and production.

The three local leaders illustrate role equivalence more sharply. In the Figure 9.1 sociogram and the structural equivalence map to the left in Figure 9.3, the head of sales is close to the salesmen who report to him, the head of marketing is close to her marketing staff, and the head of production is close to his production staff. Role equivalence presents a different picture of the organization. In the role equivalence distances mapped to the right in Figure 9.3, all three leaders are clustered together in the lower right of the map, with the heads of marketing and production right on top of one another. That is because the heads of marketing and production play identical roles in their networks: They both manage a group of completely interconnected staff and both have direct contact with the more central person 1. The head of sales also manages a group of three people and has direct contact with the central person, but the three people he manages do not talk with each other, so they are a kind of group different from the closed networks in marketing and production. Therefore, the head of sales is not role equivalent to the heads of marketing and production in Figure 9.3.

How It Works: Social Comparison and Relative Deprivation

Socialization cannot explain why equivalent people influence one another in the absence of direct communication. Socialization predicts contagion when people talk to one another so as to shape one another's opinions and behavior. In the absence of direct communication, social comparison makes more sense as the mechanism by which contagion occurs because it is not limited to people who talk to one another.

When confused about an appropriate judgment or course of action, we look around to see what people "like me" are doing. Comparison to people like me provides a benchmark for my own opinion and behavior. Ego needs to be aware of her peers to imagine herself in their position, but no direct communication is necessary. Peer pressure could be stronger with contact and discussion, but neither is required. I do not need to talk to my peers to feel that I am ahead of them or falling behind. I do not need to talk to my peers to feel that I am fortunate to have my higher compensation or that I am exploited for the relative pittance I receive. Inconsistency draws attention. If I hear, or see, or become aware of someone "like me" making an evaluation that contradicts my own evaluation, I am puzzled. Perhaps my peer has information I do not have, or vice versa. Perhaps the light is different from where he sits. If the contradiction between our evaluations is persistent or too great, perhaps we are not as similar as I thought. "Like me" is its own motivation. Ego is surprised if a peer, presented with the same stimulus, makes an evaluation obviously different from ego's. Ego feels pressure to explain the difference, moving closer to the other person's evaluation or expecting the other person to move closer to ego's evaluation. When people equivalent in a network use one another as a benchmark for their personal opinions and behavior, they come to express similar opinions and display similar behavior.

The idea that people understand themselves through comparison to others is the concept of relative advantage and deprivation, discussed as reference group theory in sociology (Merton, 1957/1968; Merton & Rossi, 1957/1968; Stouffer, 1962; Stouffer, Suchman, DeVinney, Star, & Williams, 1949), social comparison theory in psychology (Festinger, 1954), and the relative income hypothesis in economics (Duesenberry, 1949; Leibenstein, 1950).[6] The concept of relative deprivation emerged just after World War II from research conducted under Samuel Stouffer while he was serving as director of the Research Branch, Information and Education Division of the U.S. Army (more than 200 questionnaires used to interview more than half a million soldiers). Stouffer et al. (1949, p. 125) described wide differences in soldier attitudes as a preface to introducing the concept:

> To help explain such variations in attitude, by education, age, and marital condition, a general concept would be useful. Such a concept may be that of *relative deprivation*. ... The idea is simple, almost obvious, but its utility comes in reconciling data, especially in later chapters, where its applicability is not at first too apparent. The idea would seem to have a kinship to and, in part, include such well-known sociological concepts as "social frame of reference," "patterns of expectation," or "definition of the situation." Becoming a soldier meant to many men a very real deprivation. But the felt sacrifice was greater for some than for others, *depending on their standards of comparison*.

Research has accumulated on how comparisons are made, with whom, and toward what end (e.g., Buunk & Gibbons, 2007; Frank, 1985; Guimond, 2006; Ho & Levesque, 2005; Hyman & Singer, 1968; Shah, 1998; Suls & Wheeler, 2000; Walker & Smith, 2002).

Equivalence Criterion Delimits Influential Social Comparison

Social comparison has been stated in various forms, from metaphor to model. An equivalence criterion for contagion limits social comparison in two ways.

First, comparison occurs within a reference group delimited by equivalence defining the extent to which each of the individuals in the network around ego is a "like me" peer. A comparison metaphor can be based on anything—performance, language, appearance, or something else. The comparison predicted by equivalence is between people who could substitute for one another in their respective relationships. You and I are equivalent peers to the extent that we are expert in the same specialty, our work is popular with the same constituencies, we teach the same courses, and we try to place students in the same jobs. People similarly engaged in relations watch one another to see what makes someone "like me" attractive in my relationships. What style of language, lifestyle, clothing, or appearance is attractive for someone like me? The more equivalent two people are in the network around them, the more likely they benchmark against one another, and so the more likely they express similar opinion and display similar behavior.

A second restriction available is that interpersonal comparison has a specific functional form inferred from the functional form of intrapersonal evaluations observed in psychophysics. This second point is primarily a theoretical point that awaits more precise empirical research. Putting aside details available elsewhere (Burt, 1982, Chap. 5; 2009, Chap. 8), the key intuition is that ego makes evaluations with respect to her own condition and the condition of her peers in the surrounding network. Marginal interpersonal evaluation is defined by a ratio of what ego has divided by what her peers have. The result is that an individual's preferences can be "bent" by the individual's location in a network. An action can seem wise, attractive, or foolish depending on the network frame of reference within which the action is evaluated.

The functional form of relative deprivation is illustrated in Figure 9.4. The graph is taken from Burt (2009, Figure 8.3B), where the model parameters are discussed in detail. For the purposes here, it is sufficient to label the axes and focus on the two defining characteristics of the lines describing relative deprivation. The vertical axis describes how ego feels about what she has or an action she is considering. As she feels that what she has is a lot, or an action is very attractive, she is higher on the axis. The horizontal axis refers to people equivalent to ego in the surrounding network. As good things happen for ego's network peers, they move from left to right on the horizontal axis.

The lines inside the graph show what happens as good things happen for the peers while ego's situation is fixed. In the absence of peers, ego evaluates her situation with respect to her individual history. Her evaluation is independent of other people, so it is unaffected by good things happening for her peers. Ego's feelings would be described the horizontal dashed line in Figure 9.4. This is the assumption made when consumer behavior is predicted ignoring the other people in the network around the consumer.

The solid lines in Figure 9.4 describe ego's misery as peers who were below her catch up and surpass her. The heaviest solid line in the graph describes ego with just one peer. Initially ego feels terrific about what she has because it is more than her peers. The solid lines start high to the left in the graph. Ego feels intense loss as peers catch up. Ego suffers no actual loss, but she feels loss. She loses something she felt she had. The severity of the felt loss results from evaluation based on a ratio of ego to peer

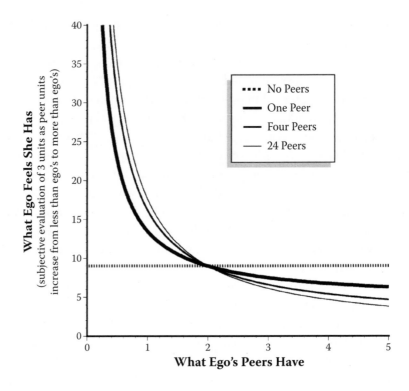

FIGURE 9.4
Ego's felt loss as peers catch up.

resources. Whatever ego has feels like a lot when her peers have very little. That inflated feeling of worth, bulging from comparison to less-fortunate peers, evaporates quickly as good things happen for the peers. Highway driving provides a familiar example. You are moving along the highway and a car comes up out of nowhere to pass you. The approaching car makes you feel as though you have slowed. We often see this in our classrooms. Students arrive from jobs in which they were smarter and faster than the people around them. It can be a shock to find oneself surrounded in the classroom by similarly able people. This is the old tension of the frog feeling small when he moves to a large pond.

Illustrative Empirical Evidence

Numerous instances of relative deprivation emerged in *The American Soldier*, and those instances are consistent with the precise predictions now possible with network models of equivalence (Burt, 2009, Chap. 8). Recent research goes further in supporting the more precise predictions. As illustration, consider two studies that illustrate features of the relative deprivation curves in Figure 9.4.

First, the severe relative deprivation ego feels as peers overtake her (illustrated by the steeply descending lines in Figure 9.4) is a stronger feeling than relative advantage. This can be discussed as a "network fear" hypothesis in that networks clearly defining peers generate a fear of obviously falling behind peers (Burt, 2009, Figure 8.4). The hypothesis is illustrated by accidents in professional car racing. Bothner, Kang, and Stuart (2007) analyzed the probability that a NASCAR driver will experience a car crash during a race as a function of competitors crowding above and below the driver. Under the assumption that "a crash is more likely if a driver attempts risky maneuvers on the track," the incidence of car crashes is an indicator of the pressure a driver feels during a race (Bothner et al., 2007, p. 211). That pressure can come from crowding ahead or behind the driver. Drivers earn points according to their finishing position in a race. The season champion is the driver with the most points from races run during the season. Bothner et al. (2007, p. 219) measured the crowding around a driver in a race by the number of competitors that the driver could surpass in the rankings if the driver did really well in the race (crowding above) and the number that could surpass the driver if they did really well in the race (crowding below). The potential gain from a race depends on crowding above the driver. If the competitors ahead of a driver are far ahead, there is no crowding above and little potential gain for the driver from pushing hard in this race. But if there is a cluster of competitors just ahead of the driver (crowding above), he has an incentive to make that little bit of extra effort in this race to pass a couple of them and move ahead in the rankings. The potential loss from a race depends on crowding below the driver. If the competitors behind the driver are way behind, it will be difficult for any of them to move ahead of the driver, whatever their performance in this race. On the other hand, if there is a cluster of competitors just behind the driver, he is at risk of one or more of them making that little bit of extra effort in this race to pass him, which could move him lower in the rankings. The research question is whether crowding around a driver increases the incidence of a car crash, and if yes, which kind of crowding is more associated with car crashes—crowding ahead of the driver or crowding behind him? Bothner et al. (2007, pp. 225–228) showed that crowding in the rankings around a driver before a race does increase the probability that the driver will crash his car during the race, and the effect is entirely from crowding below. Consistent with the network fear hypothesis, drivers are much more pushed to risky maneuvers by the possibility of being overtaken (loss) than they are drawn to risky maneuvers by the possibility of overtaking others (gain).

Second, relative deprivation is an intense but transitory discomfort. The solid lines flatten out to the right of Figure 9.4 as ego's peers pass her. This shows how feelings of relative deprivation fade as good things continue to happen for ego's peers. The bold line in Figure 9.4 decreases quickly, then continues with much slower decrease once ego's peers have surpassed her. A bubble of hubris from felt advantage is painfully burst by the success of a lesser peer followed by a rapid diminution of pain from good things continuing to happen for the peer. To continue the highway analogy about being passed by another car, your felt speed is little affected by a passing car after the car is well into the pack ahead of you.

Grinblatt, Keloharju, and Ikäheimo (2008) reported illustrative evidence. For residents in a densely populated area of Finland during 1999 through 2001, Grinblatt and his colleagues combine detailed data from tax records and car purchases. They constructed measures of car purchases by ego's closest neighbors and used those measures to predict ego's own car purchase. The research question was as follows: How does ego react to the relative deprivation of neighbors coming home in newly purchased cars? Neighbor purchases significantly increase the probability that ego will buy a car, but the effect has a strikingly short duration. The effect is strongest during the 2 days following neighbor purchases, with a weaker but still substantial effect for a week or two, and no effect thereafter (Grinblatt et al., 2008, pp. 744–745). In fact, Grinblatt and his colleagues (2008, p. 750) did not believe that keeping-up-with-the-Joneses envy is a feasible interpretation of their neighbor effects because the effects are so transitory: "It is difficult to explain how quickly the social influence of those nearest neighbors decays. Envy is a more persistent emotion." On the contrary, envy is a bent preference of short duration (baring the possibility of ego and peer resources somehow held in painful balance for a period of time). The theoretical prediction illustrated in Figure 9.4 is that the relative deprivation of falling behind the Joneses is a discomfort intense but transitory. That prediction is consistent with the intense, short-lived neighbor effects reported by Grinblatt and his colleagues.

Equivalence Criterion Implicit in Early Research

Network concepts of equivalence were not developed when the early research on social pressure was conducted, but in retrospect, the equivalence criterion can be seen in the research. For example, some methods for detecting cliques of connected people in fact detected categories of structurally equivalent people. MacRae (1960) proposed factor analyzing sociometric choice data to aggregate people into groups. A group defined by factor analysis is a cluster of structurally equivalent people because people are put into the same group (load high on the same factor) to the extent that they have similar relations with other people (Burt, 1982, pp. 47–49, 73–89). Furthermore, some people analyzed as strongly connected were structurally equivalent because of the overlap between the connectivity and equivalence criteria. Note the similar spatial distributions by connectivity in Figure 9.1 and structural equivalence in the map to the left in Figure 9.3. More generally, people within groups are structurally equivalent in a population of disconnected, cohesive groups (relation pattern is strong ties within group and no ties beyond group). The lobbyists in Figure 9.2 were such a population. At the same time that evidence of contagion within the groups is evidence supporting the connectivity criterion (left-hand graph in Figure 9.2), it is often also evidence supporting the equivalence criterion (right-hand graph in Figure 9.2), but the latter possibility went untested.

Turning from the field to the lab, equivalence was implicit in early experiments. Consider the widely cited experiments by Solomon Asch (1951, 1956) showing that social reality affects evaluations even when social reality contradicts physical reality. Asch wanted to know whether the contagion evident in Sherif's study with ambiguous stimuli was strong enough to affect evaluations of unambiguous stimuli. Figure 9.5 is a quick overview of the experiment (using the data in Asch, 1951). The perceptual task was to match line lengths between two cards. An example pair of cards is given in Figure 9.5. One card contains a single vertical line. The other card contains three lines of different lengths. The task is to match the length of the single line with the same-length line on the three-line card. In Figure 9.5, the match is with line C. Participants were asked to make 18 matches. The single lines varied from 2 to 10 inches in length. Lines on the three-line card differed on average by 1.6 inches from shortest to longest (see Asch, 1951, p. 180, for research design).

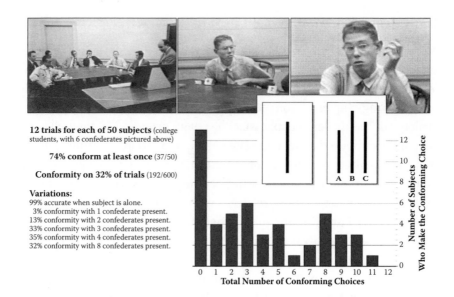

12 trials for each of 50 subjects (college students, with 6 confederates pictured above)

74% conform at least once (37/50)

Conformity on 32% of trials (192/600)

Variations:
99% accurate when subject is alone.
3% conformity with 1 confederate present.
13% conformity with 2 confederates present.
33% conformity with 3 confederates present.
35% conformity with 4 confederates present.
32% conformity with 8 confederates present.

FIGURE 9.5
The 1951 Asch experiment.

Line length in this experiment is an unambiguous stimulus. When alone as if in a psychophysics experiment, Asch's participants were accurate in reporting line length. Asch asked a control group of students to go through 12 trials writing down their matches. In 444 matches, the students made only three errors (Asch, 1951, p. 181).

Given the accurate perceptions made by people when alone, it is all the more striking to see the erroneous line lengths people report in a social setting. The left photo in Figure 9.5 shows seven students sitting around a table facing the experimenter, Asch. Asch sits next to a board on which the two stimulus cards are pasted. All but one of the students are confederates hired by Asch. The person seated second from the right at the table in Figure 9.5 is the experiment participant. On the first two trials, the confederates each verbally select the correct match. The participant comfortably goes along with what everyone else is saying. On the third trial, the confederates unanimously select the wrong line, choosing line B. The participant's reaction is illustrated in the middle picture: He cannot believe his eyes. Everyone has picked line B, but we know from the baseline results that the participant sees that line C is the correct match. One can imagine the participant in the third photo in Figure 9.5 saying to himself, "I must be blind," as he conforms to the majority in announcing that line B is the match. The experiment continues for 18 trials, of which 12 involve the majority making an erroneous match. Every so often, the majority makes a correct match to keep the participant uncertain.

The bar graph in Figure 9.5 tabulates the results (Asch, 1951, p. 181). One participant conformed to the erroneous majority opinion in 11 of 12 opportunities. Thirteen participants never conformed (zero conforming choices). In all, participants conformed to the clearly erroneous majority in 32% of 600 trials, and 74% of 50 participants conformed at least once. Conformity is less likely with two other people expressing erroneous opinion and unlikely with a single other person. As Asch (1956, p. 12) summarized the results, "The unanimously wrong majority produced a marked and significant distortion in the reported estimates." Replications of Asch's experiment show varying levels of conformity, but the experiment continues to show people conforming to the majority (Bond & Smith, 1996).[7]

The results are simultaneously evidence of social comparison between network equivalent people. First, the students are socially similar; they have what Lazarsfeld and Merton (1954) termed *homophily* (McPherson, Smith-Lovin, & Cook, 2001, provided a contemporary review). I know nothing about the social network among the students, but look at the photo in Figure 9.5. The students are all male. They are all about the same age. They are the same race. They are all enrolled in courses at the same elite New England college and familiar with the same courses taught by the same professors. They are all in the college's participant pool for psychology experiments. They likely draw female companions from the same local schools. A participant looks around the room and sees people "like me." One can imagine the photograph looking different for Sherif's experiment in the early 1930s at Columbia University, but homophily must have been similarly high.

A further point to note with respect to structural equivalence is that contagion in Asch's experiment did not require influencer and influencee to talk to one another.[8] In fact, the contagion predicted between structurally equivalent people not talking to one another—such as the salesmen in Figures 9.1 and 9.3—was familiar in social psychology long before Asch's study in 1951 or even Sherif's in 1936. It was the subject of Triplett's (1898) analysis, which is often deemed the first experiment in social psychology (Stube, 2005). Triplett described men competing in bicycle races and children competing on the speed with which they can wind a fishing reel. The racing bicyclists and competing children are structurally equivalent—standing in common relation to the rule-making authority, the goal, one another, and spectator elements in the environment. Though not talking with one another, the competitors influence one another. Consistent with the relative deprivation illustrated in Figure 9.4, Triplett (1898, p. 533) showed that people work faster when they are pitted against a competitor:[9] "The bodily presence of another contestant participating simultaneously in the race serves to liberate latent energy not ordinarily available." In Allport's (1924, pp. 260–261) influential textbook a generation later, Allport felt the need to explicitly separate evidence of social influence into two kinds, one describing influence between people not talking to one another (Triplett is cited as an example) and the other describing influence between people who talk to one another:

> Groups, in turn, may be classified under two heads: *co-acting* groups and *face-to-face* groups. In the former the individuals are primarily occupied with some stimulus other than one another. ... Pupils in a classroom reading a lesson in concert from the blackboard illustrate this type of group. In the face-to-face group, which is necessarily small, the individuals react mainly or entirely to one another. A committee of three or four directors discussing a business project is a group of this sort.

Allport (1924, p. 285) discussed at length the evidence on coacting groups and bemoaned the lack of research on face-to-face groups ("the face-to-face group has been neglected"). The neglect was corrected in the following decades, although the subsequent studies by Sherif (1936) and Asch (1951) that are today deemed classics in the midcentury research wave that established the connectivity criterion were both instances of influence in coacting groups. The point for this chapter is that influence between structurally equivalent people who do not talk to one another—a point of contention between connectivity and equivalence criteria defining "like me"—was a phenomenon familiar early in social psychology.

HOW THE MECHANISMS COMBINE

The summary results in Table 9.1 assume that contagion is a continuous function of one or the other network criterion. In fact, the two criteria combine in a systematic way. There is more here than a multiple regression model in which the two criteria are tested for their relative contribution to contagion. Rather, the two criteria interact, each affecting the other's effect.

Discovering Near-Peers

The interaction is illustrated in Figure 9.6 (from Burt & Uchiyama, 1989). The data are taken from Coleman et al.'s (1966) *Medical Innovation.* The unit of analysis is a pair of doctors practicing in the same city. The vertical axis indicates the months that pass between the first doctor's adoption and the second doctor's adoption. The minimum is zero, indicating two doctors who adopted in the same month.

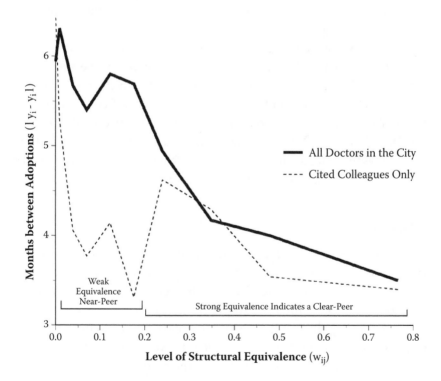

FIGURE 9.6
Detail on network conditions for contagion between the *Medical Innovation* doctors. Data are taken from *Medical Innovation*, by J. S. Coleman, E. Katz, and H. Menzel, 1966, New York: Bobbs-Merrill.

The solid line in Figure 9.6 describes contagion by structural equivalence. Doctor pairs range from nonequivalent at the left in the graph to strongly equivalent at the right. The solid line is high for nonequivalent doctors, showing that about 6 months passed between their adoptions. The solid line declines almost linearly as the network weight for structural equivalence increases. Structurally equivalent doctors tended to begin prescribing the new antibiotic at about the same time.

Now add connectivity: The dashed line describes the interval between adoptions by pairs of doctors in which one cited the other as an advisor or discussion partner. Across much of the horizontal axis, the dashed line adds nothing to the solid line. Nonequivalent doctors are separated by about 6 months, whether or not they talked together. Above a certain level of structural equivalence (network weights greater than about 0.2 in Figure 9.6), the dashed line runs parallel to the solid line, showing that equivalent doctors adopted soon after one another, whether or not they discussed cases together.

The point of the graph is the big gap between the dashed and solid lines at low levels of equivalence. A pair of doctors for whom the equivalence network weight is 0.1, for example, were separated in their adoptions by 5.79 months on average but were a month and a half closer together if they discussed cases (4.19 month average interval between adoptions for the dashed line over network weights equal to 0.1). In short, connectivity contributes to contagion in combination with equivalence. At low levels of equivalence, connectivity makes a big difference.

Z-Graphs

The same pattern occurs among the managers and lobbyists. Contagion evidence within and across the three populations is summarized in Figure 9.7. The horizontal axes distinguish levels of connection. The strongest connection measured is two people citing each other as colleagues with whom they discuss their work. The next lower level is when only one person cites the other. The next lower level is when the two people have no direct contact, but they discuss their work with colleagues who know one another such that there is *some* chain of intermediaries through whom information could travel between the two people. The lowest level of connection is when the two people discuss their work with disconnected colleagues such that there is *no* chain of intermediaries in the

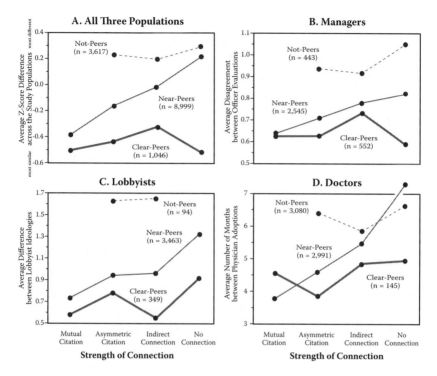

FIGURE 9.7
Summary network conditions for contagion.

observed network through whom information could travel between the two people.

The vertical axes in Figure 9.7 measure contagion. Pairs of people low on the vertical axis made similar responses on whatever variable was tested for contagion in their population. Pairs of people high on the vertical axes made widely different responses. In Figure 9.7D, for example, the vertical axis is months between doctor adoptions, as in Figure 9.6. In the Figure 9.7A graph summarizing the three populations, the vertical axis is a z-score measure of opinion or behavior within each community. The score for a pair of *Medical Innovation* doctors, for example, is the (z-score) difference between the dates when the doctors began prescribing the new drug. One doctor began prescribing the new drug in month A, and the other began in month B. The time between their adoptions ($|A-B|$), minus the average difference for other pairs of doctors in their community, divided by its standard deviation is a z-score measure of the extent to which the adoption difference between the two doctors was larger than the average in their community (high on the vertical axis) or smaller than the average (low on the vertical axis). The score for two managers is the z-score difference in their evaluations of local nonprofit organizations. The score for two lobbyists is the z-score difference between their respective opinions about national economic policy.

Figure 9.7 shows a Z-pattern within and across the three study populations. The pattern is based on the three qualitative levels of structural equivalence distinguished in Figure 9.6: not-peers, clear-peers, and near-peers.

Not-Peers: Contact Is Insufficient

Not-peers are pairs of people for whom the equivalence network weight is within rounding error of zero. Not-peers have networks as different as any in their community. The dashed lines across the top of the Z-patterns in Figure 9.7 show no evidence of contagion between not-peers, regardless of connection. On average, nonequivalent people are further apart on the contagion variable than the average pair of people in a community (0.29 mean z-score). Their difference remains if the nonequivalent people have a chain of indirect connections through whom they could communicate (0.20 mean z-score) or one of them cites the other as a discussion partner (0.23 mean z-score). There is no mean reported in Figure 9.7 for mutual citations on the dashed line because the mutual strength of connection did not occur between nonequivalent people.

Clear-Peers: Contact Is Superfluous

At the other extreme, clear-peers are pairs of people for whom equivalence is high and contagion is likely even when the two people are not connected. Most people in the three populations have a small number of these close comparison points. I selected a threshold of network weights 3 or more standard deviations greater than zero. The cutoff I use here has no theoretical foundation. It is based on comparing the three study populations to find a level of equivalence after which contagion is likely and direct contact irrelevant. Among the *Medical Innovation* doctors, the interval of the horizontal axis marked clear-peer in Figure 9.6 contains pairs of doctors who sought advice from the same colleagues, discussed cases with the same colleagues, and were themselves sought out by the same colleagues for advice and discussion.

The bold lines across the bottom of the Z-patterns in Figure 9.7 show consistent evidence of contagion between clear-peers, regardless of connection between the people. The bold lines show that structurally equivalent people who talked to one another directly were similar in their opinions and adoption dates, but no more similar than structurally equivalent people who had no direct connection with one another.[10] Contact is superfluous to alignment between structurally equivalent people. Social comparisons between equivalent people make them alert to one another such that they become similar whether or not they talk together. This point is implicit in early research conclusions about evidence recognized 30 years later to be evidence of contagion by equivalence. Merton (1949/1968, pp. 465–466) concluded,

> One gains the impression that although a relatively few people—the top influentials—exert influence upon people on all levels of the influence-structure, there occurs a secondary tendency for people to be otherwise most influenced by their peers in that structure. … People in each influence stratum are more likely to be influenced by their peers in this structure than are people in the other strata.

Katz and Lazarsfeld (1955, p. 331) concluded,

> The flow of influence in this arena tends—as it does in every arena—to remain within the boundaries of each status level, but when it does cross status lines, there is no indication that the direction of flow is any more from high to low than it is from low to high.

Near-Peers, Brokers, and Opinion Leaders

The results in Table 9.1 and Figure 9.7 show that equivalence often predicts contagion where connectivity predicts contagion, and where equivalence contradicts connectivity, equivalence is the better predictor. But near-peers are the most numerous pairs in the three study populations (8,999 of 13,662 dyads in Figure 9.7A, or 66%, are near peers), and contagion is for them clearly a function of connectivity. Near-peers are people neither equivalent nor clearly nonequivalent. The interval of the horizontal axis marked near-peer in Figure 9.6 contains pairs of doctors who had similar relations with some colleagues but also had advisors and discussion partners that the other did not. Near-peers need not be aware of their weak equivalence until they talk to one another and discover what they have in common. For example, sociologists and economists move in different academic circles, but conversations between a sociologist and economist at the same university can reveal to each the many people they know, admire, or disdain in common.

The upward-sloping thin lines in Figure 9.7 show contagion between near-peers dependent on contact. The stronger the connection between near-peers, the more likely the contagion. To the lower left in Figure 9.7A, mutual-citation near-peers are similar in opinion and behavior (–0.38 mean z-score difference on contagion variables). To the upper right in Figure 9.7A, differences between disconnected near-peers are as wide as the differences between completely nonequivalent people (0.22 mean z-score difference). The association between contagion and connection varies across the populations (managers the lowest, doctors the highest), but all three populations show contagion between near-peers more likely with stronger connection.

Once identified, the near-peers for whom personal connection is so influential are quickly recognized. They are the opinion leaders and cosmopolitans described by Katz, Lazarsfeld, and Merton in the early marketing research from Columbia University's Bureau for Applied Social Research. One of the bureau's early projects was a study of the 1940 presidential election, later published as *The People's Choice*. As so often quoted thereafter (Lazarsfeld et al., 1944, p. 151), the researchers were surprised to find almost no direct media effect on voters, instead finding "that ideas often flow from radio and print to opinion leaders and from these to the less active sections of the population." The role of opinion leaders in innovation diffusion was elaborated in Merton's (1949) contrast between cosmopolitan versus local leaders and studied in subsequent bureau projects, most notably Katz and Lazarsfeld (1955) on opinion leaders in consumer purchases. The two-step flow—a process of information moving from the media to opinion leaders, and influence moving from opinion leaders to their followers—became a guiding theme for diffusion and marketing research (Katz & Lazarsfeld, 1955, p. 309ff; Rogers, 1962/2003, p. 285). Figure 9.7 shows that the familiar two-step flow of communication is a compound of the two network mechanisms; ideas enter a group through socializing discussion between weakly equivalent near-peers on the edge of the group, then adoptions spread within the group through social comparisons between strongly equivalent clear-peers.

In other words, opinion leaders are more precisely opinion brokers who transmit information across the boundaries between status groups. These need not be leaders with superior authority or leaders in the sense of others wanting to imitate them. Defining opinion leaders by function (people whose conversations make new ideas and behaviors contagious) and structural location (people communicating with, and weakly equivalent to, the individuals they influence) removes the vertical distinction implicit in the contrast between opinion leaders and followers. Opinion leaders are not people at the top so much as people at the edge; not leaders within groups so much as brokers between groups. They are in some ways structurally similar to the people they influence, but in one important way distinct: They have strong connections to other groups. They are what Merton (1949/1968) described as cosmopolitans (see Rogers, 1962/2003, pp. 293–294, for a similar conclusion, and Rogers, 1962/2003, p. 336ff, for a discussion of change agents as linkers). They are what we today study as network brokers, or connectors, who derive competitive advantage from spanning the structural holes between groups in markets and organizations (see Burt, 1999, 2005, for review; see Burt, 2009, Table G1, for analysis showing that the near-peers between whom contagion occurs in Figure 9.7 tend to be brokers in their surrounding network).

CLOSING

This chapter is aimed at students and colleagues in marketing who are interested in a quick introduction to the two network mechanisms—socialization and social comparison—by which ideas and behaviors become contagious in a population. This seemed useful given the growing interest in social network analysis, but the chapter is also written to show that the growing interest is less a novelty than a renewed attack on foundational marketing puzzles with new tools. Marketing advocates for social network analysis can seem defensive as if introducing something novel and risky. Van den Bulte and Wuyts (2007) open their book *Social Networks and Marketing* with the chapter "Why Should Marketers Care About Social Networks?" A compelling argument is offered using contemporary facts illustrating that we live in a world increasingly based on social networks. The facts are certainly true; the turn of the century saw substantial progress in a rapid and ongoing transition from bureaucratic authority to network reputation as the mechanism governing coordination. There is another argument to be made based on intellectual history. Much of what the world knows about network effects originated in marketing and consumer research conducted during the golden age of social psychology at places like Columbia University's Bureau for Applied Social Research. Recognition of these conceptual and research foundations is particularly timely as increasingly easy access to thin data on consumers as individuals facilitates an ignorance of the social. In shadow lies the opinion and behavior of other people—friends, neighbors, colleagues, and others. Those other people are variably connected in the surrounding social network so as to affect what any one individual can do, what he or she feels obligated to do, and what he or she feels inclined to do. Something about the network around two people makes the opinion and behavior of one contagious for the other, an effect familiar in popular metaphors about word-of-mouth advertising, building the buzz, and viral marketing. My goals in this chapter were to distinguish the socialization and social comparison mechanisms by the network conditions in which they occur and to describe how the mechanisms combine in a predictable way as they generate contagion. Neither mechanism is the whole story at the same time that neither is completely wrong. Socialization turns out to describe the occasional, critical instance of opinion and behavior brokered between groups. Social comparison describes the more frequent instance of interpersonal influence within groups and indifference beyond the group. The only course of action that is clearly wrong is to ignore either one of the two mechanisms. As Van den Bulte and Wuyts (2007, p. 77) so rightly concluded their book, "There is ample evidence that the pattern of ties among people and among organizations matter."

ACKNOWLEDGMENTS

I am grateful to the University of Chicago Booth School of Business for financial support during my work on this chapter. This chapter is adapted from Burt (2009) with the permission of Oxford University Press.

NOTES

1. Sherif (1936, pp. 69–70) cited precedent experiments by Allport (1924, pp. 260–285) in which groups had what he termed a "leveling" effect, truncating the distribution of personal opinion and behavior to less extreme evaluations (which reflects a "basic human tendency to temper one's opinions and conduct by deference to the opinion and conduct of others"; Allport, 1924, p. 278). For the purposes of this chapter, Sherif's experiment seems to me the key precedent for the influential research from MIT and Columbia University during the 1950s that became the foundation for contemporary network theory on the effects of socialization. See Turner (1990) on Sherif's links to sociology more broadly.

2. The correlations in Figure 9.2 are robust to routine controls for individual differences between the lobbyists that would be expected to predict their economic ideology (Burt, 2009, Figure G3), but estimating the correlations between ego's response yi and the average response of others, yi^*, is a nontrivial statistical exercise. Ego's response is both dependent variable (when ego is the object of contagion) and predictor (when ego is the source of contagion). There is also an endogeneity issue difficult to solve even with good panel data. Did the connection captured by network weight wij cause, or result from, similar responses by ego and her discussion partners? The first issue is network autocorrelation (e.g., Leenders, 2002; Marsden & Friedkin, 1993; Ord, 1975; Strang & Soule, 1998). The second issue is network endogeneity (Mouw, 2006), nicely discussed by Manski (1993) as a reflection problem (Did you move your reflection in the mirror or did it move you?). I ignore both issues here for two reasons. First, the issues are well discussed in the works I just mentioned. Second, no statistical sophistication can correct for a misspecified model, and my point in this chapter is that the two network mechanisms—socialization and social comparison—combine in a specific way that is not captured by models based on either mechanism alone.

3. The spatial maps in Figure 9.3 are multidimensional scalings of equivalence distances between the 13 people in Figure 9.1. Distances in the two-dimensional maps are a good description of raw distances (Kruskal's stress coefficient is near-zero for both maps, .06 for structural equivalence, .01 for role equivalence; Kruskal & Wish, 1978). To compute structural equivalence distances for the spatial map to the left in Figure 9.3, I traced indirect connections from the direct connections in Figure 9.1 and used a simple fixed decay weighting to measure the relation z_{jk} from person i to person k (direct connections equal 1.0, two-step connections are 0.5, three-step connections are 0.5 squared, four-step connections are 0.5 cubed, and so on). Structural equivalence between i and j is measured by a distance, call it d_{ij}, which increases as other persons k have different relations with i and j, for example, $d_{ij}^2 = \Sigma_k (z_{ik} - z_{jk})^2 + \Sigma_k (z_{ki} - z_{kj})^2$, $i \neq k \neq j$. Distance d_{ij} is zero when i and j have identical relations with everyone else in the organization. For details on measuring structural equivalence, see a general introduction to network analysis, such as Wasserman and Faust (1994, Chap. 9), the "gently readable" Scott (2000), or the online text by Hanneman and Riddle (2005, Chaps. 12–13). To compute role equivalence distances for the spatial map to the right in Figure 9.3, I used the direct connections displayed in Figure 9.1 and computed Euclidean distances between the triad census describing each person's role in the network. The distance measure was proposed originally by Hummell and Sodeur (1987) in a book available only in German (see Burt, 1990, and Burt, 2009,

Figures 8.10 and G8, for details, literature, and illustration in English).

4. Fractional network weights w_{ij} defining the average opinion y_i^* of lobbyists structurally equivalent to person i were computed from the structural equivalence distances defined in the preceding note. People with especially low distance from person i are given especially high weight as a potential source of influence on person i's opinion and behavior (see Burt, 1982, pp. 181–184; Burt, 2009, Figure 8.8, for details and illustration).

5. Summary discussion of the evidence is provided elsewhere (Burt, 2009, Figure G4). Evidence of contagion can be detected among the doctors, but it is fragile given the complex advice and discussion networks (Table 9.1) and aggressive marketing for a drug whose adoption posed few risks (Van den Bulte & Lilien, 2001, pp. 1412–1417). For Coleman et al. (1966, pp. 114–130), doctors central in the discussion network were early adopters and socialized others, but it seems more likely that contagion was between structurally equivalent doctors regardless of direct contact (for more detail on the original Coleman et al. evidence, see Burt, 1987, pp. 1304–1306, 1313n). Either way, adoption was more determined by personal background than colleague behavior. The new drug spread without the slow-start period typical of early innovation (Burt, 1987, pp. 1304–1306), and less variance in adoption dates was predicted by contagion than by characteristics of a doctor's background and practice (respectively, 14% and 26%, Burt, 2009, Figure G4). Marsden and Podolny (1990) reported no event-history evidence of contagion when they imputed missing adoption dates from a doctor's personal background (see their appendix, pp. 210–211). The cross-sectional evidence of contagion in Burt (1987) also disappears if missing adoption dates are imputed from a doctor's personal background. Strang and Tuma (1993, pp. 633–634) reported event-history evidence of contagion by equivalence (multiplying or adding to personal background) and connectivity (additive only), but in both cases, doctor background strongly predicts adoption date. In fact, just holding constant monthly advertising on the new drug in three leading magazines can fully account for the evidence of contagion (Van den Bulte & Lilien, 2001, p. 1426), though there is an endogeneity issue in whether advertising caused or anticipated the generic diffusion curve for the spread of the new antibiotic. Contagion was correlated with aggressive advertising by the first firm into the market (Lederle, no correlation with advertising by other drug companies), and that advertising followed a generic bandwagon curve, increasing during the bandwagon phase, then slowing as diffusion reached saturation (no reason to increase advertising after the bandwagon has passed). Regardless, these analyses are similar in predicting contagion as a continuous function of equivalence or connectivity. The evidence of contagion conditional on weak equivalence highlighted in Figure 9.6 and Figure 9.7 would not be detected in any of the analyses.

6. Social comparison in psychology is similar in metaphor to reference group theory in sociology, which is not surprising because they developed together during a period of frequent cross-reference between sociology and psychology, the golden age of social psychology (House, 2008; Sewell, 1989; Pooley & Katz, 2008). More specifically, the person who created social comparison theory, Leon Festinger, led the earlier research (Festinger et al., 1950) so warmly cited in the influential Columbia University research by Lazarsfeld, Katz, Coleman, and colleagues on opinion leaders and diffusion, which together with Stouffer's *American Soldier* provided the foundation for Merton's theoretical work in sociology on reference groups—all of

which is foundation for network models of social context creating bent preferences (Burt, 2009, Chap. 8). Kindred economic theory emerged at the same time on a separate track. The relative income hypothesis and its component effects have a great deal to say about population implications of social comparison when it occurs but little to say about the situations in which social comparison is unlikely, so the work has not had much impact on network models (see Burt, 2009, Appendix G for detailed discussion).

7. It could seem reasonable to go beyond the focus of Sherif, Festinger, Lazarsfeld, Katz, and Coleman on ambiguous stimuli and argue instead that social reality can dominate physical reality—as illustrated by Asch's participants reporting perceptions consistent with social reality but clearly inconsistent with physical reality (e.g., see Hardin & Higgins, 1996, for such an argument). There is even evidence of a biological foundation for the Asch results. Berns et al. (2005) reported MRI evidence of activity in emotion areas of the brain when participants contradict the group opinion (versus activity primarily in routine perception areas of the brain when participants conform to group opinion). The authors offered the results as "the first biological evidence for the involvement of perceptual and emotional processes during social conformity." One reason for staying with the original focus on ambiguous stimuli is confidence. The paragraph quoted in the text from Festinger et al. sets up a continuum of stimuli ranging from evaluations that are clearly grounded in empirical fact (as in "this street is a dead-end road") to evaluations that have no clear empirical referent (as in "the economy will suffer if a Democrat is elected"). I am confident that people use other people as a frame of reference for evaluations that have no clear empirical referent, they feel tension contradicting a peer group of unanimous opinion, and they might be affected by other people when making evaluations clearly grounded in empirical fact—but then again they might not. A substantial number of Asch's participants showed the effects of contagion on an evaluation clearly grounded in empirical fact, but some of those participants did not believe their own reports. They went along with the majority while privately believing what their eyes told them. This public lies versus private truths phenomenon (Kuran, 1998) is illustrated by participant remarks such as "When in Rome you do as the Romans" and "I agreed less because they were right than because I wanted to agree with them. It takes a lot of nerve to go in opposition to them" (Asch, 1956, p. 32). More, participants are less likely to go along with the majority when the majority is obviously in error (Cohen, 1963, pp. 28–29), and participants are more likely to conform if they have to recall the image of the line rather than having it displayed in front of them when they evaluate its length (Deutsch & Gerard, 1955). In short, physical reality intrudes even into the social reality of complete consensus among peers, or as Asch (1951, p. 189) himself put it, "We find that the majority effect grows stronger as the situation diminishes in clarity."

8. I focus on the Asch experiment as an exemplar. Gartrell (2002) offered a broader discussion of the early research on communication and influence in the course of assuming that network connectivity defines the peers with respect to whom ego feels relative deprivation. Gartrell's chapter is useful in directing research attention to network criteria for ego's selection of peers for social comparison. For the purposes here, however, I put aside Gartrell's assumption that the peers responsible for relative deprivation are defined by connectivity, because Gartrell did not consider the structural equivalence implicit in the early research and did not have the empirical

evidence reported here supporting structural equivalence over connectivity as the criterion defining network peers.

9. Triplett presented his results in graphs and tabulations that were sophisticated for the time but can leave questions for contemporary scholars about the statistical significance of the oft-cited results (Stube, 2005). It turns out that Triplett's competitor-induced speed improvements stand up to routine statistical scrutiny (Burt, 2009, Appendix G, Footnote 7).

10. Average z-scores are well below zero for structurally equivalent people at each level of connection (–0.51, –0.32, –0.43, and –0.50 for the four points on the horizontal bold line at the bottom of Figure 9.7A). There is no statistically significant trend across the points (0.4 t-test adjusted for clustering between relations involving the same person), and the mean of 0.47 for the people in direct contact is not significantly higher than the mean of 0.38 for the people with no direct contact to one another (1.4 t-test adjusted for clustering between relations involving the same person). The clustering adjustment was applied using the CLUSTER option in STATA.

REFERENCES

Allport, F. H. (1924). *Social psychology*. New York: Houghton Mifflin.

Asch, S. E. (1951). Effects of group pressure upon the modification and distortion of judgments. In H. Guetzkow (Ed.), *Groups, leadership and men* (pp. 177–190). Pittsburgh, PA: Carnegie Press.

Asch, S. E. (1956). Studies of independence and conformity: A minority of one against a unanimous majority. *Psychological Monographs, 70*(416).

Berelson, B. R., Lazarsfeld, P. F., & McPhee, W. N. (1954). *Voting*. Chicago: University of Chicago Press.

Berns, G. S., Chappelow, J., Zink, C. F., Pagnoni, G., Martin-Skurski, M. E., & Richards, J. (2005). Neurobiological correlates of social conformity and independence during mental rotation. *Biological Psychiatry, 58*, 245–253.

Bond, R., & Smith, P. B. (1996). Culture and conformity: A meta-analysis of studies using Asch's (1952b, 1956) line judgment task. *Psychological Bulletin, 119*, 111–137.

Bothner, M. S., Kang, J.-H., & Stuart, T. E. (2007). Competitive crowding and risk taking in a tournament: Evidence from NASCAR racing. *Administrative Science Quarterly, 52*, 208–247.

Burt, R. S. (1982). *Toward a structural theory of action*. New York: Academic Press.

Burt, R. S. (1987). Social contagion and innovation, cohesion versus structural equivalence. *American Journal of Sociology, 92*, 1287–1335.

Burt, R. S. (1990). Detecting role equivalence. *Social Networks, 12*, 83–97.

Burt, R. S. (1999). The social capital of opinion leaders. *Annals, 566*, 37–54.

Burt, R. S. (2005). *Brokerage and closure*. Oxford: Oxford University Press.

Burt, R. S. (2009). *Neighbor networks*. Oxford: Oxford University Press.

Burt, R. S., & Janicik, G. A. (1996). Social contagion and social structure. In D. Iacobucci (Ed.), *Networks in marketing* (pp. 32–49). Newbury Park, CA: Sage.

Burt, R. S. & Uchiyama, T. (1989). The conditional significance of communication for interpersonal influence. In M. Kochen (Ed.), *The small world* (pp. 67–87). Norwood, NJ: Ablex.

Buunk, A. P., & Gibbons, F. X. (2007). Social comparison: The end of a theory and the emergence of a field. *Organizational Behavior and Human Decision Processes, 102*, 3–21.

Carrin, G. (1987). Drug prescribing—A discussion of its variability and (ir)rationality. *Health Policy, 7*, 73–94.

Centola, D., & Macy, M. (2007). Complex contagions and the weakness of long ties. *American Journal of Sociology, 113*, 702–734.

Cohen, B. P. (1963). *Conflict and conformity*. Cambridge, MA: MIT Press.

Coleman, J. S., Katz, E., & Menzel, H. (1957). The diffusion of an innovation among physicians. *Sociometry, 20*, 253–270.

Coleman, J. S., Katz, E., & Menzel, H. (1966). *Medical innovation*. New York: Bobbs-Merrill.

Davis, G. F., Morrill, C., Rao, H., & Soule, S. A. (2008). Introduction: Social movements in organizations and markets. *Administrative Science Quarterly, 53*, 389–394.

Deutsch, M., & Gerard, H. B. (1955). A study of normative and informational social influences upon individual judgment. *Journal of Abnormal and Social Psychology, 51*, 629–636.

DiMaggio, P., & Louch, H. (1998). Socially embedded consumer transactions: For what kinds of purchases do people most often use networks? *American Sociological Review, 63*, 619–637.

Duesenberry, J. S. (1949). *Income, saving, and the theory of consumer behavior*. Cambridge, MA: Harvard University Press.

Festinger, L. (1954). A theory of social comparison processes. *Human Relations, 7*, 117–140.

Festinger, L., Schachter, S., & Back, K. W. (1950). *Social pressures in informal groups*. Stanford, CA: Stanford University Press.

Frank, R. H. (1985). *Choosing the right pond*. Oxford: Oxford University Press.

Frenzen, J. K., & Davis, H. L. (1990). Purchasing behavior in embedded markets. *Journal of Consumer Research, 17*, 1–12.

Galaskiewicz, J. (1985). *Social organization of an urban grants economy*. New York: Academic Press.

Galaskiewicz, J. (1997). An urban grants economy revisited: Corporate charitable contributions in the Twin Cities, 1979–81, 1987–89. *Administrative Science Quarterly, 42*, 445–471.

Galaskiewicz, J., & Burt, R. S. (1991). Interorganization contagion in corporate philanthropy. *Administrative Science Quarterly, 36*, 88–105.

Gartrell, C. D. (2002). The embeddedness of social comparison. In I. Walker & H. J. Smith (Ed.), *Relative deprivation* (pp. 164–184). Cambridge: Cambridge University Press.

Grinblatt, M., Keloharju, M., & Ikäheimo, S. (2008). Social influence and consumption: Evidence from the automobile purchases of neighbors. *Review of Economics and Statistics, 90*, 735–753.

Guimond, S. (Ed.). (2006). *Social comparison and social psychology*. Cambridge: Cambridge University Press.

Hanneman, R. A., & Riddle, M. (2005). *Introduction to social network methods*. Riverside: University of California, Riverside. Retrieved from http://faculty.ucr.edu/~hanneman

Hardin, C. D., & Higgins, E. T. (1996). Shared reality: How social verification makes the subjective objective. In R. M. Sorrentino & E. T. Higgins (Eds.), *Handbook of motivation and cognition* (Vol. 3, pp. 28–77). New York: Guilford.

Heinz, J. P., Laumann, E. O., Nelson, R. L., & Salisbury, R. H. (1993). *The hollow core.* Cambridge, MA: Harvard University Press.

Ho, V. T., & Levesque, L. L. (2005). With a little help from my friends (and substitutes): Social referents and influence in psychological contract fulfillment. *Organization Science, 16,* 275–289.

House, J. S. (2008). Social psychology, social science, and economics: Twentieth century progress and problems, twenty-first century prospects. *Social Psychology Quarterly, 71,* 232–256.

Hummell, H., & Sodeur, W. (1987). Strukturbeschreibung von positionen in sozialen beziehungsnetzen. In F. U. Pappi (Ed.), *Techniken der Empirischen Sozialforschung, 1, Methoden der Netzwerkanalyse* (pp. 177–202). Munich: Oldenbourg.

Hyman, H., & Singer, E. (Eds.). (1968). *Readings in reference group theory.* New York: Free Press.

Katz, E., & Lazarsfeld, P. F. (1955). *Personal influence.* New York: Free Press.

Kruskal, J. B., & Wish, M. (1978). *Multidimensional scaling.* Newbury Park, CA: Sage.

Kuran, T. (1998). *Private truths, public lies.* Cambridge, MA: Harvard University Press.

Lazarsfeld, P. F., Berelson, B., & Gaudet, H. (1944). *The people's choice.* New York: Duell, Sloan and Pearce.

Lazarsfeld, P. F., & Merton, R. K. (1954). Friendship as a social process: A substantive and methodological analysis. In M. Berger, T. Abel, & C. H. Page (Eds.), *Freedom and control in modern society* (pp. 18–66). New York: Van Nostrand.

Leenders, R. T. A. J. (2002). Modeling social influence through network autocorrelation: Constructing the weight matrix. *Social Networks, 24,* 21–47.

Leibenstein, H. (1950). Bandwagon, snob, and Veblen effects in the theory of consumers' demand. *Quarterly Journal of Economics, 64,* 183–207.

Lorrain, F. P., & White, H. C. (1971). Structural equivalence of individuals in social networks. *Journal of Mathematical Sociology, 1,* 49–80.

MacRae, D., Jr. (1960). Direct factor analysis of sociometric data. *Sociometry, 23,* 360–371.

Manski, C. F. (1993). Identification of endogenous social effects: The reflection problem. *Review of Economic Studies, 60,* 531–542.

Marsden, P. V., & Friedkin, N. E. (1993). Network studies of social influence. *Sociological Methods and Research, 22,* 127–151.

Marsden, P. V., & Podolny, J. M. (1990). Dynamic analysis of network diffusion processes. In J. Weesie & H. Flap (Eds.), *Social networks through time* (pp. 197–214). Utrecht, the Netherlands: ISOR.

McPherson, M., Smith-Lovin, L., & Cook, J. M. (2001). Birds of a feather: Homophily in social networks. *Annual Review of Sociology, 27,* 415–444.

Merton, R. K. (1968). Patterns of influence: Local and cosmopolitan influentials. In R. K. Merton (Ed.), *Social theory and social structure* (pp. 441–474). New York: Free Press. (Original work published 1949)

Merton, R. K. (1968). Continuities in the theory of reference groups and social structure. In R. K. Merton (Ed.), *Social theory and social structure* (pp. 335–440). New York: Free Press. (Original work published 1957)

Merton, R. K., & Rossi, A. S. (1968). Contributions to the theory of reference group behavior. In R. K. Merton (Ed.), *Social theory and social structure* (pp. 279–334). New York: Free Press. (Original work published 1957)

Monge, P. R., & Contractor, N. (2003). *Theories of communication networks.* New York: Oxford University Press.

Mouw, T. (2006). Estimating the causal effect of social capital: A review of recent research. *Annual Review of Sociology, 32,* 79–102.

Ord, K. (1975). Estimation methods for models of spatial interaction. *Journal of the American Statistical Association, 70,* 120–126.

Orzechowicz, D. (2008). Privileged emotion managers: The case of actors. *Social Psychology Quarterly, 71,* 143–156.

Pooley, J., & Katz, E. (2008). Further notes on why American sociology abandoned mass communication research. *Journal of Communication, 58,* 767–786.

Rao, H., Greve, H. R., & Davis, G. F. (2001). Fool's gold: Social proof in the initiation and abandonment of coverage by Wall Street analysts. *Administrative Science Quarterly, 46,* 502–526.

Rogers, E. (2003). *Diffusion of innovations.* New York: Free Press. (Original work published 1962)

Sawai, K. (1994). A study on how Coleman's book on diffusion of new drugs has been cited in subsequent published articles. *Library and Information Science, 32,* 105–122.

Schachter, S. (1959). *The psychology of affiliation.* Stanford, CA: Stanford University Press.

Schachter, S., & Singer, J. E. (1962). Cognitive, social, and physiological determinants of emotional state. *Psychological Review, 69,* 379–399.

Scott, J. P. (2000). *Social network analysis.* Newbury Park, CA: Sage.

Sewell, W. H. (1989). Some reflections on the golden age of interdisciplinary social psychology. *Social Psychology Quarterly, 52,* 88–97.

Shah, P. P. (1998). Who are employees' social referents? Using a network perspective to determine referent others. *Academy of Management Journal, 41,* 249–268.

Sherif, M. (1935). A study of some factors in perception. *Archives of Psychology, 27*(187).

Sherif, M. (1936). *The psychology of social norms.* New York: Harper & Brothers.

Stouffer, S. A. (1962). The concept of relative deprivation. In S. A. Stouffer (Ed.), *Social research to test ideas* (pp. 13–38). New York: Free Press.

Stouffer, S. A., Suchman, E. A., DeVinney, L. C., Star, S. A., & Williams, R. M., Jr. (1949). *The American soldier: Adjustment during Army life.* Princeton, NJ: Princeton University Press.

Strang, D., & Soule, S. A. (1998). Diffusion in organizations and social movements: From hybrid corn to poison pills. *Annual Review of Sociology, 24,* 265–290.

Strang, D., & Tuma, N. B. (1993). Spatial and temporal heterogeneity in diffusion. *American Journal of Sociology, 99,* 614–639.

Stube, M. J. (2005). What did Triplett really find? A contemporary analysis of the first experiment in social psychology. *American Journal of Psychology, 118,* 271–286.

Suls, J., & Wheeler, L. (Eds.). (2000). *Handbook of social comparison.* Boston: Kluwer Academic/Plenum.

Triplett, N. (1898). The dynamogenic factors in pacemaking and competition. *American Journal of Psychology, 9,* 507–533.

Turner, R. H. (1990). Some contributions of Muzafer Sherif to sociology. *Social Psychology Quarterly, 53,* 283–291.

Van den Bulte, C., & Lilien, G. L. (2001). *Medical Innovation* revisited: Social contagion versus marketing effort. *American Journal of Sociology, 106,* 1409–1435.

Van den Bulte, C., & Wuyts, S. (2007). *Social networks and marketing.* Cambridge, MA: Marketing Science Institute.

Walker, I., & Smith, H. J. (Eds.). (2002). *Relative deprivation.* Cambridge: Cambridge University Press.

Wasserman, S., & Faust, K. (1994). *Social network analysis.* Cambridge: Cambridge University Press.

White, H. C., Boorman, S. A., & Breiger, R. L. (1976). Social structure from multiple networks, I. Blockmodels of roles and positions. *American Journal of Sociology, 81,* 730–780.

Zucker, L. G. (1977). The role of institutionalization in cultural persistence. *American Sociological Review, 42,* 726–743.

10

Viral Marketing: What Is It, and What Are the Components of Viral Success?

Ralf van der Lans and Gerrit van Bruggen

Firms are reallocating their marketing communication budgets to word-of-mouth (WoM) marketing. PQ Media (2007) reported that total U.S. marketing expenditures on WoM marketing climbed 35.9% in 2006, and similar growth is projected for the 2007–2011 period. This makes WoM marketing the fastest-growing marketing communication segment. Key drivers of the popularity of WoM marketing are the decreasing effectiveness of the traditional marketing communication tools and the developments on the Internet that enhance consumers' abilities to exchange information.

Viral marketing is probably the most important online marketing communication tool that fully exploits the effectiveness of WoM communications. In a viral marketing campaign, consumers spread online information about products and services to their peers by forwarding e-mail. Because online WoM spreads rapidly and is not hampered by geographical boundaries, it has the potential to reach many customers in short time periods. It is not surprising that major organizations develop viral marketing campaigns to promote their brands and products. For instance, in December 2007, OfficeMax launched the viral campaign "Elf Yourself," which generated more than 110 million visitors to its Web site, and the campaign Web site is ranked in the top 1,000 Web sites in about 50 countries (Morrissey, 2008). Likewise, during the Democratic nomination elections, candidate Barack Obama's viral marketing campaign reached 258,000 people, who donated more than $10 million (Tumulty, 2007). For every high-profile example of a successful viral product, however, there are many more attempts that fail. For example, a viral film of Kate Moss in her underwear for Agent Provocateur, a lingerie maker, had what would appear to be the recipe for a viral sensation. It was viewed, however, fewer than 75,000 times in 3 months after it was uploaded (Morrissey, 2007).

This shows the predicament facing marketers who vie for consumer attention with campaigns they hope will go viral. What seems less well understood is that most viral attempts are likely to fail (Kalyanam, McIntyre, & Masonis, 2007).

An important reason of the many viral failures is the common misunderstanding that viral campaigns are random and that successful campaigns happen by luck. This belief in combination with the fact that viral campaigns can be launched relatively cheaply stimulates marketers to upload videos at YouTube without a thoughtful strategy, hoping that their message will go viral. Just as any other marketing communication campaign, however, viral marketing campaigns need to be carefully designed and actively managed to become successful (Kalyanam et al., 2007). The reason for the misassumption that success of viral campaigns happens by luck is that viral campaigns are relatively new and that marketers frequently do not understand the complex underlying mechanism of the spread of information in viral marketing campaigns. The goal of this chapter is therefore twofold. First, we define viral marketing and review its advantages and disadvantages. Second, by illustration of a successful and nonsuccessful viral campaign, we explain the components of success in viral marketing campaigns and subsequently discuss variables that affect these components, that is, the drivers of viral success.

This chapter is structured as follows. The first section defines viral marketing campaigns and its advantages and disadvantages compared to traditional communication campaigns such as advertising. The second section describes the key components that determine the spread of viral marketing campaigns. Based on this discussion, the third section describes the drivers that influence these components and hence the success of viral marketing campaigns. In the fourth section, we explore two real-life viral marketing campaigns and explain why one is more successful than the other. Finally, the last section concludes this chapter with a short summary and avenues for future research.

WHAT IS VIRAL MARKETING?

Viral marketing is a form of peer-to-peer communication in which individuals are encouraged to receive and process but also pass on promotional messages within their social networks (Bampo, Ewing, Mather, Stewart, & Wallace, 2008). In a viral marketing campaign, an organization develops a marketing message and stimulates customers to forward this message electronically (i.e., by e-mail or text messaging) to their social network contacts (e.g., friends, colleagues, or family). These contacts are subsequently motivated to forward the message to their contacts, and so on. Because messages from friends are likely to have more impact than advertising, and information spreads rapidly over the Internet, viral marketing is potentially a very powerful marketing communication tool that may reach many customers in a short period of time (De Bruyn & Lilien, 2008). Furthermore, next to plain text messages, the nature of the Internet allows marketers to use many different forms of communication such as videos, games, and interactive Web sites in their viral campaigns.

Although viral marketing campaigns can be very different in nature, they possess two important characteristics. First, attractive or interesting content for a target group is developed and placed on a Web site. This content can be of hedonic nature, such as short funny movies, commercials, or exciting video games, but it can also be more functional such as e-mail platforms (Hotmail, Yahoo!, and Gmail), chat boxes, and blogs. The viral content can be placed on a platform that is specifically developed for the campaign, but it can also be placed on existing Internet platforms such as YouTube. Second, to stimulate electronic WoM and to attract more visitors to the campaign, the Web site contains facilities for visitors to inform friends (i.e., spread the campaign) by e-mail, such as a "Tell a Friend" or "Share Video" button. Viral marketing by this exploits the many-to-many communication opportunities so-called hypermedia computer-mediated environments (Hoffman & Novak, 1996) offer.

What Makes Viral Marketing Campaigns Attractive?

Viral marketing campaigns have numerous advantages over more traditional marketing communication campaigns that make it an attractive communication tool (Bampo et al., 2008). First of all, viral marketing campaigns may simultaneously serve several communication goals that traditional advertising tools are not able to obtain. Next to the creation of awareness, positive attitudes, and promoting products, viral campaigns may, because of their interactive nature, obtain interesting consumer information, such as demographics, preferences, and opinions.

In addition, and frequently most important, during a viral marketing campaign, a consumer is asked to forward the message by e-mail. This results in large databases with additional consumer information, including e-mail addresses, that the company may use to target those consumers in future campaigns.

Second, viral marketing campaigns incur very little expense because the individual passing on the referral carries the cost of forwarding the brand message (Woerndl, Papagiannidis, Bourlakis, & Li, 2008). Furthermore, many Web sites such as YouTube provide marketers free opportunities to upload their viral messages. Despite these cheap opportunities, however, nowadays marketers need to invest increasingly higher amounts in viral marketing campaigns to attract consumer attention and to motivate them to spread the marketing message.

A third advantage of viral marketing campaigns is that these campaigns are based on WoM communications that have proved to have more impact than nonpersonal communications. Because of WoM's effectiveness, marketers have always recognized it as an important antecedent of consumer behavior (Katz & Lazarsfeld, 1955). Interpersonal influence in computer-mediated settings of viral marketing, however, is significantly different from that occurring in conventional contexts (Subramani & Rajagopalan, 2003). Scale and scope of influence is considerably expanded. Computer mediation allows a much larger number of individuals to be connected by informational linkages than is feasible through face-to-face contact or through conventional media such as the telephone. This allows consumers to easily reach their peers all over the world who may read their messages at different times if more convenient. This substantially increases the speed and reach of WoM in viral marketing campaigns.

A fourth advantage of viral marketing is that this form of marketing communication is highly targeted. Influencers are not only able to accurately anticipate interests of connected others (Subramani & Rajagopalan, 2003) but also better able to write a personal persuasive message in which they promote the viral message. The use of these relationships between people makes viral marketing potentially more profitable than direct marketing. Turning customers into a marketing force is thus crucial for viral marketing (Phelps, Lewis, Mobilio, Perry, & Raman, 2004).

Finally, and probably the most important advantage of viral marketing, is that marketers can exactly monitor who is forwarding a message to whom, whether consumers respond to a viral message, how long they spend on the campaigns Web site, and so on. This provides marketers with the unique opportunity to fine-tune the campaign after its launch, and online experimentation is therefore common practice to improve viral marketing campaigns (Kalyanam et al., 2007). For instance, many viral marketing campaigns provide incentives, such as sweepstakes, to motivate consumers to forward a message to friends. It is frequently not clear whether this incentive should be presented in the subject line of the viral e-mail. By randomly changing the content of the viral e-mail, marketers can relatively straightforwardly optimize the effectiveness of viral marketing campaigns.

Viral Marketing: Threats

Next to the advantages mentioned in the previous paragraph, marketers need to be aware of potential risks connected to viral marketing campaigns. Once a message spreads as a virus over the Web, it is impossible to further control this process. In addition, because consumers are free to forward any message, it is difficult to control what message consumers are writing to their peers. A frequently used solution is that consumers are allowed only to forward a message but not allowed to edit it. A disadvantage of this approach is of course that the message is less personal and that consumers are less likely to forward the message, making the campaign less effective. If the information starts to spread as a virus, and the process gets out of control, it may lead to logistical problems such as slow Web sites or very high costs, as Starbucks experienced when it offered a free coffee to every recipient of a viral e-mail (Dilworth, 2006).

As viral marketing gets more popular, consumers are getting used to the messages, and it becomes harder for them to get through the clutter and be motivated to forward messages. At the same time, spam-e-mail-based viruses and the like have cluttered electronic communications, which makes viral marketing campaigns increasingly more challenging to deploy (De Bruyn & Lilien, 2008).

In sum, viral marketing is a powerful marketing communication tool that can reach a large set of customers. But developing a successful viral marketing campaign requires a thorough understanding of how marketing messages spread and how marketers can influence this spread, which will be discussed in the remainder of this chapter.

HOW DOES INFORMATION IN VIRAL MARKETING SPREAD?

Figure 10.1 graphically depicts how information spreads in viral marketing campaigns. In this figure, each e-mail symbol (📨) corresponds to one customer in the viral marketing campaign. The viral process is started by one customer in generation 0, and grows rapidly in each subsequent generation. As becomes clear from this figure, a viral marketing campaign contains two types of customers. First, there are customers who are not informed by a viral e-mail of a friend about the campaign (indicated by the symbol 📨). These customers (in Figure 10.1 there is only one such customer) join the campaign because of seeding activities of the company. They initiate the viral process by forwarding an invitation to join the campaign by e-mailing some of their acquaintances. These acquaintances can become customers as well (indicated by the symbol 📨), and they may forward an e-mail to invite their friends to join the campaign.

As such, messages in viral marketing campaigns may spread like a virus (Watts & Peretti, 2007). An "infected" customer forwards a message to

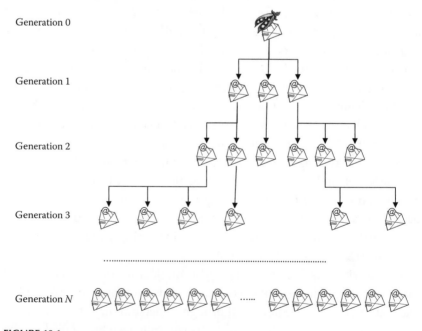

FIGURE 10.1
Spread of information in viral marketing campaigns.

another customer, who may become "infected" as well by joining the campaign. Similarly, the spread of information in Figure 10.1 can also be compared to the growth of families and populations over time (Harris, 1963; Kendall, 1949). In this case, a female may give birth to children who may give birth to their children, and so on. Therefore, insights from epidemics and biology have proved to be extremely useful to explain the spread of information in viral marketing campaigns. For instance, standard results in these literature streams suggest that the number of customers should grow exponentially if the average number of "infected" friends exceeds one for each customer who joins the campaign (Athreya & Ney, 1972; Hartmann et al., 2008). This average number, which plays a crucial role in the spread of viruses and growth of populations, is frequently called reproduction rate, infection rate, or offspring.

Building on insights of epidemics and population growth, van der Lans, van Bruggen, Eliashberg, and Wierenga (2008) developed a model that exactly describes stochastically the reach S_t of viral marketing campaigns at time t. This model, based on the theory of branching processes (Athreya & Ney, 1972; Harris, 1963), shows that the reach at time t of viral marketing campaigns depends on (a) the number of seeded customers; (b) the seeding acceptance, that is, the probability that a seeded customer joins the campaign; (c) the forward rate, that is, the average number of e-mail forwarded by a customer in the campaign; (d) the viral acceptance, that is, the probability that a customer joins the campaign after receiving a viral e-mail; and (e) the response time, that is, the time a customer takes to join the campaign after receiving a viral e-mail. Note that in this model, the reproduction rate is the product of the forward rate and the viral acceptance. The strength of this model is that it uses detailed information of the underlying viral process to predict the number of customers in a viral marketing campaign. Because marketers are able to store detailed information of each online customer (Bonfrer & Drèze, 2009; Chevalier & Mayzlin, 2006), information on all parameters becomes available in large quantities early in a campaign. Therefore, this information allows for first applications of the stochastic branching processes on actual data, as these data are usually not available or impossible to measure in the offline world.

Because detailed data of the underlying viral process are available only recently, researchers traditionally used deterministic models to describe the spread of information and the diffusion of rumors and innovations. These deterministic models assume random mixing of two or more populations.

The Bass model, the most well-known of these models, especially in business, assumes two populations: adopters and those who did not adopt yet (Bartlett, 1960; Bass, 1969). In these models, S_t is used directly to infer and optimize model parameters (in the Bass model p and q). In contrast, branching processes do *not* use information on S_t and estimate model parameters using the underlying process data. These parameter estimates are subsequently used to infer the reach S_t using its closed-form equation (van der Lans et al., 2008). An advantage of using the underlying viral process is that parameters are estimated based on larger quantities of data and are therefore much more accurate. As a comparison, suppose a small campaign is online for 10 days and generates a thousand customers. In this case, deterministic models such as the Bass model would have 10 observations to derive the underlying parameters, that is, each day serves as 1 observation. In contrast, the parameters of the branching process are determined by 1,000 observations, as in this case customers are treated as the unit of observation. More interesting, however, the parameters of branching processes have a one-to-one relationship with the underlying viral process. Hence, researchers get a much better understanding of why some campaigns are more successful than others. For instance, van der Lans et al. (2008) used their model to execute what-if analyses by, for example, assuming that the company seeds an additional amount of customers. In addition, this approach could also be used to find out why one campaign is more successful compared to another campaign, as we will do later in this chapter.

In sum, the reach or success of viral marketing campaigns is composed of five important factors: (a) number of seeded customers, (b) seeding acceptance, (c) forward rate, (d) viral acceptance, and (e) response time. An important feature of viral marketing campaigns is that marketers are able to directly observe these important factors as they are able to monitor the viral process. In the following section we will discuss drivers that marketers may use to control these five important factors.

—————

DRIVERS OF VIRAL MARKETING CAMPAIGN SUCCESS

As mentioned in the previous section, the reach of a viral marketing campaign over time is composed of five factors. The last factor (response time) influences the speed of the process. The first four factors (number of seeded customers, seeding acceptance, forward rate, and viral acceptance) directly influence the number of customers. The first two factors related to seeding (number of seeded customers and seeding acceptance) have a direct linear effect on the number of customers in the campaign. Thus, if a marketer doubles the number of seeded customers, the total reach should double as well. In contrast, the factors related to the viral spread (forward rate and viral acceptance) have an exponential effect on the campaign's reach. As shown in the following sections, however, the drivers to increase these two viral factors are generally much more complex and costly than the drivers to improve the seeding factors.

Number of Seeded Customers

In general, marketers can choose from three distinct categories to seed their viral marketing campaigns: (a) seeding e-mail, (b) online advertising, and (c) offline advertising. Seeding e-mail are usually sent by the company itself or by a specialized marketing agency to customers who gave permission to receive promotional e-mail (Bonfrer & Drèze, 2009). Using this seeding tool, a marketer can target individual customers who are potentially interested in the campaign. The design and content of the e-mail are crucial because customers easily categorize such e-mail as spam and quickly delete them. For this reason, seeding e-mail can also be expected to be less effective than viral e-mail that are sent by friends or acquaintances of the recipient.

Online advertising is another important seeding tool that marketers can use to influence the viral process. There are many different online advertising formats, such as banners, pop-ups, skyscrapers, large rectangles, floating ads, and interstitials (Burns & Lutz, 2006). The effectiveness of these formats may differ across customers as well as across the Web sites on which the ads are placed. Interestingly, marketers can directly observe when a specific online ad generates a visitor to the viral campaign. Hence, the effectiveness of each advertising format can be monitored accurately, and on the basis of the advertisement's performance, a marketer can decide to adapt its online advertising strategy. Furthermore, online advertising agencies may offer contracts that guarantee a predetermined number of clicks to the campaign's Web site within a certain time window. In such cases, organizations usually pay for each realized click. Because online ads may be perceived as less obtrusive than promotional e-mail, this seeding tool may be very attractive.

Finally, besides using online seeding tools, marketers may still use "traditional" offline advertising to seed their campaigns. Examples are magazine or TV ads that refer to the Web site of the viral marketing campaign and package labels or coupons that try to attract visitors to the campaign's Web site. Because customers cannot directly visit the campaigns Web site by clicking a link, offline seeding activities are less popular and can be expected to be less effective. Another disadvantage of offline activities is that it is more difficult to measure their effectiveness, as one cannot directly observe that customers visit campaigns because of these activities. Possible solutions for this problem are asking customers on the Web site how they got informed or asking for the bar code of the product or coupon that they used to enter the Web site.

Seeding Acceptance

Seeding acceptance, that is, the probability that someone who receives an invitation by seeding joins the campaign, strongly depends on the seeding source. As discussed previously, online advertising through banners is usually more effective than promotional e-mail, as marketers frequently pay for each realized click on a banner. Hence, most consumers who click on a banner arrive at the landing page of the campaign, whereas consumers receiving a promotional e-mail have a much lower probability of visiting the landing page. In support of this, van der Lans et al. (2008) found in their empirical application that the seeding acceptance is higher for banners compared to promotional e-mail. Furthermore, online seeding tools are expected to be more effective than offline seeding tools as it is much easier for customers to join the viral campaign as they are already online.

Other important factors that positively influence seeding acceptance are incentives, the structure and content of the campaign, attracting consumer's attention, and targeting. As incentives and the structure and content of the campaign also influence the forward rate and viral acceptance, we will discuss these drivers next. Attracting consumer's attention gets increasingly difficult. As consumers are bombarded with online ads and receive many promotional e-mail, it is difficult to get through this clutter with seeding activities. Moreover, as many computers have spam filters, it is getting even more difficult to reach consumers at all. An advantage of the online environment, however, is that marketers can track the success of their seeding activities in real time. This allows marketers to adapt their marketing activities depending on the seeding acceptance, which even allows for field experiments that are commonly executed. In addition, the seeding acceptance of specific marketing tools may also vary across consumers. For instance, Phillip and Suri (2004) showed that females react differently to promotional e-mail than males. Other researchers have distinguished specific groups of consumers that are more likely to respond or to participate in viral marketing campaigns, such as viral mavens or opinion leaders (Phelps et al., 2004). Marketers should therefore carefully target their seeding activities.

Forward Rate

Marketing activities that aim to influence the forward rate should focus on motivating customers to forward marketing messages to their contacts. As suggested by Godes et al. (2005), motivations to forward messages are either intrinsic or extrinsic. Intrinsic motivations can be triggered by the content of the viral marketing campaign. Phelps et al. (2004) identified several campaign characteristics that stimulate consumers to forward a message. They suggested that campaigns that spark strong emotion— humor, fear, sadness, or inspiration—have a higher tendency to be forwarded. In agreement with this observation, marketers frequently develop Web sites that contain videos and games that attract consumers' attention and are surprising or funny. In addition, Welker (2002) mentioned that providing effortless transmission to others increases the forward rate. To accomplish this, Web sites usually facilitate the viral process by providing tools to easily forward e-mail to friends, such as "Tell a Friend" or "Share Video" buttons. Other ways to increase the intrinsic motivation of consumers is to get them more involved or loyal to the campaign. For instance, nowadays marketers develop viral games in which consumers are motivated to challenge their friends by achieving higher scores on a specific game. This stimulates consumers to repeatedly visit a campaign's Web site and to invite more friends.

Examples of extrinsic motivations to forward marketing messages are rewards, such as prizes, free products, and other monetary incentives (Biyalogorsky, Gerstner, & Libai, 2001). Rewards are found to increase the forwarding rate especially for referring to weak ties and for weaker brands. It is also important to consider the receiver of the reward. Overall, for weak ties and weaker brands, giving a reward to the provider of the recommendation is important. For strong ties and stronger brands, providing at least some of the reward to the receiver of the referral seems to be effective (Ryu & Feick, 2007).

Viral Acceptance

To control the viral acceptance, that is, the probability that a customer joins the campaign after receiving a viral e-mail, it is important to understand the decisions that a consumer needs to make before joining the campaign (De Bruyn & Lilien, 2008). Figure 10.2 schematically presents the process of viral acceptance. This process consists of four stages: (a) receiving a viral e-mail, (b) reading a viral e-mail, (c) visiting the landing page of the viral campaign, and (d) joining the viral campaign. Viral acceptance corresponds to the probability that a consumer goes through all four stages, that is, from receiving a viral e-mail to joining the campaign. Note that seeding acceptance consumers go through a similar process, the main difference being the source of invitation. Therefore, to increase seeding acceptance, marketers should take into account this process for seeding as well.

To increase the viral acceptance, marketers should therefore examine each stage of the viral acceptance process. First, a marketer should stimulate consumers to read the e-mail. As electronic mailboxes become more crowded, response rates are falling. Consumers often hit the delete key when they know the message is from a marketer. They are much more reluctant to delete a message from a person they know. This fact is a key component in understanding the potential power of viral marketing (Phelps et al., 2004). According to Leskovec, Adamic, and Huberman (2007), strong ties (between families or friends) are more likely to be activated and are also more influential than weak ties. As a person sends out more and more recommendations past a certain number for a product, the success per recommendation declines. This seems to indicate that

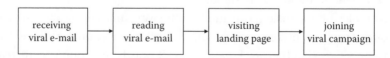

FIGURE 10.2
Process of viral acceptance.

individuals have influence over a few of their friends but not everybody they know (Leskovec et al., 2007). It implies that higher response rates can be expected if people are encouraged to forward their e-mail messages to persons they know well.

Important drivers to open and read the viral message are characteristics of the sender and the subject line. De Bruyn and Lilien (2008) showed that viral messages from strong ties have a higher likelihood to be opened and read. Although the sender source relationship is difficult to control for the marketer, a marketing researcher could stimulate consumers to invite a fixed number of friends. The first few invited friends are probably stronger ties than the last invited friend. Marketers can control the content of the subject line directly, compared to sender characteristics. In many situations, consumers have to provide only the names and e-mail addresses of their friends to forward a viral message. In such situations, a marketer has to decide on the content of the message and the subject line. An important decision here is whether to include in the subject line incentives or only the purpose of the campaign and/or brand name. Personal messages, however, gain more credibility than those coming directly from the self-interested advertiser (Pousttchi & Wiedemann, 2007). Therefore, marketers should consider whether senders are allowed to write their own message. Disadvantages of allowing consumers to write their own viral messages are that it could lower the forward rate, and marketers lack control to prevent consumers from writing insulting messages to peers.

Next to stimulating opening and reading of viral messages, it is important that consumers visit the landing page of the campaign by clicking a link in the viral e-mail. Important here are the content and style of the message (Bonfrer & Drèze, 2009). Again, marketers need to consider whether they allow consumers to write the viral message. Marketers, however, frequently write the message themselves to mention rewards and to include a proper link to the campaigns Web site. Finally, marketers need to develop an attractive Web site to stimulate visitors of the landing page to join the campaign by viewing a video or playing a game. An important decision here is whether consumers need to register to join the campaign. Registering is frequently necessary as consumers are promised an incentive such as winning a prize or a free product after joining the campaign.

Although viral acceptance is higher than seeding acceptance (van der Lans et al., 2008), these percentages are usually very low, resulting in infection rates below 1 (Watts & Peretti, 2007). To increase acceptance, marketers could consider sending reminder e-mail and allowing consumers to send viral e-mail to consumers who already received a viral e-mail. It is unclear whether such a strategy is successful, as consumers may get annoyed and perceive the messages as spam.

Response Time

The final factor, response time, influences the speed of the viral process rather than its reach. As information spreads rapidly online, viral marketing campaigns spread relatively fast. Marketers have therefore little control on the response time of consumers. Responses, however, seem to be quicker at certain time periods. For instance, van der Lans et al. (2008) showed that responses during weekends are slower than during weekdays. This suggests that marketers should time their marketing activities carefully, as seeding activities during weekends might be less effective.

In sum, it is a misunderstanding to portray viral marketing as a random ground-up phenomenon over which marketers have little control. The viral process, although complex, depends on only a few key parameters that can be continuously monitored and influenced by marketers. In the next section, using two real-life viral marketing campaigns, we show how marketers can monitor and manage viral campaigns in real time.

TRACKING VIRAL CAMPAIGN SUCCESS

We will now describe the way we can analyze and diagnose the success of viral marketing campaigns. To do so, we explore two real-life viral marketing campaigns. These two campaigns were selected based on the reach the campaigns obtained. The first campaign is very successful, whereas the second campaign is not. The next paragraph gives a short description of both campaigns. To find out why the first campaign is more effective than the second one, we analyze and compare the forward rate and viral acceptance of both campaigns. Finally, we also present the speed of the campaigns by comparing the response times of the campaigns.

Descriptions of the Viral Marketing Campaigns

The successful campaign reached 97,561 customers in 116 days, whereas the less successful campaign reached 2,085 customers in 188 days. For both campaigns, a professional e-marketing agency tracked the viral process on a daily basis. Hence, we know for both campaigns exactly the moment in time a customer joins the viral campaign and to which e-mail addresses each customer forwards a viral e-mail. Unfortunately, the e-marketing agency did not record the seeding activities, so we are able to analyze only the viral factors for these two campaigns.

The successful campaign was executed for one of the biggest dairy manufacturers in the Netherlands. The goals of the campaign were to stimulate sales, activate the brand, and rejuvenate the target group. The viral campaign consisted of a game. In the game, a player first chooses one of the recognizable characters from a brand family and then starts to dance around a table with the other virtual family members. The table contains puddings for all but one of the family members. During the game, as the music stops, the family members stop dancing and need to obtain a pudding. If the player is not able to get a pudding, the game is over. Otherwise the dance starts again with one family member less. The goal of the game is to beat all the family members and to make it to the last round, in which the player wins a prize. Consumers are allowed to play the game more than once if they forward viral e-mail to friends about the viral game. This means that there is an incentive to provide e-mail addresses, forward e-mail, and thus stimulate the viral process. We refer to this campaign as "Pudding."

The nonsuccessful viral campaign was developed to stimulate awareness and purchase of a DVD release of a TV show. The DVD release was marketed by a large independent movie distributor in Western Europe. Similar to the successful campaign, this campaign developed a game to promote the DVD release. In the game, a short video extracted from the series is shown. Participants could click on the Laugh-O-Meter to activate the laughter in the video. By finishing the game, consumers could win prizes such as the DVD box. We refer to this campaign as "DVD." In both campaigns participants received a reward for forwarding e-mail, that is, a so-called tipping incentive.

In Figure 10.3 we graphically present the difference in the cumulative number of consumers reached by the two campaigns during the first 10 weeks. The data in Figure 10.3 show that for the Pudding campaign, the

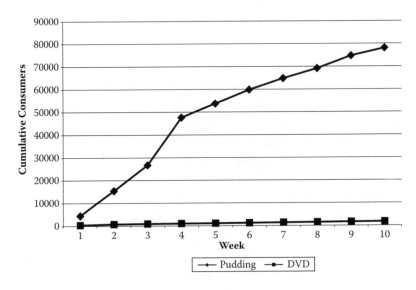

FIGURE 10.3
Cumulative number of participants for successful and nonsuccessful viral campaigns.

number of participants, the reach, increases quickly between Week 1 and Week 4, after which the number of new participants per week decreases. This also becomes clear from Figure 10.4, which presents the incremental number of participants by week. This is the way the reach of successful viral marketing campaigns typically develops. Initially, the number of participants grows rapidly, after which the viral process dies out slowly. For the DVD campaign, the pattern is different as this campaign never really took off, and probably most of the visitors are due to seeding.

The following paragraphs compare the viral factors to find out why the Pudding campaign is much more successful than the DVD campaign.

Comparison of Forwarding Rates

In viral campaigns, consumers are free to send an e-mail to any other e-mail address. As consumers have incentives to send as many e-mails as possible, they often send messages to invalid e-mail addresses. In addition, as the campaign attracts more consumers, the probability that a consumer invites a friend who already joined the campaign increases as well. Therefore, to count only potentially effective viral e-mail, we computed the forward rate by counting the net number of viral e-mail forwarded. This number is computed by subtracting invalid e-mail and e-mail to people

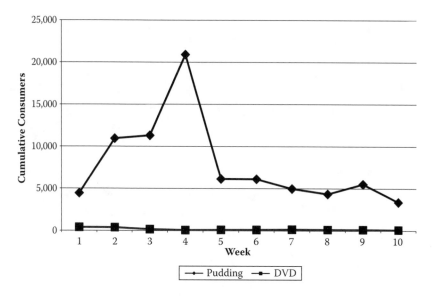

FIGURE 10.4
Number of participants by week for successful and nonsuccessful viral campaigns.

who already received an e-mail from the gross number of e-mail sent. This leads to a forward rate of 1.21 in the Pudding campaign and 0.36 in the DVD campaign.

Figure 10.5 graphically presents the forward rate for both campaigns by week. Clearly, the successful campaign has a significantly higher forward rate, which is more than three times higher than the less successful campaign. Over time, the forward rates seem to decrease slightly, especially for the Pudding campaign. This is because the number of consumers joining the campaign increases over time, and hence the likelihood that someone forwards a viral e-mail to a consumer who already joined the campaign increases over time as well. It is also interesting to mention that the number of redundant or irrelevant e-mail is larger for the Pudding campaign than for the DVD campaign. Apparently the Pudding campaign was more effective in stimulating people to forward messages than the DVD campaign. This, however, also caused people to send away more e-mail to e-mail addresses that did not exist or to people who already received an e-mail.

Because the forward rate is an extremely important success factor, both campaigns stimulated the forward rate by allowing consumers to play multiple times. Stimulating such repeat behavior may be attractive because it makes it possible for the organization to more effectively communicate

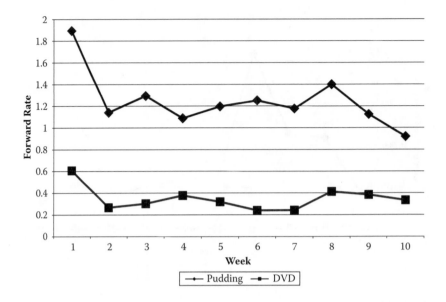

FIGURE 10.5
Forward rate for successful and nonsuccessful viral campaigns.

its messages and reinforce its awareness and brand image. Also, repeat behavior will be effective for further stimulating the viral process by increasing the forward rate. The results in Figure 10.6 show that in the Pudding campaign, repeat behavior turned out to be a very effective tool to increase the forward rate. Overall, the forward rate for consumers who played the game for the first time equals 1.09, but if those consumers came back and played the game again, they tended to forward an additional 2.82 viral e-mail. A similar effect is found for the DVD campaign, although less pronounced. First-time players forwarded on average 0.42 viral e-mail. If those consumers decided to play again, they tended to forward an additional 0.23 viral e-mail.

Comparison of Viral Acceptance

If we compare the viral acceptance of the two campaigns in our data set, Pudding and DVD, we find that the Pudding campaign is clearly better able to make people respond to e-mail. The overall viral acceptance for the Pudding campaign is 0.35, whereas it is 0.19 for the DVD campaign. Multiplying these viral acceptances with the forward rates as discussed previously, we find reproduction rates of 0.42 for the Pudding campaign

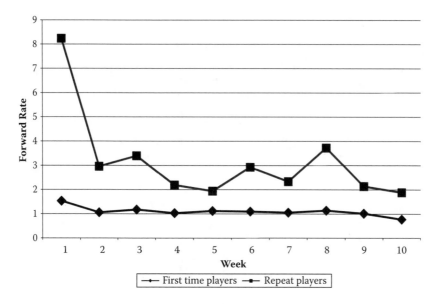

FIGURE 10.6
Forward rate for first-time and repeat players in the "Pudding" campaign.

and 0.068 for the DVD campaign. Using these reproduction rates, we are able to compute how many additional customers each customer will generate on average, by the following equation (Watts & Peretti, 2007):

$$\text{Expected number of additional customers} = \frac{\text{Reproduction Rate}}{1 - \text{Reproduction Rate}}$$

Application of this formula shows that each seeded customer in the Pudding campaign generates on average 0.73 additional consumers, which is over 10 times higher than the average number of additional consumers in the DVD campaign, which equals 0.07.

Figure 10.7 presents the viral acceptance rates over time. This figure shows that although variation in time exists, there is no clear increase or decrease in the response rates over time. In fact, the variability in the forwarding rate for the DVD campaign is due to the few observations, especially in later stages of the campaign.

We also examined whether viral acceptance is different for e-mail forwarded by consumers who play for the first time and repeat players. Interestingly, although repeated behavior led to a strong increase in the

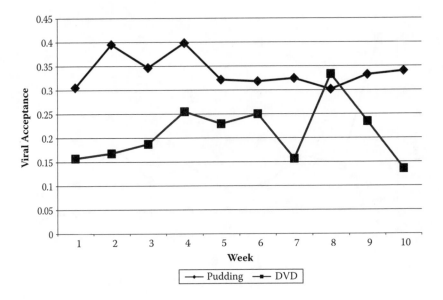

FIGURE 10.7
Viral acceptance for successful and nonsuccessful viral campaigns.

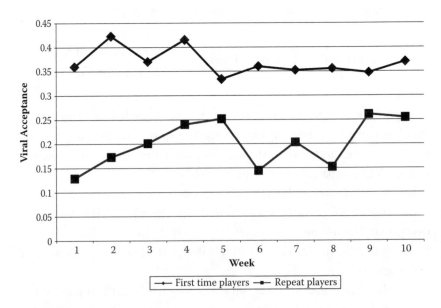

FIGURE 10.8
Viral acceptance for first-time and repeat players in the "Pudding" campaign.

forward rate, the viral acceptance is much lower for the Pudding campaign (0.38 vs. 0.20), whereas the viral acceptance of the DVD campaign seems to be stable (0.19 vs. 0.21). These results are in correspondence with the observations of Leskovec et al. (2007), who suggested that later e-mail are sent to weak ties that have a lower probability to open and respond these e-mail. The fact that consumers in the DVD campaign invited only a few friends probably results in equally effective viral e-mail for repeat and first-time players.

Comparison of Response Time

The success of a viral marketing campaign will often be measured in terms of its reach. This reach will thus depend on the forwarding activities of participants and on the responses of recipients. It may also be important, however, that this process evolves quickly. To make the campaign grow fast, the response time will also matter. On average the median response time for both campaigns seems to be fairly equal: The median response time of the Pudding campaign was 0.38 days, whereas it was 0.46 days for the DVD campaign. Figure 10.9 illustrates a similar pattern over time, although the response time for the DVD campaign shows more variation because of

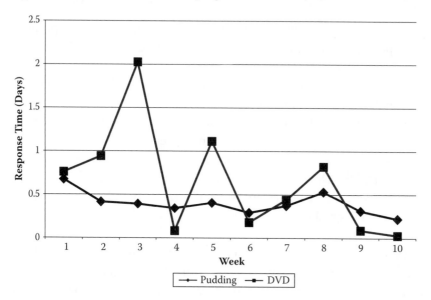

FIGURE 10.9
Median response time (in days) for successful and nonsuccessful viral campaigns.

the fewer observations. These results stress the speed of viral marketing campaigns, as consumers respond to viral e-mail rapidly. Furthermore, as response times are relatively stable across campaigns, marketers have fewer possibilities to control the speed of the viral process.

CONCLUSIONS

Summary

In this chapter we dealt with viral marketing and how these campaigns may become successful. In a viral marketing campaign, an organization develops a marketing message and stimulates customers to forward this message by e-mail to their social network contacts (e.g., friends, colleagues, or family). These contacts are subsequently motivated to forward the message to their contacts, and so on. The viral spread of information in viral marketing seems complex, leading to the common misunderstanding that the success of viral marketing campaigns is more a matter of luck. In this chapter we showed that there are five important components of success of viral marketing campaigns:

- *Number of seeded customers:* A sufficient number of appropriate people should be targeted with an appealing and attractive message through seeding activities.
- *Seeding acceptance:* The seeded customers should be incentivized to join the viral campaign.
- *Forward rate:* Customers who join a viral campaign should be motivated to forward viral e-mail to their peers.
- *Viral acceptance:* It should be made attractive for recipients of viral e-mail to respond to them.
- *Response time:* Receivers of viral e-mail should be motivated to respond quickly.

As marketers are able to observe online consumer behavior in detail, these factors can be measured in real time during viral marketing campaigns. For instance, in two empirical examples we showed how marketers tried to improve the forward rate and viral acceptance by providing incentives and stimulating repeat playing of a game.

Opportunities and Challenges for Future Research on Viral Marketing

Viral marketing is a relatively new phenomenon, and little research has been done. In addition, viral marketing provides marketers with detailed data of actual behavior. This opens many interesting avenues for future research. First, there is a need for more sophisticated and targeted seeding experimentation (Bampo et al., 2008), because targeting the right people is essential to any viral effect (Phelps et al., 2004). Should "hubs" or influentials who have many connections be targeted? Intuitively this seems to be an attractive and effective strategy. Watts and Dodds (2007), however, debated the influential hypothesis. Because people seem to show lower response rates to seeding activities than to viral e-mail from persons they are familiar with, it could be a waste to approach influentials with seeding marketing activities. To fully exploit influentials, future research could test whether influentials are indeed most effective to target.

Second, as discussed in a previous section, there are many drivers that may affect the success of viral marketing campaigns. There is little research, however, that links these drivers to the five components of success of actual viral campaigns. Cross-sectional research on a large number of viral campaigns is needed to identify important generalizations of which campaign characteristics are useful under which circumstances. Such research not only should focus on the reach of viral marketing campaigns but could also focus on other important performance measures. For instance, how much time do consumers spend on a viral Web site, and does this increase sales? In addition, it is unclear how viral marketing campaigns affect other marketing communication objectives such as awareness, brand image, and memory and how they interact with other marketing communication tools such as advertising and sales promotions. Future research should investigate the position and importance of viral marketing campaigns in the total marketing communication mix.

Third, as consumers are getting increasingly annoyed with promotional e-mail and classify them as spam, it is important that future research investigates possible negative effects of viral marketing campaigns. It is important to find out when customers get annoyed and/or irritated and how this affects the brand. For instance, do customers get annoyed when they receive more than one viral e-mail? If so, marketers should inform senders of viral e-mail whether a friend already received a viral e-mail or already participated in the viral campaign.

Fourth, in this chapter we did not take the actual network structure into account. Such a structure can be expected to affect the viral process. Three of the variables that determine the way a virus spreads (the forward rate, the viral acceptance, and the response time) will most likely depend on the network structure. For example, we can expect the forwarding rate to be higher in a densely connected network than in a sparse network, and the same may be true for the viral acceptance and the response time. An important feature of viral marketing processes is that these components of its spread are directly observable. After a few days of the launch of the campaign, one can already obtain figures about the forwarding and acceptance rates and use these to predict the way the campaign will further develop. One thus does not need information about the network structure to make these types of forecasts. Also, observing the actual network structure will probably be quite difficult for the large-size populations through which typical marketing viruses spread. At the same time, having information about the network structure could be a useful addition because this might be instrumental in forecasting the development of the forwarding rate, the acceptance rate, and the response time over time. For instance, as illustrated in Figure 10.5, the forward rate decreases over time. The rate of this decrease is likely to depend on network structure. In future research it would, therefore, be interesting to investigate the relationship between network characteristics and the various components of viral marketing success.

Finally, viral marketing is a specific form of online WoM, which is probably the most influential form of communications. Traditionally, research on WoM has been hampered by the fact that it is an unobserved process, and marketers frequently rely on simple experiments and survey data. In a viral marketing campaign, large amounts of data come available on actual WoM of consumers. This allows marketing researchers to test important theories of WoM behavior (Godes et al., 2005). In addition, viral marketing campaigns offer unique opportunities to execute large-scale field experiments in which exogenous variables of interest are easily manipulated.

In sum, a viral marketing campaign is a powerful tool that has the potential to reach many consumers in an era in which they are increasingly difficult to reach. We hope that this chapter helps practitioners to improve their viral marketing campaigns and to further stimulate research in the area of viral marketing.

NOTE

The authors thank Klaas Weima and Ayse Geertsma of Energize for providing the data set and for their helpful suggestions during this project. They also thank Melissa Nguyen for analyzing the data.

REFERENCES

Athreya, K. B., & Ney, P. E. (1972). *Branching processes.* Berlin, Germany: Springer-Verlag.

Bampo, M., Ewing, M. T., Mather, D. R., Stewart, D., & Wallacem M. (2008). The effects of the social structure of digital networks on viral marketing performance. *Information Systems Research, 19*(3), 273–293.

Bartlett, M. S. (1960). *Stochastic population models in ecology and epidemiology.* London: Methuen.

Bass, F. M. (1969). A new product growth for model consumer durables. *Management Science, 15*(5), 215–227.

Biyalogorsky, E., Gerstner, E., & Libai, B. (2001). Customer referral management: Optimal reward programs. *Marketing Science, 20*(1), 82–95.

Bonfrer, A., & Drèze, X. (2009). Real-time evaluation of email campaign performance. *Marketing Science, 28*(2), 251–263.

Burns, K. S., & Lutz, R. J. (2006). The function of format: Consumer responses to six on-line advertising formats. *Journal of Advertising, 35*(1), 53–63.

Chevalier, J. A., & Mayzlin, D. (2006). The effect of word-of-mouth on sales: Online book reviews. *Journal of Marketing Research, 43*, 345–354.

De Bruyn, A., & Lilien, G. L. (2008). A multi-stage model of word of mouth through viral marketing. *International Journal of Research in Marketing, 25*(3), 151–163.

Dilworth, D. (2006). Starbucks holds fast forwarded e-mail promotion. *DMNews.* http://www.dmnews.com/starbucks-halts-fast-forwarded-e-mail-promotion/article/92533/

Godes, D., Mayzlin, D., Chen, Y., Das, S., Dellarocas, C., Pfeiffer, B., Libai, B., Sen, S., Shi, M., & Verlegh, P. (2005). The firm's management of social interactions. *Marketing Letters, 16*(3–4), 415–428.

Harris, T. E. (1963). *The theory of branching processes.* Berlin, Germany: Springer-Verlag.

Hartmann, W. R., Manchanda, P., Nair, H., Bothner, M., Dodds, P., Godes, D., Hosanagar, K., & Tucker, C. (2008). Modeling social interactions: Identification, empirical methods and policy implications. *Marketing Letters, 19*(3–4), 287–304.

Hoffman, D., & Novak, T. P. (1996). Marketing in hypermedia computer mediated environments: Conceptual foundations. *Journal of Marketing, 80*(3), 50–68.

Kalyanam, K., McIntyre, S., & Masonis, J. T. (2007). Adaptive experimentation in interactive marketing: The case of viral marketing at Plaxo. *Journal of Interactive Marketing, 21*(3), 72–85.

Katz, E., & Lazarsfeld, P. (1955). *Personal influence.* Glencoe, IL: Free Press.

Kendall, D. G. (1949). Stochastic processes and population growth. *Journal of the Royal Statistical Society, Series B, 11*(2), 230–282.

Leskovec, J., Adamic, L. A., & Huberman, B. A. (2007). The dynamics of viral marketing. *ACM Transactions on the Web, 1*(1), 1–39.

Morrissey, B. (2007). Clients try to manipulate 'unpredictable' viral buzz. *Adweek*, 48 (March 19), p. 12.

Morrissey, B. (2008, January 7). The rules of viral Web success, at least for now. *Adweek*, p. 13.

Phelps, J. E., Lewis, R., Mobilio, L., Perry, D., & Raman, N. (2004, December). Viral marketing or electronic word-of-mouth advertising: Examining consumer responses and motivations to pass along email. *Journal of Advertising Research*, 44, 333–348.

Phillip, M. V., & Suri, R. (2004, December). Impact of gender differences on the evaluation of promotional emails. *Journal of Advertising Research*, 44, 360–368.

Pousttchi, K., & Wiedemann, D. G. (2007). *Success factors in mobile viral marketing: A multi-case study approach*. Paper presented at the Sixth International Conference on the Management of Mobile Business, IEEE Computer Society. Toronto, Canada, November.

PQ Media. (2007). *Word-of-mouth marketing forecast 2007–2011: Spending, trends and analysis*.

Ryu, G., & Feick, L. (2007, January). A penny for your thoughts: Referral reward programs and referral likelihood. *Journal of Marketing*, 71, 84–94.

Subramani, M. R., & Rajagopalan, B. (2003). Knowledge-sharing and influence in online social networks via viral marketing. *Communications of the ACM*, 46(12), 300–307.

Tumulty, K. (2007, July 5). Obama's viral marketing campaign. *Time*. July 16, pp. 38–39.

Van der Lans, R., van Bruggen, G., Eliashberg, J., & Wierenga, B. (2008). A viral branching model for predicting the spread of electronic word-of-mouth. *Marketing Science*, in press.

Watts, D. J., & Dodds, P. S. (2007, December). Influentials, networks, and public opinion formation. *Journal of Consumer Research*, 34, 441–458.

Watts, D. J., & Peretti, J. (2007, May). Viral marketing for the real world. *Harvard Business Review*, 22–23.

Welker, C. B. (2002). The paradigm of viral communication. *Information Services and Use*, 22, 3–8.

Woerndl, M., Papagiannidis, S., Bourlakis, M., & Li, F. (2008). Internet-induced marketing techniques: Critical factors in viral marketing campaigns. *International Journal of Business Science and Applied Management*, 3(1), 33–45.

11

Social Connectivity, Opinion Leadership, and Diffusion

Jacob Goldenberg, Sangman Han, and Donald R. Lehmann

One of the earliest accounts of the impact of word-of-mouth information in social networks comes from the book of Exodus (Weimann, 1994). While leading his people through the desert to the Promised Land, Moses turns to God for help. God instructs Moses to appoint a number of influential individuals (the 70 elders) to spread Moses' critical instructions to the entire community. According to Weimann, this represents "the first documentation of the multi-step flow of communication where personal networks and social positions are used for disseminating the messages from a single source ... to the vast public." The story highlights one of the defining features of social networks that is consistent with popular intuition and experience: Social groups are structured around individuals who enjoy above-average influence over other members of their community. In this chapter, we use the terms "opinion leaders" and "influentials" interchangeably to describe individuals who have more than proportional influence on the attitudes and actions of others.

Research demonstrating that a relatively small number of people have a substantial influence on the opinions and decisions of the majority can be traced back at least 50 years to the studies of Katz and Lazarsfeld (1955). Focusing on the effect of media messages, they developed the notion of a "two-step" flow of information, in which group members and their relationships mediate the effects of media messages. Although today we know that their two-stage model is an imperfect representation of information flow in a social system (Van den Bulte & Wuyts, 2007), some of its concepts and findings are still relevant. In particular, their study found that opinion leaders are more active than others both in *seeking* information and in *conveying* it to others. Another fundamental assumption that we adopt in this chapter is that diffusion, or product adoption, is an inherently *social process*.

Three groups of traits have been identified with influentials: strong social communication (e.g., charisma, empathy), expertise, and social connectivity (many social ties). Although the connections between these groups of traits have been studied to some degree, it is our argument here that these traits are fundamentally independent. That is, influentials who are experts do not necessarily have extensive social ties, and influentials who are strong in communication are not necessarily product experts. In this chapter, we focus on a specific group of influentials—*social hubs*—who have a unique impact on the rest of the consumer network by virtue of their social connectivity. This is a measurable trait, network dependent, and although it may be correlated with communication, it is, as we show, orthogonal to expertise and relevant in innovation adoption.

PRODUCT DIFFUSION: A SOCIAL PROCESS

Diffusion theory, as well as most diffusion modeling efforts in marketing, suggests that the process in which a social system adopts an innovation is largely based on interactions among potential adopters. The transition from a potential adopter to an adopter is attributed to two information sources. *External* sources include advertising, sales force, and other marketing efforts, as well as mass media, and are unrelated to the number of previous adopters. Consumers are, however, also influenced by *internal* sources of information: These are previous adopters of the innovation who can influence potential adopters by digesting, analyzing, filtering, customizing, and spreading word-of-mouth and functioning as role models in the market. Practitioners and academics alike acknowledge the significant role of internal sources of information, or opinion leaders, in the dissemination of market information (Eliashberg, Jonker, Sawhney, & Wierenga, 2000; Godes & Mayzlin, 2004; Herr, Kardes, & Kim, 1991; Krider & Weinberg, 1998; Mahajan, Muller, & Kerin, 1984; Mahajan, Muller, & Wind, 2000; Reichheld, 1996).

Not all researchers or practitioners, however, subscribe to the social influence paradigm. Although they do not deny that some people have a disproportionate influence on others, some reject the thesis that a handful of people are responsible for trends or for product success or failure, sometimes referred to as the influentials theory or Gladwell's Law of the Few (Gladwell, 2002). Watts and Dodds (2008), for example, challenged the claim that a small number of highly connected people shape the world. In their opinion, this is an overly simplistic explanation for the success or failure of products, and it is one that has gained support not least because it plays up to marketers' own sense of importance through their ability to execute strategies that trigger and manipulate widespread influence by tapping into a kernel of influential individuals. In a series of simulations, Watts and Dodds offered a more complex—and perhaps egalitarian—understanding of the complicated fabric of social forces that influence market outcomes. They showed that ordinary people can have just as much chance if not more to trigger a product success or failure. Note that both sides in this debate over "the randomness of success" concede that some individuals are more highly connected than others: The debate focuses on the extent of influentials' impact on the attitudes and purchase decisions of the general public and their ability to influence market outcomes.

A major thrust of criticism against influentials theorists is directed against the murkiness of the theory and its failure to elaborate exactly how the mechanism of social influence actually works. Our aim in this chapter is to shed light on how one specific group of influential consumers, whom we call social hubs, affects both the extent and the rate of adoption. To do so, we first elaborate on what we know about influentials.

DIFFERENT KINDS OF INFLUENTIALS

Currently, researchers employ a number of labels to identify influential individuals. The 70 elders to whom Moses passed God's commands would variously be termed "opinion leaders," "influentials," "network hubs," "social hubs," "brand advocates," "mavens," "experts," "salesmen," or "connectors" depending on the particular characteristics highlighted in each study or paper. The literature is replete with multiple labels—some synonymous, some contradictory, some complimentary—to describe opinion leaders, partly because authors and researchers are describing different facets of opinion leaders or different dimensions of the influence process.

In the past 60 years, researchers have suggested that the influence of opinion leaders, whatever label is used to describe them, is based on several distinct but possibly related components: communications or social ties, personal traits, and expertise. Most work on influentials to date has focused on discovering the personal traits or expert knowledge that characterize influential individuals.

Accepting this tripartite distinction, researchers have the simple task to create some order in the chaos of the literature that comes under the general heading of opinion leadership. Several studies have reported correlations between opinion leadership and several product-related attributes. Of these, two correlates with opinion leadership have received the most attention: *product involvement* and *product knowledge*. Coulter, Feick, and Price (2002) outlined the logical connection between opinion leaders' high level of product involvement and their expertise: Because opinion leaders are involved in the product category and spend time shopping, they also acquire general marketplace expertise. Many researchers (e.g., Arbatt, Nel, & Nezer, 1995; Coulter et al., 2002; Engelland, Hopkins, & Larson, 2001; Feick & Price, 1987; Goldsmith, Flynn, & Goldsmith, 2003; Steenkamp & Gielens, 2003) have highlighted influentials' knowledge about kinds of products and places to shop as well as their tendency to initiate discussions with consumers and offer market information. The literature has suggested that to some extent, opinion leaders are both expert and innovative (e.g., Childers, 1986; Coulter et al., 2002; Feick & Price, 1987; Flynn, Goldsmith, & Eastman, 1994, 1996; Goldsmith & Desborde, 1991; Goldsmith & Hofacker, 1991; Myers & Robertson, 1972; Summers, 1970). They are also highly aware of (Coulter et al., 2002; Goldsmith & Desborde, 1991), involved with, and interested in products (e.g., Coulter et al., 2002; Myers & Robertson, 1972; Richins & Root-Shaffer, 1988; Summers, 1970; Venkatraman, 1990). Opinion leaders have more extensive product category knowledge than others (e.g., Coulter et al., 2002; Flynn et al., 1994, 1996; Myers & Robertson, 1972; Summers, 1970; Venkatraman, 1990), are confident in their product-related choices (Coulter et al., 2002), and tend to be loyal (Godes & Mayzlin, 2004). In fact, the majority of researchers, applying self-designation scales, have described opinion leadership as unidimensional, generally slanted toward the knowledge aspect.[1] Several studies, however, have shown that product knowledge is not synonymous with opinion leadership. In other words, opinion leaders have something *more* than mere knowledge.

Another stream of research has focused on the personal traits of opinion leaders. Opinion leaders have been found to be gregarious and socially active (Myers & Robertson, 1972, Weimann, 1994), variety seekers

(Coulter et al., 2002), high in self-esteem (Goldsmith & Desborde, 1991), and not risk averse (Chan & Misra, 1990; Childers, 1986). Opinion leaders also have a cognitive orientation (Lennon & Davis, 1987; Levy, 1978), are dogmatic (Chan & Misra, 1990), and are typically information seekers and innovative (Chan & Misra, 1990; Coulter et al., 2002; Feick & Gierl, 1996; Feick & Price, 1987; Katz & Lazarsfeld, 1955, 1964; Summers, 1970).

We argue that at least some of the confusion in literature is the result of researchers focusing on different classes of influentials. We further argue that these classes can be distinguished by the source of their influence on the product diffusion process. For some, special expertise accounts for their influence, others have unique personal traits that transform them into influential sources of information, and some opinion leaders enjoy special social status because of their extensive social ties with others.

Although previous work on the correlates of social influence helps flesh out a picture of a typical opinion leader, it does little to explain *how* a small number of individuals in a group influences a large number of other individuals. As we noted, this has been a point of criticism directed at researchers who subscribe to the opinion leadership paradigm. We believe that the identification of different types of influentials can contribute to our understanding of the process, and we specifically contend that one of the most critical traits for opinion leaders in marketing in general, and the diffusion process in particular, is their social position and high social connectivity. Others, such as Gladwell (2000), have also acknowledged the importance of social connectedness and described a specific type of influential ("connector") who has mega-influence on his or her surroundings because he or she is acquainted with others on an order of magnitude greater than other people. Connectors' extensive connections create a powerful (sometimes invisible) network of interpersonal communications that ultimately determine systemwide changes. In the remainder of this chapter, we describe how this network of influence operates and several of its interesting implications. We begin with a brief summary of network analysis.

THE SOCIAL HUB: THE KEY TO NETWORK PROCESSES

Network analysis offers the key to describing social hubs in a precise manner that makes it easier to define and empirically study the product diffusion process and the role played by social hubs in that process. Although the notion of using social networks to analyze marketing processes is rather recent, the study of propagation in networks and the role of hubs in propagation dates to as early as the 1950s (Rapaport, 1953). By propagation or diffusion, the network literature refers to the transport from node to node of some quantity, for example, information, opinion, or an epidemic. The spread of socially transmitted diseases is one example (see Newman, 2002, for a modeling approach based on theoretical physics and Eames & Keeling, 2002, for an approach from the biomathematics perspective). Rapaport established the influence of network characteristics such as transitivity of node-linking on disease propagation. Different measures of centrality, or connectedness, have also been used by researchers (i.e., embeddedness; see Coleman, Katz, & Menzel, 1966; Freeman, 1978).

A social hub can be depicted as a node in a network connected to a large number of other nodes. We say that the number of ties represents a hub's social connectivity because the connections function as pathways on which socially relevant information is transmitted and shared. Influence is a function of a hub's number of connections, defined as the degree of a node. The distribution of individuals' degrees in a network often follows a power law with a few individuals who possess a large degree and are considered hubs. Barabasi and Albert's scale-free model illustrates how a small number of nodes dominate network connectivity because of their extremely large number of ties.

SOCIAL HUBS ACTIVATE THE NETWORK BY SEEKING AND CONVEYING ATTRACTIVE INFORMATION

Just because two people are connected in a network does not mean they will communicate about a particular topic. Rather, two separate events must occur: (a) One party must transmit information, and (b) the other party must receive it (i.e., listen). Stephen and Lehmann examined the impact of a number of factors on the likelihood a person would transmit new product information (in this case about a new movie). The factors included whether the information was based on firsthand experience ("initial transmission") or received secondhand ("retransmission") and whether the reaction was positive or negative. For each type of information, separate samples indicated how likely potential transmitters would be to transmit information about the movie to 16 potential recipients (described on four characteristics: transmitter–recipient tie strength, fit of message with the recipient's interest [relevance], recipient's past receptivity to information, and social connectivity of the recipient). Tie strength and fit were important for all types of transmission. Interestingly, however, past receptivity was more important for initial transmissions, whereas recipient's social connectivity was more important for transmitting secondhand information.

A study by Goldenberg et al. (2006) also illustrates the perceived importance of the social hub as an information source. It compared two types of information sources: *technical experts*, people who have knowledge and understanding in a specific product category (i.e., know details about technical aspects, operation, models, etc.), and *socially connected individuals*, people who have multiple connections and tend to communicate with others about products. Participants were asked to think of a person they consult with before purchasing a new product and rate the extent to which this person influenced their decision and how well a series of items describes that person in terms of expertise, social connectivity, and personal innovativeness. In the second part of the questionnaire, participants were asked to think of a (different) person who typically has no effect on their purchase decisions and answer the same set of questions referring to that person.

A factor analysis (Table 11.1) produced three factors with eigenvalues over 1 and accounted for 75.8% of the variance. The six expertise items loaded on the first factor, the five social connectivity items loaded on the second factor, and the three innovativeness items loaded on the third factor. Cronbach's alphas of the six items of expertise and the five items of the social connectivity were .95 and .88, respectively, whereas the alpha of the innovativeness scale was .83.

To test the effect of expertise and social connectivity on the tendency to consult with an individual before purchasing a new product, the researchers performed a regression analysis. The influence of the person the participants were rating was the dependent variable (measured on a 1 to 7 scale), and that person's connectivity, expertise, and personal innovativeness were the independent variables (measured by the average of their items). Gender and age were also controlled for.

TABLE 11.1

Factor Loadings of Opinion Leadership Dimensions

	1 Expertise	2 Social Connectivity	3 Innovativeness
Social Connectivity			
Is connected to the key players in his environment	.320	.662	.295
Has a large circle of friends	.228	.799	.140
Is connected to people from different social circles	.116	.796	.111
Tends to talk to a large variety of people	.172	.881	.124
Loves to talk to people he doesn't know	.141	.804	.111
Expertise			
Knows about different versions of the product	.774	.125	.349
Knows how to operate the product	.848	.149	.219
People ask him about the operations of the product	.891	.221	.118
People consult with him about purchasing the product	.825	.263	.245
Is an expert on the product	.822	.227	.283
Provides information about the technical details of the product	.840	.211	.213
Innovativeness			
Buys the product immediately when it is launched on the market	.226	.147	.853
Likes to try new and different things	.290	.229	.789
Is one of the first people to know about a new product	.462	.212	.707

TABLE 11.2

Regression of Tendency to Consult With an Information Source

	Coefficient	Standardized Beta Coefficient
Expertise	.36*	.37*
Social connectivity	.29*	.27*
Innovativeness	.19*	.18*
Gender	.19	.09
Age	.00	−.13
Adjusted R^2	.51	.51

* Significant at the $p < .01$ level.

Expertise had the largest effect (Table 11.2) with a standardized coefficient of .37, followed by social connectivity (.27), and then innovativeness (.18). Gender and age were not significant. Although participants tended most to consult with technical experts, social connectivity also has a significant and relatively strong effect, supporting the claim that having more social ties makes a person a more desirable information source.

SOCIAL HUBS ARE ATTRACTIVE INFORMATION SOURCES

Social hubs are considered an important source of consumer information because of several distinct information-related advantages, the first of which is the scope of information they possess. We argue that individuals with an exceptionally large number of social ties benefit from an elevated social status that transmits signals about their knowledge, behavior, and relevance in the context of innovation adoption. Keller and Berry (2003) discussed people who influence others and their relatively large numbers of social links. Because connections can provide indirect information, highly connected individuals will possess greater information. Schott (1987), in examining interpersonal influence in science, suggested that a national community's influence is enhanced by its expertise (indicated by its number of Nobel laureates) and that the influence of one community on another is related to the collegial and educational ties between them (indicated by coauthorships and student exchanges, respectively). Similarly, Weimann (1994) suggested that centrally positioned scholars, that is, scientific opinion leaders, determine the direction of scientific progress because innovations adopted by central figures are more widely accepted by other members of the profession. Opinion leaders in a field tend to be connected, thus creating an "invisible college" that dominates the adoption or the rejection of new scientific models, ideas, and methods (p. 205).

Consequently, consumers seek out and are more receptive to information from social hubs. Consumers act as decision makers who, according to information acquisition research (e.g., Biggs, Bedard, Gaber, & Linsmeier, 1985; Creyer, Bettman, & Payne, 1990; Johnson, Payne, & Bettman, 1988; Payne, Bettman, & Johnson, 1993; Redd, 2002; Sundstrom, 1987), actively consider the costs and benefits of various decision strategies and attempt to select the strategy that provides the most accurate information for any given effort level.

Social hubs not only possess a great deal of knowledge but also offer knowledge that is especially attractive for main market consumers. Goldenberg, Lehmann, Shidlovski, and Matser-Barak (2006) illustrated several specific circumstances in which social hubs offer uniquely beneficial information to main market consumers. This study demonstrated that under certain conditions, main market consumers prefer social hubs over technical experts as their source of product-related information. More precisely, when the innovation is radical, less innovative (main market) consumers prefer to seek advice from social hubs instead of technical experts. The explanation offered is that people's differences in their own innovativeness may lead them to seek different kinds of information. Innovators are less concerned with technology risks and may have confidence in their own skills and knowledge so they are mainly interested in the new benefits or attributes a new product has to offer. If consumers are less skilled, their lack of understanding may decrease a product's utility.

Less innovative consumers, or main market consumers, are generally aware of their shortcomings and lower level of technological training and skills. For them, those attributes that require learning and skill development demand more attention, and the complexity of a new product is driven mainly by what they have to do to use it. Consequently, they worry that they will "get stuck" because there is a mismatch between their own skills and those that are needed to properly use the product (in a more extreme case, this can be viewed as a tech phobia). As a result of the perceived risk that they will fail to be able to use a product (rather than the risk the product will fail to work), they may be deterred from purchasing it.

For information about how to use a new product, it can be pointless for nonexperts to seek advice from experts because of the communication and knowledge gaps between them. For information on such attributes, social connectors may be more helpful because they may have both the same skill level and the required information about usage problems. Therefore for complex or radical innovations, we expect less innovative consumers will reduce their reliance on expert advice and seek information from social hubs who may have knowledge about the satisfaction of other previous adopters from the main market and the problems they encountered. Secondhand usage information may be particularly relevant to consumers who want to understand the potential difficulties in using a new product before deciding to adopt it.

When an innovation is incremental, that is, based on current products or technology, risk and the need to learn new skills are lower, and the differences between using the new product and the current one become smaller and more predictable. Therefore mainstream consumers are likely to be less concerned about risks, uncertainties, procedural knowledge, and compatibility in this case than in the case of a radical innovation. In such cases, an expert's advice may be more desirable because it contains details of new features and their benefits. Consider a new version of the Palm Pilot. At least for consumers who are considering upgrading from an earlier generation of a PDA, the information that is most relevant to their purchase decision involves specifications, features, and which product version or generation would be most sensible to purchase. For factual product traits (e.g., speed of a computer), experts are the preferred information source because this type of information needs no "translation."

In addition to the information they possess and their ability to use language that main market consumers understand and can identify with, social hubs also impact product diffusion as a result of their unique ability to connect disparate sections of a network that typically do not share information or communicate with each other. To fully understand social hubs' bridging capabilities, we briefly review the dual-market phenomenon in the following section.

BRIDGING THE CHASM

Since Moore (1991) identified a discontinuity in the diffusion process that effectively creates what has become known as a dual market, researchers and practitioners have concurred that communications between early adopters and others are extremely limited, at least for high-tech products. As a result of the gap in communications between these two groups (early adopters and main market consumers), a break in the diffusion curve is evident after about 16% of the population adopts an innovative product. At this point, the contagion process slows because later adopters are reluctant to rely on the early adopters for product-related information. This finding meshes well with high-tech market intuition that adopters in the *early market* are materially different from *main market* adopters and require a significantly different product and/or marketing strategy. Early adopters' influence over other potential adopters is limited precisely because of the limited communications between these two consumer groups.

Social hubs have a special type of information advantage, which Burt (1997) called "social capital." This social capital allows social hubs to bridge structural holes in social networks, that is, connect unconnected sections of a network. Burt's study illustrated, in a managerial context, how the value of social connectivity is related to social capital and demonstrated how managers who have high average values of social capital are poised at the crossroads of organizations and have the ability to bring together otherwise disconnected individuals in the network.

From a network point of view, social hubs have not only a high "degree" centrality (a large number of connections to actors) but also a high "betweenness" centrality (links with others in different groups). These two centralities are typically correlated because people with an extremely high degree have a higher probability of being connected to different social circles. Not only do connections to many interconnected people allow one to *collect* more diverse information sooner than the average network member (Van den Bulte & Wuyts, 2007), high connectivity also unleashes the power of communications that are *disseminated* over increasing and expanding groups of connected individuals by connecting otherwise unconnected network members. In general, the extent to which someone has an information advantage depends on crossing structural holes, which means linking separate parts of the network (Burt, 1992).

Because of their unique position within the main market, social hubs transmit information that is considered extremely reliable by the main market. The following illustration of an adoption process of a really new product and an incrementally new product summarizes the information advantages of social hubs and their role in product diffusion.

ACTIVATING THE SOCIAL NETWORK

In the case of really new products, consumers can seek out or receive information from people who have firsthand experience with the new product, people who have expert knowledge in the field, or the few people who *know* people who have firsthand experience with the new product although they themselves may not have used the product themselves. As a result of the substantial differences between early adopters and main market consumers, early adopters are a costly source of information for main market consumers: The latter may be put off by the technical and sometimes incomprehensible language of early adopters and technophiles. Technical or product experts simply do not speak the same language as noninnovators. Main market consumers also suspect that they have different utility functions than early adopters and therefore view the latter's advice as less relevant. In fact, studies that identify a disconnection in communications between main market consumers and technical experts confirm that these groups use a different language to describe really new products and have a different perspective on product usage and benefits.

Fortunately, main market consumers have a more cost-effective source of information available to them. In many cases, noninnovators or main market consumers prefer to seek information on product innovations from people who are most similar to them in terms of product conceptualizations, technical understanding, risk aversion, and so on. Social hubs are not necessarily technical experts and hence may share the same perspective on the new product as other main market consumers who differ from them only in that they preceded others in obtaining product information through their extensive social ties, which include both technical experts and early adopters.

In the initial stages of product growth, few people inside the social circle of any given individual have already adopted it. In such cases, the individual turns to people who may not have adopted the product but have information from others about it, that is, those who are widely connected.

Furthermore, social hubs may benefit from additional traits that affect their attractiveness as a source of information, such as source credibility, language, empathy, and similarity (homophily). It is hard not to observe a similarity between these characteristics and social activity, and therefore it seems reasonable to predict that those who have strong social relations are high on these traits as well.

SOCIAL HUBS ARE NOT EARLY ADOPTERS, BUT THEY ADOPT EARLY

Until now, many researchers have suggested that the early adopters share certain traits. We argue that although social hubs are not necessarily innovators (we do not discount the possibility that some social hubs are early adopters by nature), they do adopt early.

Consider a hub who is not innovative and an innovator who has an average number of social ties. Innovators by nature require little exposure to make a decision to adopt. Because hubs are well connected, however, the number of their indirect exposures to the new product is large during the early stages of diffusion. As a result, hubs may reach their adoption threshold before innovators do. In other words, even hubs who are not innovative may be persuaded to adopt in the early stages of the process because of their large number of contacts rather than their propensity for innovative new products. Consequently, the early adopter group may contain both innovative individuals and hubs.

Furthermore, if hubs adopt early, because of their having a large number of links that connect them to a large number of other individuals, their adoption should increase the speed of adoption in the period after they adopt (if the product adopted performs satisfactorily). Assume the probability of adoption by an individual (see Goldenberg, Libai, & Muller, 2004) is as follows:

$$P = 1 - (1 - p)(1 - q)^{\alpha(t)}$$

Here P is the probability an individual adopts, p is the effect of exposure to external forces (e.g., marketing efforts), q is the impact of word-of-mouth (network effects), and $\alpha(t)$ is the number of links to current adopters. The number of the adopters at time t would then be $E(P) \times (M - N(t))$. An individual with a large number of links (e.g., 500) was shown to contribute much more to adoption through word-of-mouth interactions than an individual with a moderate number of links (e.g., 25). Even if social hubs are not more persuasive than other individuals or do not actively contact those they are linked to, more connections to them will be activated once they adopt, resulting in a significant increase in the adoption rate. In addition, because innovator hubs adopt earlier than follower hubs, they have more time to influence the network. Empirical support for this claim is found in two studies (Goldenberg, Han, Lehmann, & Weon-Hong, 2008; Goldenberg, Lehmann, et al., 2006).

TRACKING THE INFLUENCE OF SOCIAL HUBS

Although it has been clear for a long time that network analysis is important for understanding growth processes and that network analysis of field experiments is a promising direction for diffusion studies, the effect of hubs has rarely been tested empirically, partially on account of a lack of appropriate data on both networks and the multiple diffusion processes over them. Without data on the various diffusion processes on the same network, the role of different actors (e.g., social hubs) is difficult to analyze, and it may be even harder to argue that this role is consistent and stable over different processes.

Because researchers often had to collect network data manually, they were limited to networks consisting of several hundred nodes at most. Since these humble beginnings in 1995, researchers now have available data sets comprising mapped networks as large as 100,000 nodes. Recently it has become possible to document both network development and the adoption process and specifically locate when each member (or node) of the network adopted. But even this is not sufficient: To properly analyze how network properties influence adoption, we need data on multiple adoption processes over the same network.

Goldenberg et al. (2009) were able to analyze multiple adoptions in the same network using Cyworld data, which allowed them to examine both the aggregate growth process and what happens at the individual level in a network. Their work is consistent with the general perspective of examining an interpersonal network first used by Brown and Reingen (1987), although it concentrates on the impact of individuals on the aggregate diffusion process rather than on individual adoption. In 2006, Cyworld was Korea's major online social network, which included as many as 90% of Koreans in their 20s. One third of Korea's total population is registered with Cyworld. As of September 2006, there were about 19 million registered members in Cyworld.

The data set contained information about the timing of individual (node) adoption for multiple diffusion processes. A key aspect of the service allows people to customize their home pages by including documents, photos, and other "goodies" for free and to decorate their Mini-hompy (personal home page) with paid items such as virtual household items—furniture, electronics, wallpaper, and so on. People can also adopt items such as pictures or video clips directly from the Mini-hompies they visit. The study focused on this second type of adoption of items, known in Cyworld as "scraping."

To test whether hubs adopt earlier than the rest of the population, the researchers divided each diffusion process into five categories—t5%, t16%, t30%, t50%, and t100%—where t5% is the time when the first 5% of total adoption is reached, t16% is the time it takes for the first 16% of total adoption to occur, and so on. Hub adoption patterns are shown in Figure 11.1. As can be seen, the percentage of adoption by hubs has a tendency to slowly decline. Thus the concentration of hubs among first adopters is significantly ($p < .001$) larger than among later adopters; that is, hubs on average adopt sooner than nonhubs. In summary, socially connected individuals were more likely to adopt than less connected individuals. In addition, when social hubs adopted a new item, they did so at an earlier stage in the diffusion process compared to other adopters. That is, on average, hubs adopted earlier than nonhubs.

The study also compared the adoption of 100 randomly selected hubs and 100 nonhubs. The number of neighbors who adopted before them and the proportion who did so for 60 items are presented in Table 11.3. As expected, hubs adopt earlier in their neighborhood in terms of the proportion of their neighbors who have adopted. Consistent with our argument that the number of exposures drives adoption, however, hubs are not more innovative per se because they on average had 1.68 neighbors adopt first

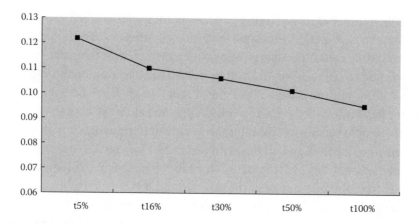

FIGURE 11.1
Percentage adoption by social hubs over time.

TABLE 11.3

Hub and Nonhub Adoption Timing Within Their
Neighborhood: Mean (and Standard Deviation)

	Number of Neighbors Who Adopt Earlier	Proportion
Hubs	1.68 (2.10)	0.01 (0.01)
Nonhubs	0.61 (0.96)	0.25 (0.36)

versus only 0.61 for nonhubs. Thus, hubs appear to adopt early because of their large number of connections (contacts) rather than any innate innovativeness (which in one sense is below average).

An alternative explanation is that hubs adopt because of their innovativeness rather than because their connectivity, and because of their innovativeness, social hubs tend to be more connected to innovators than are "ordinary" people. This explanation was refuted by another study, described next, that used an agent-based model to demonstrate that in realistic networks, social hubs can adopt very early even if they are not innovative.

Agent-based modeling (ABM) has many names. One of the first applications in the social sciences was coined *cellular automata*. The conception of cellular automata is typically attributed to John von Neumann as a formal model of a self-reproducing biological organism. The history of the use of cellular automata in a variety of disciplines has been well documented (e.g., Sarkar, 2000).[2] Basically, one can envision ABM as a grid of cells. In the ABM environment, time is discrete, and a cell can be in one of a finite number of possible states at each point in time. A cell can change its state in each period in response to (or as a function of) the state of its surrounding cells. The algorithm by which cells change their state is usually called "local rule" or "transition rule." The collection of all states at a given point in time is called the "global state." In each period, application of the local rule of the ABM to a cell changes the global state of the matrix. In the simple version of ABM, local rules are deterministic: A global state determines the next global state with certainty. One can also use *stochastic* ABM, however, in which the state of the cells changes based on some probability function of the state of the cells around it.

Using the Cyworld data set, Goldenberg et al. compared the 30 most successful items and the first 30 items just below average of the top 1,067 in terms of eventual adoption. They regressed the number of adopters at time t as a function of time, cumulative number of adopters at $t - 1$, the squared cumulative number of adopters at $t - 1$, and the number of hubs adopting at $t - 1$. The scraping process is fairly rapid, and the entire adoption process is often concluded within several months during which millions of people may adopt an item. Separate regressions were performed using time periods of 1 day, 6 hours, and 2 hours.

The model provided fairly good fit ($R^2 = .55$ to $.75$), especially for the 2-hour time interval, suggesting that imitation occurs rapidly. Importantly, a hub that has adopted in the previous time period has a stronger impact on the process compared to a typical adopter, suggesting hubs are indeed critical to the adoption process. Most important, the number of adopting hubs adds predictive power to the terms represented by cumulative adopters and cumulative adopters squared in the discrete Bass (1969) model.

Goldenberg et al. (2009) also randomly selected 30 items from the same list of 1,067 items and ran the regression analysis. The results are consistent with one exception. Here, adoption is better predicted using the daily window, reflecting the relatively slower growth of some products.

DISCUSSION

One of the most serious challenges in introducing new products to the market is the gap between early adopters and main market consumers. Moore (1991) was one of the first to identify a discontinuity in the diffusion process after about 16% of the population adopts an innovative product. The contagion process slows at this point because later adopters (the main market) are reluctant to rely on the early adopters for information. At least for high-tech products, this implies that early adopters have limited influence over others who have yet to adopt the product (Moore, 1991, 1995). In high-tech markets, a common premise is that adopters in the *early market* are meaningfully different from *main market* adopters and thus require a significantly different product and/or marketing strategy. Early adopters are often characterized as technophiles, fascinated by cutting-edge technology and applications, whereas main market consumers are described as more utilitarian, risk-averse, and value-conscious individuals who view learning about new products as a burden. A fundamental characteristic of this dual-market concept is strong word-of-mouth effect *within* each market and weaker communication ties *between* them.

Socially connected individuals, or social hubs, function as opinion leaders by virtue of their multiple social connections. If marketers are able to identify social hubs, not only will they be better positioned to predict new product success, but by directly marketing activities specifically to social hubs, they may also be able to bridge the chasm between the early market and the main market and overcome one of the key obstacles to new product take-off. In either case, social hubs have an important impact on sales and revenues.

As in any such area of study, there are numerous open research questions involving the role of social connectivity and opinion leadership in new product adoption:

1. How does one become a hub or opinion leader? Is it an innate trait, or does a person become one over time, perhaps in the fashion of a cascade where having one conversation or opinion leads to having more?
2. Are opinion leaders influential because they engage in more information-seeking and broadcasting behaviors, or do they become involved in communication-related behaviors because they are perceived as influential members of their society and hence sought out by others?
3. How does one stop being a hub or opinion leader? Is this decision a choice of the hub or of some other network role player, perhaps a member of a different type of influential?

4. What roles do information accuracy, consistency with existing knowledge, and novelty play in the search for and transmission of product-related information? What other factors affect the search and transmission process?
5. What is the relative impact of tie strength on the likelihood of conveying and/or receiving information? What factors affect this relationship?

We hope this chapter will encourage others to address these and other fascinating relevant and complex issues.

NOTES

1. On the bias of self-designation scales in the context of influentials, see Van den Bulte (2009).
2. Cellular automata are models of computation that can generate complex aggregate behaviors using a limited number of simple individual-level rules. Cellular automata were publicly recognized when proposed by John von Neumann as formal models of self-reproducing organisms. The first attempt to understand complex system behavior, however, can be traced to the Ising model, first proposed in 1924 by Ernst Ising. Despite its deceptively simple appearance, this well-established model explains and predicts deterministic phenomena in nature.

REFERENCES

Abratt, R., Nel, D., & Nezer, C. (1995). Role of the market maven in retailing: A general marketplace influencer. *Journal of Business and Psychology, 10*(1), 31–55.
Bass, F. M. (1969). A new product growth for model consumer durables. *Management Science, 15*(5), 215–227.
Biggs, S. F., Bedard, J. C., Gaber, B. G., & Linsmeier, T. J. (1985). The effects of task size and similarity on the decision behavior of bank loan officers. *Management Science, 31*(8), 970–987.
Brown, J. J., & Reingen, P. H. (1987). Social ties and word-of-mouth referral behavior. *Journal of Consumer Research, 14*(3), 350–362.
Burt, R. S. (1992). *Structural holes: The social structure of competition.* Cambridge, MA: Harvard University Press.
Burt, R. S. (1997). The contingent value of social capital. *Administrative Science Quarterly, 42*(2), 339–365.
Chan, K. K., & Misra, S. R. (1990). Characteristics of the opinion leader: A new dimension. *Journal of Advertising, 19*(3), 53–60.
Childers, T. L. (1986). Assessment of the psychometric properties of an opinion leadership scale. *Journal of Marketing Research, 23*(2), 184–188.

Coleman, J. S., Katz, E., & Menzel, H. (1966). *Medical innovation: A diffusion study.* Indianapolis, IN: Bobbs-Merrill.

Coulter, R. A., Feick, L. F., & Price, L. L. (2002). Changing faces: Cosmetics opinion leadership among women in the new Hungary. *European Journal of Marketing, 36*(11), 1287–1308.

Creyer, E. H., Bettman, J. R., & Payne, J. W. (1990). The impact of accuracy and effort feedback and goals on adaptive decision behavior. *Journal of Behavioral Decision Making, 3*(1), 1–16.

Eames, K. T. D., & Keeling, M. J. (2002). Modeling dynamic and network heterogeneities in the spread of sexually transmitted diseases. *Proceedings of the National Academy of Sciences of the United States of America, 99*(20), 13330–13335.

Eliashberg, J., Jonker, J. J., Sawhney, M. S., & Wierenga, B. (2000). MOVIEMOD: An implementable decision-support system for prerelease market evaluation of motion pictures. *Marketing Science, 19*(3), 226–243.

Engelland, B. T., Hopkins, C., & Larson, D. A. (2001). Market mavenship as an influencer of service quality evaluation. *Journal of Marketing Theory and Practice, 9*(4), 15–26.

Feick, L., & Gierl, H. (1996). Skepticism about advertising: A comparison of East and West German consumers. *International Journal of Research in Marketing, 13*(3), 227–235.

Feick, L. F., & Price, L. L. (1987). The market maven: A diffuser of marketplace information. *Journal of Marketing, 51*(1), 83–97.

Flynn, L. R., Goldsmith, R. E., & Eastman, J. K. (1994). The King and Summers Opinion Leadership Scale: Revision and refinement. *Journal of Business Research, 31*(1), 55.

Flynn, L., Goldsmith, R., & Eastman, J. (1996). Opinion leaders and opinion seekers: Two new measurement scales. *Journal of the Academy of Marketing Science, 24*(2), 137–147.

Freeman, L. C. (1978). Social networks. In *International network for social network analysis.* Lausanne: Elsevier Sequoia.

Gladwell, M. (2000). *The tipping point: How little things can make a big difference.* Boston: Little, Brown.

Godes, D., & Mayzlin, D. (2004). Using online conversations to study word-of-mouth communication. *Marketing Science, 23*(4), 545–560.

Goldenberg, J., Han, S., Lehmann, D. R., & Weon-Hong, J. W. (2008). *The role of hubs in the adoption processes.* Unpublished manuscript.

Goldenberg, J., Lehmann, D. R., Shidlovski, D., & Matser-Barak, M. (2006). *The role of expert vs. social opinion leaders in new product adoption.* Jerusalem, Israel: Hebrew University of Jerusalem.

Goldenberg, J., Libai, B., & Muller, E. (2004). Complex, yet simple: Cellular automata as an enabling technology in marketing strategy research. In *Assessing marketing strategy performance* (pp. 229–246). Cambridge, MA: Marketing Science Institute.

Goldenberg, J., Moldovan, S., & Chattopadhyay, A. (2006). *What drives word-of-mouth? The roles of product originality and usefulness* (MSI Working Papers Series, 06–111). Cambridge, MA: Marketing Science Institute.

Goldsmith, R. E., & Desborde, R. (1991). A validity study of a measure of opinion leadership. *Journal of Business Research, 22*(1), 11–19.

Goldsmith, R. E., Flynn, L. R., & Goldsmith, E. B. (2003). Innovative consumers and market mavens. *Journal of Marketing Theory and Practice, 11*(4), 54–65.

Goldsmith, R. E., & Hofacker, C. F. (1991). Measuring consumer innovativeness. *Journal of the Academy of Marketing Science, 19*(3), 209–221.

Herr, P. M., Kardes, F. R., & Kim, J. (1991). Effects of word-of-mouth and product-attribute information on persuasion: An accessibility-diagnosticity perspective. *Journal of Consumer Research, 17*(4), 454–462.

Johnson, E. J., Payne, J. W., & Bettman, J. R. (1988). Information displays and preference reversals. *Organizational Behavior and Human Decision Processes, 42*, 1–21.

Katz, E., & Lazarsfeld, P. F. (1955). *Personal influence: The part played by people in the flow of mass communications.* Glencoe, IL: Columbia University Bureau of Applied Social, Research, Free Press.

Katz, E., & Lazarsfeld, P. F. (1964). *Personal influence: The part played by people in the flow of mass communications.* New York: Free Press.

Keller, E. B., & Berry, J. L. (2003). *The influentials.* New York: Free Press.

Krider, R. E., & Weinberg, C. B. (1998). Competitive dynamics and the introduction of new products: The motion picture timing game. *Journal of Marketing Research, 35*(1), 1–15.

Lehmann, D. R., & Stephen, A. T. (2008). *Recipient characteristics and product-related word-of-mouth transmission: The role of social capital.* Paper presented at the INFORMS Marketing Science Conference, Columbia University Graduate School of Business, Vancouver.

Lennon, S. J., & Davis, L. (1987). Individual differences in fashion orientation and cognitive complexity. *Perceptual and Motor Skills, 64*, 327–330.

Levy, M. R. (1978). Opinion leadership and television news uses. *Public Opinion Quarterly, 42*(3), 402–406.

Mahajan, V., Muller, E., & Kerin, R. A. (1984). Introduction strategy for new products with positive and negative word-of-mouth. *Management Science, 30*(12), 1389–1404.

Mahajan, V., Muller, E., & Wind, Y. (2000). *New-product diffusion models.* New York: Kluwer Academic.

Moore, G. A. (1991). *Crossing the chasm: Marketing and selling technology products to mainstream customers.* New York: HarperBusiness.

Moore, G. A. (1995). *Inside the tornado: Marketing strategies from Silicon Valley's cutting edge.* New York: HarperBusiness.

Myers, J. H., & Robertson, T. S. (1972). Dimensions of opinion leadership. *Journal of Marketing Research, 9*(1), 41–46.

Newman, M. E. J. (2002). Spread of epidemic disease on networks. *Physical Review E, 66*(1), 16128.

Payne, J. W., Bettman, J. R., & Johnson, E. J. (1993). *The adaptive decision maker.* New York: Cambridge University Press.

Rapaport, A. (1953). Spread of information through a population with sociostructural bias: Assumption of transitivity. *Bulletin of Mathematical Biophysics, 15*, 523–533.

Redd, S. B. (2002). The influence of advisers on foreign policy decision making: An experimental study. *Journal of Conflict Resolution, 46*(3), 335–364.

Reichheld, F. F. (1996). *The loyalty effect: The hidden force behind growth, profits, and lasting value.* Cambridge, MA: Harvard Business School Press.

Richins, M. L., & Root-Shaffer, T. (1988). The role of involvement and opinion leadership in consumer word-of-mouth: An implicit model made explicit. In M. J. Houston (Ed.), *Advances in consumer research* (Vol. 15, pp. 32–36). Provo, UT: Association for Consumer Research.

Sarkar, P. (2000). A brief history of cellular automata. *ACM Computing Surveys, 32*(1), 80.

Schott, T. (1987). Scientific productivity and international integration of small countries: Mathematics in Denmark and Israel. *Social Network, 9*(1), 351–375.

Steenkamp, J.-B. E. M., & Gielens, K. (2003). Consumer and market drivers of the trial probability of new consumer packaged goods. *Journal of Consumer Research, 30,* 368–384.

Summers, J. O. (1970). The identity of women's clothing fashion opinion leaders. *Journal of Marketing Research, 7*(2), 178–185.

Sundstrom, G. A. (1987). Information search and decision making: The effects of information displays. *Acta Psychologica, 65*(2), 165–179.

Van den Bulte, C., & Wuyts, S. (2007). *Social networks and marketing.* Cambridge, MA: Marketing Science Institute.

Venkatraman, M. P. (1990). *Opinion leadership, enduring involvement and characteristics of opinion leaders: A moderating or mediating relationship?* Boston: Boston University School of Management.

Watts, D. J., & Dodds, P. S. (2007). Influentials, networks, and public opinion formation. *Journal of Consumer Research, 34*(4), 441–458.

Weimann, G. (1994). *The influentials: People who influence people.* Albany: State University of New York Press.

12

The Effect of Negative Word-of-Mouth in Social Networks

Andre Bonfrer

An understanding of how customers communicate with one another can substantially improve marketing communication performance. Marketing practitioners and researchers are extremely interested in understanding and harnessing network effects to improve marketing effectiveness and efficiency. At the heart of this issue is how, and how often, people talk to one another about the company's products. We refer to this type of communication as "word-of-mouth." For the purpose of this chapter, word-of-mouth is defined as some type of communication between two or more connected customers or potential customers. Such communication can take the form of verbal, face-to-face communication or many other means, including e-mail, telephone, cell-phone-based text messages, blogs, instant messaging, social network software (e.g., Facebook, Friendster, LinkedIn), and so on.

Word-of-mouth is frequently talked about in the context of its positive impacts. Many marketing models have explicitly or implicitly included word-of-mouth communication within a group of customers in understanding how information flows through a target group. Marketers are interested in understanding how to harness the power of positive word-of-mouth, for example, in maximizing the chances of the success of a new product. Early models include Bass (1969; see the review by Mahajan, Muller, & Bass, 1990). Another, more recent, review in Van den Bulte and Wuyts (2007) examines a number of different ways that social influence can spread through networks among customers.[1] They focused on how social influence works for new products and identified the types of contagion that occur in such networks, ranging from awareness and interest, belief updating, normative pressure, and competitive concerns. Their construct of contagion, however, is broader than what we are focusing on here because they allowed communication to occur simply through what has been sometimes referred to as "conspicuous consumption" (see Bearden & Teel, 1983).[2]

Although less prevalent, there is also a growing literature on negative word-of-mouth and its effects. The overarching goal of this chapter is to discuss the impact of negative word-of-mouth. To set this chapter apart from similar research, particularly in the social contagion or innovation diffusion literature, we further restrict our attention on products that are established, and we focus our attention on customers who regularly use the product class, for example, cell phone users, credit card users, laundry detergent users, and so on. Most people either have experience in such established markets or are unlikely to ever have experience in these categories. This dichotomy is explicitly recognized in new products in split hazard models of product adoption (e.g., Kamakura, Kossar, & Wedel, 2004). For new products, because many customers have not yet tried the product, customers rely on people who have experience with the product to help them make informed purchase decisions. In contrast, most buyers for established products tend to have their own well-established attitudes about the product, and any word-of-mouth information must be integrated into this.

Although many people talk about negative word-of-mouth being harmful to a marketer's business, it is puzzling to see that many bad service encounters are ignored by marketers. It is equally puzzling to observe that customers avoid reporting their negative encounters, if companies actively solicit and welcome such feedback. Is word-of-mouth really harmful to companies?

To examine this issue, we highlight that negative word-of-mouth is frequently recognized as being strongly intertwined with two other related literatures: generally, the literature on customer complaints and the literature on customer satisfaction. This chapter draws on these bodies of work to understand the effects of negative influences stemming from dissatisfied customers (through word-of-mouth communication). The purpose is to assess the magnitude of these effects based on available empirical evidence rather than to provide a comprehensive review of the literature in these areas.

The objectives of this chapter are as follows:

1. to understand where negative word-of-mouth comes from and identify key constituents of negative word-of-mouth,
2. to assess the overall impact of negative word-of-mouth and draw a comparison with the impact of positive word-of-mouth, and
3. to explore some of the ways marketers can manage and control negative word-of-mouth.

Why is it important to know the impact of negative word-of-mouth? One possible reason involves marketer's choices of the allocation of resources. Firms could allocate resources toward resolving customer complaints, monitoring and tracking possible incidents (see the last section in this chapter), and quality testing and improvement programs with the primary goal of preventing product and service failures. They could also allocate resources toward producing experiences that exceed expectations, for example, by providing some customers with additional services such as bonuses, upgrading their service classes, training customer service and salespeople, and so on.

A second reason to study negative word-of-mouth is the recent interest that has involved understanding the contagion of attitudes among customers organized in social networks. Considerable attention by marketing researchers is now being focused on understanding the role of interdependencies among customers, and a few word-of-mouth researchers have studied social network theory to understand information flows through studied networks (see, e.g., Brown & Reingen, 1987; Reingen, 1987; Reingen & Kernan, 1986). Much of the recent work in this area is driven by information technology that enables the organization of customers into social networks and allows marketers to track a rich set of activities of such social groups (e.g., Chen & Xie, 2008; Godes & Mayzlin, 2004). Marketers are very interested in harnessing the power of such networks (e.g., understanding how best to target advertisements on Facebook). To guide marketers in this domain, we need to understand the nature of the communication among customers about their consumption experiences.

We also restrict the scope of our study to the type of negative word-of-mouth arising from basic product failures and/or dissatisfaction rather than some specific events that ended up being international brand-damaging stories. For example, consider the damage caused to the Audi brand by the few customers who brought about false accusations of the uncontrolled acceleration of their cars. A more recent example is a large dairy company in China (the Sanlu Group) that was found to add melamine to its products, causing many children to become ill (*New York Times*, September 19, 2008).

Examples abound of scenarios where companies have launched products or grown products with a high reliance on word-of-mouth to complement their traditional communication through advertising. The Apple launch of the iPhone, for example, was preceded by advertising specifically engineered to elicit positive word-of-mouth. It started with a teaser advertisement called "Hello," which only briefly featured the product being advertised and thereby generated much speculation and discussion about the nature of the product itself. Starbucks, until relatively recently, engaged in very little traditional advertising for its outlets. There are also numerous examples where marketers, either deliberately or serendipitously, harness the power of positive word-of-mouth by engaging in practices likely to induce such behavior. Some direct attempts include the movie *The Blair Witch Project*, the positive word-of-mouth for which was induced by the marketers of the film placing information strategically on the Internet. Other direct attempts include the promotion for Steven Spielberg's 2001 *Artificial Intelligence* movie, which involved planting clues in various promotions (starting with the trailer), leading to an elaborate underground puzzle game that many customers ultimately became involved with (*Los Angeles Times*, July 13, 2001).

There also exist more subterfuge attempts to spread word-of-mouth. Marketers need to be careful using such methods, however, because sometimes these methods backfire. An example is the classic McDonald's attempt at a viral marketing campaign dubbed the "Lincoln Fry" campaign (CNN/Money, February 18, 2005). It started with a McDonald's french fry that resembled Abraham Lincoln. A blog was set up, supposedly by a couple (Mike and Liz) who reported on their experiences after finding the Lincoln resemblance of the french fry. It was subsequently featured in a McDonald's advertisement during the Super Bowl. The fry was actually molded from polyurethane plastic, and it was later auctioned for charity, fetching a price of $75,100. The methods used by McDonald's, in collaboration with Yahoo!, which allowed the key word *blog* to be associated with Lincoln Fry, were designed to generate a high degree of media exposure. Many customers, however, were outraged by the misleading use of the fake blog.

In the United States, a self-regulation body, the Word of Mouth Marketing Association (WOMMA), was started up and publishes a code of ethics. For example, "We encourage word-of-mouth advocates to disclose their relationship with marketers in their communications with other consumers" (WOMMA Web site, womma.org). Although many of these attempts are focused on stimulating positive word-of-mouth to enhance the growth of new products, campaigns aimed at generating a high degree of discussion for established goods (typically known as teaser campaigns) can also be effective.

Although so much attention is paid on analyzing the positive effects of word-of-mouth, negative word-of-mouth, however, is clearly not desired. For new products, negative word-of-mouth can stifle the growth of a new product (e.g., Menzel & Katz, 1955), and in established product categories, it can result in significant damage to the marketer's brands. In the case of negative word-of-mouth, it is clearly in the marketer's best interest to learn how to minimize the damage caused.

The starting point for managing negative word-of-mouth is to understand its constituents. To do so, we next review relevant literature on word-of-mouth, paying particular attention on negative word-of-mouth and its antecedents, including a brief review of the customer satisfaction and dissatisfaction and complaints literature. We highlight some issues with respect to customer networks and assess the possible net impact of negative word-of-mouth. Finally, we draw our conclusions and raise some key issues that could be fruitful areas for further investigation.

WHAT WE HAVE LEARNED ABOUT WORD-OF-MOUTH

Word-of-Mouth Defined

It has long been recognized that word-of-mouth is an important source of information that customers use to make purchase decisions (e.g., Arndt, 1967). Broadly speaking, the word-of-mouth construct captures any communication not stemming directly from the marketer. This broader definition can include unbiased third-party reviews (e.g., in movies) and consumer reports magazine (see Chen & Xie, 2008; Chevalier & Mayzlin,

2006; Godes & Mayzlin, 2004). In this broader definition, word-of-mouth can also include the many reviews available on Web sites such as Amazon. com, eBay, or special-purpose industry-based Web sites such as GameSpot for videogames. Reviews are a slightly different type of word-of-mouth, in that they are available not just to people "close" to one another (in a network sense) but to everyone. For example, anyone who wants to purchase a book can go to Amazon.com to read the reviews—there is no need for the customer to have forged some tie with the various authors of the reviews. In our discussion, however, we are specifically interested in negative word-of-mouth that arises from communicating with people who have experience with the product. For this, there needs to be some relationship already in place that acts as a channel through which information and influence can flow.

Much of the literature on word-of-mouth talks about the use of "opinion leaders" (e.g., Engel, Blackwell, & Kegerreis, 1969; Rogers, 1962). Such influential people in the network, typically people with high degrees of centrality in the network, tend to have a disproportionately high influence on others. It is not very practical to consider word-of-mouth for just opinion leaders, however. Because what marketers need to guide policy is to understand what resources to allocate to ensure some minimum product consistency or service quality, it is difficult to target just those customers they believe are influential in spreading positive or negative word-of-mouth (a point also raised in Van den Bulte & Wuyts, 2007). Instead, we must be concerned with considering the expected effect on all existing customers. In a social network context, negative word-of-mouth could spread to anyone who is "close" to the affected customer. This involves understanding the likelihood of someone being affected by bad service, their likelihood to complain to other customers, and the expected number of people they then tell. Finally, the impact of the negative word-of-mouth on the final recipients can be assessed to understand how brand preferences may be impacted by the word-of-mouth.

Accordingly, the starting point for our discussion involves a consideration of the source of negative word-of-mouth. Our assumption is that people satisfied with a product are unlikely to generate negative word-of-mouth, so it is important at this point to consider the literature on customer satisfaction and dissatisfaction.

The Source of Word-of-Mouth: Dissatisfaction and Complaining Behavior

Customer Satisfaction and Dissatisfaction

The source of negative word-of-mouth typically is thought of as dissatisfaction, sometimes regarded as "service failure," which we more broadly consider as the occurrence of a breach of the firm's promise to deliver some quality level. Although positive word-of-mouth typically comes from product performance on some dimension, negative word-of-mouth stems from some breakdown in the company's ability to deliver expected performance (Andreasen, 1977). Landon (1977) conceptually established that dissatisfaction is a function of expectations minus benefits, that is, where expectations are not met. Bearden and Teel (1983) found evidence to suggest that customer dissatisfaction and complaints are caused by the disconfirmation of expectations that customers may have about the product or service. Satisfaction and dissatisfaction may further be considered as either a single incidence of dissatisfaction or some gestalt dissatisfaction "score." For example, consider rating a restaurant based on a meal that you just ate (and the service you just received) versus answering the question about how satisfied you are, on average, with your financial advisor. The latter involves an assessment of the average based on a set of experiences, whereas the former typically involves a single purchase or consumption incidence. Indeed, many customer satisfaction measures ask individual customers for a point estimate for a satisfaction scale, rather than a distribution metric, for example, asking customers about the level of variation in the delivered product or service quality. The average performance of a service provider can be considered as an expectation of the performance on any subsequent transaction. If the service provider underperforms on this average, there is the chance of a dissatisfaction encounter.

A simplifying assumption implicit in much of the literature is that the event of dissatisfaction is discrete. This is consistent with much of the observations of behavior dealing with dissatisfaction (e.g., the critical incidents technique asks customers to recall incidents where they have been very dissatisfied). Furthermore, a complaint usually means that dissatisfaction has exceeded some basic threshold. This could, of course, be invalid. There may be many degrees of dissatisfaction, for example, see Anderson (1998), who reported the number of people that word-of-mouth is spread to, for all levels of customer satisfaction. In this discussion we talk in the context of the literature discussed previously and think of discrete product or service failures. One could think about such failures as extreme dissatisfaction, although satisfaction may be a measure of the product category as a whole, not just customers' satisfaction with an individual transaction or service encounter.

To the extent that firms manage expectations through communication (directly) using advertising and/or product releases, dissatisfaction can be somewhat managed (see, e.g., Cardozo, 1965). Advertising claims that exceed the product's ability to deliver will directly raise likely expectations, and therefore the firm has control over not only dissatisfaction but also its impact on complaints, because complaints can be regarded as a function of the gap between expectations and benefits derived (Landon, 1977). We will return to how companies can manage this source of negative word-of-mouth later in our discussion section.

Complaining Behavior

Given customer dissatisfaction, the customer may complain. A number of different outlets for complaining have been identified (Day & Landon, 1977; Landon, 1977), including complaining to the marketer, complaining to other customers, or using more formal channels for complaints such as consumer regulation bodies or legal channels. Not all dissatisfied customers complain, however. This is a fairly robust finding throughout the complaints literature—only a small proportion of customers complain directly to the provider of the product or service that is the source of their dissatisfaction, compared with the proportion of customers who complain to their friends, family members, and colleagues. For example, in a survey focusing on customer dissatisfaction of retailing transactions, Hoch (2006) reported that around 6% of the shoppers who experienced a problem actually contacted the company about it. In a study by Diener and Greyser (1978), the number of people who reported complaining to the company was very small, for example, only 12% complained to the store, and only 9% returned the product to the store or to the manufacturer.

Many factors could explain why some dissatisfied customers complain to the firm and why they complain only some of the time. As testimony to the richness of this issue, Folkes (1984) highlighted that the reasons for product or service failures (i.e., attribution) yield different outcomes and expectations from the firm. For example, if a newly purchased set of bookshelves collapses, a customer may either blame the firm for poor construction or himself or herself for poor installation or use. Folkes suggested that the outcome of the failure will depend on such attribution. She found that consumers are more likely to demand some resolution or feel angry if the failure is due to the firm and if the firm has perceived control over the product failure.

It is important to note that the field of complaining is much broader than just customers complaining about specific incidents (either to the firm or through word-of-mouth). There may be intrinsic qualities in individual people that cause them to complain. Kowalski (1996) discussed complaining behavior and put forward a theory of complaining that continues some of the points made in Landon (1977) about the perceived benefits versus costs of complaining about negative affectivity (dissatisfaction). This type of work suggests that we can expect there to be considerable heterogeneity in the intrinsic likelihood that customers will complain. Individual factors such as age (e.g., Romaniuk, 2007), introversion and extraversion, and gender (e.g., Kowalski, 1996, suggests that women complain more than men) could help explain this heterogeneity.

A link can be established between complaining behavior and negative word-of-mouth. As discussed previously, an important outlet for customer redress, following a dissatisfactory experience with a product or service, is complaining to friends, relatives, or other social acquaintances. For established products, it is likely that a significant proportion of the recipients of such complaints are also customers of the product or service. Thus, any factors that have been found to explain the likelihood of a customer complaining may be relevant in considering whether a customer is likely to engage in negative word-of-mouth.

The Impact of Negative Word-of-Mouth

We now turn to the issue of what happens given that satisfied or dissatisfied customers complain to other customers. The evidence for whether positive or negative word-of-mouth has a larger absolute effect appears to be somewhat controversial. Classic statements are often made about how dissatisfied customers will tell more people about their negative experience than satisfied customers will tell about their positive experience. Sometimes statements are made that suggest that customers are more likely to tell someone else about an unfavorable experience than a favorable experience. To help clarify this issue, we separate out the effect of word-of-mouth in several ways. Because the starting point for negative word-of-mouth is dissatisfaction, we should perhaps also consider the likelihood that someone obtains a negative experience. This likelihood is likely to be very industry or firm specific, however. Customer satisfaction indexes could be a good proxy of this (see, e.g., Fornell et al., 1996), although the reporting of simple averages of satisfaction across customers may mask the true proportion of dissatisfied customers.

Given the level of satisfaction with the product or service (either negative or positive), what is the net impact of negative versus positive word-of-mouth?[3] Holmes and Lett (1977) looked at customers receiving free samples of instant coffee and asked them how many people with unfavorable experiences versus favorable experiences told others about their experiences. They found that significantly more "favorable experience" people than "unfavorable experience" people told others about their experiences. East, Hammond, and Wright (2007) reported that negative word-of-mouth is less likely to occur than positive word-of-mouth. Their argument is based on the level of incidence of satisfaction that occurred in the categories they studied. They argued for some asymmetric distribution in service or product quality, that is, that there are more occurrences of extremely satisfactory experiences than extremely unsatisfactory experiences, and therefore positive word-of-mouth is more likely to occur than negative word-of-mouth. A particularly interesting finding in their study is that individuals who engage in more negative word-of-mouth also engage in more positive word-of-mouth.

Throughout East et al.'s (2007) study, the premise is that there is word-of-mouth based on observations of the entire distribution of the brand. Because most brands give, on average, some positive experiences, it is not easy to isolate the effect of word-of-mouth (positive versus negative) given a bad consumption experience. We highlight, however, that to understand the magnitude of the net impact, we should study its composition more carefully. To do so, we will discuss a few articles that talk about the conditional probability that someone dissatisfied with the product will tell someone else about it.[4] Second, we identify how many people that word-of-mouth tends to be transmitted to. The final component we examine is the impact of word-of-mouth on the recipient.

The Incidence of Word-of-Mouth

The incidence of word-of-mouth is examined at an individual customer level and is conditional on a negative or positive (dissatisfaction or satisfaction) experience outcome. More formally, we could think of this in terms of simple probabilities: p_{nn}= Prob(negative word-of-mouth | negative experience) versus p_{pp} = Prob(positive word-of-mouth | positive experience). For completeness we should also consider the off diagonals Prob(positive word-of-mouth | negative experience) and Prob(negative word-of-mouth | positive experience). It is difficult to imagine scenarios wherein this can occur, however, so we assume they are both zero. One may argue that Prob(positive word-of-mouth | negative experience) can occur where there is resolution of the complaint (i.e., this would be the service recovery paradox), but for our purposes we consider the net effect to be equal to zero.

To get some idea of what is the magnitude of p_{nn} and on whether $p_{nn} > p_{pp}$, we draw on findings from a few studies that explicitly provide some numbers on this metric for word-of-mouth. Diener and Greyser (1978) reported that of those people who had a negative experience, around 34% told others about their dissatisfaction. Richins (1983) reported that 34% of dissatisfied customers told only other customers without complaining to the firm.[5] Holmes and Lett (1977) reported that 20% of people with unfavorable experiences communicated their brand experiences with others, compared with 38% for people with favorable experiences.

Engel, Kegerreis, and Blackwell (1969) ran a survey on a set of first users of a new automotive diagnostic center. These first users were defined as innovators for the purpose of the study. The authors measured both the innovators' levels of satisfaction and the level of word-of-mouth these innovators engaged in after their experience. Although they did not report the composition of the number of satisfied versus dissatisfied customers, they did report a pooled number of around 105 out of the 213 (around 50%) innovators who told at least one other person. Engel, Blackwell, et al. (1969) specifically tested the hypothesis that dissatisfied customers are more likely to engage in negative word-of-mouth than are satisfied customers, and they found no support for this in their data.

The Number of People Influenced by Word-of-Mouth

Although sometimes confused with the incidence of word-of-mouth, a separate component of word-of-mouth communication that can be identified is the number of people that a customer relates their negative experience to. It is important to reiterate here that this is the number of people told, conditional on telling at least one person. Unfortunately, for established products we have very little evidence available, and we need to draw on the literature involving new products to get any idea of the number of people that satisfied and dissatisfied customers tend to talk to.

In their study on customers adopting a new auto diagnostic service, Engel, Blackwell, et al. (1969) found that around one in three of their respondents tell at least two people. Although it is not valid to generate an average from their frequency distribution (more than four people are combined into the four-plus group), we do find that the majority of people tell at least two people; in only one out of three cases, given word-of-mouth has been given, is only one other person told.

What was missing from their research is whether dissatisfied people talk to more (or fewer) people than satisfied customers, conditional on providing word-of-mouth. Richins (1983) reported that customers experiencing dissatisfaction with a clothing item told an average of five other people. Hoch's (2006) report from the Wharton School's Jay H. Baker Retailing Initiative ran a survey before and after Christmas 2005 and reported that of those people who complained, 26% told one person, another 26% told two people, and the remainder told three or more people about their experience.

Anderson's (1998) study on the customer satisfaction barometer, described earlier, sheds a little light on the relative numbers of people told by satisfied customers versus dissatisfied customers. Their evidence suggests that, on average, satisfied customers tell more people about their satisfaction than dissatisfied customers tell about their dissatisfaction. For the Swedish sample, the number of people that dissatisfied people told (those who scored a one on the customer satisfaction index) was around 12; in the United States, this number was around 10. These word-of-mouth numbers are just marginally lower for satisfied customers. Anderson (1998) thought of satisfaction on more of a continuous scale, ranging from *very dissatisfied* to *very satisfied*. This recognizes that there exists a utility of word-of-mouth that increases at either extreme of the satisfaction with a product. This continuous scale yields an inverted U-shape relationship whereby any neutral product experience (i.e., the product or service simply matched expectations) has a low likelihood of spreading word-of-mouth, and any extreme satisfaction or dissatisfaction results in a higher likelihood of word-of-mouth. It is important to point out that although both tails of the satisfaction score distribution are present (i.e., the firms whose average score is either 1 or 9 out of 10 for satisfaction), Anderson (1998) did not report the number of people with positive probability of giving word-of-mouth for these levels, and so we cannot directly report these numbers for his study. There is, however, some indication that given word-of-mouth occurs, the average number of people that extremely dissatisfied customers and extremely satisfied customers tell about their experiences is higher than those who have just neutral levels of experience.

In summary, there is not much consensus about the number of people that dissatisfied customers tell about their experience and dissatisfaction. The range of the number of people communicated with is from around 2 to 12 people. Clearly there is also heterogeneity here—different people tell different numbers of people, and this may be related to their position in a network, for example, their degree of centrality. Similar to the notion that personality traits may explain the extent to which people complain (e.g., Kowalski, 1996), it is reasonable to expect these traits to also be factors when it comes to explaining how many people a given individual will tell about any negative experience. There is also scant empirical evidence to support that dissatisfied customers, conditional on engaging in word-of-mouth, tell more or less than satisfied customers (Anderson, 1998, seems the exception here).

Purchase Intentions of the Recipients of Word-of-Mouth

In this section we are interested in how negative word-of-mouth may impact the recipient's preferences. Again, we are focusing on the context of regular purchase patterns, so we have to think in terms of two customers of the same firm talking to one another about a brand or product category. In this context, how will the negative experience of one customer affect the purchase decision of the recipient after being told about a negative experience?

Arndt (1967) measured word-of-mouth communication and created an overall index for each customer who received word-of-mouth feedback. His results suggest that customers who receive a positive word-of-mouth score tend to be much more likely to purchase the product than customers who receive negative word-of-mouth. In Arndt's sample, 54% of the people who reported receiving positive word-of-mouth adopted the product, whereas 18% of those customers receiving a negative word-of-mouth score were likely to purchase the product.

The other effect of negative word-of-mouth is that such information may be weighted more heavily than positive word-of-mouth. This has been found in studies of diffusion of innovation (Lutz, 1975; Wright, 1974). It is also relevant to a more general insight about the nature of negative information—that unfavorable information is stronger in its effect than positive information (Mizerski, 1982; Weinberger, Allen, & Dillon, 1981). Opposite to positive word-of-mouth, negative word-of-mouth may act to stifle the adoption of new technologies (e.g., Leonard-Barton, 1985). In the context of established products, it is easy to see that negative word-of-mouth may have a significantly greater impact on other customers than positive word-of-mouth, because the latter merely reinforces the current positive attitudes.

More recent evidence carries the surprising finding that it is possible that purchase likelihood of recipients of the negative word-of-mouth are affected more than the person originally faced with the dissatisfaction (Hoch et al., 2006). Intuition for this result is based on the dissatisfied customer exaggerating the experience, making the entire situation seem much worse than was actually faced. Another possible reason for such a result is the feeling that the customer, offended by the firm's poor treatment, wants to hurt the firm's business by telling people about the bad experience.

Attribution theory may also lend an explanation to this result. Attribution theory involves causal attribution, or the perceived cause for which the information was transmitted from sender to receiver (e.g., Mizerski, 1982). Thus, in any dyad, how the person perceives the sender may impact on how the word-of-mouth is integrated into his or her own beliefs about the product. As an example, the opinion of a friend complaining about airline food may be taken differently if that person has a lot of dietary issues or is a very fussy eater than if that person is more relaxed and has fewer dietary constraints.

Managing Negative Word-of-Mouth

For the marketer, the most practical issue involves what to do about negative word-of-mouth. We discuss two broad avenues here. The first is how to avoid negative word-of-mouth in the first place. Clearly, because word-of-mouth stems from customer dissatisfaction, managing the source for dissatisfaction deserves attention. As discussed earlier, typically dissatisfaction arises from some (negative) expectation disconfirmation. Expectations may be built up from previous experience, advertising, and so on. We highlight two key levers to manage the sources of negative word-of-mouth: product performance and quality, and marketing communications. Although marketers strive to deliver consistency in quality, problems can occur, and it is important to understand recovery efforts by marketers to avoid the possibility of negative word-of-mouth. The second avenue involves identifying what managers should do when confronted by negative word-of-mouth. We speculate on some guidance for marketers on this question.

Reducing Variations in Product Quality

The product or service industry context is important to how much control firms can have over this process. Most products and services carry some level of variation in performance. Although a good quality control program can help in reducing this variation, it is difficult to completely remove all negative encounters. This is especially likely in some products and services that are more susceptible to such variation, for example, the quality of fresh produce or baked goods, the level of friendliness of the person checking in the customer for a flight, and so on. The variability in product or service quality directly impacts the incidence of negative experiences versus positive experiences. As the level of variability increases, the chances of a "significant" negative draw versus positive draw increases. (This of course ignores the heterogeneity among customers for the quality attractiveness.) In the Bitner, Booms, and Tetreault (1990) critical incidents study, customers were more easily able to recall incidents carrying a great deal of dissatisfaction than they were able to recall incidents that were highly satisfactory. Furthermore, and as discussed earlier, not all customers complain about bad service encounters—they internalize. It would also be good to understand more about whether customers with very positive experiences are more likely to share their positive experiences than customers with a similar magnitude negative experience. This is an empirical question that needs to be considered in various product categories.[6]

The Effect of Marketing Communications on Word-of-Mouth

Marketing communications can affect the amount of word-of-mouth customers engage in, either directly or indirectly. For the indirect route, marketing communications designed to raise expectations will increase the likelihood of a disconfirmation of an expectation. Consider, for example, an airline that advertises its broad entertainment system and world-class cuisine but neglects to make it clear to customers that this is available only in business and first-class cabins. Economy-class customers exposed to such communication end up having high expectations and relatively poor service performance, increasing the likelihood of negative word-of-mouth.

There is some question of whether marketing communications (e.g., advertising) can directly stimulate word-of-mouth communications. Even if it does, this is likely to be positive. An interesting perspective is provided by Rossiter and Percy (1997, Chap. 16), who suggested that advertisers need to measure the "personal influence" component of their advertising. This is defined as a multiplier on any person reached by an advertising message, that is, the amount that the customer tells other people about the advertised message.

The question of the direct effect of marketing communications has been tested directly. For example, and in a novel field experiment, Bayus (1985) conducted a series of tests for recruitment of U.S. naval personnel in 1978. The experiment involved varying the amount of advertising and the number of recruiting salespeople across two experimental waves. Measures were collected on the number of discussions reported among the target market (males and females of recruiting age) through a telephone survey. They also asked about how certain the potential recruits were about joining the U.S. Navy. The results suggest that increased advertising is able to increase the amount of word-of-mouth that is generated, particularly among male recruits who were unsure about their military enlistment likelihood. For female recruits, however, a decreased amount of advertising increased the likelihood of word-of-mouth.

Service Recovery and Its Ability to Mitigate Negative Word-of-Mouth

As we saw in the previous discussion, available empirical evidence suggests that dissatisfied customers rarely complain to the firm. We next examine the issue of what are the responses by companies to these complaints, and how successful they are in resolving the complaints. On the basis of a study of 700 critical incidents, Bitner et al. (1990) found that around 50% of incidents were not resolved successfully. They also claimed that many customers would be satisfied and repurchase if the manufacturer responded with some type of remedy (other than with a letter apologizing). Unsatisfactory service recovery remedies have been found to be more susceptible to the spread of negative information through word-of-mouth than the positive effects of satisfactory service recovery attempts (e.g., Technical Assistance Research Programmes, 1979).

This raises the issue of how effective are service recovery efforts. Some authors have described the possibility of a service "recovery paradox," defined as the positive experience that one gets from service failure followed by service recovery efforts—typically such customers give an overall positive experience assessment of the company. The evidence for this phenomenon is mixed—Gilly and Gelb (1982) did not find evidence that successful service recovery enhances the amount of brand repurchase. Smith and Bolton (1998) found that service recovery efforts can completely reverse dissatisfaction and even improve satisfaction scores. Hart, Heskett, and Sasser (1990) provided a number of anecdotes consistent with positive service recovery yielding more satisfied customers. McCollough, Berry, and Yadav (2000), however, found no support for their hypothesized service recovery paradox and, instead, found some evidence that service recovery does not fully mitigate the initial decrease in satisfaction caused by service failures.

This variability in the efficacy of firms' service recovery begs the question of how to improve service recovery for customers. This question was examined Gilly and Gelb (1982). The authors studied a sample of 521 customers of a major oil company who had previously complained about some aspect of this company's service. They found that an important issue revolved around whether a monetary loss versus nonmonetary loss was experienced. Although perhaps costly, it is straightforward for a marketer to satisfy someone who has suffered monetary loss—just compensate them. They did indeed find that people experiencing a monetary loss tended to be more satisfied with the organization's response than those facing a nonmonetary loss. No evidence was found that the absolute amount of monetary loss led to lower satisfaction with the organization's response, but they did find that the monetary loss as a percentage of the monetary loss reimbursed is associated with higher customer satisfaction with firm's response to complaints. The speed of response was found to be important for the nonmonetary losses but not for monetary losses.

There could be the case of a customer complaint being resolved after the negative word-of-mouth has spread to others. Because Gilly and Gelb (1982) also highlighted the effect of time, a recommendation highlighted by such research is that the service recovery must be done as fast as possible. This will minimize the possible effect of negative word-of-mouth spreading before the company has had a chance to solve the problem. Any delay raises the chance the customer talks to more people.

Clearly, the service recovery process is intricately related to the negative word-of-mouth incidence and quantity. What appears to be important is whether the initial dissatisfaction was caused by the firm, how quickly the firm responds, and how it responds. These will act to possibly reduce negative word-of-mouth. For example, consider the airline industry; nonweather-related long delays in travel often mean the airlines offers additional meals and drinks and sometimes overnight hotel stays. Delaying these recovery efforts or not making travelers sufficiently comfortable (or out of pocket) on such delays means travelers will remain very dissatisfied.

Measurement Issues

As discussed previously, because not all dissatisfied customers complain, the collection of data from companies' feedback (or complaints) systems may be biased because it does not contain a metric for the number of customers that are dissatisfied. Thus, any estimate of the proportion of dissatisfied customers will be biased. This is commonly called a "self-selection" bias (e.g., Heckman, 1979). This observation has led some authors to suggest methods developed in quality control to infer the true level of dissatisfaction that exists based on complaint behavior (e.g., Kurth, 1965).

Nonpassive tracking techniques may be possible to infer the extent to which negative word-of-mouth exists among customers. Survey methods are commonly used for this purpose. For example, Romaniuk (2007) surveyed viewers of TV programs and asked about their receipt of negative word-of-mouth versus positive word-of-mouth. Keaveney (1995) and Mangold, Miller, and Brockway (1999) asked people about their previous satisfaction with service experiences.

Possibly the best mechanism to use for the measure of the word-of-mouth construct (and its valence) involves monitoring what is actually said among a group of customers. A promising direction involves the use of social networking information technologies through the Internet or other communication devices including smart phones. One such example is the study by Godes and Mayzlin (2004) of online conversations. Detailed activities by customers interacting with one another can be tracked, including the content of actual conversations. To the extent that these platforms fully capture everything that is said (or not said) about a product or service consumption experience, at least for a representative sample of customers, it could be possible to quantify the degree to which word-of-mouth permeates throughout the network. This is probably applicable, however, only for products that are sold and consumed through the same medium, for example, the Internet. Perhaps virtual worlds such as Second Life could provide a good lens to study this issue.

In assessing the validity of negative word-of-mouth, the point is sometimes made that it could be biased because the customer embellishes the negative experience, and it is a one-sided view. There may also be no attribution to the company in such circumstances, depending on how the customer telling the story about his or her dissatisfaction is perceived by the recipient.

Another interesting point made by a few researchers (e.g., Engel, Kegerreis, et al., 1969) is that positive word-of-mouth may arise because of dissonance the customer faces with a product. This is likely to amplify the effect of positive word-of-mouth in the dimension of the number of people told of this experience. This view was also put forward by Dichter (1966, p. 148):

> The most effective Word-of-Mouth for the advertiser is the post-decision speaker who is bent on eliminating all dissonance in his post-decision situation.

From a marketer's perspective, however, unless such conversations are monitored and analyzed, it is difficult to implement any tracking system around it. In that case it is recommended to monitor the *source* of the negative word-of-mouth—customer dissatisfaction.

DISCUSSION

It is often perceived that word-of-mouth is not in direct control of market-ers, that is, they cannot control exactly what is said. It is clear that positive word-of-mouth benefits marketers and that negative word-of-mouth harms marketers. Some of the literature on word-of-mouth has been focused on measuring these positive and negative effects. The question addressed in this chapter is, for established products, how much does negative word-of-mouth harm a marketer's business, and how much does positive word-of-mouth benefit a firm's business?

Our perusal of the literature in this area has identified several mech-anisms through which word-of-mouth can impact a marketer's sales or market share for established products. The first mechanism is dissatisfac-tion, which we find arises when the benefits of a product or service fall short of some expectations of customers. As with Landon (1977), however, we find that dissatisfaction is only a necessary, but not a sufficient, condi-tion for customers to turn to some method for resolution of such gaps between product and service performance and expectations. Most cus-tomers just stay silent and do nothing to resolve the negative utility that arises from dissatisfactory product and service outcomes.

Given that customers do something about their dissatisfaction, the two main outlets for redress include making a complaint to one of the stake-holders involved in the provision of the product or service or to complain to their friends, colleagues, and associates. It is this latter outlet for redress that is the main interest for this chapter. We find widespread agreement that very few customers complain directly to the company if there is some problem. Typically the most frequently turned to outlet for redress is com-plaining to friends, colleagues, and associates. Indeed, we find that many articles suggest that around one in three dissatisfied customers complain to these members of their social networks.

A common comparison made in the trade and academic literatures is how satisfied customers are more or less likely to engage in word-of-mouth. We highlighted the need to study this as a conditional statement of the likelihood to engage in word-of-mouth, given the experience the customer received was highly positive or negative. Although less evidence is available for such comparable findings in the case where customers are highly satis-fied, we found only a couple of studies that suggest that more people engage in word-of-mouth after a positive experience than after a negative experience (Engel, Kegerreis, et al., 1969; Holmes & Lett, 1977). Clearly, more evidence spanning more product or service categories would be useful to enable us to draw more generalizable conclusions for this important issue.

The other components of the effect of dissatisfaction and word-of-mouth involve the number of people that are told by each dissatisfied or satisfied customers and the impact on each of these people in terms of their future purchase behavior. Although a number of studies do report such figures, we unfortunately do not find much agreement on the number of people that word-of-mouth is spread to for any one person. Numbers reported range from around 2 or 3 up to around 12 people told about experiences. This evidence suggests that such numbers could be highly dependent on factors such as the situation, the type of product or service, or how dissatisfaction versus satisfaction is measured.

For the third component of the conditional impact of word-of-mouth, how do recipients of word-of-mouth (positive or negative) react to this? Although clearly one could think of this issue in a more complicated analytical fashion, for example, by allowing such customers to update their belief structure, a simplified way to look at this is simply to document the extent to which the word-of-mouth influences repeat purchase behavior. Some researchers have argued for an asymmetry in negative information versus positive information, stemming from the finding that negative information is weighted more heavily than positive information in purchasing decisions. Some research has pointed out that the effect on the purchase decision may be larger for recipients of the information than for the person initially affected by the product or service failure.

Combining these effects, we can begin to make some rough initial assessments as to the potential magnitudes of any negative service encounter. As an illustration of this, after a negative product or service encounter, we can expect around one in two people will not purchase the product again. This is our benchmark "naive" expected loss of business a company is placing at risk from poor performance, because it does not consider the full ramifications of a negative service encounter through the channel of word-of-mouth.

A company that considers the impact of these dissatisfied customers, however, may wish to also consider the expected negative impact resulting from negative word-of-mouth. There is some consensus in the literature that around one in three dissatisfied customers will spread negative news about the company. Again, on the basis of what we have seen from the literature, we further assume that each of the recipients of negative word-of-mouth tell another five people. Finally, although there are few findings on this (Arndt, 1967; Hoch, 2006), we also consider that the recipients of negative word-of-mouth information are equally likely to stop purchasing from the company. In terms of the number of customers, the expected impact is slightly greater than one additional customer that could be expected to be lost from a negative experience by the company, in addition to the direct impact on the affected customer. Even if we consider some of the higher numbers reported in the literature as to how many people are told about a negative experience, we still see at most two customers lost because of word-of-mouth, in addition to the chance of losing the affected customer. Again, these numbers are conditional on a "dissatisfaction" encounter.

Let us contrast this with what may happen in the case of a very positive customer experience. We should highlight that we do not consider this the same as a net positive service encounter arising from a negative service encounter that a company successfully resolves. Other than the direct effect of a positive experience (which will be to keep the customer), the positive effect of word-of-mouth also is a function of the number of people they tell and the effect on those people. We speculate that in established products, positive word-of-mouth will have less impact on customers' attitudes and beliefs than in the case of new products, because stronger prior beliefs developed from many other sources are likely to exist (past product experience, advertising information, other sources of word-of-mouth, and so on). Although one could anticipate that there would be multiple customers who are affected in a positive way, it is not likely that the net impact would be much greater.

Our discussion therefore suggests that in established product categories, negative word-of-mouth will have a greater negative impact on the customer base than positive word-of-mouth will have a positive effect. Even so, we find that the effect of negative word-of-mouth is unlikely to be very large, even conditional on a customer being dissatisfied. We next consider what implications we draw for companies wishing to reduce the impacts of negative word-of-mouth.

What Can Marketers Do About Negative Word-of-Mouth?

Marketers strive to understand the catalysts for each type of word-of-mouth. Thus, a key issue is, what can the company do about negative word-of-mouth? Negative word-of-mouth is not directly under the control of the company, because many customers do not directly communicate with the company (see the discussion in previous sections). Clearly, improving product performance is a direct way to address this issue, striving, for example, for "Six Sigma" quality. There may be technological constraints, however, that inhibit the ability to make such changes in the short run. Also, for service-dominated marketers (restaurants, stores), reducing the variation may be very costly.

We also discussed that the other way to view the control that a marketer has over the amount of negative word-of-mouth involves managing customer expectations. Because dissatisfaction is the source for much of complaining behavior (Landon, 1977), reducing dissatisfaction involves either improving the benefits to the customer by raising product or service quality or managing expectations by avoiding overinflated claims about the product or service quality. An interesting tension therefore arises— to help increase the likelihood that customers will purchase the product, marketers must make effective claims about the benefits of the product or service. On the other hand, this raises the likelihood of increasing dissatisfaction and therefore negative word-of-mouth. It is thereby important for firms to recognize such trade-offs explicitly in deciding on the content of communication programs.

What advice can we draw for marketers to manage negative word-of-mouth? We draw three key recommendations from our discussion:

1. *Monitor customer word-of-mouth.* Although interpersonal contact is difficult, if not impossible, for a marketer to monitor (without engaging in immoral espionage), more and more customer discussion is emerging through platforms that the marketer can monitor, such as blogs, discussion boards, customer review sites, and so on. Because customers often tend to complain more to other customers than to the firm itself, many incidents many go undetected by a company's regular complaints systems. The more popular sites should be monitored by the marketer to detect when a problem occurs. When a problem occurs, marketers need to assess the likelihood of the customer telling more people and assess how best to assuage the customer and reverse the dissatisfaction experienced.

2. *Proactively manage negative word-of-mouth discussion.* This is very much like handling any complaint directed at the firm by the

customer. That is, the marketer should assess whether the dissatisfaction can be mitigated by fixing the problem (e.g., exchanging the product), offering monetary compensation or an apology, and so on. Because negative word-of-mouth is often undetectable until it occurs, however, the marketer may need to manage both the sender and the receiver of the negative word-of-mouth.

3. *Act fast.* The longer the marketer takes to take action, the more people that may be affected by the negative word-of-mouth (Gilly & Gelb, 1982).

Naturally any action taken to counter negative word-of-mouth should carefully balance the costs against the benefits of doing so. A metric useful to guide such policy is Customer Lifetime Value (CLV). Because we discussed the impact of negative word-of-mouth in terms of the loss of customers, the question becomes, what are these customers worth to the firm? CLV can be useful in providing an upper bound to the resources that should be allocated to negating such word-of-mouth effects.

Measuring Word-of-Mouth in Social Networks

The key idea behind social network theory is that both the location of a customer and his or her influence with network neighbors will influence how information and attitudes will diffuse through the network of customers. That is, the distance (or tie strength) among customers will impact how negative or positive word-of-mouth will spread through the network (Brown & Reingen, 1987). Although we refer to other reviews on specifics of social network theory, we do draw in some key issues here. The basic point is that customers who are "close" to one another are likely to talk to one another. Sociologists and statistics researchers have highlighted that transitivity is important in considering the influences among network actors who are not directly connected. In a network context, transitivity simply means that if A and B are "connected," the probability that A is connected to friends of B is higher. That means we can expect that the influence of information travels beyond the observed dyad to other customers linked to that dyad.

On the basis of knowledge of the network structure, we see what happens to customer dissatisfaction if, as is reported in the literature, negative word-of-mouth ensues from product or service failures. Negative word-of-mouth may diffuse (i.e., the influence of a dissatisfaction will carry toward other people, either directly or indirectly), and the speed of such diffusion may be slower than the diffusion of positive information. Unfortunately, we find little evidence of the networkwide consequences of negative word-of-mouth, beyond the dyadic relationship that is represented in many of the studies discussed earlier.

Can Negative Word-of-Mouth Information "Cascade"?

A key issue is the unknown phenomenon of how negative word-of-mouth could influence customers beyond the immediate network neighbors of the complainers. Some authors have suggested that complaining behavior is contagious (e.g., Kowalski, 1996) and that a complaint by one customer will ignite the recipient of that complaint to pass on that complaint to others. These examples, however, tend to be discussed in the context of group dynamics rather than the possibly more typical dyadic interactions that are faced in many networks. Also this contagion relies on the recipients of the information to also have experienced dissatisfaction with the marketer concerned, and it seems unlikely that this discussion will continue beyond the dyad or group discussing the complaint.

Nevertheless, we do not rule out the possibility of this type of behavior and could consider what would be the effect of negative word-of-mouth, if this information spreads beyond just the customer concerned and his or her immediate network neighbors. To get an estimate of the possible impact, we raise the following questions: How far through a network will negative information spread, and how much influence will this information have on deeper levels of the network? Although this has not been covered in the literature, it clearly has arisen in extreme situations. A few very popular anecdotal examples exist where the negative experience of a small number of customers affected many more customers, for example, the false accusations made by a few customers about Audi vehicles that accelerated out of control. Perceived unfair treatment by a company may spark a one-person campaign that is designed to damage a company's brand and reputation.

Some authors are drawing some of the findings from the literature on negative word-of-mouth into the realm of CLV. Because the impacts discussed previously have the direct impact of losing not only the affected customer but also customers connected to that customer, the question, again, is, how far into the network will this impact reach? This is a crucial question, but it has not been studied in the context of negative word-of-mouth for established goods. Thus the discussion of the research on negative word-of-mouth suggests that the total impact of negative word-of-mouth, for any dissatisfied customer, is quite limited.

CONCLUSION

This chapter studied the effect of negative word-of-mouth with the goal of assessing what would be the likely spillover impact on a company's performance of a single dissatisfied customer. Starting with identifying the sources of dissatisfaction and the likely impact on that customer, we then highlighted the separate roles of several different components of the impact of negative word-of-mouth.

We speculate from our study of the findings given in the literature on word-of-mouth that firms can expect around one to two customers to be lost from any extremely dissatisfied customer. This number combines various factors (incidence of word-of-mouth, number of people told, and impact on these people).

What are the recommendations for any marketer wanting to minimize this impact of dissatisfaction through negative word-of-mouth? We identified two broad recommendations. The first is to manage the variation in quality, to the extent that the product or service "breakdowns" are minimized. The other is to develop an effective outlet for customers to air their dissatisfaction. It may be difficult to reduce the variation in quality, as there will always be a lower tail of dissatisfaction in products or services, so long as there is variation in quality. Customers will build up their expectations, and even good companies can end up with dissatisfied customers.

To minimize the impact of negative word-of-mouth, in terms of losing both the affected dissatisfied customers and their social ties, probably the strongest recommendation from the previous analysis involves an effective complaint system. The goal of a complaint system is to identify the most dissatisfied customers. What is the recommendation for such a complaint system? The advice here from the literature is quite basic: Lower the cost of submitting to this feedback system, and increase the expected benefit from providing the feedback. The costs to registering a complaint, however, should be considered based on more than just the time or "hassle" factor involved. The costs should include any perceived psychological impact, for example, facing a customer service agent that appears to be personally offended by someone registering a complaint. The benefits can be either monetary or nonmonetary but very much depend on the nature of the dissatisfaction.

From a measurement perspective, our knowledge of the impact of negative word-of-mouth could benefit from more consistency in the quantitative measures underlying the word-of-mouth construct and its impacts. We essentially are asking to sharpen our quantitative tools to better assess the expected impact of poor product or service quality. The decomposition of the impact of word-of-mouth into components discussed previously is a useful starting point. One example is to improve the reporting of aggregated (across customers) data such as variance of the satisfaction scores, because a proxy for dissatisfaction for any company may be product or service performance that is some number of standard deviations below what is expected.

NOTES

1. It is important to recognize that besides the literature reviewed here, there is a lot of relevant work that could be included from consumer behavior. Some of this work is covered in more depth by Richins (1983), covering aspects of the effectiveness of communication among people.
2. The term *conspicuous consumption* traces back to Veblen (1899), who defined it as any consumption of products designed to display wealth to others. The signals given by such consumption choices (e.g., wearing Prada clothing, carrying Gucci handbags, or driving Lamborghini automobiles) do not require any direct, dyadic communication with others.
3. Neutral satisfaction is, of course, the case where expectations are confirmed by product consumption or service experience. This could lead to fairly neutral word-of-mouth or no word-of-mouth. A potentially interesting question for research involves how customers update their beliefs given they observe no word-of-mouth.
4. In expectation, of course, this is directly linked to the number of people told. For some studies, however, this conditional probability is not reported, so this could be used as a proxy.

5. We can only speculate what is the number and effect of people who both complain to the firm and spread word-of-mouth. On the one hand, it could be that customers who complain receive a positive remedy from the manufacturer and go on to spread positive word-of-mouth.

6. Some observers have referred to customer complaints as "gifts" because they provide direct information about quality breakdown, something that could be a prelude to a bigger problem. Of course, that assumes companies are sufficiently farsighted to monitor and react to such complaints.

REFERENCES

Anderson, E. W. (1998). Customer satisfaction and word of mouth. *Journal of Service Research, 1*(1), 5–17.

Andreasen, A. R. (1977). A taxonomy of consumer satisfaction/dissatisfaction measures. *Journal of Consumer Affairs, 11*(2), 11–24.

Arndt, J. (1967, August). Role of product related conversations in the diffusion of a new product. *Journal of Marketing Research, 4*, 291–295.

Bass, F. M. (1969). A new product growth for model consumer durables. *Management Science, 15*(5), 215–227.

Bayus, B. L. (1985). Word of mouth: The indirect effects of marketing efforts. *Journal of Advertising Research, 25*(3), 31–39.

Bearden, W. O., & Teel, J. E. (1983). Selected determinants of consumer satisfaction and complaint reports. *Journal of Marketing Research, 20*(1), 21–28.

Bitner, M. J., Booms, B. H., & Tetreault, M. S. (1990, January). The service encounter: Diagnosing favorable and unfavorable incidents. *Journal of Marketing, 54*, 71–84.

Brown, J. J., & Reingen, P. H. (1987). Social ties and word-of-mouth referral behavior. *Journal of Consumer Research, 14*(3), 350–362.

Cardozo, R. N. (1965). An experimental study of consumer effort, expectations and satisfaction. *Journal of Marketing Research, 2*(3), 244–249.

Chen, Y., & Xie, J. (2008). Online consumer review: Word-of-mouth as a new element of marketing communication mix. *Management Science, 54*(3), 477–491.

Chevalier, J. A., & Mayzlin, D. (2006, August). The effect of word of mouth on sales: Online book reviews. *Journal of Marketing Research, 43*, 345–354.

CNN/Money (2005). "Abe" Fry Fetches $75,100. *CNN/Money*, February 18, 2005. (http://money.cnn.com/2005/02/18/news/funny/lincoln_fry/index.htm)

Day, R. L., & Landon, E. L., Jr. (1977). Toward a theory of consumer complaining behavior. In A. G. Woodside (Ed.), *Consumer and industrial buying behavior*. North Holland: Elsevier Science.

Dichter, E. (1966). How word-of-mouth advertising works. *Harvard Business Review, 44*(6), 147–166.

Diener, B. J., & Greyser, S. A. (1978). Consumer views of redress needs. *Journal of Marketing, 42*(4), 21–27.

East, R., Hammond, K., & Wright, M. (2007). The relative incidence of positive and negative word of mouth: A multi-category study. *International Journal of Research in Marketing, 24*, 175–184.

Engel, J. F., Blackwell, R. D., & Kegerreis, R. J. (1969). How information is used to adopt an innovation. *Journal of Advertising Research, 9*(4), 3–8.

Engel, J. F., Kegerreis, R. J., & Blackwell, R. D. (1969, July). Word-of-mouth communication by the innovator. *Journal of Marketing, 33,* 15–19.

Folkes, V. S. (1984). Consumer reactions to product failure: An attributional approach. *Journal of Consumer Research, 10*(4), 398–409.

Fornell, C., Johnson, M. D, Anderson, E. W, Cha, J., & Bryant, B. E. (1996). The American Customer Satisfaction Index: Nature, purpose, and findings. *Journal of Marketing, 60*(4), 7–18.

Gilly, M. C., & Gelb, B. D. (1982). Post-purchase consumer processes and the complaining consumer. *Journal of Consumer Research, 9*(3), 323–328.

Godes, D., & Mayzlin, D. (2004). Using online conversations to study word of mouth communication. *Marketing Science, 23*(4), 545–560.

Hart, C. W. L., Heskett, J. L., & Sasser, W. E., Jr. (1990, July–August). The profitable art of service recovery. *Harvard Business Review,* 148–156.

Heckman, J. J. (1979). Sample selection bias as a specification error. *Econometrica, 47,* 153–161.

Hoch S. J. (2006) Beware of dissatisfied consumers: They like to blab. *Knowledge@Wharton* (http://knowledge.wharton.upenn.edu/article.cfm?articleid=1422). March 8, 2006.

Holmes, J. H., & Lett, J. D., Jr. (1977). Product sampling and word of mouth. *Journal of Advertising Research, 17*(5), 35–40.

Kamakura, W. A., Kossar, B. S., & Wedel, M. (2004). Identifying innovators for the cross-selling of new products. *Management Science, 50*(8), 1120–1133.

Keaveney, S. M. (1995, April). Customer switching behavior in service industries: An exploratory study. *Journal of Marketing, 59,* 71–82.

Kowalski, R. M. (1996). Complaints and complaining: Functions, antecedents, and consequences. *Psychological Bulletin, 119*(2), 179–196.

Kurth, R. (1965). Testing the significance of consumer complaints. *Journal of Marketing Research, 2*(3), 283–284.

Landon, E. L. (1977). A model of consumer complaint behavior. In R. L. Day (Ed.), *Consumer satisfaction, dissatisfaction and complaining behavior* (pp. 31–35). Bloomington: Indiana University School of Business.

Leonard-Barton, D. (1985). Experts as negative opinion leaders in the diffusion of a technical innovation. *Journal of Consumer Research, 11*(4), 914–926.

Lutz, R.J. (1975). Changing brand attitudes through modification of cognitive structure. *Journal of Consumer Research, 1,* 49–59.

Mahajan, V., Muller, E., & Bass, F. M. (1990, January). New product diffusion models in marketing: A review and directions for research. *Journal of Marketing, 54,* 1–26.

Mangold, W. G., Miller, F., & Brockway, G. R. (1999). Word of mouth communication in the service marketplace. *Journal of Services Marketing, 13*(1), 73–84.

McCollough, M. A., Berry, L. L., & Yadav, M. S. (2000). An empirical investigation of customer satisfaction after service failure and recovery. *Journal of Service Research, 3*(2), 121–137.

Menzel, H., & Katz, E. (1955, Winter). Social relations and innovation in the medical profession: The epidemiology of a new drug. *Public Opinion Quarterly, 19,* 337–352.

Mizerski, R. W. (1982, December). An attribution explanation of the disproportionate influence of unfavorable information. *Journal of Consumer Research, 9,* 301–310.

Phan, M. (2001). Studios turning to elaborate internet games for promotion. *Los Angeles Times*, July 13, 2001. http://articles.latimes.com/2001/jul/13/entertainment/ca-21935

Reingen, P. H. (1987). A word of mouth network. *Advances in Consumer Research*, *14*(1), 213–217.

Reingen, P. H., & Kernan, J. B. (1986, November). Analysis of referral networks in marketing: Methods and illustration. *Journal of Marketing Research*, *23*, 370–378.

Richins, M. L. (1983, Winter). Negative word of mouth by dissatisfied customers: A pilot study. *Journal of Marketing*, *47*, 68–78.

Rogers, E. (1962). *Diffusion of innovations*. New York: Free Press.

Romaniuk, J. (2007). Word of mouth and the viewing of television programs. *Journal of Advertising Research*, *47*(4), 462–471.

Rossiter, J. & Percy, L. (1997). *Advertising communications and promotion management*, Second edition, New York:McGraw-Hill.

Smith, A. K., & Bolton, R. N. (1998). An experimental investigation of customer reactions to service failure and recovery encounters. *Journal of Service Research*, *1*(1), 65–81.

Technical Assistance Research Programmes (1979). *Consumer complaint handling in America: summary of findings and recommendations*. U.S Office of Consumer Affairs, Washington DC.

Van den Bulte, C., & Wuyts, S. (2007). *Social networks and marketing*. Cambridge, MA: Marketing Science Institute.

Veblen, T. (1899). *The theory of the leisure class*. New York: Mentor Books.

Weinberger, M. C., Allen, C. T., & Dillon, W. R. (1981). Negative information: Perspectives and research directions. *Advances in Consumer Research*, *8*, 398–404.

Wong, E. (2008). China says more milk products show signs of being tainted. *New York Times*, September 19, 2008. http://www.nytimes.com/2008/09/19/world/asia/19milk.html?_r=1&scp=2&sq=Sanlu+group&st=nyt

Wright P. (1974). The harassed decision maker: Time pressures, distractions, and the use of evidence. *Journal of Applied Psychology*, *59*(5), 555–561.

Author Index

A

Aaker, D. A., 39
Aaker, J. L., 50
Abbratt, R., 286
Adamic, L. A., 268, 269, 277
Aggarwal, P., 50
Agrafioti, I., 27
Albers, S., 25
Albrecht, S. L., 165
Algesheimer, R., 87
Allatta, J. T., 22
Allen, M. P., 92
Allport, F. H., 240
Alper, B. S., 107, 122
Alphonso, C., 163
Altemeyer, B., 173, 200
Ambler, R., 205
American Healthways, 129
Anderson, A. R., 313
Anderson, E. W., 318
Antia, K., 79, 85
Arbia, G., 25
Ariely, D., 152
Armstrong, K., 186, 187, 189, 190
Asch, S. E., 237, 238, 239
Athreya, K. B., 263
Azari, R., 123

B

Bagozzi, R. P., 54
Bailenson, J. N., 156
Balmer, R., 167
Bampo, M., 259, 279
Barrot, C., 25
Bartels, R., 164
Bartlett, M. S., 264
Bass, F. M., 264, 300, 307
Batra, R., 143
Baum, A., 119, 120

Baysinger, B. D., 93
Bayus, B. L., 322
Beardon, W. O., 40, 307
Bearman, P., 26
Bechara, A., 145, 147, 149, 151
Becker, M. H., 10
Beckfield, J., 98
Belk, R. W., 164, 169
Bell, D. R., 23, 24
Bell, R. A., 110, 119, 120, 123, 128, 132
Benlter, P. M., 185
Berger, H., 91
Berger, J., 12
Beringer, J., 58, 59
Berntson, G. G., 155
Berrelson, B. R., 219
Bettman, J. R., 149, 166, 173, 182, 189, 193, 199, 292
Bishop, D., 145
Bkashi, N., 13
Bonacich, P., 19
Bond, R., 239
Bonfrer, A., 263, 264, 269
Bonfret, A., 22
Bonoguore, T., 163
Boorman, S. A., 224
Borgatti, S. P., 89
Bothner, M. S., 235
Boulding, W., 205
Boyle, E., 50
Brantley, P., 93
Brass, D. J., 89, 120
Braudel, F., 77
Breiger, R. L., 224
Brewer, D. D., 26
Brody, D. S., 108, 124
Bronnenberg, B. J., 25
Brown, J. J., 309, 333
Burnkrant, R. E., 40
Burns, K. S., 264
Burroughs, J. E., 169, 170, 181, 190

Burt, R. S., 14, 25, 82, 96, 120, 226, 228, 229, 233, 235, 237, 241, 250, 251, 252
Burton, M. L., 25
Buskens, V., 80, 86, 89
Butler, H. N., 93

C

Cacioppo, J. T., 155
Campbell, D. T., 52, 53
Cannon, J. P., 18
Caputo, G. C., 108, 124
Carley, K., 15
Carpenter, J. A., 167
Carrin, G., 228
Carrington, P. J., 7
Carter, W. C., 26
Cassileth, B. R., 128
Chadhrui, A., 171, 180, 182, 199
Chan, K. K., 287
Chaplin, L. N., 52
Charles, C., 108, 111, 134
Chen, Y., 280
Chevalier, J. A., 263, 311
Chiangm J., 22
Childers, T. L., 287
Ching, A., 112
Chonko, L. B., 18
Chou, C. P., 185
Christensen, H. K., 204
Chun, W. Y., 180, 192
Cleanthous, P., 112
Cliff, A. D., 23, 25
Clinton, H. R., 121
CNN/Money, 310
Coleman, J., 79
Coleman, J. S., 20, 113, 219, 220, 241, 288
Conrwall, M., 165
Cook, J. M., 231
Cook, K. S., 27, 79
Cosmides, L., 145
Costenbader, E., 26
Coulter, R. A., 8, 286, 287
Court, D., 39
Cousineau, A., 40
Cowles, D., 40, 53
Crabtree, B. F., 123

Creyer, E. H., 292
Crosby, L. A., 40, 53
Cunningham, M. T., 18, 19
Cunningham, P. H., 165
Cunningham, R. M., 191

D

Dahlstrom, R., 40, 52
Damasio, A. R., 145, 146, 147, 149, 150, 151
Damasio, H., 149, 146146
Danes, J. E., 52
Danzon, P. M., 121
Das, S., 280
Davis, G. E., 90
Dawes, P. L., 90
Day, G. S., 43
Day, R. L., 314
De Bruyn, A., 11, 259, 261
De Silva, E., 27
DeGrada, E., 180, 192
Delener, N., 164, 167, 168
Dellande, S., 124
Deutcsch, M., 97
Deutcsch, Y., 97
Dholakia, U. M., 87
Diener, B. J., 314, 317
Diener, E., 150
DiMaggio, P., 20, 95, 96
DiMatteo, M. R., 108
Ding, M., 112
Dixon, A., 18
Djupe, P. A., 168
Dodds, P. S., 10, 27, 285
Dollinger, M. J., 85
Donahue, J. M., 119, 126
Dong, X. J., 112
Dooley, P. C., 92, 93
Douglas, M/, 12
Dow, M. M., 25
Dowling, G. R., 90
Dreze, X., 22, 263, 264, 269
Durkheim, E., 164
Duttam S., 94, 95, 99

E

Eames, K. T. D., 288

East, R., 316
Ebaugh, H. R., 163, 164
Ekland-Olson, S., 15
Eliashberg, J., 288
Elkins, D. N., 170
Emerson, R. M., 27, 79
Emirbayer, M., 15, 80
Emmanuel, E. J., 107, 108, 110
Emmanuel, L. L., 107, 108, 110
Emmons, R. A., 150
Engel, J. F., 312, 318, 327
Engelland, B. T., 286
Epstein, R. E., 110, 119, 128, 132
Epstein, R. M., 107, 122
Erdem, T., 51
Escalas, J. E., 173, 182, 189, 193, 199
Eurobarometer, 163
Evans K. R., 40, 53, 54
Everitt, B. J., 145
Ewing, M. T., 259, 279

F

Faden, R. R., 121
Fahey, L., 204, 205
Fang, E., 53
Fastnow, C. J., 164
Feick, L., 16
Feick, L. F., 286, 287
Feld, S. L., 26
Feldman, M. D., 110, 119, 128, 132
Fiscella, K., 122
Fligstein, N., 93
Flocke, S. A., 123
Flynn, K. E., 128
Folkes, V. S., 315
Ford, G. T., 40–41, 56, 58
Fornell, C., 175, 183
Fournier, S., 50, 52, 180, 189, 191
Francis, L. J., 164, 173, 174, 180
Frank, R., 146
Frank, R. E., 191
Franses, P. H., 21, 27, 79, 83
Frazier, G. L., 79, 85
Freelang, A., 39
Freeman, L., 89
Frels, J. K., 43

G

Gabarino, E. C., 166
Gafni, A., 108, 111, 134
Galaburda, A. M., 146
Galaskiewicz, J., 120
Gargiulo, M., 83
Gaski, J. F., 98
Gaudet, H., 219
Gawande, A., 121
Gelberg, L., 108
Gielens, K., 9
Gil, R. B., 57, 66
Gillmore, M. R., 27
Glock, C. Y., 165, 167, 173, 180
Gneezy, U., 149
Godes, D., 8, 12, 18, 280, 309, 312
Golden, P. A., 85
Goldenberg, J., 3, 8, 10, 289, 292, 296, 297
Goldsmith, E. B., 286
Goldsmith, R. E., 286
Golin, C. E., 108
Goodwin, J., 80
Gopalakrishna, S., 40, 53, 54
Gorn, G. J., 143
Gould, R. V., 86, 96
Grabowski, T., 146
Graduate Center of the City University of New York, 173
Granovetter, M. S., 77, 80, 85, 92, 96
Grant, R., 57, 60
Grant, T., 164
Greeley, A., 191
Greely, A., 174
Green, J. C., 170
Green, J. R., 148
Greene, J., 68
Gregory, S., 67, 68
Greve, H. R., 120
Greyser, S. A., 314, 317
Gross, J. J., 156
Grundy, S, M., 114
Guadagnoli, E., 125
Gulati, R., 94, 97
Gupta, C., 203
Gupta, S., 16
Guth, J. L., 170
Gwinner, K. P., 11

H

Hakansson, H., 19
Hall, J. A., 114, 121, 128
Hall, M. A., 123
Hamilton, D. L., 53, 54
Hammond, K., 316
Hannon, M. T., 25, 120
Hanssens, D. M., 205
Harlow, J. M., 146
Harris Interactive, 163
Hartmann, W. R., 259
Haunschild, P. R., 92, 94
Hawke, A., 54
Haygreeva, R., 93
Hazel, E., 108
Heath, C., 12
Heide, J. B., 78–79, 112
Heider, F., 83
Heinz, J. P., 222
Herrmann, A., 87
Hesterly, W. S., 89
Hill, P. C., 166
Hill, S., 22
Hinz, O., 22
Hirschman, E. C., 164
Ho, V. T., 232
Hodges, S. D., 150
Hoeffler, S., 39
Hoffman, B. R., 8, 11
Hogan, J., 203
Hogan, J. E., 16
Hogarth, J. M., 41, 42, 45, 50, 56
Holbrook, M. B., 171, 180, 182, 199
Hollon, M. F., 119
Holt, D. B., 14, 189
Homse, E., 18, 19
Hood, R. W. , Jr., 165, 168
Hopkins, C., 286
Hosanagar, K., 13
Houghton, D. C., 180, 182
Houston, M. B., 40, 53, 54
Huismans, S., 166, 167, 169
Hunsberger, B., 173, 200
Hunt, S. D., 204
Hutcherson, C. A. C., 156
Hutt, M. D., 18, 19

I

Iacobucci, D., 2
iCrossing, 115
Ingram, P., 27
Innis, D. E., 143
Isherwood, B., 12
Iyengar, R., 9

J

Jabon, M E., 156
Jap, S. D., 91
Jarvis, C. B., 174
Jasper, J. M., 15
Jaworski, B. J., 142
Johlke, M. C., 53
John, D. R., 52
John, G., 81, 91
John, O., 156
Johns Hopkins, 129
Johnson, E. J., 149
Jones, C., 89
Jones, E., 18
Jones, M. H., 92
Jones, R., 56
Jonker, J. J., 288
Joshi, Y., 12

K

Kaldor, P., 163, 173, 174
Kalyanam, K., 258, 261
Kang, J.-K., 235
Kardes, F. R., 180
Katz, E., 113, 219, 220, 241, 245, 246, 260, 283, 288, 311
Kaufman, J., 22
Kavanaugh, J. F., 169
Keeling, M. J., 288
Keeney, R. L., 41
Keller, K. L., 39, 40, 46, 52, 65, 142, 143, 155, 157, 171, 172, 203, 205
Khanna, P., 93
Kihlstrom, J. F., 155
Kilduff, M., 80
Kim, Y., 182

Klaaren, K. J., 150
Klein, L. R., 40–41, 56, 58
Kleine, R. E., III, 52
Kliatchko, J. G., 60, 62
Kogut, B., 207
Kohlberg, L., 145
Kossowska, M., 180, 191
Kowalski, R. M., 315, 319, 331
Koza, M. P., 80
Krackhardt, D., 22
Kravitz, R. L., 110, 119, 120, 123, 128, 132
Krishnan, R., 22
Krishnan, V., 207
Kruglanski, A. W., 180, 192
Krupat, E., 123
Kulatilaka, N., 207
Kumar, V., 16, 22, 205

L

LaFeur, S. J., 150
Lagace, R. R., 40, 52
Lambkin, M., 43
Landon, E. L., 313, 315, 326, 327
Landsman, V., 128
Lang, J. R., 92
Larsen, R. J., 150
Larson, A., 86
Larson, D. A., 286
Lazarsfeld, P. F., 219, 239, 245, 246, 260, 283
Lee, D. Y., 90
Lee, E., 205
Lee, J., 16, 24, 41, 42, 45, 50, 56
Lee, S. H., 27
Leeflang, P., 112
Lehmann, D. R., 46, 52, 65, 203
Leiter, M., 39
Lemon, K. N., 16
Leone, R. P., 16
Lerman, C. E., 108, 124
Leskovec, J., 22, 27, 268
Levesque, L. L., 232
Lewin, A. Y., 80
Lewis, K., 22
Lewis, R., 260, 267, 268
Li, N., 53

Libai, B., 16
Lilien, G. L., 11, 218, 259, 261
Lin, Q., 24, 41
Lisle, D. J., 150
Little, P., 108
Lockhart, D. E., 93
Loewenstein, G., 149
Lorrain, E. P., 237
Louch, H., 20
Luce, M. F., 150, 166
Lusch, R. F., 91
Lutz, R. J., 264

M

Macauley, S., 77, 91
MacInnis, D., 142
Macy, M. W., 89
Mahajan, V., 284
Manchanda, P., 33, 112
Mannetti, L., 180, 192
March. V., 128
Mariolis, O., 92
Markovsky, B., 79
Markus, H., 143, 145, 157, 166
Marsden, P. V., 26
Martin Gutierrez, S., 39, 50
Marx, K., 164
Mas-Colell, A., 148
Mather, D. R., 259, 279
Mayzlin. D., 8, 12, 263, 280, 311
McCarty, C., 27
McLean, P. D., 15
McPhee, W. N., 219
Mela, C. F., 16
Meloy, M. G., 152, 153, 155
Menzel, H., 113, 219, 220, 241, 288, 311
Merino, M., 203
Merton, R. K., 231, 239, 245, 246, 247
Mick, D. G., 174
Miller, C. M., 13
Miller, S. M., 108, 124
Miller, W. L., 123
Milo, R., 19
Miniard, P. W., 143
Misra, S., 112
Misra, S. R., 287

Mitchell, A. A., 143
Mizerski, R. W., 320
Mizik, N., 112
Mizruchi, M. S., 93
Mobilio, L., 260, 267, 268
Mochon, D., 152
Molnar, V., 12
Moore, G. A., 294
Moore, J. F., 40, 43, 44, 53, 54
Morgan, M., 107, 110, 113
Morgan, R. M., 204
Morrissey, B., 257
Muass, I. B., 156
Muhamad, R., 27
Mulvaney, S., 155
Muniz, A. M., 15
Murtha, B. R., 19

N

Nadel, S., 15
Naqvi, N., 147
Narayanan, S., 112
Nass, C., 156
Nasu, Y., 164
Nel, D., 286
Newman. J., 80
Ney, P. E., 264
Nezer, C., 288
Niedenthal, P. M., 156
Noorderhaven, N. C., 91
Nooteboom, B., 91
Norton, M. I., 152

O

Obama, B., 121
Obstfield, D., 96
Oliver, R. L., 171, 191, 192, 199, 200
Olson, J. C., 143
Ord, J. K., 23, 25
Ornstein, M. D., 92
Ortberg, C., 19

P

Paez, A., 23
Pala, O., 152

Palmatier, R. W., 40, 53, 54
Parigi, P., 26
Park, C. W., 142
Park. S. H., 80
Parsons, A. J., 39
Patton, T., 79
Payne, J. W., 142, 166, 292
PBienenstock, E. J., 19
Percy, L., 322
Perry, D., 260, 267, 268
Peterson, J. A., 16
Pew Forum, 163
Pharmaceutical Executive, 116
Phelps, J. E., 260, 267, 268
Pierro, A., 180, 192
Pitcher, B. L., 165
Podolny, J. M., 21, 66, 120
Pontikakis, E.D., 156
Portes, A., 20
Posluszny, D. M., 119, 120
Potters, J., 149
Poulsen, J. D., 15
Powell, W. W., 80
Price, L. L., 286, 287
Provan, K. G., 89
Provost, F., 22

Q

Quill, T. E., 107, 122
Quinn, C., 43, 44

R

Raman, N., 260, 267, 268
Rangaswamy, A., 25
Ratner, R. K., 58
Raub, W., 89
Ray, M. L., 143
Reinartz, W., 203
Reingen, P. H., 15, 308, 309
Reitz, K., 25
Rhoads, G. K., 52
Rice, R. E., 22
Richardson, M., 17
Richins, M. L., 286, 318
Roberts, J., 205
Roccas, S., 165, 167, 179

Rogers, E., 219, 247, 315
Rogers, E. M., 8, 9
Ross, T., 97
Rossiter, J., 322
Roter, D., 114, 121, 128
Rudolph. T. J., 164
Russo, J. E., 152, 153, 155

S

Sabol, B., 40, 53
Salancik, G. R., 99
Sanchez, R., 207
Sarkar, P., 299
Saroglou, V., 165, 166, 167, 168, 169, 186
Sawai, K., 228
Saxon, T., 85
Schachter, S., 220
Scheer, L. K., 40, 53, 54
Schooler, J. W., 150
Schott, T., 291
Schwartz, S. H., 165, 166, 167, 168, 169,
        173, 179
Scott Morton, F., 61
Scott, D. M., 23
Scott, J. P., 7, 81
Sebastian, J. G., 89
Sensenbrenner, J., 20
Shah, P. P., 232
Shaikh, N. I., 25
Sherif, M., 218, 219
Sherry, J. F., Jr., 164, 169
Shervani, T., 204, 205
Shervant, T., 43
Shiv, B., 147, 149
Sigourev, S. V.l, 11
Silva-Risso, J., 75
Singer, J. E., 220
Singh, J., 40, 52, 53
Sirdeshmukh, D., 40, 53, 143
Sirgy, M. J., 52
Sirsi, A. K., 15
Sivakumar, K., 93
Skvoretz, J., 89
Smith, D. G., 108, 124
Smith, H., 167, 169, 188
Smith, H. J., 232
Smith, M. A., 128

Smith, M. C., 126
Smith, P. B., 239
Smith, R. E., 41
Snow, D. A., 15
Song, S., 23, 24
Sood, J., 164
Spann, M., 22
Spilka, B., 165
Spiro, J., 97
Srinivasan, S., 205
Srivastava, R., 203, 204, 205
Srivastavam R. K., 43
Staelin, R., 205
Stamper, C. L., 53
Star, A., 231, 232
Stark, R., 165, 167, 173, 180
Steenkamp, J.-B. E. M., 9
Stephen, A. T., 22
Stern, I., 99
Stern, L. W., 81
Stevenson, W. B., 80
Stewart, D., 259, 279
Stewart, T. E., 120
Stouffer, S. A., 231, 232
Street, R. L., 128, 132
Stremersch, S., 21, 27, 79, 83, 119, 128, 132,
        133
Strogatz, S. H., 89
Stuart, J. A., 203
Stuart, T. E., 235
Stube, M. J., 239
Stumpf, M. P. H., 27
Sugden, R., 149
Suls, J., 232
Summer, J. O., 286
Sutton-Smith, K., 128
Swait, J., 51
Swanson, S. R., 11
Swire, J., 27

T

Tassinary, L. G., 155
Taylor, S., 110
Teel, J. E., 307
Tellis, G. J., 164
Thibaut, J. W., 96, 97
Thom, D. H., 123

Thomas, J., 203
Thompson. C., 10
Thorne, T., 27
Titchener, E. B., 157
Tobias, B. A., 155
Tobis, I. P., 155
Tooby, J., 145
Toubia, O., 22
Triplett, N., 239
Tsai, W., 80, 120
Tucker, W. T., 191

U

Ustuner, T., 18
Uzzi, B., 93, 97

V

Valente, T. W., 8, 9, 11, 26
van Bruggen, G., 263, 264, 266, 267
Van den Bulte, C., 2, 9, 12, 13, 14, 19, 21, 24, 27, 40, 44, 45, 55, 56, 57, 59, 79, 83, 90, 120, 134, 218, 247, 248, 307, 311
Van der Lans, R., 263, 264, 266, 267
Van Dyck, W., 133
Van Hill, A., 180, 192
Vanness, D., 128
Venkataraman, S., 119, 128, 132
Verhoef, P., 203
Vidal-Sanz, J. M., 16
Volinsky, C., 22

W

Walker, R., 12, 13, 14, 15
Wallacem, M., 259, 279
Wallendorf, M., 164, 169
Walsh, G., 11
Ward, J. C., 15
Wasserman, S., 7
Wathne, K. H., 112
Watt27s, D. J.
Watts, D. J., 10, 89, 262, 275, 285
Webster, D. M., 180, 192
Weesie, J., 89

Weimann, G., 8, 9, 10, 283, 292
Weiss, A. M., 78
Welker, C. B., 267
Wernerfelt, B., 204
Westphal, J. D., 93
Wheeler, L., 232
Whelan, T., 108, 111, 134
Whinston, M. D., 148
White, D. R., 25
White, H. C., 224
Whitmeyer, J. M., 79
Wilde, M. J., 191
Wilkes, M. S., 119, 120
Wilkes, R. E., 164, 168, 191
Wilkinson, I. F., 19
Wilks, T. J., 152, 153, 155
Willder, D., 79
Wilson. T. D., 150
Wipperfurth, A., 15
Wittink, D. R., 112
Wiuf, C., 27
Wolff, K. H., 82
Wong, N., 170, 181
Wootz, B., 19
World Health Organization, 133
Wosinka, M., 124, 133
Wrightm M., 316
Wrong, D., 80
Wulff, D. M., 166
Wuyts, S., 2, 14, 21, 27, 40, 44, 45, 55, 56, 57, 59, 79, 83, 86, 87, 90, 91, 94, 95, 99, 120, 134, 248, 307, 311

X

Xie, Y., 33

Y

Yamagishi, T., 27
Yin, E., 164
Youn, N., 33
Young, H. N., 110, 119, 128, 132

Z

Zajonc, R. B., 143, 145, 157, 166

Zaltman, G., 122
Zerhouni, E., 116
Zettelmeyer, F., 61
Zimmer, H., 169
Zinnbauer, B. J., 164, 168

Zucker, L. G., 219
Zuckerman, E. W., 11, 122
Zupkis, R. V., 128
Zurcher, L A., Jr., 15

Subject Index

A

Affect Intensity Measure scale, 150–151
Agent-based modeling, 299–300
Apple
    iPod nano, 68
    Nike + cross-company team, 67–69
Attribution theory, 320

B

Boundary spanners
    affiliations, 53
    customers, relationship between,
      53–54
    description of, 52–53
    marketing, importance to, 54–55
    trustworthiness, 53–54
Brain, human
    emotional circuitry, 146, 147*f*
    neurological cases, behavior changes
      learned from, 147–148
    Phineas Gage case, 145–146, 147
    ventromedial prefrontal cortex, 146
Brand emotions. *See also* Brands;
      Customer value proposition
      (CVP)
    attachment, brand, 191
    connection, 171
    customer connections, link to. *See*
      Customer connections
    impact on decision making. *See*
      Decision making
    loyalty, 42–43, 154, 158–159, 171–172,
      181
    overview, 144–145
    physiology, 220
    power of, 154
    religion. *See* Religiosity and branding
    self-brand connection, 172, 181
    somatic marker hypothesis, 151–154

Brands. *See also* Brand emotions
    believability, 51
    communities of, 14–16
    creation, 50
    credibility, 50–51
    customer value perception (CVP) and
      choice, 143–144
    customers, relationship between, 50
    emotion. *See* Brand emotions
    engagement, role of, 15–16
    equity, 71
    fashion, "cool" factor of, 12–13
    inertia of, 52
    luxury, 12
    purchasing decisions, influence on,
      39–40
    relational ecosystem, as part of, 45–46
    relational entities, as, 46, 50–52
    religiosity. *See* Religiosity and
      branding
    trustworthiness, 51
Business-to-business marketing, 18–19
Buzz marketing, 1. *See also* Viral
      marketing

C

Cellular automata, 299
Connectivity
    criterion, 218–220, 221
    dissemination of information, impact
      on, 294
    equivalence, predictions regarding,
      225–226
    horizontal. *See* Horizontal
      connectivity
    initiatives, 1
    opinion leadership, relationship
      between, 301–302
    overview, 223–224
    vertical. *See* Vertical connectivity

Customer connections
  brand equity, link to, 203
  business performance, relationship
    between, 210–212
  value of, 210–212
Customer networks
  densely knit, impact of, 19–21
  social in-groups, 56–57
Customer value proposition (CVP)
  beta weights, adding, 1158
  customer satisfaction, 154
  E, measuring, 155–156
  E, retrieving, during decision-making
    process, 157–158
  E, shaping, 156–158
  emotional component, measures of,
    155–156
  endowment effects, 157
  historical perspective, 142–144
  overview, 142
  second-wave view, 143
  third-wave view, 143–144, 155
Customers
  connections to. *See* Customer
    connections
  decision making, 37–38
  early adopters *versus* main market,
    300–301
  gatekeepers, as, 66
  marketplace network, relationship to,
    59
  networks. *See* Customer networks
  social in-group of, 55–58, 60–61
  valuing, 16

D

Decision making
  emotional circuitry, role of, 150,
    152–153
  normative benchmarks, 148, 149
  output side to decisions, 149–150
  predecisional distortion paradigm,
    153
  somatic marker hypothesis, 151–154
Diffusion theory, 9
  discontinuity in process of diffusion,
    294

  overview, 284–285
  social hubs, influence of, 293
Direct-to-consumer pharmaceutical
    advertising, 107, 119–121
Dominance, 148

E

Edwards, Trevor, 67
Equivalence criterion
  Asch experiment, 237–240
  connectivity, predictions regarding,
    225–226
  contact requirements, 244–245
  influence arenas, 45
  overview, 224
  role, 224
  social comparison, relationship
    between, 232–234, 237–240
  structural, 224

G

Gage, Phineas, 145–146, 147
Gatekeepers, customers as, 66–67
Gossip
  effect of negative, 79, 81
  expansion to larger networks, 89
  motivational conditions for, 85–86
  personal network control mechanism,
    as, 84–85
  triadic conditions for, 85
Group norms, 79
  closure, role of, 89
  connectivity, role of, 89–90
  control mechanism, as, 86–87
  motivational conditions for, 86–87
  triadic conditions for, 86
  trust conventions, 81

H

Health system network
  connected patients as part of. *See*
    Patients, connected
  demographic changes, impact of,
    113–114

e-health, rise in, 114–115
genomics, impact of the, 114, 116
Internet, impact of the, 114–115
lifestyle changes, impact of, 113–114
malpractice suits, impact of, 121
overview, 112–113
patient-physician ties, 113
personalized medicine, impact of the, 116
prescription drug sales, 117–118*t*
regulatory changes, impact of, 116
Horizontal connectivity, 3
description, 17
social influence within, 29
suppliers, 19–21, 29
Hubs, social. *See* Social hubs

I

Iacobucci, Dawn, 2
Influentials. *See* Opinion leaders

L

Loyalty, brand. *See* Brand emotion

M

Marketing
market-based assets, 206–207
product platforms. *See* Product platforms
shareholder impact, 204, 205
strategy decisions, 204
viral. *See* Viral marketing
Marketplace networks
consumer decisions, influence on, 40–41
credibility, 60
customers, relationship between, 59
Internet, role of, 61
intimacy, lack of, 60–61
limitless nature of, 42–43
media channels, role of, 58–59
relational entity, as, 58–61
technology, role of, 58
McDonald's "Lincoln Fry" blog, 310

Microsoft's marketing strategy
leveraging of customer base, 208, 209
risk mitigation, 208

N

Need for cognitive closure (NFCC), 180, 182, 186–187, 193
Negative word-of-mouth
cascading, 331–332
customer complaints, linked to, 308, 314–315
customer dissatisfaction, linked to, 308, 312, 313–314, 317–318, 319, 326–327, 332
impact of, 315–317, 320
marketers, reaction of, 328–330
marketing communications, impact of, 322, 329
marketing research, importance to, 308–311
measuring, 324–325, 330–331
positive, *versus,* 307–308
product quality, controlled, as antidote for, 321–322
service recovery, as mitigating factor, 323–324
subterfuge attempts, 310
Network analysis
electronic data, 22–23
experiments, 27–28
geographical analysis, 23–26
overview, 21–22
surveys, 26–27
Network constraints. *See also* Network controls
board interlocking, role of, 93–95
controls, relationship with, 90–91
opportunity, relationship between, 96–97
overview, 90–92
self-centered behavior, 93–94
simultaneous deployment with controls, 91
subtle variant of, 92–93
Network controls. *See also* Network constraints
control mechanisms, overview of, 80–83

expansion to larger networks, 88–90
governance, 79
group norms. *See* Group norms
impersonal control mechanisms,
    80–81, 82
negative gossip. *See* Gossip
network levels, 81–82
overview, 78–80
personal control mechanisms, 80, 82
research, future, 96
tertius gardens. *See* Tertius gardens
triadic structures, 82–83
two-step leverage, 83–84
Neumann, John von, 299
Nike +, 67–69

O

Opinion leaders
    contagion, influence on, 245–247
    identifying, 10
    influence of, 9–10, 28–29
    personal traits of, 286–287
    persuading, 11
    preexisting social ties, activating, 11
    product involvement, 286
    product knowledge, 286
    social connectivity, link between,
        301–302
    social influence, 287
    types of, 285

P

Patient-centered marketing
    defining, 125
    direct-to-consumer pharmaceutical
        advertising, 107, 119–121,
        127–128, 132–133
    expectations, based on, 129
    mass therapy approach, 126–127, 130
    needs, based on, 129
    niches, patient, 130
    patient involvement, level of, 127–128
    philosophy of, 129–130
    physician communications, 126
    physician responsiveness, 128

segmentation, market, 125–126
    treatment goals, patient, 131–132
Patients, connected
    compliance, role of, 124
    consumerist model, 110
    decision making, 108, 111
    disordered model, 111
    health improvements, role of, 124–125
    health system network. *See* Health
        system network
    informed, 107
    overview, 107, 122
    participation, increased, 108–109
    patient-centered marketing. *See*
        Patient-centered marketing
    pharmaceutical direct-to-consumer
        advertising, 107, 119–121
    physicians, dialogue with, 107–108
    physicians, ties to, 113
    preventive behaviors, impact of, 124
    reactive physicians, 110–111
    satisfaction (patient), role of, 123
    strategic implications of, 132–134
    treatment plan, adherence to, 123–124
    trends, 127
    trust, role of, 122–123
    white-coat model, *versus*, 108,
        109–110
Peer product review sites, 22
Product platforms
    benefits of, 209*t*
    GE, 209–210
    Intel x86, 208, 209
    Microsoft's strategy. *See* Microsoft's
        marketing strategy
    overview, 207–208
    Pentium, 208

R

Red Bull, 15
Reference group theory, 231–232
Relational channels, 38*t*, 39
    distinguishing properties of, 63–64*t*
    frequency, role of, 65
    overview, 61–62
    power of activity, role of, 65–66
    primary, 62

research directions, 70
side relational channels, 66–67, 70
Relational ecosystems
    definition, 37, 38*t*
    diversity of elements, 45–46
    evolution, role of, 44–45
    integration, 44
    overview, 37–38, 43–44
    research directions for, 69–72
    time, role of, 44
Relational entities
    boundary spanners, 52–55
    brands, 46, 50–52
    distinguishing properties, 47–49*t*
    information searches, relationship
        between, 41
    marketplace network. *See* Marketplace
        networks
    overview, 37–40
    social in-group, 55–58, 60–61
Religiosity and branding
    brand avoidment, 189
    brand loyalty, 181
    Buddhism, 169, 184
    Christian Broadcasting Network, 189
    Christianity, 169, 178, 184
    church affiliation, 191
    church attendance, 191
    cognitive traits, relationship between,
        179–180
    contemporary social life, role in,
        163–164
    fundamentalism, 166, 167–168, 173,
        174, 176–177, 180, 186–187, 188
    influence of, 164–165
    Islam, 184
    loyalty, impact on, 177, 178
    managerial implications, 191–192
    need for cognitive closure (NFCC),
        link to, 180, 182, 186–187, 193
    overview, 163
    religious affects, 165
    religious behavior, 165
    religious cognitions, 165
    robustness, testing across religions,
        184–187
    secularism, verus, 187
    self-brand connection, 181

spirituality, 166, 168–170, 173, 174,
    176–177, 190
study 1, measures and validation,
    171–175
study 1, participants and procedures,
    170–171
study 1, replication, 184
study 2 (Singapore) overview,
    179–180
study 2 (Singapore), measures and
    validation, 181–183
study 2 (Singapore), participants and
    procedures, 181
values, 173
values theory, 179

S

Simmel, Georg, 12
Six Sigma, 221
Social comparison
    benchmarks, as, 231
    ego, role of, 231, 233–234
    equivalence criterion, relationship
        between, 232–234
    overview, 217
    reference group theory, 231–232
    relative deprivation, relationship
        between, 234–236
    socialization, *versus*, 231
Social contagion
    assumptions regarding, 8, 28
    customers, impact on, 7
    leveraging, 10–11
    status, impact of, 12–13
Social hubs, 3
    adoption patterns, 296–297
    influence of, 297–300
    information transmission source,
        291–293, 295
    innovativeness, 299
    network activation, 288–289, 291
    overview, 287–288
    product diffusion, influence on, 293
    social capital, 294
Social network theory
    actors, influences of, 120
    DTCA, 120

Social networking
    activating, 295–296
    board interlocking, 92–93, 94–95
    constraints. *See also* Network
        constraints
    controls inherent in, 77–78. *See also*
        Network controls
    cross-fertilization, 98
    denseness, 97
    distribution channels, impact on, 21
    emotions, role of, 97–98
    inferior exchange conditions, 92–93
    marketers, for, 2
    motivations, role of, 97
    terms of trade, 95
    theory of. *See* Social network theory
    ties, depth of, 22–23
    valuing, 16–17
Social status, 13
Social ties
    activating, in social contagion, 11
    asymmetric nature of, 13–14
Socialization
    connectivity contradictions, 226,
        228–230
    connectivity criterion, 218–220, 221
    contagion correlations, 226, 228,
        240–241, 242
    contagious opinion, 219
    evidence, empirical, 221–223
    overview, 217, 218
    social comparison, *versus*. *See* Social
        comparison
    Z-graphs, 242–244
Somatic marker hypothesis, 151–154
Spock, as emotionless customer, 141–142,
    159
Stochastic agent-based modeling, 300
Surveys, network, 26–27
Sustainability, 208

T

Tertius gardens
    competition, role of, 96
    description, 87
    global level, operating at, 88–89

motivational conditions for, 87–88
    triadic conditions for, 87
Transitivity, 148

V

Vertical connectivity, 3
    description, 17–18
Viral marketing, 3
    acceptance, viral, 268–270, 274–275,
        277, 278
    advantages, 259–261
    Agent Provocateur viral film, failure
        of, 257
    assumptions regarding, 8–9
    attractiveness over traditional
        campaigns, 259–261
    Barack Obama, use by, 257
    costs of, 260
    drivers to reading viral messages, 269
    email reminders, 270
    extrinsic motivators, 267–268
    failed campaigns, reasons for, 257–258
    forward rate, 267–268, 272–274, 278
    information spread, 262–264
    monitoring, 260–261
    OfficeMax "Elf Yourself" campaign,
        257
    overview, 258–259
    potential, future, 279–280
    reallocation of marketing budgets to,
        257
    response time, 277–278
    risks, 261
    seeded customers, 264, 265–266, 269,
        278
    seeding acceptance, 266–267, 278
    successful *versus* unsuccessful, analysis
        of, 271–275, 277–278
    underlying process, 263–264
    viral games, 267–268
    viral-for-hire services, effectiveness
        of, 12

W

White-coat model, 108, 109–110

Word of Mouth Marketing Association,
311
Word-of-mouth
definition, 311–312
dissonance, 325
earliest accounts of, 283
effectiveness, boosting, 10–11
incidence of, 317–318

influence of, 318–319
marketing, reallocation of budget to,
257
negative. *See* Negative word-of-mouth
purchasing decisions based on,
319–320
revival of concept's importance, 1, 4
social contagion. *See* Social contagion